CW00819061

CAMBRIDGESHIRE RECORDS SOCIETY

(formerly Cambridge Antiquarian Records Society)

VOLUME 20

THE TOPOGRAPHY OF MEDIEVAL ELY

Edited by

Anne Holton-Krayenbuhl

CAMBRIDGE 2011

THE TOPOGRAPHY OF MEDIEVAL ELY

Edited by

Anne Holton-Krayenbuhl

Cambridgeshire Records Society

Volume 20

2011

Published by the Cambridgeshire Records Society

County Record Office, Shire Hall, Cambridge CB3 0AP

British Library Cataloguing in Publication Data

A catalogue record for this book
is available from the British Library

ISBN 978-0-904323-22-1

Printed in Great Britain by the MPG Books Group,
Bodmin and King's Lynn

CONTENTS

LIST OF ILLUSTRATIONS

Tables

Maps

Plate

ACKNOWLEDGEMENTS

My interest in medieval Ely was kindled some twenty-five years ago when I organised excavations at the Three Blackbirds in Broad Street, Ely. This building, incorporating a medieval hall house, had been purchased by the Ely Preservation Trust whose chairman invited members of the Ely and District Archaeological Society to investigate the presumed site of the open hearth, in conjunction with an architectural survey of the building. On preparing the report, it became clear that there was very little published material on the development of the medieval town. I consulted the late Mr R. Holmes who had undertaken a considerable amount of documentary research on the history of Ely, and he introduced me to the 1417 survey. The late Dr D. M. Owen, then Keeper of the University Archives and of the Ely Diocesan Records and Dean and Chapter Archives, guided me towards the relevant manuscripts in the cathedral archives, and the report on the Three Blackbirds was eventually completed, with contributions from many other people. I pursued the search, in conjunction with other projects, and the transcripts accumulated. I was wondering what to do next, when, in 2003, a conversation with the late Mr A .P. Baggs, then president of the Cambridge Records Society, resulted in a meeting with Dr R. E. Horrox, editor of this Society, and a discussion on the contents of a possible volume in this series. The suggestion, by Dr E. S. Leedham-Green, to reproduce in facsimile one of the copies of the 1417 survey has determined the format of this volume. I have much appreciated the contribution of all those involved in the initial stages.

Thanks are due to Dr Horrox for her encouragement and constructive comments at various stages in the preparation of this volume, to Dr Leedham-Green for discussing with me the layout of the text and helping with IT matters, and to Ms S. Wroot for transforming my drawings into presentable maps. I am grateful to the staff of the Cambridge University Library, especially Mr P. M. Meadows, Keeper of the Ely Diocesan Records and Dean and Chapter Archives, and Mr G. Waller and his colleagues at the Manuscripts Room, and the staff at the departments of Rare Books, and of Maps for their unstinting help. Thanks are also due to the staff at the County Record Office and Cambridgeshire Archaeology at Shire Hall, Cambridge, and to the staff at the Cambridgeshire Collection, the library of Gonville and Caius College, the Manuscripts Department at the British Library and the The National Archives. The contribution of Dr A. S. Bendall, Miss P. Blakeman, Mrs E. M. Davis, Dr J. Fairweather and Mr P. Edwards is gratefully acknowledged. Finally, thanks are due to Dr Wilfrid Holton, my husband, without whose support this volume would not have been completed.

I am particularly grateful to the British Library for granting permission to reproduce Harleian 329, fos 10–24v, 28v, and publish the Ely section of Cotton Tiberius BII, and to the Keeper of the Ely Diocesan Records and Dean and Chapter Archives for permission to publish parts of CUL EDR G7/27 and CUL EDC 1/C/7.

Anne Holton-Krayenbuhl
Witchford
August 2008

ABBREVIATIONS

AFU	Archaeological Field Unit, Cambridgeshire County Council
BL	British Library
C	BL Cotton Claudius C XI
CAU	Cambridge Archaeological Unit
CLR	*Calendar of Liberate Rolls*
CPR	*Calendar of Patent Rolls*
CRO	Cambridgeshire Record Office
CUL	Cambridge University Library
EAA	*East Anglian Archaeology*
G	Gonville and Caius Manuscript 489/485
H	BL Harleian 329, fos 10-24v
J	BL Harleian 329, fos 25-32
LE	*Liber Eliensis*: E.O. Blake, ed., *Liber Eliensis* (Camden Society Third Series, 92, 1962); J. Fairweather, trans., *Liber Eliensis: a history of the Isle of Ely from the seventh century to the twelfth* (Woodbridge, 2005). References to *Liber Eliensis* will give book and chapter number, followed by page number in Fairweather.
LPFD	*Letters and Papers Foreign and Domestic*
M	'Liber M': CUL EDR G3/28
PCAS	*Proceedings of the Cambridge Antiquarian Society*
P	PRO C66/401
R	'Liber R': CUL EDR G3/27
T	BL Cotton Tiberius B II
TNA	The National Archives
V	BL Cotton Vespasian A XIX
VCH	*The Victoria History of the Counties of England. Cambridgeshire and the Isle of Ely* (10 vols, 1938-2002)

Unpublished excavation reports are held at the Cambridgeshire Archaeology Department, Shire Hall, Cambridge.

Note: Most of the medieval documents are in Latin. In this volume, medieval sources are quoted in translation, followed by the original text, in italics, where relevant. Post-medieval references are quoted in their original form.
The maps are based on the 1880s maps of Ely, retaining the street layout and names of that period (most of which have remained unchanged).

Notes on the transcripts and translations

The 1417 survey is reproduced in facsimile, the remaining three documents are transcribed, and in each case there is a translation on the facing page.

In the transcript, abbreviations are expanded silently unless the expanded form is uncertain. Modern punctuation is introduced and the layout of the manuscript is modified, as specified in the sub-sections below.
The following editorial symbols are used:
\ / inserted material, apparently in the same hand as the manuscript
< > inserted material, superscript, in a different hand from that of the manuscript
[ ] editorial insertions; for the use of square brackets in the 1417 survey, see below
[italics] editorial comments
... illegible word or part of word

In the translations, Christian names are translated and surnames transcribed, except in the thirteenth-century surveys where occupational surnames and most locative and descriptive surnames are translated, and untranslated descriptive surnames are in italics. Place-names are translated in standardised form. Significant marginalia and variant readings are included in the endnotes, which are generally keyed to the translation. The exceptions are variant readings which do not significantly affect the meaning of the text and which are keyed to the transcript, except for the 1417 survey where all variants are keyed to the translation.

The thirteenth-century surveys
R is transcribed and significant variants in C and G are indicated in the endnotes. The text is in two columns and the second column is indicated thus [col. 2]. Thirteenth-century spelling is retained in the transcripts, if common throughout the manuscript (e.g. 'i' for 'j' in 'iusticiarius'); thorn is transcribed 'th'. Headings and initial letters in red ink are reproduced in bold type.

The 1417 survey
The layout of the translation follows that of the original manuscript as closely as possible, but some adaptation has been necessary. Marginalia have been incorporated in the body of the text, as follows: indications in the left-hand margin, recording whether tenements belong to the bishop or to the prior, are printed in italics at the head of each group of holdings listed within the vertical brackets; the name of the obedientiary to whom rent is payable on a specific holding, usually written next to the bracket, is printed after the name of the tenant and description of the holding, in square brackets and abbreviated form; a key to the abbreviations is given below. Topographical references on the left or right of the text are incorporated in the translation, in bold type, at the point where they occur. Measurements and other details about a group of tenements, noted within vertical brackets on the right-hand part of the page, are printed below the relevant list of tenants, with an indented left-hand margin.

Key to the abbreviations for the names of the obedientiaries, the Latin word is in brackets where it differs significantly from the English

[c]	keeper of the Lady Chapel (capella)
[cel]	cellarer

[cam]	chamberlain (camerarius)
[can]	precentor (cantor)
[e]	almoner (elemosinarius)
[f]	shrine-keeper (feretrarius)
[h]	hosteller (but may refer to the steward of the prior's household, see chapter 2, note 45)
[i]	infirmarer
[p]	pittancer
[pri]	prior
[s]	sacrist
[sh]	steward of the prior's household (senescallus hospitii)
[t]	treasurer

Variant readings and significant additions or omissions occurring in the other four copies of the survey are recorded in the endnotes. These are given in translation only, unless the meaning is not clear. A variant reading for a proper noun is spelt as it occurs in the first-listed copy of the survey; there may be minor variations in the other copies.

The sixteenth-century priory rentals

Variations from standard medieval Latin spelling and grammar occur in this manuscript but have been standardised. These include *capud, (de) fiodo, percella, perochia, (ex) perte, tenuera, venetum; uno* occurs as an indeclinable numeral. The only non-standard word that has been retained is *scituatur* as a synonym of *iacet*. *Redd' ass'* is expanded to *redditus assisus* on the basis of an entry on fo 71: *Red' ass' et firmus* implying the use of *assisus* as an adjective.

The transcript reproduces numerals as they occur in the manuscript. In the translation, arabic numerals are used for measurements and sums of money; regnal years are translated in abbreviated form, followed by the modern equivalent in square brackets. The layout of the manuscript is reproduced, but the spacing is modified. Bold type and italics are introduced to indicate the main articulations within the text.

The rentals include references to holdings outside Ely, and material not relevant to the topography of the medieval town. Such entries are noted in summarised form within square brackets.

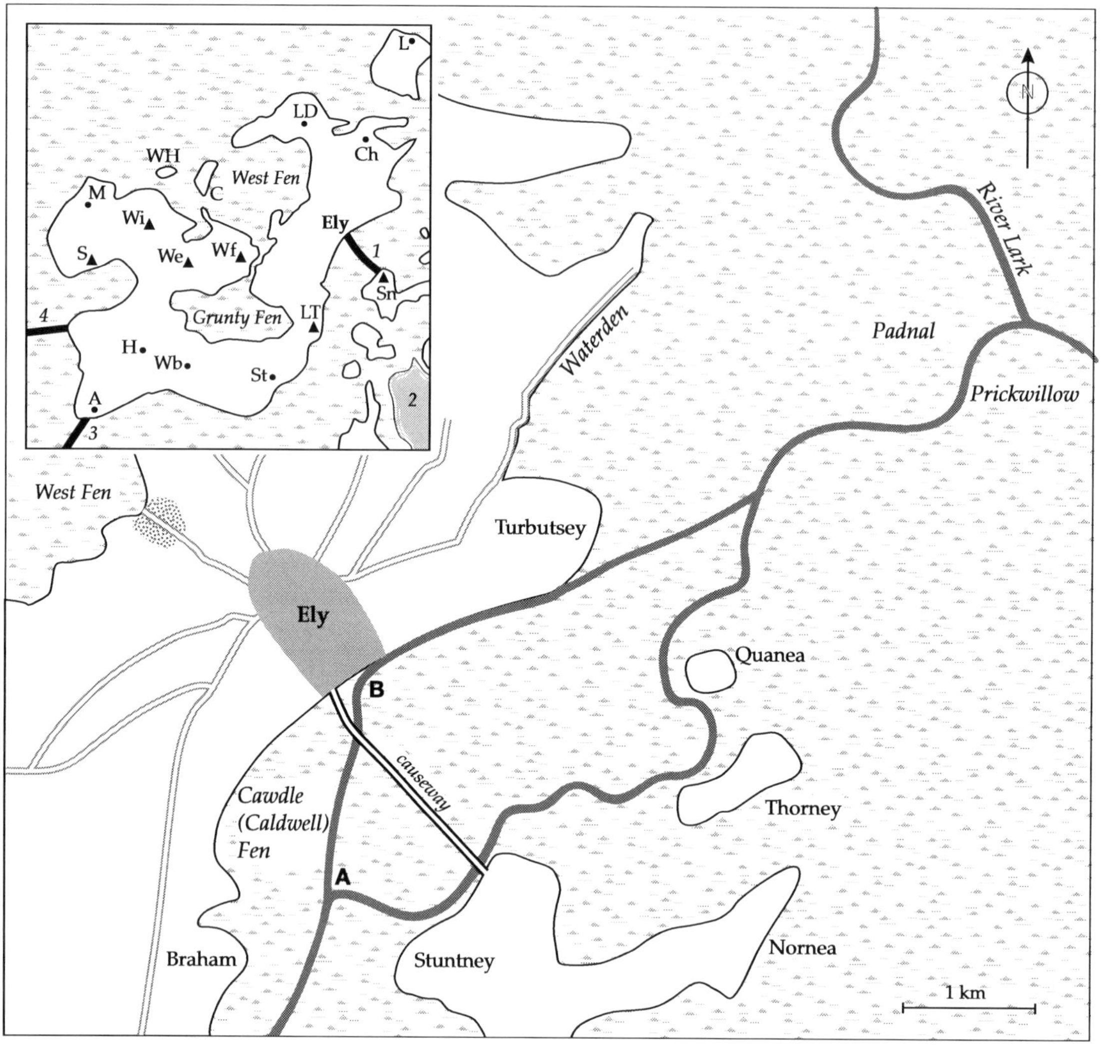

Map 1

Ely and environs. A – B: conjectured line of the cut diverting the river to Ely; stippled: Saxon site at West Fen Road. Inset. The Isle of Ely. Key. 1: Stuntney causeway. 2: Soham mere. 3: Aldreth causeway. 4: Earith causeway. A: Aldreth. C: Coveney. Ch: Chettisham. H: Haddenham. L: Littleport. LD: Little Downham. LT: Little Thetford. M: Mepal. S: Sutton. Sn: Stuntney. St: Stretham. Wb: Wilburton. We: Wentworth. Wf: Witchford. WH: Wardy Hill. Wi: Witcham. Triangles denote priory manors. (Map based on Hall, *Fenland Project*, p. 34, fig. 19 and p. 160, fig. 89, with permission of English Heritage.)

INTRODUCTION

The documents presented in this volume span a period of three hundred years, from the early stages in the development of the medieval town to the eve of the Dissolution. The two thirteenth-century surveys are lists of bishops' tenants, subdivided into sections according to tenurial status; the dues attached to each type of holding are enumerated. The 1417 survey is mainly concerned with the holdings of the priory; it is a street-by-street survey of Ely, showing the town at or just after it had reached its peak, and lists all the tenants of the priory and those of the bishop where these are adjacent to priory holdings. The sixteenth-century priory rentals record lands, tenements and other sources of priory income on the Isle of Ely and beyond in the final years of the priory; many entries include topographical references and the names of former holders some of which occur in the 1417 survey.

The Benedictine abbey, founded *c.* 970, became a cathedral priory in 1109 following the establishment of the see of Ely. The bishop became titular abbot, granting lands and rights to the priory in piecemeal fashion after an initial general grant towards the middle of the twelfth century; he remained, however, the major landholder in medieval Ely. The framework for the development of medieval Ely was provided by the two ecclesiastical bodies, the bishop and the priory, and the manuscripts that form the subject of this volume illustrate some aspects of their involvement in the affairs of the medieval town. The tenurial organisation implied in the documents is outlined, and the form, purpose and contents of each of these manuscripts are described.

HISTORICAL BACKGROUND

The medieval landscape

The Isle of Ely stood out from a marshy expanse crossed by a network of meandering waterways that have been diverted or straightened in the course of the past millenium. The wealth of natural resources is described in *Liber Eliensis*, and the opening sections of the 1250 survey show how the marsh was exploited for its fish, grazing and fuel, while the upland provided arable and meadow, and was quarried for stone and clay.[1] The latter was used in the Middle Ages for the manufacture of pottery, brick and tile.

Ely lies on the eastern edge of the Isle; the monastic precinct and the main part of the town lay on the high ground, while Forehill and Back Hill, running steeply down to the river, provided a link with the area of settlement developed along the riverside in the second half of the twelfth century and in the thirteenth century (maps 1 and 2). The underlying geology consists of Lower Greensand overlying Kimmeridge Clay, the latter being exposed along the flank of the hill; the greensand is a water-bearing stratum, and its waters fed wells and streams.[2] Babylon, the area east of the Great Ouse, lies on firm ground formed by a south–north band of alluvium bounded to the east by the peat of Middle Fen.[3]

The Great Ouse is a major feature in the topography of the town, but its present course is the result of medieval engineering activity undertaken some time between the tenth and the late twelfth century. This involved the diversion of the main channel of the river from its former course that had meandered past the foot of Stuntney hill, Thorney and Quanea, on the eastern edge of the

[1] *LE* ii.105: pp. 213–14; R, fo 1r and v; see p. 26 for a discussion on the date of the 1250 survey.

[2] C. P. Chatwin, *British regional geology: East Anglia and adjoining areas* (1961), p. 21; R. W. Gallois, *Geology of the country around Ely* (British Geological Survey, Memoir for 1:50000 geological sheet 173, 1988), p. 49.

[3] Geological maps of England and Wales (Solid and Drift) 1:50000 (1980, 1981), sheets 173 and 188.

flood-plain, to flow along the western edge of the flood-plain, past Ely (map 1). The former course of the river remains visible as a roddon, or raised bank, in the black fen soil west of Stuntney.[4] Documentary evidence suggests that the river was diverted in the twelfth century. The narrative of Abbot Brihtnoth's expedition to East Dereham in 974 to seize the relics of St Withburga seems to imply that there were no landing stages in the vicinity of Waterside. On the return journey, Brihtnoth had embarked at Brandon and travelled by water as far as Turbutsey; there he had disembarked and the relics had been placed onto a cart and taken to the abbey, some 1½ miles (2½ km) away, a somewhat longer journey than the 700 yards (*c.*1 km) from a landing stage at Waterside, had it existed at the time.[5] A charter concerning a holding next to Stuntney causeway dating to the reign of Richard I (1189–99), provides a *terminus ad quem* for the diversion of the river. Station Road reflects the line of the western end of the causeway, and the holding therefore lay in the Annesdale area (map 2). The document records that Richard, son of Lambricht, grants to the almonry a holding lying 'in the marsh beyond the water ... it stretches lengthwise from the causeway to the great water that is at the northern boundary of the messuage' (*in marisco ultra aquam ...cuius mesagii longitudo incipit a calceta et durat usque ad magnam aquam que est in fine ipsius mesagii versus aquilonem*); it measured in breadth 'nineteen yards of King Richard'.[6] The 'water' that marked the edge of the marsh was a stream, now extinct, flowing from Cawdle (or Caldwell) Fen and along Annesdale into the bend of the Great Ouse. The 'great water' at the north end of the holding was the diverted river Great Ouse. Although this grant was made in the reign of Richard I, the messuage may have been established earlier. A date during the episcopate of William Longchamp (1189–97) is, however, possible; this bishop had been involved in the diversion of the course of the river Lea, having granted the abbot of Waltham permission to divert it 'for ease of navigation'.[7] In the Middle Ages, the river was not known as the Great Ouse; it was 'the great water', as noted above, 'the common watercourse in Ely', or 'the river flowing between Ely and Lynn'.[8]

Medieval Ely was drained by ditches and streams for which there is documentary and archaeological evidence. Three watercourses ran into the flood-plain to the east, two of which may have been incorporated in the course of the diverted river (map 3). The southernmost has been mentioned above. It flowed northwards from Cawdle Fen into the bend of the Great Ouse; it was connected with Castle Hithe and the stone bridge, the latter still marking an entrance to Ely in the eighteenth century, being the site of a turnpike gate in 1764–5.[9] The course of the stream and the river at their confluence east of Annesdale suggests that the river was a secondary element, and that the cut made to bring the Great Ouse to the foot of the Ely escarpment utilised the bed of the stream along a short stretch north of Annesdale. At the northern end of the riverside area, a watercourse called the 'long lode', the 'ancient lode' or the 'common ditch' flowed into the Great Ouse.[10] The topography suggests that the bed of this watercourse may also have been incorporated in the channel of the diverted river. Between the two watercourses was a third one that ran across The Park where a marked dip in the ground reflects its course. It was recorded as the 'common

[4] D. Hall, *The Fenland Project, Number 10: Cambridgeshire Survey, Isle of Ely and Wisbech* (*EAA*, 79, 1996), p. 30.

[5] R. C. Love, ed. and trans., *Goscelin of Saint-Bertin: the hagiography of the female saints of Ely* (Oxford Medieval Texts, Oxford, 2004), pp. 70–75; Wihtburh is the Old English form for Withburga.

[6] M, p. 510.

[7] N. Karn, ed., *Ely 1109–1197* (English Episcopal Acta, 31, 2005), pp. 209–10.

[8] CUL EDC 1/A/2, fos 78v–79 (this cartulary was repaginated in 2007 and the new folio nos are used); M, p. 507.

[9] CRO T/E/AT 1.

[10] CUL EDC 1/B1/219, 220, 297; H, fo 15.

gutter' in the 1417 survey, and is marked 'ancient watercourse' on Bacon's manuscript 'Plan of Drains to the Western portion of the Cathedral'.[11] A document of 1482–3 recording that 'the bishop must clean the common watercourse in Lardeners Lane at the corner of his palace' indicates that the upper stretch of the watercourse ran past the bishop's palace complex, possibly rising from a spring on the higher ground south-west of St Mary's church.[12] Archaeological evidence for this watercourse has been found on the Hayward Theatre site, west of The Gallery, and on the east side of Broad Street, at number 25.[13]

Three causeways linked the Isle of Ely with the uplands to the south-east and south-west (map 1: inset). Stuntney causeway provided the main land route from the Isle of Ely to East Anglia; the flood-plain at this point is about one mile (1.8 km) wide. Settlement on Stuntney hill lasting from the Bronze Age into the late Roman period testifies to the importance of this route from an early date, and William I's demand that the causeway be properly maintained shows his appreciation of the value of this point of access, of particular importance before the river was diverted to Ely.[14] At the south-west end of the Isle were the causeways of Aldreth and Earith, both associated with the manor of Linden, later absorbed into the manor of Haddenham. Aldreth causeway crossed over to Willingham providing the land route to Cambridge, while that at Earith provided a link with the East Midlands.

Piecemeal land reclamation was undertaken over much of the fenland between the tenth and thirteenth centuries. In the late twelfth century, Bishop Longchamp granted the monks more than 2000 acres of reclaimed land in Wisbech and surrounding hamlets.[15] The bishops' surveys of 1222 and 1250 show an increase of some 265 acres in arable and 78 acres in meadow on the episcopal manor of Ely over this twenty-five year period, while 214 acres of arable had been lost to quarrying and other uses. Expansion into the waste was reaching its limits by the mid-thirteenth century, as neighbouring landlords started quarrelling over boundaries, and Matthew Paris records the settlement of the dispute between the bishop of Ely and the abbot of Ramsey concerning a common boundary in the fen, under the year 1256; he continues with a description of the improvements resulting from reclamation, 'A wonderful circumstance took place on these marshes in our time, which was, that in places which … had been pathless and inaccessible…those places were now converted into vast meadows and even into arable land. And those parts of the same which did not produce corn or hay supplied an abundance of sword-grass, turf and other materials for burning, useful to the inhabitants'.[16] Reclamation could be ephemeral, as was the case for the bishop's demesne at Leverington, where the acreage in 1250 was recorded as being variable depending on the sea.[17]

The present landscape results from the large-scale drainage of the Fens carried out in the seventeenth century, and nineteenth-century engineering works have obliterated the medieval land-

11 J. Bacon, *A record of the restorations, repairs, etc., done in and about Ely Cathedral since 1818* (1871): CUL EDC 4/6/2, p. 12.

12 CUL EDR G2/1, column 297.

13 P. Whittaker, *Archaeological excavation at King's School, Ely, Cambridgeshire* (CAU Report 343, 1999), p. 23; D. McConnell *et al.*, *25 Broad Street, Ely, Cambridgeshire* (Archaeological Solutions Ltd Report 1991, 2005), pp. 30–32.

14 Hall, *Fenland Project*, Number 10, pp. 34–6; S. Keynes, 'Ely Abbey 672–1109', in P. Meadows and N. Ramsay, eds, *A history of Ely Cathedral* (Woodbridge, 2003), p. 49.

15 E. Miller, *The abbey and bishopric of Ely* (Cambridge, 1951), p. 97.

16 J. A. Giles, trans., *Matthew Paris's English History* (3 vols, 1852–4), iii, p. 182.

17 Miller, *Abbey and Bishopric*, p. 96 n.

scape both at Turbutsey and in the area south of Annesdale. At Turbutsey, extraction of clay by the Bedford Level Corporation has resulted in the creation of artificial lakes; Sandalls Cut channelling the river to Littleport, and the construction of the railway loop have also affected this area.[18] Similarly, at the foot of Back Hill, construction of the railway station and associated works have modified the topography in the area south-east of Annesdale, a triangle of drained land in the Middle Ages, bounded to the south by Stuntney causeway.

c. *970*–c. *1280: From village to small town*

The Benedictine abbey whose records provide much of the evidence for the development of medieval Ely had Saxon antecedents. Etheldreda, daughter of Anna king of the East Angles, had founded *c.* 673 a double house of which she was the first abbess; she was succeeded by her sister Sexburga. The succession then passed from mother to daughter, from Sexburga to Ermenhilda to Werburga, although the last two may be tenth-century interpolations.[19] No other abbesses are recorded and St Etheldreda's religious house may have failed before 870, in which year the Danes are said to have burnt down the monastery.[20] When organised religious observance resumed at Ely, the framework was provided by secular clerics, expelled *c.*970 on the foundation of the Benedictine abbey.

Ethelwold, bishop of Winchester, founded Ely abbey and King Edgar provided the initial endowment. To this was added an extensive estate in Cambridgeshire and East Anglia following large-scale purchases by Bishop Ethelwold and Brihtnoth, the first abbot. Later acquisitions took the form of scattered gifts of land, and the abbey estate reached its maximal extent in the early decades of the eleventh century, with holdings over much of East Anglia. The connection with the former kingdom of the East Angles was emphasised by Abbot Brihtnoth; he promoted the cult of the four Saxon saints, Etheldreda, Sexburga, Ermenhilda and Withburga, probably inventing the ties linking Etheldreda and Sexburga with Withburga, their supposed sister, having seized Withburga's body as described above to join the relics of the saints already venerated at Ely.[21]

The buildings of St Etheldreda's seventh-century double house have not been located. Continuity of site is implied in *Liber Eliensis* where the chronicler records that, on the foundation of the Benedictine abbey, St Etheldreda's church, though in a ruinous state, was restored by Abbot Brihtnoth.[22] The antiquity of the church restored by Brihtnoth is not clear, and it is possible that the church restored in the tenth century was not of seventh-century origin.

Etheldreda's monastery had been established on a site about one mile distant from the settlement of Cratendune.[23] The name occurs in the bishops' thirteenth-century surveys, and refers to a field that was probably situated south-west of the medieval town. The monastery may well have stood on the site of the Benedictine abbey, but other locations might be considered. Excavations carried out since the 1990s have yielded evidence for mid- and late-Saxon occupation on the west-

18 S. Wells, *The history of the drainage of the Great Level of the fen called Bedford Level* (2 vols, 1828–30), i, p. 590n; *VCH* 2, p. 78, fig. 10; T. Kirby, 'Railways', in T. Kirby and S. Oosthuizen, eds, *An atlas of Cambridgeshire and Huntingdonshire history* (Cambridge, 2000), no. 68.

19 The Latin names are used, the Old English equivalents are Aethelthryth, Seaxburh, Eormenhild and Waerburh; *LE* i.25, 36, 37: pp. 56–7, 69–70; Love, *Goscelin of Saint-Bertin*, p. xv.

20 *LE* i.40: pp. 73–4.

21 Miller, *Abbey and bishopric*, pp. 23–4; Keynes, 'Ely Abbey' in Meadows and Ramsay, *Ely Cathedral*, pp. 24–6.

22 *LE* ii.52: pp. 143–4.

23 *LE* i, preface: pp. 4–5.

ern edge of Ely, between West Fen Road and West End, a block of land that slopes gently down to the medieval embayment of West Fen (maps 1 and 2). The site at West Fen Road has yielded evidence for a settlement established in the early eighth century that expanded until the mid-twelfth century; from that time, the ground appears to have been turned over to agricultural use.[24] The date of the settlement points to a link with the monastery founded some decades previously, and possible alternative locations for the monastery might be sought on the high ground overlooking it. The site of St Mary's church and that of the two hospitals on the western edge of Ely are possible alternatives. It should be noted that mid- and late-Saxon material has also been found on a few sites east of the cathedral, but the associated excavations yielded limited data as they were much less extensive.

The tenth-century abbey probably stood on the site of the medieval buildings that remain to this day; possible traces include a barrel-vaulted structure incorporated into the twelfth-century infirmary.[25] By the time of the Norman Conquest, Ely was the second wealthiest Benedictine abbey in England, with a large village that numbered 88 households in 1086.[26] The Isle served as a refuge for the opposition to William I; Hereward's revolt of 1070–71 was crushed, and the king left a garrison at Aldreth to guard the Isle.[27] The abbey's involvement in this revolt had led to the temporary loss of estates and privileges, but most were recovered by Simeon, the first Norman abbot of Ely, appointed in 1082. Simeon died in 1093, and there was a seven-year vacancy before the appointment of his successor, Richard (1100–1107). Ely had been part of the see of Lincoln since 1072, and the bishops of Lincoln claimed the right to consecrate abbots within their diocese, but both Simeon and Richard objected to being subordinate to Lincoln. Plans to elevate Ely to episcopal status came to fruition in 1109 and the see was established on 17th October, the feast-day of the Translation of St Etheldreda. The diocese, coterminous with the county of Cambridgeshire, was carved out of the see of Lincoln, and Hervey, a Breton, was appointed first bishop of Ely, in which capacity he became titular abbot.[28] The abbey was turned into a cathedral priory and its endowment made over to the bishops who subsequently granted property and rights to the monks. Thus the monks received back from the bishops part of the original possessions of Ely abbey.

Bishop Nigel, Hervey's successor, appears to have established the foundations for the development of the medieval priory and town, despite reverses due to his involvement in the politics of his time. His grant to the monks of 1138x1139 provides the earliest statement of landholdings and rights awarded to the cathedral priory, an earlier charter attributed to Bishop Hervey being considered spurious.[29] Bishop Nigel's grant included the lands and the churches pertaining to these lands in Sutton, Witcham, Witchford, Wentworth, Turbutsey, Whittlesey, Stuntney with 23000 eels, all profits from the altars of the cathedral church and of St Mary's church in Ely, with the lands and tithes pertaining to St Mary's church, the tithe of the bishop's barton, and the monks' vineyard in Ely 'as they held it before I became bishop'; he also granted lands and income in Cambridgeshire, Suffolk and Norfolk. Bishop Nigel granted the monks possession of their servants

24 R. Mortimer, R. Regan and S. Lucy, *The Saxon and Medieval settlement at West Fen Road, Ely: the Ashwell site* (EAA, 110, 2005), pp. 2–3, 25–49 *passim*.

25 A. Holton-Krayenbuhl, 'The infirmary complex at Ely', *Archaeological Journal*, 154 (1997), 135–7.

26 D. Knowles, *The monastic order in England* (Cambridge, 2nd ed., 1963), p. 102; A. Rumble, ed., *Domesday Book: Cambridgeshire* (History from the Sources. Domesday Book, 18, 1981), 5.57.

27 *VCH* 2, pp. 384–5.

28 Keynes, 'Ely Abbey' in Meadows and Ramsay, *Ely Cathedral*, pp. 48–9, 51–2; Karn, *Ely 1109–1197*, pp. liii–liv.

29 Karn, *Ely 1109–1197*, pp. 11–14, 48–52.

Map 2

Ely, with modern street names and some sites and features mentioned in the text. (Based on the first edition of the OS map at 1:2500, 1887 and 1888, omitting railway features.)

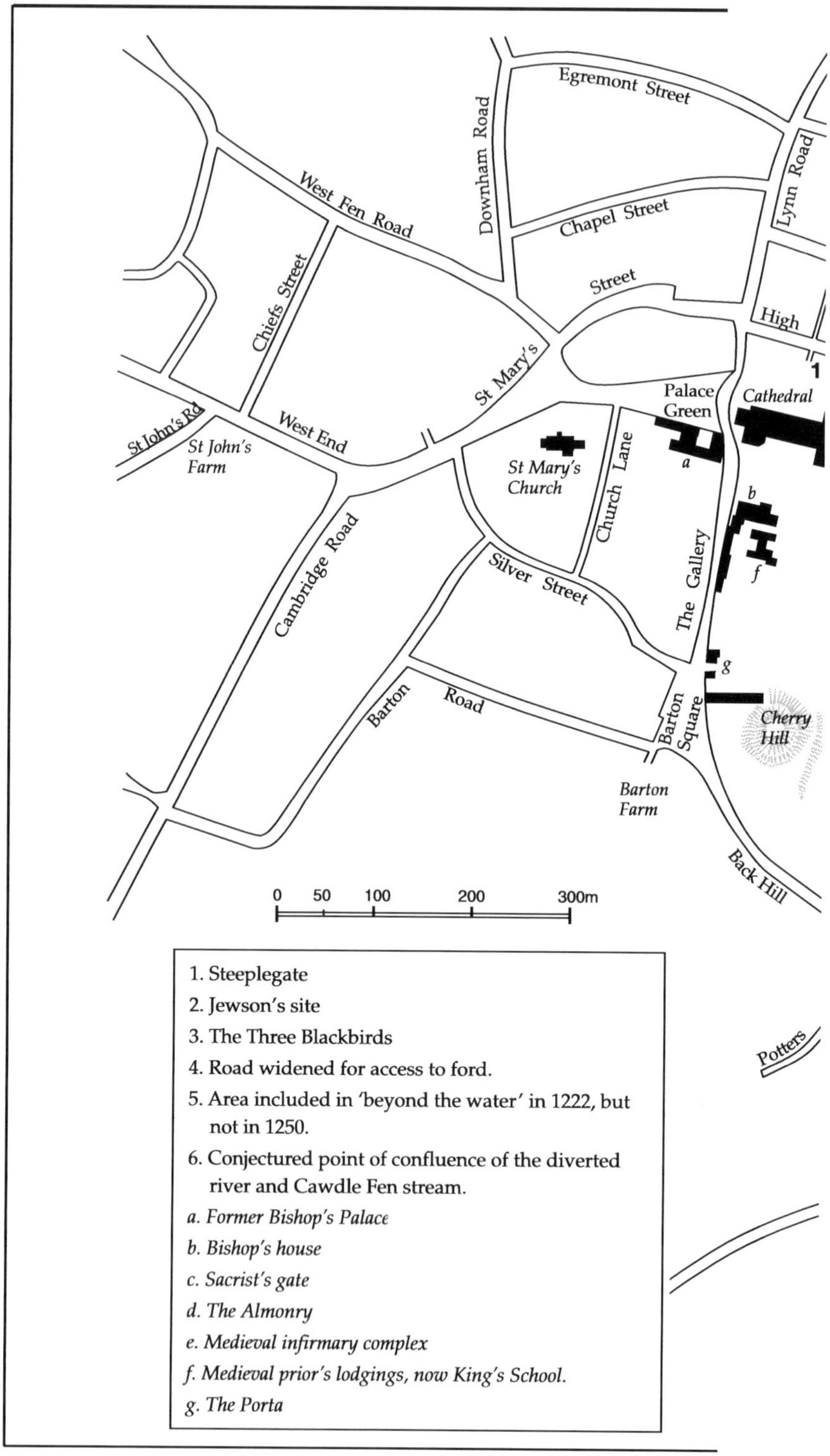

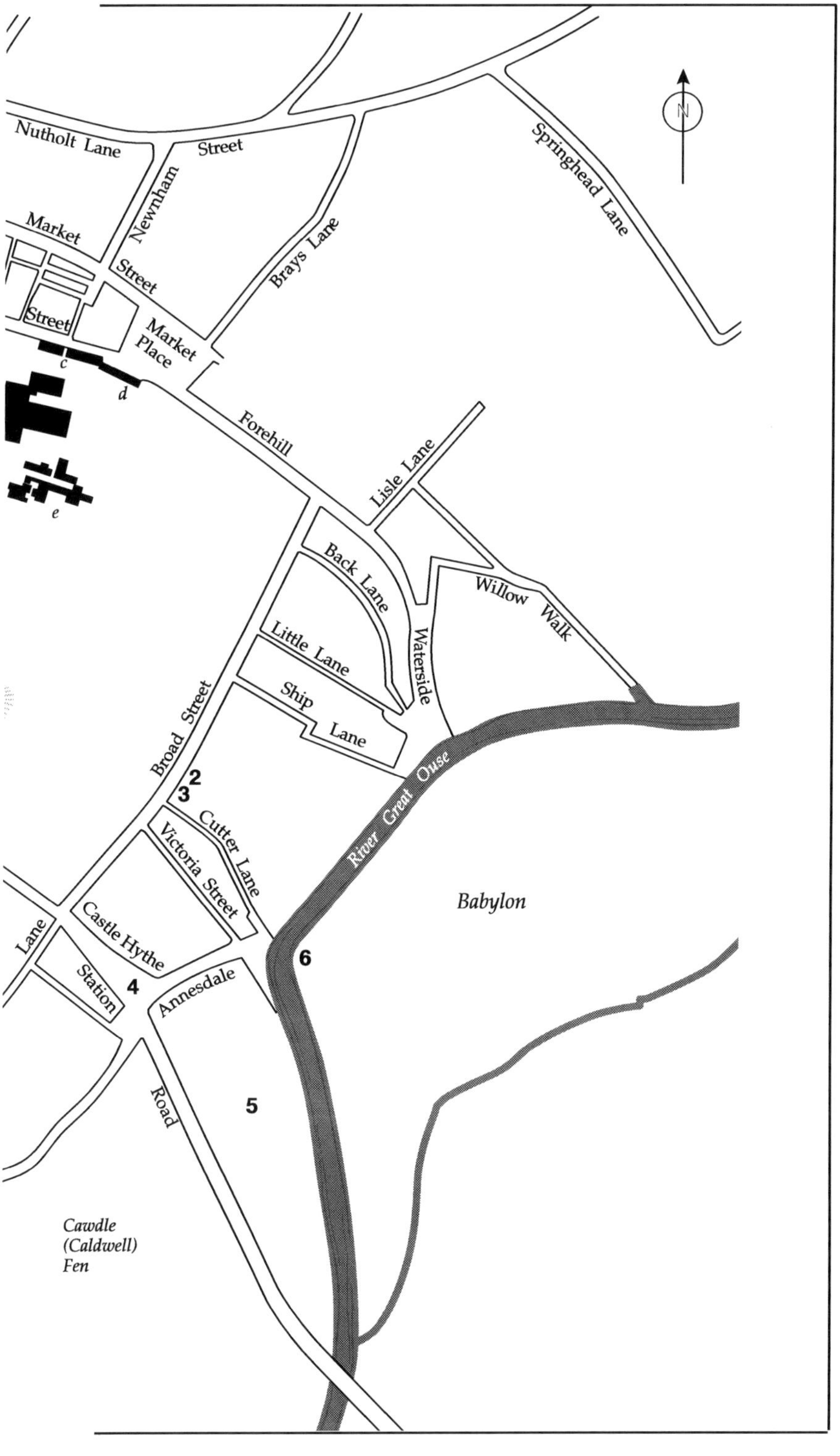
N
Nutholt Lane
Newnham
Street
Market
Street
Street
Brays Lane
Springhead Lane
Market
Place
c
d
e
Forehill
Lisle Lane
Back Lane
Willow Walk
Waterside
Little Lane
Ship
Lane
Broad Street
2
3
Cutter Lane
Victoria Street
River Great Ouse
Babylon
Castle Hythe
Lane
Station
4
Annesdale
6
Road
5
Cawdle
(Caldwell)
Fen

and the houses in which they lived, and of all gifts received before, during or after his episcopate 'whether they be lands, churches, tithes, fisheries, cash or whatever revenue any of the faithful have given them or might give them in future'. The monks were granted their court with all liberties and customary dues in the lands within the bishop's jurisdiction. On the Isle of Ely, Nigel's award to the priory comprised manors extending in a belt across the central part of the Isle (map 1: inset), together with income from tithes and offerings, but apart from the vineyard, no Ely holdings were specified.

A deed of Bishop Nigel dated 1133x1145 is the only documentary evidence for the mid-twelfth-century replanning of the settlement at Ely although there is archaeological evidence for such a process in this period.[30] The document is a grant to Livitha, sister of Wlmann a monk, of a house in exchange for the one that her father and grandfather had held, 'because the sites in front of St Etheldreda's church (*ante ecclesiam Sancte Etheldrede*)[31] are being cleared on account of the fear of fire or other hindrances (*propter timorem ignis vel aliorum impedimentorum*)'.[32] This suggests the removal of houses in the vicinity of the cathedral, construction of which was reaching completion, although the upper stages of the west tower and transepts had yet to be built.[33] Displacement of settlement from the vicinity of a great church occurred elsewhere at this time. At Peterborough, removal of the settlement to a new site was instigated by the abbot, Martin de Bec in 1145, and archaeological evidence shows that the precinct of Norwich cathedral priory overlay late Saxon settlement.[34]

Nigel was involved in the troubles of King Stephen's reign. He led the rebels against Stephen in 1139, while Geoffrey de Mandeville played this role in 1143–4; both men exploited the natural defences provided by the Isle, as Hereward had done some eighty years previously. On all three occasions the castle at Aldreth (*Alrehede*) was the main point of defence. The Isle was to serve as a refuge in two further revolts against the Crown. During the revolt in King John's reign, the rebel barons withdrew to the Isle in 1215–16, having fortified the entrances, but moved on when the royalists entered the Isle. Falk de Breaute, entering from Stuntney, is said to have taken and destroyed a castle in 1216, the cathedral and town were ravaged by King John's men, and the bishopric was seized by Robert of York. The revolt against Henry III was a more protracted affair, starting in 1256 when Henry III had ordered the stewards of both the bishop and the prior to fortify and guard the entrances to the Isle; it ended in 1268 with Prince Edward's capture of Ely. This was the last great revolt associated with the Isle of Ely.[35]

The location of the castle at Ely is problematic and the evidence suggests that there were two. Cherry Hill, a mound facing the cathedral across the former valley, may well have been the site of a Norman motte, and the castle may have been raised in the aftermath of Hereward's revolt to serve a royal garrison.[36] Cherry Hill provided a good vantage point over the Stuntney causeway

30 Mortimer *et al.*, *West Fen Road, Ely*, p. 39; A. Holton-Krayenbuhl, 'Excavations on the Paddock, Ely, Cambs.', *PCAS*, 77 (1988), 122.

31 Not '*circa ecclesiam*' as transcribed in Karn, *Ely 1109–1197*, p. 93.

32 BL Egerton 3047, fo 18v, published in Karn, *Ely 1109–1197*, pp. 92–3.

33 K. Fearn *et al.*, *The south-west transept of Ely Cathedral: archaeological interpretation* (unpublished archive report, 1995): CUL EDC 4/10B/3.

34 D. Mackreth, *Peterborough history and guide* (Stroud, 1994), p. 24; B. S. Ayers, 'The Cathedral Site before 1096', in I. Atherton *et al.*, eds, *Norwich Cathedral: church, city and diocese, 1096–1996* (1996), pp. 64–8.

35 *VCH* 2, pp. 386–97; S. J. A. Evans, ed., *Ely Chapter ordinances and visitation records: 1241–1515* (The Camden Miscellany, Third Series, 17, 1940), p. viii.

36 P. Dixon, 'The monastic buildings at Ely' in Meadows and Ramsay, *Ely Cathedral*, p. 145; *LE* ii.111: pp. 229–30.

entrance to the Isle, and William's interest in this access to the Isle, noted above, supports the hypothesis of a Norman motte on this hill. The stone castle built by Bishop Nigel may also have been on Cherry Hill; it it is recorded that, as this castle was being repeatedly damaged during hostilities, Nigel replaced it with a timber fortification 'towards the water' (*ad aquam*) that was subsequently used by Geoffrey de Mandeville.[37] The description suggests that the second castle lay at Castle Hithe, at the Ely end of the causeway, and may well have been the castle destroyed by the royalists in 1216. A grant of 1220×1225 refers to a messuage 'on the bank at the bridge (*super ripam ad pontem*) where the castle formerly stood', and the 1250 survey refers to a messuage on the site of the 'old castle'.[38]

The Great Ouse had been diverted to the foot of the Ely escarpment in the latter half of the twelfth century, and the ground on either side was drained and parcelled out. The area 'beyond the water' (*ultra aquam*) had been apportioned by 1222; it was bounded to the east by Middle Fen. This area remained peripheral to the development of the medieval town, whereas the low-lying ground west of the river became a major element of medieval Ely. It was bounded by Broad Street to the west, Castle Hithe to the south, and the 'ancient lode' or 'common ditch' to the north (maps 2 and 3). Although there is a considerable amount of documentary evidence, the medieval topography is difficult to reconstruct, particularly in the area north of Waterside, as streams, ditches and other features for which there is documentary evidence have now disappeared. The following description is therefore tentative, and uses documentary, archaeological and topographical evidence.

There is documentary evidence for land reclamation, and material evidence for this process has been found in excavations near Ship Lane. The documentary evidence includes a grant to the almoner Nicholas (1261×1271) concerning a plot of land measuring eighteen perches in length (90.5 m); he is also entitled to keep all the ground that he manages to reclaim towards the river bank in the same way as his neighbours on either side (*cum tota conquiciscione quam elemosinarius poterit conquirere versus aquam secundum quod vicini ex utraque parte conquisierint*); the grant includes 'common rights on the lode' (*cum communi lade*) on the northern boundary of this land.[39] The process of reclamation is implied in four entries in the bishops' thirteenth-century surveys. Two record plots of reclaimed land (*purprestura*), and two record holdings described as new tenancies (*de novo*) in 1222, and messuages in 1250. The archaeological evidence observed at The Maltings, south of Ship Lane, consisted of a series of deposits dumped beyond successive river banks, pushing the waterfront further east; this was being carried out between 1200 and 1400, judging by the pottery evidence.[40]

Bishop Eustace's confirmation of the grant of a messuage next to Broad Hithe (*bradehide*) made by Bishop Ridel (1174–89) to Robert of Wells shows that the development of the Waterside area had already begun in the last quarter of the twelfth century.[41] The lode north of Waterside possibly flowed along the line of Willow Walk; it was called the 'long lode' in two charters of 1402, and the evidence from these documents suggests that the stream flowed south-eastward into the river.[42] The lode provided shipping access to Stock Hithe, itself next to the gate of Liles estate. The street layout north of Waterside suggests more than one phase of development, while Waterside forms a link between the foot of Forehill and the bend in the Great Ouse, and was possibly established after the diversion of the river.

37 *VCH* 4, p. 30; H. Wharton, *Anglia sacra* (2 vols, 1691), i, pp. 620–21.

38 M, p. 169 *iterata*.

39 M, pp. 492–3.

40 T. Reynolds, *A medieval waterfront at The Maltings, Ely* (AFU Report 096, 1994).

41 M, p. 161 *iterata*.

42 CUL EDC 1/B1/219 and 220.

The 'common gutter' divided the area between Broad Street and the river into a northern part that became more densely occupied, and a southern part where occupation remained limited to the street frontage (map 3). Adjoining the 'common gutter' was Sedgwick, a landmark frequently mentioned in medieval documents. It probably lay south of the gutter, if '*Sedgewickes ditch*' recorded in the Parliamentary Surveys of 1649 and the 'common gutter' mentioned in 1417 are the same watercourse. The entry concerned '*Sidgwicks Lease*', describing it as being bounded by the river on the south-east and by '*Sedgewickes ditch*' on the north-east.[43]

The ground between Broad Street and the river was gradually drained. Evidence for a ditch parallel to Broad Street has been found on a number of sites east of this street, particularly clearly on Jewson's site where it lies some seventy metres from the street frontage (map 2).[44] Buildings were constructed in this newly drained area. At 41 Broad Street, The Three Blackbirds incorporates a late thirteenth-century hall, standing at right-angles to the street. Some fifty yards north, on the Jewson's site, excavations have uncovered evidence for an aisled hall running parallel with the street frontage, and in Jubilee Terrace (formerly Cutter Lane) there was evidence for a rectangular building parallel with the lane, both structures dating to the thirteenth century.[45] The riverside became a centre of activity; landing stages catered for persons and goods transported by boat, while occupations that required water were situated there. Castle Hithe marked the south end of the riverside area, near the point where Stuntney causeway crossed Cawdle Fen stream. There are many thirteenth-century references to a bridge over the stream, but initially the stream would have been forded; the irregular triangle formed by Castle Hithe may represent the fanning-out approaches to an earlier ford, possibly remaining in use after construction of the bridge.[46] Potters Lane probably predates the diversion of the river; it does not line up with Broad Street. It occurs frequently as the potters' street or lane (*vicus or venella figulorum*) in thirteenth-century documents, and there is evidence for the manufacture of pottery here from the thirteenth to the fifteenth century.[47]

The framework for medieval Ely was established by *c.*1250. In the upper part of the town, it incorporated earlier elements (map 3). The bishop's private land lay in three separate blocks; his palace complex lay west of the cloister, his vineyard north of Forehill, and the barton farm south of Barton Square. The home farm probably predates the creation of the see, but the palace complex and the vineyard may well have been laid out in the latter half of the twelfth century, in connection with the postulated redevelopment of the settlement initiated by Bishop Nigel. The bishop's grant to Livitha suggests former occupation in the vicinity of the west end of the cathedral, and burials excavated in front of the old bishop's palace imply a former cemetery.[48] West of the cathedral, an open area (now Palace Green) formed a focus upon which roads from other Isle settlements converged. The parish church of St Mary and the associated tithe barn stood west of the bishop's palace complex. The church had been rebuilt by Bishop Eustace *c.*1200, and the adjacent tithe barn,

43 CUL EDC 8A/1/13, p. 13.

44 C. Cessford, M. Alexander and A. Dickens, *Between Broad Street and the Great Ouse: waterfront archaeology in Ely* (EAA, 114, 2006), p. 10.

45 A. P. B. Holton-Krayenbuhl, ed., *The Three Blackbirds: a medieval house in Ely, Cambridgeshire* (Ely, 1984); Cessford *et al.*, *Between Broad Street and the Great Ouse*, pp. 7–8, 14.

46 Broadening of a roadside verge may reflect the approach to a former ford, often remaining in use after construction of the bridge, and providing access up or downstream of the bridge: M. Cook, *Medieval bridges* (Princes Risborough, 1998), p. 6.

47 P. Spoerry, *Ely wares* (EAA, 122, 2008), pp. 11–12.

48 Although limited pottery evidence suggests a fourteenth-century date: R.M. Regan and M. Alexander, *Archaeological investigations: the old Bishop's Palace, Ely* (CAU Report 141, 1995), pp. 5–8.

demolished in 1842, was of mid-thirteenth-century date.[49] Both were the sacrist's responsibility, and for this reason the tithe barn is usually known as the sacrist's barn. The hospitals of St John the Baptist and St Mary Magdalene stood at the western limits of the town, on the road to Witchford; of obscure origin, they were united by Bishop Hugh of Northwold (1229–54) to form the hospital of St John *c.* 1240. The residents were to consist of a master and thirteen chaplains and brethren. The presence of paupers is implied in the foundation statutes, and the presence of sisters in a later thirteenth-century document; but numbers seem to have dwindled by the end of the century, and the mastership became a sinecure in the fifteenth century.[50] Bishop Northwold was also responsible for establishing a chantry for four priests, and he provided them with a house on the green opposite his palace complex. The medieval market place formed an elongated rectangle north of the monastic precinct, and the butchers' stalls stood within this area.

Produce of local origin was exchanged at the market, whereas the fairs provided a venue for the exchange of goods from further afield. Reference to purchases at the fair in Ely illustrates the involvement of the town in long-distance trade. In the mid-thirteenth century these included furs and silk, and the merchants involved came from *Erneburg*, Gotland and Lynn.[51] This seven-day fair had been granted by Henry I to Bishop Hervey, to be held on the feast of St Etheldreda (23rd June), and on the three days preceding and following it.[52] Two more fairs were granted in the fourteenth century, one to be held at the feast of St Lambert (17th September), granted in 1312, and the other at Ascension-tide, granted in 1318.[53] In the fourteenth century, the sacrist received income from 'stalls at the great bank, at the time of the fair'.[54]

Street names are mentioned in many thirteenth-century deeds, providing evidence for the status of roads within the urban network, and for the existence of tenements along these streets (maps 2 and 3). Forehill and Back Hill were major thoroughfares, the former was 'the street (*vicus* or *magna strata*) extending from the monks' gate to the great bank', the latter was 'the street (*vicus*) that leads to the castle bank'. Broad Street provided a link between them. A deed of 1292 refers to it as 'the street that leads from the king's highway running from the cathedral to the great bank, to the king's highway running from the bishop's barton to the castle bank', suggesting that it was secondary to Forehill and Back Hill.[55] Another deed, of 1297, refers to it as 'the street called *le Brodelane* leading from the castle bank to the broad bank'; Broad Street also occurs as 'Castle Lane' and as 'the street that leads from the great bank to the castle bank'.[56] 'Great bank' and 'broad bank' were used interchangeably to denote the Waterside area. Of the lanes running between Broad Street and the river, only Barkers Lane, now Ship Lane, is mentioned in thirteenth-century documents. In the upper part of the town, Egremont Street and Chapel Street occur as 'Acreman Street' (ploughman's street) and 'Cats Lane'. The south-west branch of Newnham Street was 'the lane (*venella*) leading towards Newnham', and the eastern branch was 'Newnham'. Nutholt Lane occurring as 'Shendforth Lane' was a secondary lane, linking Newnham with 'the street (*vicus*) leading towards

49 T. D. Atkinson, *An architectural history of the Benedictine monastery of St Etheldreda at Ely* (2 vols, Cambridge, 1933), i, pp. 167–9; F. R. Chapman, ed., *Sacrist rolls of Ely* (2 vols, Cambridge, 1907), i, p. 114.

50 M, pp. 186–7; W. M. Palmer, 'The Hospitals of St John the Baptist and St Mary Magdalene at Ely, part II', *PCAS*, 36 (1936), 81, 85, 86.

51 *CLR* 1245–51, pp. 257, 262, 315, 316.

52 M, p. 84.

53 *VCH* 4, p.50.

54 Chapman, *Sacrist Rolls*, ii, pp. 36, 74, etc.

55 CUL EDC 1/A/2, fo 53v.

56 CUL EDC 1/B1/74; CUL EDC 1/A/2, fos 78v–79.

Map 3

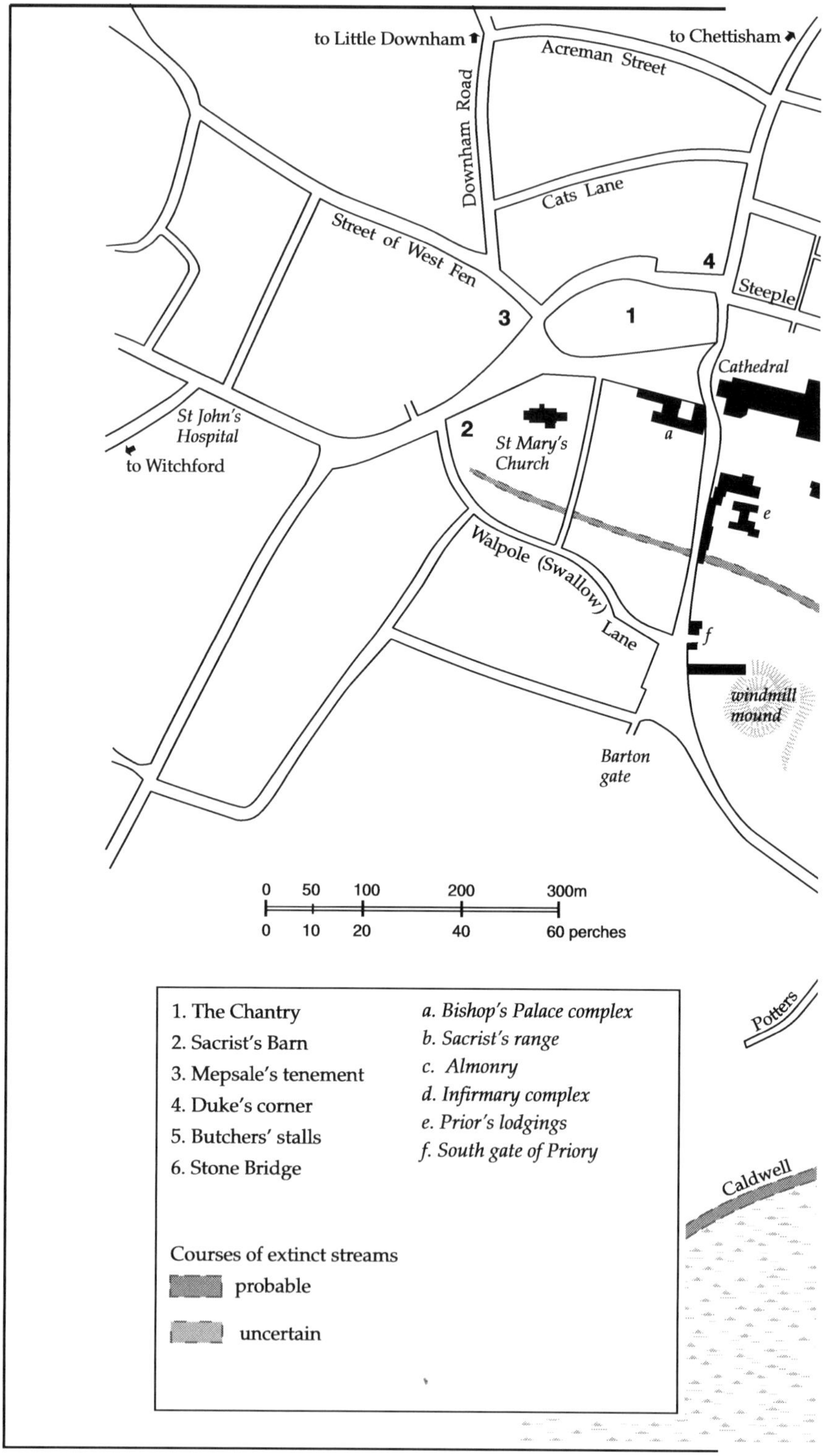

Ely in 1417. A reconstruction, with medieval street names, and the conjectured course of extinct streams.

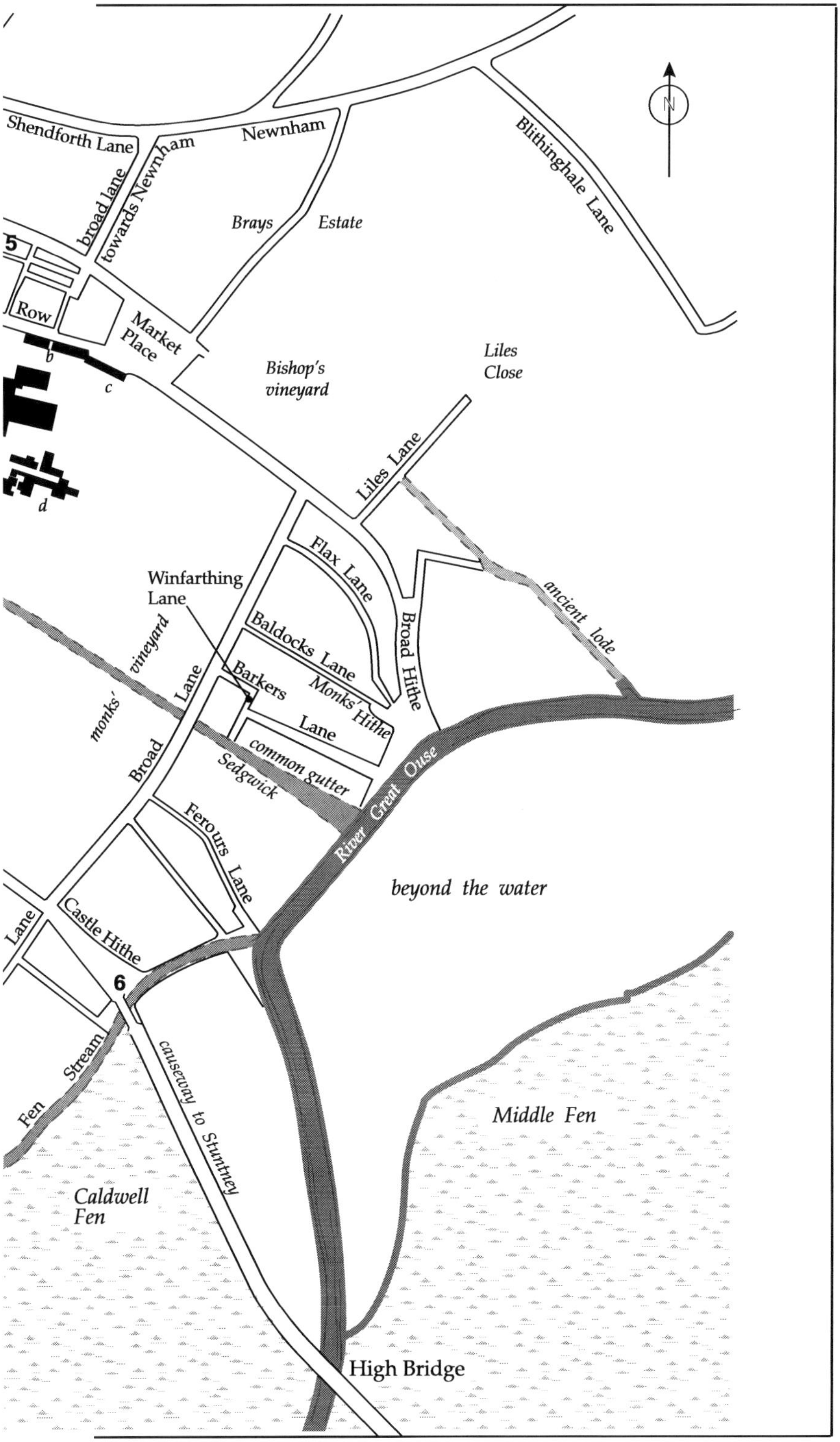

Shendforth Lane
broad lane
towards Newnham
Newnham
Blithinghale Lane
Brays Estate
5
Row
Market Place
b
c
d
Bishop's vineyard
Liles Close
Liles Lane
Flax Lane
Winfarthing Lane
Baldocks Lane
Broad Hithe
ancient lode
monks' vineyard
Broad Lane
Barkers Lane
Monks' Hithe
common gutter
Sedgwick
River Great Ouse
Ferours Lane
beyond the water
Lane
Castle Hithe
6
Fen Stream
causeway to Stuntney
Middle Fen
Caldwell Fen
High Bridge

Chettisham', now Lynn Road. South of St Mary's church was 'Swallow Lane' (*Swaulewe Lane*), later Walpole Lane and now Silver Streeet, and east of Newnham was 'Blithinghale Way' (*via de Blythynghale*) or Lane, now Springhead Lane. The spelling of all these names varied considerably.

Bishop Nigel had laid the basis for the landholdings and rights of the medieval priory, and his grant of 1138x1139 was confirmed by successive bishops.[57] Among the earliest grants of holdings in Ely were Nigel's grant of a *mansura* and house for the monastic *scriptorium*, and Bishop Longchamp's confirmation of a grant to the sacrist of four stalls on either side of St Peter's tower, later known as Steeplegate.[58] Priory acquisitions were particularly numerous in the period between 1230 and 1270, under Prior Ralph and Prior Walter, and, *c.* 1261–71, when Nicholas was almoner. In expanding their holdings, the prior and convent had the support of Bishop Northwold.[59] Some of this bishop's grants to the priory are recorded in the 1250 survey.

Abbot Simeon had started rebuilding the abbey church *c.* 1082, and the eastern arm was completed by 1106 when the body of St Etheldreda was translated to the new choir together with the remains of the other three Saxon saints. Construction reached completion during the episcopate of Geoffrey Ridel (1173–89). Bishop Northwold rebuilt the eastern arm, providing a more splendid setting for the shrines of the Saxon saints and improved circulation for pilgrims. The cathedral was rededicated to the Virgin Mary, St Peter and St Etheldreda when the new presbytery was consecrated in 1252 in the presence of Henry III, his son Edward and a large gathering of prelates, nobles and laymen.[60] The first phase in the construction of the medieval claustral buildings saw the gradual build-up of structures, *c.* 1150–*c.* 1280, beginning with the construction of the prior's hall (map 3).[61] Initially, the boundary between the bishop's land and the priory had been fluid, as is illustrated by thirteenth-century grants to the priory of sites near the south-west corner of the cloister, but it was stabilised by the mid-fourteenth century.[62] The prior's department lay south of the refectory and monastic kitchen, the ranges of the sacrist and almoner formed the northern boundary of the precinct at the interface with the town, while the remaining buildings followed the standard Benedictine plan. The outer court lay in the southern part of the precinct and opened onto Barton Square; it comprised buildings such as the monastic barn and was a centre of activity for laymen associated with the priory. By the 1270s, the monastic enclosure contained a six-acre vineyard, a two-acre garden, and a windmill, presumably on Cherry Hill, the site of a windmill on Speed's map of 1610.[63]

The thirteenth-century evidence implies that, by *c.* 1280, the priory had gained increased institutional independence from the bishop, and the buildings associated with its various departments had all been constructed. Ely had become partly urban, with a population engaged in service activities and crafts, much more numerous than the rural population recorded in the Domesday Book.

57 Karn, *Ely 1109–1197*, p. 50.

58 M, pp. 160, 168.

59 Evans, *Ely Chapter ordinances*, pp. vii–viii; S. Evans, *The medieval estate of the Cathedral Priory of Ely: a preliminary survey* (Ely, 1973), p. 7; the almoner's cartulary: CUL EDC 1/A/2, *passim*.

60 P. Draper, 'Bishop Northwold and the Cult of St Etheldreda' in *Medieval Art and Architecture at Ely Cathedral* (British Archaeological Association Transactions, 2, 1979), pp. 11, 15, 21; Wharton, *Anglia sacra*, i, p. 636.

61 Many of these buildings were re-examined in the course of the restoration programme of 1987–96; some of the findings have been published: Holton-Krayenbuhl, 'The Infirmary Complex', 118–72; A. Holton-Krayenbuhl, 'The Prior's Lodgings at Ely', *Archaeological Journal*, 156 (1999), 294–341.

62 Holton-Krayenbuhl, 'Prior's Lodgings', 334.

63 M, p. 612.

The first of the Ely gilds was also founded at about this time; it was the gild of St Etheldreda.[64] The population expansion is reflected in Bishop Balsham's order of 1277 forbidding the sacrist to continue giving each inhabitant a candle at Candlemas because this would now require more than 700 pounds of wax.[65]

By this date, Ely was part of a wide network of river communications that included not only the fenland, but also the ports of eastern England and north-west Europe, accessible through the harbour town of Lynn, founded *c.* 1100 by the bishop of Norwich, Herbert of Losinga.[66] In the course of the twelfth century, Lynn had developed into the main port on the Wash, replacing Wisbech whose estuary was silting up, necessitating changes in the course of the fenland rivers. The Nene with its East Midlands tributaries and the Western Ouse had been diverted at Outwell in Norfolk to flow eastwards along Well Creek. Beyond Well Creek, these watercourses entered the north – south channel created between Littleport and Wiggenhall; they merged with the other fenland rivers at Wiggenhall, to flow into the Wash estuary at Lynn. The diversion along Well Creek probably occurred in the final decades of the thirteenth century, while the cut from Littleport northwards may have been completed a century earlier.[67]

c. 1280–1539: Expansion and transformation of the medieval town

The fourteenth century saw major building activity in the monastic precinct, while the prior and convent increased their holdings in Ely and built houses and shops. Both bishop and priory were affected by the agrarian crisis, the onset of the Black Death and the Peasants' Revolt. Discord between the bishop and the priory that had been simmering since the end of the century was resolved in the arbitration of 1417 which includes the street-by-street survey of the town. Expansion ceased in the fifteenth century and Ely became a minor town. In the decades around 1500 there was renewed building activity in the monastic precinct, in the bishop's palace complex, and in the town. The monastery was dissolved in 1539.

Three personalities dominated the fourteenth-century building campaign in the cathedral priory: Bishop Hotham (1316–37), Prior Crauden (1321–41) and Alan of Walsingham (sacrist 1321–41, then prior 1341–*c.* 1364), and the good relationship between the three men contributed to the success of this undertaking. Construction of the Lady Chapel had started in 1321, but was interrupted in the following year by the need to replace the Norman crossing-tower, in a state of imminent collapse; this resulted in the construction of the octagon, completed *c.* 1340, together with the three westernmost bays of the presbytery. The Lady Chapel was completed between 1349 and 1353.[68] In the 1360s a lean-to parish church was built against the north side of the cathedral, and was dedicated as the church of St Cross by Bishop Langham (1362–6). This was a belated response to a visitation injunction of 1315.[69] Until then, the eleven westernmost bays of the cathedral nave had served as the parish church of St Peter, being separated from the monks' choir by a screen; this

64 W. M. Palmer, 'The village gilds of Cambridgeshire', *Transactions of the Cambridgeshire and Huntingdonshire Archaeological Society*, 1 (1904), 376.

65 M, p. 203.

66 The town was also called Bishop's Lynn, and became King's Lynn after the Reformation: H. Clarke and A. Carter, *Excavations in King's Lynn 1963–1970* (1977), pp. 1–2.

67 H. C. Darby, *The medieval fenland* (Newton Abbot, reprinted 1974), pp. 96–8.

68 P. G. Lindley, *The monastic cathedral at Ely* c. *1320–*c. *1350: art and patronage in medieval East Anglia* (Unpublished Ph.D. thesis, 2 vols, Cambridge, 1985), i, pp. 4–5; Wharton, *Anglia sacra*, i, pp. 643–4, 651–2.

69 BL Egerton 3047, fos 31v–32.

caused inconvenience when the parishioners' services were in progress at the same time as the monks' offices. The church of St Cross was demolished *c.* 1566 and its exact location is not known.[70]

The claustral buildings were remodelled and extended. At the north end of the precinct, Alan of Walsingham rebuilt the sacrist's enclosure; in a corner he constructed the Goldsmith's Tower, a two-storey block housing his accounting office over a ground-floor workshop for the goldsmith; he also built a hall in the infirmary for the use of the monks' female relatives, a structure forming the northern arm of the L-shaped range that replaced the north aisle of the infirmary hall.[71] Major work was carried out in the prior's department, resulting in a system of interconnected ranges. The prior's hall was extended by the construction of Prior Crauden's chapel and study, and Queen's Hall was built; other ranges were extensively remodelled, with the addition of porches, passages and stairs to enable circulation throughout the department at ground- and first-floor level. In the fourteenth century, the prior's household included some twenty-one domestic servants, as well as secular chaplains, squires and grooms.[72] The west range of the prior's complex provided accommodation for high status guests with their retinue, which included Edward III's queen, Philippa, a frequent visitor to the priory; Queen's Hall was probably built for her use. There was a separate kitchen and dining-hall for lay visitors not subject to the restrictions of Benedictine diet. By *c.* 1350, the monastic precinct had been modernised, and the accommodation adapted for increased comfort and privacy.[73] At the south end of the precinct, in the area forming the outer court of the monastery, the barn was built in the 1370s, and the Porta *c.*1400, both presumably replacing earlier structures.[74]

Funding for all this building activity came from several sources. The bishops financed cathedral building projects while the sacrist was responsible for routine maintenance. In view of the extensive financial requirements of this period, additional funding was obtained through borrowing, and through gifts and legacies of laymen. Ely also benefited from royal patronage which included the lease of the manor of Soham that the priory had obtained from Queen Philippa.[75]

Priory holdings increased considerably in the fourteenth century. Brays estate was purchased in 1314 during the priorate of John Fressingfield; the estate included holdings accumulated by Payne, Alexander's son and his descendants, listed among the free tenants in the surveys of 1222 and 1250.The estate of Braham was purchased in 1336; it included tenements in Ely as well as Braham farm where the goldsmiths of Ely had received part of their income, as recorded in the 1250 survey. Bishop Hotham bequeathed lands and tenements in Ely, later known as 'the cellarer's rents', and attached to the cellarer's department; some time after 1362, the cellarer purchased Ketons manor, on the south side of Silver Street.[76] The prior and convent acquired the manor of Liles Place in 1398.[77]

[70] Chapman, *Sacrist rolls*, i, pp. 102–4; Atkinson, *Monastic buildings of Ely*, ii, Sheet IV.

[71] A. Holton-Krayenbuhl, T. Cocke and T. Malim, 'Ely Cathedral precincts: the north range', *PCAS*, 78 (1989), 63–5; Holton-Krayenbuhl, 'Infirmary complex', 144–8, 169; Wharton, *Anglia sacra*, i, p. 646.

[72] Evans, *Ely Chapter ordinances*, pp. xi, 26.

[73] Holton-Krayenbuhl, 'Prior's lodgings', 334–6.

[74] Atkinson, *Monastic buildings of Ely*, i, pp. 150, 153.

[75] Lindley, *Monastic cathedral at Ely*, pp. 4, 13; S. Raban, *Mortmain legislation and the English church 1279–1500* (Cambridge, 1982), pp. 107–8.

[76] Evans, *Medieval estate*, p. 17; J. Bentham, *The history and antiquities of the conventual and cathedral church of Ely* (Cambridge, 1771), p. 158; *VCH* 4, p. 49.

[77] BL Egerton 3047, fos 113v, 117v.

The claustral buildings stood on the high ground between the cathedral and Cherry Hill and the vineyard occupied the east-facing slope below (maps 2 and 3). The pittancer's account rolls show that both wine and verjuice were being produced in the fourteenth century; accounts of 1510–11 show that the vineyard was enclosed with a ditch and wall.[78] On the north side of Forehill, in the bishop's vineyard, stood a wine press (*domus pro pressura*) according to the inventory of the bishop's manors made in 1356–8; the same document records, on the Barton estate, a hall, three barns, two oxhouses, a dovehouse, two windmills and a prison.[79] There is material evidence for fourteenth-century buildings. This includes the standing building at 23 Broad Street, and an aisled hall traces of which were excavated on the Jewson's site, replacing the earlier structure; both are aligned at right-angles to the street.[80] The cellarer's account rolls for 1337–8 record the construction by this obedientiary of thirteen stalls (*selde*), nine on a plot that had been William Tilly's, opposite the Porta, four next to the bishop's vineyard; they were all paying rent the following year.[81]

Speed's map of 1610 shows a stone bridge at Castle Hithe and, beyond, a drawbridge carrying the causeway over the Great Ouse. The stone bridge 'at the castle bank' was constructed in 1339–40 replacing a postulated thirteenth-century structure.[82] There is late medieval documentary evidence for the drawbridge; during the reign of Henry VI, the keeper of the 'high bridge' was entitled to bread and beer whenever he raised the bridge to allow the prior's barge to pass through, and in 1516–17 a cable was bought for the 'great bridge'.[83]

The bishop and the prior and convent were not immune to the disasters of the age. The agrarian crisis that started in 1315 appears to have seriously affected sheep rearing. Most of the wool exported from Lynn and Boston came from the fenland, and customs returns from these ports show that the volume of wool exported between 1315 and 1335 was half that exported in the period between 1305 and 1315. Changes in the management of sheep farming may have been a contributory factor. On the bishop's manor of Wisbech Barton in the 1330s sheep were grazing on the fen because the demesne pasture was being leased out, and the food allowance for lambs had been considerably reduced, thus making the flock more susceptible to diseases such as liverfluke. Grain production seems to have been unaffected initially, and men of Lincolnshire were buying corn in Cambridgeshire and Huntingdonshire in 1316.[84] By 1341, however, the acreage of arable in Cambridgeshire had shrunk. The returns of the *Nonarum Inquisitiones* show that, in 1341, some 1420 acres had been lost to flooding, and over 3450 acres had been abandoned for a variety of reasons including shortage of seed corn and the inability of tenants to till the land due to extreme poverty.[85] The Black Death reached Ely in 1349, and mortality was high both in the town and in the priory where the number of monks was reduced to twenty-eight, from a total of fifty-four in 1347–8; num-

78 CUL EDC 1/F/8/4, 16 and 21.

79 PRO E 143/9/2, membrane 36.

80 E. M. Davis, pers. comm.; Cessford *et al.*, *Between Broad Street and the Great Ouse*, p. 17.

81 CUL EDC 1/F/2/4, and 5B; although the heading of Roll 4 refers to the construction of thirteen stalls on William Tilly's plot, Roll 5B has income from nine new stalls on this site.

82 Chapman, *Sacrist rolls*, ii, p. 91; Wharton, *Anglia sacra*, i, p. 644.

83 D. J. Stewart, *On the architectural history of Ely Cathedral* (1868), p. 178; CUL EDC 1/F/10/44.

84 I. Kershaw, 'The great famine and agrarian crisis in England 1315–1322' in R. H. Hilton, ed., *Peasants, knights and heretics* (Cambridge, 1976), pp. 91, 104–5; D. Stone, *Decision-making in medieval agriculture* (Oxford, 2005), pp. 76–7.

85 A. R. H. Baker, 'Evidence in the "Nonarum Inquisitiones" of contracting arable lands in England during the early fourteenth century', *Economic History Review*, Second Series, 19, no. 3 (1966), 527–8.

bers were already recovering in 1352–3 when they had risen to thirty-five.[86] Likewise, the population of Ely seems to have replenished itself, probably through immigration from the countryside, but by the early fifteenth century recurrent epidemics had started to affect population levels.[87]

The final decades of the fourteenth century witnessed discord both between the tenants and their ecclesiastical landlords, and between the landlords themselves. In June 1381, the Peasants' Revolt caused brief but destructive upheavals in Ely; this included an attack on the bishop's prison. The ringleaders were punished while minor participants were pardoned.[88] Part of the Ely archive had been destroyed in the revolt, and a fire of the Ely muniments in 1401 caused further loss; the dispute between the bishop and the priory over their respective rights and duties was probably exacerbated by this, but it had earlier antecedents.[89] These included claims of the archdeacon of Ely to the sacrist's jurisdiction over the Isle and Cambridgeshire; in the 1320s and 1330s the sacrist had incurred legal expenses to support his rights. A settlement reached in 1401 was unsatisfactory, and the rival claims of archdeacon and sacrist, together with other causes of discord, were finally settled in 1417 in the king's court. The street-by-street survey of Ely that forms part of this agreement provides the framework for a reconstruction of the town at, or just after, its maximal medieval extent (Map 3).[90]

The development of the village at Ely had been part of the general spate of town foundations of the thirteenth century, resulting in a dense network of market centres. The more successful had continued to expand, and their range of influence increased to the detriment of lesser towns, such as Ely.[91] Income from offerings at St Etheldreda's shrine had peaked in 1408–9, although the shrines continued to attract pilgrims until the Dissolution.[92] The fairs likewise continued to attract traders in the fifteenth century, iron and timber being particularly sought after, but the town was turning into a minor centre.[93] Ely suffered for several reasons. Strong ecclesiastical lordship was a disincentive for entrepreneurs. Besides, communications by land were poor, and the town was dependent on the river and the trading facilities provided by Lynn. This port was in decline; the Hanse had taken control of much of the North Sea and Baltic trade, and, by 1424, had its own warehouses at Lynn; the port had been unable to adapt to the change from export of wool to that of finished cloth due to the lack of manufacturing facilities in its hinterland; additionally, the harbour was silting up.[94]

Fifteenth-century Ely appears to have remained moderately prosperous. The priory continued to purchase property in unspecified places, judging by the continued grants of alienation in mortmain until 1534.[95] Although the rentals indicate a drop in the value of holdings towards the mid-fifteenth century, this may be due both to a shortage of potential tenants who were thus able to apply downward pressure on rent levels, and to the fact that the upkeep of the property, hitherto

86 *VCH* 4, p. 34 n; Evans, *Ely Chapter ordinances*, p. ix.

87 A. Dyer, *Decline and growth in English towns. 1400–1640* (1991), pp. 13–14.

88 *VCH* 4, p. 34.

89 N. Ramsay, 'The library and archives 1109–1541' in Meadows and Ramsay, *Ely Cathedral*, p. 164.

90 M. Aston, *Thomas Arundel: a study of church life in the reign of Richard II* (Oxford, 1967), pp. 83–6.

91 Dyer, *Decline and growth in English towns*, pp. 20, 26.

92 D. M. Owen, 'Ely 1109–1539: priory, community and town' in Meadows and Ramsay, *Ely Cathedral*, p. 70.

93 *VCH* 4, p. 50.

94 V. Parker, *The making of King's Lynn* (1971), pp. 11, 37; Clarke and Carter, *Excavations in King's Lynn*, p. 423.

95 *LPFD 1534*, p. 109.

undertaken by the landlord, had become the responsibility of the tenant.[96] Buildings of fifteenth-century origin include the houses at 47 Forehill, 7–11 Silver Street, and 3 West Fen Road.[97] There is some evidence for movement of population. In 1436, three immigrants from Flanders and Holland were granted permission to settle in Ely.[98] The population, estimated at 3367 in 1377, had shrunk to some 1950 by 1524–5.[99] Agricultural opportunities had been reduced by the enclosure of arable land to create pasture, a practice developed towards the end of the fifteenth century.[100] An inquiry of 1548 records the chronology of enclosure in Ely, listing acreages of land taken out of the open fields; this included land on Ketons manor, the almonry barn, and New Barns farm, north of Newnham; the now redundant farm dwellings associated with these estates had been allowed to fall into disrepair. The inquiry also records the blocking up of thoroughfares, another source of grievance for the smallholder.[101]

The decades around 1500 saw a final burst of building activity in the bishop's palace complex and in the monastic precinct. Following his appointment in 1486, Bishop Alcock rebuilt the bishop's palace around a brick gatehouse, now blocked and forming the east wing of the present building; to the east was a range that straddled The Gallery.[102] In the monastic precinct, remodelling aimed at further privatisation of space. The two principal ranges in the prior's department, the Bishop's House and Priory House, were each turned into self-contained houses with internal subdivisions and a kitchen in the undercroft, thus breaking up the links created between the ranges in the fourteenth century. The priory continued to provide education into the sixteenth century in the cloister and in the almonry school. Selected monks received further education at the University of Cambridge as they had done since the 1330s; they included Robert Wells, the last prior, who had been a student at Cambridge in 1510–12, and obtained his BA in 1516–17.[103] The priory remained a dynamic institution into the last decade of its existence, attracting new recruits shortly before 1534 when ten monks were professed; twenty-four remained at the time of the Dissolution in 1539.[104]

Although the priory was dissolved in 1539, the institution persisted in a new form through the establishment, in 1541, of the College of the Holy and Undivided Trinity which was endowed with much of the estate of the late priory.[105] Robert Wells, the last prior, became dean, assuming the name of Robert Steward, having taken on the surname of his father, Nicholas Steward of Wells.[106] Three of the obedientiaries became canons; most of the remaining monks obtained minor posts,

96 Dyer, *Decline and growth in English towns*, pp. 46–7.

97 M. Alexander, 'A medieval and post-medieval street frontage: investigations at Forehill, Ely', *PCAS*, 92 (2003), 143–4; E.M. Davis, pers. comm.

98 *CPR 1429–36*, pp. 539, 541.

99 Dyer, *Decline and growth in English towns*, p. 73, table 3.

100 C. Dyer, 'Peasants and farmers: rural settlements and landscapes in an age of transition' in D. Gaimster and P. Stamper, eds, *The age of transition: the archaeology of English culture 1400–1600* (Oxford, 1997), p. 71.

101 W. M. Palmer, 'Enclosures at Ely, Downham, and Littleport. AD 1548', *Transactions of the Cambridgeshire and Huntingdonshire Archaeological Society*, 5 (1936), 369–81.

102 Atkinson, *Monastic buildings of Ely*, i, pp. 161–4.

103 J. Greatrex, 'Benedictine observance at Ely: the intellectual, liturgical and spiritual evidence considered' in Meadows and Ramsay, *Ely Cathedral*, pp. 80–81; J. Greatrex, *Biographical register of the English cathedral priories of the Province of Canterbury, c. 1066–1540* (Oxford, 1997), pp. 457–8.

104 Greatrex, *Biographical register*, p. 383; *LPFD 1539*, part 2, pp. 189–90.

105 Evans, *Medieval estate*, p. 18.

106 Greatrex, *Biographical register*, p. 458.

and all were awarded accommodation within the precinct.[107] The personnel and buildings of the priory had escaped the fate of many other religious houses, but the social and religious functions associated with it disappeared, and the cult of St Etheldreda and the other saints was abolished, bringing to an end a tradition that had originated in mid-Saxon times.

TENURIAL ORGANISATION

Feudal hierarchy

The Domesday Book records eighty-eight tenants. In 1222, there were, on the bishop's manor of Ely, five knights, some 160 free tenants, eleven holders of butchers' stalls, fifty-one serfs and ninety-eight cottars; in addition, there was an unspecified, though lesser, number of priory tenants. This implies a significant increase in population over this period of some 140 years. The bishops' thirteenth-century surveys record the appearance of new classes of tenants whose status and obligations had developed in the course of the twelfth century.

The earliest mention of knights associated with Ely abbey is in connection with William I's campaign in Scotland of 1072. The abbot, together with all the other tenants-in-chief, had to provide the king with a specific quota of knights to perform military service or castle guard. Ely abbey contributed forty knights who initially were resident within the abbey precinct, and subsequently were granted parcels of abbey land to hold in fee in return for their service.[108] When the see was created, the bishop took over the abbot's responsibilities which, by the early twelfth century, involved provision of forty knights to serve at the royal castle in Norwich. Henry I relieved Bishop Hervey and his successors of this burden and of associated dues, on payment of a fine of £1000, and allowed the bishops of Ely to retain the services of their knights for their own use.[109] On the bishop's manor of Ely, the number of knights was reduced from five in 1222 to four in 1250, Henry Muschet having recently relinquished his holding in Ely in exchange for payment of the rent that he owed at Fen Ditton where he is listed as a knight.[110] The 1250 survey records the duties required of the Ely knights showing that guard duty was still expected of this class at that time.

In the bishops' thirteenth-century surveys, there are two categories of free tenant below the rank of knight, the 'free men beyond the water' having the lightest obligations; they were among the minority of free tenants who were exempt from payment of wite pound, while the majority had to pay this customary rent, possibly as an annual insurance against punishment for minor offences.[111] Additionally, some free tenants had to dig in the bishop's vineyard, the number burdened with this duty increasing between 1222 and 1250. Two holdings were attached to serjeanties. In 1250, these were held by John the helmsman whose duty was to transport the bishop by boat, and John of Hatfield responsible for the bishop's bakehouse; a third, connected with the office of keeper of the rushes, had formerly belonged to this category. In 1250, five free holdings had services attached to them, suggestive of serf origin. Of the four that involved performance of certain labour-services, two also included judicial obligations; the fifth required judicial duties only. These involved meeting the justices in eyre and serving as coroner, functions established in the last decades of the

107 I. Atherton, 'The Dean and Chapter, Reformation to Restoration: 1541–1660' in Meadows and Ramsay, *Ely Cathedral*, p. 170; D. J. Stewart, 'Distribution of the buildings of the dissolved monastery at Ely', *Archaeological Journal*, 54 (1897), 174–85.

108 Miller, *Abbey and bishopric*, pp. 67–8.

109 *VCH* 4, p. 30; Bentham, *History and antiquities of the Church of Ely*, p. 132.

110 R, fo 61v.

111 N. Neilson, *Customary rents* (Oxford, 1910), pp. 177, 184–5.

twelfth century, providing a *terminus post quem* for the creation of these holdings.[112] The degree of freedom was linked to the status of the holding rather than to the status of the tenant, as is illustrated by the case of Payne, Alexander's son in 1222, and his three grand-daughters in 1250. Payne and his grand-daughters paid rent on sixteen free holdings, nine of which required payment of wite pound, and two involved digging in the vineyard, one was formerly subject to labour-service but paid no wite pound; holdings exempt of wite pound included a plot of reclaimed land and a water-meadow.

The status of the serf had deteriorated towards the end of the twelfth century, as leasing was replaced by demesne agriculture, and landowners resumed direct exploitation of parts of their estates. While a few former serf holdings became free, as noted above, the majority became burdened with labour-services on the lord's demesne as well as with various customary dues. On the bishop's manor of Ely the full-land holders, with eighteen ware acres, performed the most onerous duties, while the duties of holders of half lands or portions thereof were proportionally lighter. The ware acre was a fiscal area, probably measuring 1½ acres.[113] The cottars with their one-acre holding performed minimal labour-services; they hired themselves out as their holdings were inadequate for subsistence.

The total amount of labour-services required on the bishop's manors as a whole increased by some 10% between 1222 and 1250, the latter date marking the zenith of demesne agriculture; in the century after 1250, serf labour was gradually replaced by wage labour, as land was taken out of demesne and leased out again. The serf released from labour-service paid a monetary compensation. In 1299 one third of the labour-services due from the bishop's manors had been sold, and between 1297 and 1347, more than 1000 acres of demesne had been leased on six of these manors.[114] By the fifteenth century labour-services had been commuted to money rents. The accounts for the bishop's manor of Barton in Ely for the years 1436–7 and 1440–41 show how the bishop's manor had evolved in the two hundred years since the 1250 survey; the demesne had been rented out, and payment was required for commuted services, but wite pound was still due; the serfs holding full lands (*terra nativa*) and portions thereof paid a total of £35 19*s* 8*d*, while the cottars (*cotarii*) paid £7 18*s* altogether.[115] By the late Middle Ages, former serf tenures had been converted into copyhold tenures.

At Ely, knights, free tenants, serfs and cottars all held of the bishop or of the prior and convent. These ecclesiastical landlords were themselves tenants-in-chief, holding their estates of the Crown. Their estates and rights fell into two categories: *temporalia* and *spiritualia*. The temporalities provided income from manors, estates, markets, tolls and the like; while the spiritualities yielded income from tithes, appropriated churches, and offerings at shrines.[116] On the death of a bishop or of a prior, the temporalities attached to their office were liable to be taken into the king's custody, while the monks, forming a self-regenerating body, still required income for their maintenance. During a vacancy of the see, the king was entitled to the bishop's revenues, appointing keepers to administer the episcopal estates.[117] On a number of occasions in the thirteenth century, the keep-

112 Miller, *Abbey and bishopric*, pp. 124–5.

113 Miller, *Abbey and bishopric*, p. 87 n.

114 Miller, *Abbey and bishopric*, p. 101; E. Miller and J. Hatcher, *Medieval England – Rural society and economic change 1086–1348* (1978), p. 236.

115 CUL EDR D 10/1/1 and 2.

116 E.U. Crosby, *Bishop and Chapter in twelfth-century England: a study of the Mensa Episcopalis* (Cambridge, 1994), pp. 371–2.

117 Crosby, *Bishop and chapter*, p. 365; R. Graham, 'The Administration of the diocese of Ely during the vacancies of the see, 1298–9 and 1302–3' in *Transactions of the Royal Historical Society*, 4th series, 12 (1929), 51.

ers of the see also took the priory into the king's hands, following the death of a prior in 1229 and 1271, during a vacancy of the see in 1286, and in 1298 in connection with the disputed election of a bishop.[118] The matter was resolved the following year by a royal charter granting that the prior and convent should hold the priory with its liberties and revenues separately from the bishopric, and that in future vacancies of the see these should not be taken into the king's hands; for this, the prior and convent paid a fine of 1000 marks.[119] In 1329, Bishop Hotham obtained of Edward III that the priory should also have custody of the temporalities of the see during a vacancy with the profits thereof; for this privilege the prior and convent would pay in proportion to the duration of the vacancy, at a rate of £2000 per annum.[120] This arrangement seems to have prevailed until 1533 but was then challenged, as recorded in two letters addressed to Thomas Cromwell.[121]

The perpetual nature of the monastic community deprived the king of revenues from lands belonging to the priory which would normally have accrued on the death of a secular tenant, and it was in this context that the Statute of Mortmain was passed in 1279. The statute forbade further acquisition of property by religious bodies, and Ely priory incurred fines for flouting the statute in 1298, 1311 and in the early 1320s.[122] A licencing system was developed allowing religious institutions to override this restriction, permitting the acquisition of property up to a specified annual value; the prior and convent of Ely made use of this facility on numerous occasions in the fourteenth and fifteenth centuries, and as late as 1534.[123] A licence was necessary even if the religious house intended to acquire land of a tenant of its own fee because this might deprive the king of his rights over the said tenant.[124] The listed holdings, in excess of one hundred, for which the priory paid a fine in 1371 included some of the prior's fee.[125] The other two religious institutions in Ely also acquired licences for alienation in mortmain, the brethren of St John's hospital on five occasions between 1319 and 1392, and the four chaplains of the chantry on the green in 1387.[126]

The method of appointment of bishops, priors and monastic officials reflects the ranking of these ecclesiastical posts. The bishop was usually appointed by the king. From the thirteenth century, the monks were allowed to select the candidate, although their freedom of choice was probably limited. There were many disputed elections. These include that of John de Keton in 1310, and that of Simon de Montacute in 1337; the former had been almoner at Ely priory and was the monks' candidate, his appointment was confirmed by the archbishop of Canterbury despite the Crown's selection of a rival nominee; the latter was the pope's nominee, appointed instead of Prior Crauden who had been elected by the monks.[127]

118 P. Meadows, 'The Priors of Ely' in Meadows and Ramsay, *Ely Cathedral*, pp. 393–4; Graham, 'The administration of the diocese of Ely', 52–3.

119 *CPR 1292–1301*, pp. 457–8.

120 Bentham, *History and antiquities of the Church of Ely*, p. 158.

121 *LPFD 1533*, pp. 509, 604.

122 Raban, *Mortmain legislation*, p. 95.

123 *LPFD 1534*, p. 109.

124 T. A. M. Bishop, 'Monastic demesnes and the Statute of Mortmain', *English Historical Review*, 49 (1934), 304–5.

125 *Calendar of Inquisitions Miscellaneous* 3 (1937), pp. 294–5.

126 *CPR 1317–21*, p. 319; *CPR 1327–30*, p.144; *CPR 1358–61*, p. 15; *CPR 1381–85*, pp. 298–9; *CPR 1391–96*, p. 144; *CPR 1385–89*, p. 310.

127 Wharton, *Anglia sacra*, i, pp. 641–2, 649.

Most bishops had held high office at court, and several retained these functions after their elevation to the see, among them Bishops Ridel and Longchamp in the twelfth century, and Bishop Hotham in the fourteenth.[128] As landowner, the bishop was involved in the management of extensive estates, scattered throughout six counties, which were run by the bishop's stewards, bailiffs and reeves in the age of demesne farming. These estates are recorded in the thirteenth-century surveys, while an inventory of episcopal manors made in 1356–8 provides a picture of the buildings at the centre of these estates a century later. This inventory records some forty properties, some centred on a palace, others on a manor house.[129] The former group includes the estates at Holborn, Somersham and Hatfield, as well as those at Ely and Little Downham, the latter being a favoured place of residence when the bishop had to be in Ely on episcopal business. The bishop's episcopal duties included the performance of ordinations and visitations, he chaired hearings of the consistory court and held diocesan synods. The diocesan administration was based both in Ely and in Cambridge, and 1374–82, during the episcopate of Thomas Arundel, all meetings of the consistory court were held in Cambridge.[130]

The prior was probably appointed by the bishop until 1271 when Bishop Balsham, previously subprior at Ely, granted the monks the right to elect their prior. The subprior, sacrist, cellarer and chamberlain were nominated by the bishop, and the remaining obedientiaries by the prior.[131] In the later fourteenth and fifteenth centuries, out of an average of forty-five monks about twenty were obedientiaries. Additionally, there were clerks, chaplains, and lay residents that included servants and workmen, adding to a total population of some 150 residents within the monastic precinct; their numbers would be increased by the arrival of visitors to the priory and their retinues.[132] In contrast to the bishop's peripatetic life-style, the monks were confined to the monastic precinct. After a probationary year, the novice made his monastic profession, undertaking to follow the Rule of St Benedict, with a life centred on prayer, the performance of the daily offices, communal living and the provision of hospitality.[133] Infringements of the Rule recorded in the bishop's visitation injunctions probably provide a more realistic picture of life in the priory.[134]

The income of the priory

Bishop Nigel's grant to the priory had included both temporal and spiritual sources of income, and documents provide evidence for the subsequent accumulation by the monks of both types of assets; the sixteenth-century priory rentals records the late medieval situation.

Spiritualia might form part of the endowment of an obedientiary, in the same way as *temporalia*. The sacrist received, by the early fourteenth century, income from both parish churches in Ely, and from the churches of Wentworth and St Andrew's in Cambridge; he received a pension from the church of Little Downham, and the offerings made at five shrines and altars in the cathedral and at the altar in St Mary's church, Ely, besides income from tenements, lands and granges in various places.[135] Out of this, the sacrist paid for the upkeep of the fabric within the precinct and for

128 Karn, *Ely 1109–1197*, pp. lxxx–lxxxii, lxxxiii–lxxxix; Bentham, *History and antiquities*, pp. 156–7.

129 PRO E 143/9/2; Aston, *Thomas Arundel*, p. 264.

130 Aston, *Thomas Arundel*, pp. 25, 38–41.

131 Greatrex, *Biographical register*, pp. 380, 378.

132 Greatrex, *Biographical register*, p. 378; Evans, *Ely Chapter ordinances*, pp. x–xii.

133 Greatrex, 'Benedictine observance at Ely' in Meadows and Ramsay, *Ely Cathedral*, pp. 78–9.

134 Evans, *Ely Chapter ordinances*.

135 Chapman, *Sacrist rolls*, i, pp. 111–23.

the expenses of his department. The monks' rights over a church ranged from possession of the advowson, that is the right to appoint the incumbent, to appropriation whereby the monks became owners of the land, tithes, offerings and other sources of income attached to that church; in cases of appropriated churches, the monks had to provide a vicar who could be a secular priest or might be a fellow-monk.[136] The latter option was discouraged but became common from the late fourteenth century, and at Ely the pittancer appears to have become *ex officio* vicar of Sutton. An undated entry in Bishop Wren's transcripts states that the pittancer of Ely is the parson of Sutton; the title 'pittancer of Sutton' occurs in the heading of a charter of Agnes Raven, copied into the fifteenth-century priory cartulary, where the pittancer is the beneficiary of an annual rent of 2s, and the title occurs in the sacrist's rolls from 1349–50 onwards, in the 1417 survey and in the sixteenth-century priory rentals.[137] Assessment of the priory's revenue for the taxation of 1291 suggests that at that date *spiritualia* yielded just over half the income derived from *temporalia*, although the figures of £351 and £635 respectively are considered to be an underestimate.[138]

The endowment of an obedientiary was proportionate to the level of expenditure required of his department, while the treasurer provided for departments that lacked a specific endowment. The earliest extant account rolls are those of the sacrist, for the year 1292–3, and account rolls survive for fourteen obedientiaries altogether, mostly of the fourteenth and of the first half of the fifteenth century. Only the account rolls of the treasurer, sacrist, granger and pittancer survive for the sixteenth century.[139] The obedientiary account rolls have been used to calculate the average annual income for the departments of the priory in the fourteenth and fifteenth century; the assets of the treasurer's department yielded some £600 per annum, those of the sacrist some £200, the almoner's about £100, and the steward of the prior's household some £90 to which was added money from the treasurer.[140] The administration of an estate might be transferred to a specific obedientiary, as occurred with the Braham estate, granted to the almoner in a deed dated 1362. The grant included specific instructions as to how the money should be spent; the sacrist being among the recipients of these annual payments.[141] The holdings forming Braham estate are listed in the sixteenth-century priory rentals, in the section recording the almoner's rents.

While the obedientiary account rolls provide evidence for the income and expenditure of the departments in the priory, the visitation records provide information about the standards expected in the administration and management of the estate of the priory over the period between 1241 and 1515 for which the records have been published; these cover ten visitations. The treasurers were the chief financial officers throughout the period. The early fourteenth-century injunctions stipulated that the obedientiaries and other officers should present their accounts annually soon after Michaelmas, in the presence of the prior, the subprior and three monks appointed to serve as auditors; in 1314, the sacrist, the shrine-keeper and the keeper of the altar of the Virgin Mary were specifically requested to account for income from shrines. The requirement that obedientiaries render annual accounts was repeated in 1466.[142] Most of the money was then handed over to the two treasurers, selected by the prior and convent, who then distributed it among the departments;

[136] R. H. Snape, *English monastic finances in the later Middle Ages* (Cambridge, 1926), pp. 76–9.

[137] CUL EDR G2/1, column 306; BL Egerton 3047, fo 145v; Chapman, *Sacrist rolls*, ii, p.141; for the date of the Egerton cartulary: Ramsay, 'The library and archives' in Meadows and Ramsay, *Ely Cathedral*, p. 165.

[138] Evans, *Ely Chapter ordinances*, p. xii.

[139] The call numbers for the obedientiary account rolls are CUL EDC 1/F/1–14.

[140] Evans, *Ely Chapter ordinances*, p. xii.

[141] BL Egerton 3047, fo 244 r and v.

[142] Evans, *Ely Chapter ordinances*, pp. 4, 28, 30–31, 38, 39, 59–60.

the visitation records suggest that redistribution of this income evolved in the course of the period, as well as the expenditure required of each obedientiary. The injunctions of 1403 specified that the income from all the obedientiaries except for the almoner should be handed over to the treasurers.[143]

Administration of priory manors had initially been in the hands of two monks, but in 1304, the prior was required to appoint a monk as steward of the manors (*senescallus forinsecus*), and this official is mentioned again in 1307 and 1403.[144] In the visitation injunctions of 1466, two items are concerned with the upkeep and administration of priory goods. The first deals with the unsatisfactory state of buildings in the precinct and on priory manors and granges, as well as the state of disrepair into which the chancels of churches pertaining to the priory had fallen. The second item is concerned with leases; the prior and convent were required to draw up indentures of leases for all their houses, manors, granges and rectories, indicating the sums to be paid and the duration of the lease.[145] The priory rentals show that the monks had documentary evidence for leases on their holdings that went back to the first half of the fifteenth century. The *Valor Ecclesiasticus* of 1535 gives the net annual value of the priory at £1084 6s 9d.[146]

THE DOCUMENTS

The thirteenth-century surveys of the bishops of Ely

The surveys of 1222 and 1250 take the form of an inquiry into the sources of revenue on all the manors of the see, a type of document that first appeared in the late twelfth century and became increasingly common in the thirteenth, as demesne farming was taken up over much of England. The surveys record the holdings of the bishop's fee only. There is one extant copy of the 1222 survey; three copies of the 1250 survey survive.

The 1222 survey (T) is in BL Cotton Tiberius B II, fos 86–233v; it begins with the manor of Ely (fos 86–93), the other manors in Cambridgeshire, and those in Norfolk, Essex, Herfordshire and Suffolk are then listed, not entirely in topographical order. The manuscript is parchment; the written page measures 20x10.6 cm and there are thirty-seven or thirty-eight lines per page; headings are in red ink. There are blank lines and incomplete entries throughout the document, but the text of the Ely section is complete. The inquiry was carried out in the second year of the episcopate of John of Fountains (1220–25), following a five-year vacancy of the see; it may therefore have been undertaken to establish which holdings belonged to the bishop, and what dues could be expected of the tenants on the episcopal manors after this interregnum.

There are three copies of the 1250 survey; R, also known as the Old Coucher or Liber R, is transcribed in this volume (CUL EDR G3/27). The inquiry is on fos 1–206, opening with the section on the manor of Ely on fos 1–7v; it continues with the other manors in Cambridgeshire, Hertfordshire, Essex, Norfolk and Suffolk, in topographical order. The other two copies of the 1250 survey are C (BL Cotton Claudius C XI), fos 25–312, the Ely entry being on fos 25–34v, and G (Gonville and Caius MS 489/485), fos 19–366, beginning with the Ely entry on fos 19–29v.[147]

All three copies of the 1250 survey are on parchment, the text is in double columns and the head-

143 Evans, *Ely Chapter ordinances*, pp. 26–7, 52–3, 53–4.

144 Evans, *Ely Chapter ordinances*, pp. 24, 35, 53.

145 Evans, *Ely Chapter ordinances*, pp. 61–2, 62–3.

146 Evans, *Ely Chapter ordinances*, p. xiii.

147 There is a translation in abbreviated form of the initial part of this survey, up to and including the section on full-lands: J. H. Crosby, 'Ely Episcopal Manor', *Fenland Notes and Queries*, 3 (1897), 190–96, 275–9.

ings are in red ink. In R, the written page measures 30x19 cm and has fifty-five to fifty-seven lines per column. C and G are of similar dimensions; in each, the written page is 23½ cm high, it is 16 cm wide in C, 17 cm in G; both have thirty-seven lines per column. The contents of C and G seem to belong to an earlier stage in the transmission of the text, and generally have common variants in relation to R. Among the variants, C and G both have *Newedik* while R has *Nowedik*, and in the case of numerals the variant is usually common to C and G. The readings in C and G appear to be more reliable than in R, where it is possible to check through internal evidence. R is of a much later date than C.[148]

Alternative dates have been proposed for the 1250 survey. The opening sentence of the survey records that the inquiry was made in the twenty-first year of the episcopate of Bishop Hugh by his steward Roger of Abington. Bishop Hugh of Northwold was enthroned in June 1229, and Ramsay has pointed out recently that the twenty-first year of his episcopate therefore fell in 1249–50. The survey was probably completed in 1250, the inquiry having been made some time between June 1249 and June 1250, but the latter half of 1249 is also possible. Hitherto, Miller's date of 1251 had been taken up in most printed works, while 1256 and 1277 also occur. The date 1277 stems from a note in C inserted by Cole in the eighteenth century; he assumed that the inquiry belonged to the episcopate of Hugh of Balsham (1257–86), dating the survey to 1277; this date was also inserted in G. The inquiry must however belong to the episcopate of Hugh of Northwold, because Roger of Abington is known to have been his steward. Douglas considered that R and C were distinct surveys and dated the former to 1256, the latter to 1277, without discussing the evidence.[149]

The surveys of 1222 and 1250 record a changing landscape, as land next to the recently diverted river was developed, and drainage and assarting progressed. Demesne farming was reaching its zenith in 1250, and demands on the free and customary tenants increased somewhat in the twenty-five year period between the two surveys. The survey of 1222 is less detailed than that of 1250, and omits a few sections, as is shown in the table below, but both record a relatively constant number of holdings.

Table 1. Contents of the 1222 and 1250 surveys of Ely, with folio numbers

1222 [T] fos 86–93	1250 [R] fos 1–7
Introduction, 86	Introduction, 1
Demesne, 86	Demesne, 1
Meadow, 86	Hay meadow, 1
	Marsh, 1–1v
	Livestock, 1v
	Mills, 1v
Fisheries, 86v	Fisheries, 1v–2
Knights, 86v	Knights, 2
Free tenants,[150] 86v–89v	Free tenants, 2–4v
Customary obligations subject to	Free men beyond the water, 4v–5
labour-service, 89v–9	Butchers' stalls, 5
Full lands, 90v	Full lands, 5–6
Half lands, 90v–91v	Half lands, 6–6v
Cottars, 91v–92v	Cottars in Ely, 6v–7
Free men beyond the water, 92v	Reeves and beadles, 7
Butchers' stalls, 92v–93	

148 N. Ramsay, 'The library and archives 1109–1541' in Meadows and Ramsay, *Ely Cathedral*, p. 160 n 20.

149 Wharton, *Anglia sacra*, i, pp. 635–6; Ramsay, 'The library and archives 1109–1541' in Meadows and Ramsay, *Ely Cathedral*, p. 160 n 19; Miller, *Abbey and bishopric*, pp. 5–6 n; D. C. Douglas, *The social structure of medieval East Anglia* (Oxford, 1927), p. 7.

150 Strictly: 'men holding freely' (*De libere tenentibus*).

Units of measurement used on the manor of Ely are defined in the 1250 inquiry. At the end of the section on the demesne, the jurors state that the Ely perch measured 16½ ft; this is reiterated in the initial section of the 1417 survey. A document of 1649 regarding holdings of the Dean and Chapter records two values for the Ely perch or pole, depending on the type of ground that was being measured: 'the fens are layd out by the 18 foot pole & arable & pasture by the 16½ foot'.[151] In the course of the thirteenth century, measurements were being introduced into surveys, the measured acre was equivalent to an area of forty perches long by four perches wide.[152] Arable land was divided into long narrow strips scattered among the open fields of the settlement, the area of each strip ranging from ¼ acre to ½ acre; thus the eighteen acres of the full-land holder in the bishop's surveys were distributed among the open fields of Ely that lay north and south of the town. Such a distribution is illustrated in a late thirteenth-century grant of ten acres of land made by Ralph of Chatteris and his wife Agnes to Andrew, son of Nicholas of Ely; about one third lay in the 'fields towards Little Downham', the remainder lay in the fields 'towards Witchford' the land mostly divided up into half-acre strips.[153]

The surveys of 1222 and 1250 open with a description of the topography of the manor and the associated natural resources; the acreage within each field is recorded together with the totals.[154] Both lists begin with the arable in Grunty Fen field, but subsequently the order is not consistent; Cratendon, the name of the settlement that pre-existed St Etheldreda's seventh-century foundation occurs among the arable fields listed. Despite the loss of some 200 acres of arable in Roueshill and Weld over the twenty-five years between the surveys, due to quarrying and other factors, there was an overall increase of 42 acres in arable and 78 acres in meadow between the two surveys; assarts at Chettisham account for most of the increase. It is suggested that Roueshill can be identified with Rosewell Hill, *le Rougemont* and the Red Mount of medieval documents. The 1250 survey provides a detailed record of the extent of the marsh, and of the rights of the bishop and of other users on fen produce; these covered mowing, grazing and fishing rights, as well as gathering of reeds for thatching and digging of turves. Both surveys record the renders from fisheries which included fishing from boats along the stretch of the river between Little Thetford and Prickwillow; five boats are recorded in 1222, six in 1250, and it is possible that in 1222 the sixth boat fishery is that pertaining to John of Pulham's messuage for which he renders 3*s*, listed under 'free tenants'.[155] These boat fisheries occur as *boatgangs* in the sixteenth-century rentals. The renders from fisheries were in money or in kind in the form of eels, and remained constant from 1222 to 1250.

The bishops' tenants were divided into categories according to the condition of their tenure. Exemption from payment of wite pound is common to all plots of reclaimed land recorded in the surveys, as well as to the holdings of the 'free tenants beyond the water', underlining the special status of these tenements that were held on lighter terms.There are few topographical references in the section on free tenants, apart from the group whose holdings abutted upon the bishop's vineyard, and therefore can be located on the north side of Forehill; some names occur as former holders in the 1417 survey, suggesting that the thirteenth-century surveyors proceeded uphill, from east to west. Comparison between the two surveys shows that the eight holdings at the head of 'Free men beyond the water' in 1222 occur at the end of 'Free tenants' in 1250; one refers to a

151 CUL EDC 8A/1/15.

152 P. D. A. Harvey, *Manorial Records* (1999), p. 16.

153 CUL EDC 1/B1/44.

154 In the 1222 survey, the total of 1482½ acres of arable land is incorrect; the field-by-field acreages add up to 1473 acres.

155 T, fo 87v.

holding in Soham, leaving seven holdings in Ely whose classification changed between 1222 and 1250. It is suggested that these lay in the area south of Annesdale, between Stuntney causeway and the recently diverted course of the river (map 2). Although documentary evidence indicates that the river had been diverted by the last decade of the twelfth century, it appears that the area considered 'beyond the water' in 1222 still comprised ground beyond Cawdle Fen stream. By 1250 the course of the diverted river was a well-established fact and the holdings listed 'beyond the water' all lay on the east side of the river. In the 1222 survey, the section on tenants 'beyond the water' occurs at the end of the survey, together with the butchers' stalls, suggesting perhaps a recent addition.

The customary tenants had specific duties attached to their holdings in the township of Ely, which included the hamlet of Chettisham. This part of the surveys is not transcribed in this volume and the main features are summarised here.[156] The focal points in the farming year were Michaelmas, Whitsun and Lammas. The 18-acre holders had to provide three days' work per week, except for the period between Whitsun and Lammas where they gave two days' work; the 12-acre holders worked two days per week, except for the period between Lammas and Michaelmas when three days' work was required; those holding fractions of 12 acres provided a fraction of the work. The cottars performed one day's labour-service per week throughout the year. Thus, the greatest number of labour-service days were owed in the period between Lammas and Michaelmas.

Customary obligations for the full- and half-land holder included ploughing, harrowing and hoeing; hay had to be mowed and stacked, corn reaped, bound and carted, threshed and winnowed; barley had to be winnowed and made into malt. The serf had to provide his cart or his plough, or his share of the same; and he was required to undertake carrying services by land and water to specified locations. Besides, the serf had to mow reeds and carry them to the bishop's brewhouse for the Feast of St John, if the bishop was to be in Ely at that time. The serf might also have to make hurdles, or wash and shear sheep; he was also required to repair ditches or dig new ones; but the requirement for the whole vill to make eighty perches of ditch and fence round the bishop's park at Little Downham was stated to have no precedent by the jurors of 1250, and the jurors said that the serfs could not be asked to undertake this task. The cottars had to hoe and reap, bind, stook and thresh corn, but they had no carrying duties. Customary tenants were entitled to a food allowance when performing certain duties; this included provision of a loaf and two herrings on each day that the serf harrowed the lord's land. The length of the working day was specified, as was remission of work days in case of illness. The serf and the cottar had to pay tallage, leyrwite, a fine when his daughter married, and suit of mill; additionally, the serf paid heriot.

The 1417 survey

The survey was drawn up in response to a specific situation, namely the dispute between the bishop, and the prior and convent regarding their respective rights over lands and tenants on the Isle of Ely and within the diocese. It was appended to the arbitration and its aim was to identify all the holdings of the prior and convent in Ely; reference to bishop's holdings was incidental.

The chronology of the processes leading to the settlement of the dispute can be reconstructed from internal evidence. In January 1417, Richard Hildersham and Thomas Hervy, accountant and bailiff of the prior respectively, carried out the street-by-street survey. By December 1417, the king's representatives, Henry Ware, William Hankford and Roger Horton, had heard the claims of both parties regarding spiritual and temporal jurisdiction on the Isle and in the diocese, had inspected the documentary evidence for these, and pronounced judgement acceptable to both parties. The

[156] The sections omitted in this volume are T, fos 89v–90v, 90v–91, and R, fos 5 r and v, 6 r and v.

agreement took the form of a tripartite indenture. The king's three representatives affixed their seals on all three parts of the indenture on 6th December 1417 (the Feast of St Nicholas, bishop), on 8th December (the Feast of the Conception of the Blessed Virgin Mary) the bishop affixed his seal on two parts of the indenture, namely those of the Crown and of the prior and convent, and the prior and convent affixed theirs on the parts of the indenture of the Crown and of the bishop on 13th December (the Feast of St Lucy the Virgin). In February 1418, an enquiry confirmed that the survey of the priory holdings in the town was correct; it was carried out by the archdeacon of Ely and by brother Peter, a monk of Ely, on behalf of the three Crown arbitrators. The arbitration was enrolled on 20th April 1418.

There are six copies of part or all of the arbitration and town survey, as listed in Table 2.

Table 2. The manuscripts containing all, or part of the arbitration of 1417, with folio numbers

	Arbitration	*Town survey*
BL Cotton Claudius C XI [C]	fos 321–326v	fos 327–332v
BL Harleian 329, fos 1–24v [H]	fos 1–9v	fos 10–24v
BL Harleian 329, fos 25–32 [J]		fos 25–32 (incomplete)
PRO C66/401 [P][157]	membranes 5–3	membranes 3–1
BL Cotton Vespasian A XIX [V][158]	fos 61–75	fos 76–98v
CUL EDC 1/C/8	fos 3–8v	–

H has been selected for publication; it is the most detailed version of the survey. It contains many insertions, including the name of the obedientiary receiving rent from the holding, and the names of former holders. The document is therefore pivotal for reconstructing the medieval town plan in areas where most of the holdings belonged to the priory. The four other copies of the survey provide complementary information and variant readings; cross-reference with other documentary sources add to the comprehension of the data provided by H. Although now both part of the same volume, H and J were distinct documents originally, as is clear when comparing the facsimile of J, fo 28v (plate, p. 30), with that of H in Chapter 2. J is incomplete; fo 25 begins in the middle of the entry for tenements near the corner of Broad Street and Forehill, and breaks off in the middle of an entry for a holding on the north side of the High Street.

All five copies of the town survey are parchment. All but H use red ink for headings. In C, the written page measures 24x16 cm, and there are double columns with thirty-seven lines per column; this copy of the 1417 survey is in the same volume as the bishop's survey of 1250, and has a similar layout, but the hand is different. The written page in H measures on average 19x14 cm, the script frequently encroaching upon the margins, there is an average of twenty-nine lines per page. In J, the dimensions are 18½x13½ cm, and in V 14x9¼ cm, both manuscripts have twenty-four to twenty-five lines per page. P comprises the last five membranes of a roll. The manuscripts fall into two groups. P, C and probably J are copies of the original tripartite indenture made between the Crown, the bishop, and the prior and convent, listing all the priory holdings and those of the bishop where these are adjacent to the former; the lists of holdings and the sub-headings form a continuous text. H and V have a common layout and contain a more extensive list of bishop's holdings; V is the more finished of the two, possibly a copy of H. This grouping is supported by the analysis of common variants where C J and P form one group, H and V another.

As noted above, each copy of the tripartite indenture was sealed on a different date in December

157 This copy is translated in abbreviated form in *CPR 1416–22*, pp. 183–95.

158 Transcribed by Bentham in the eighteenth century: CUL Add. 2948, fos 9–22v.

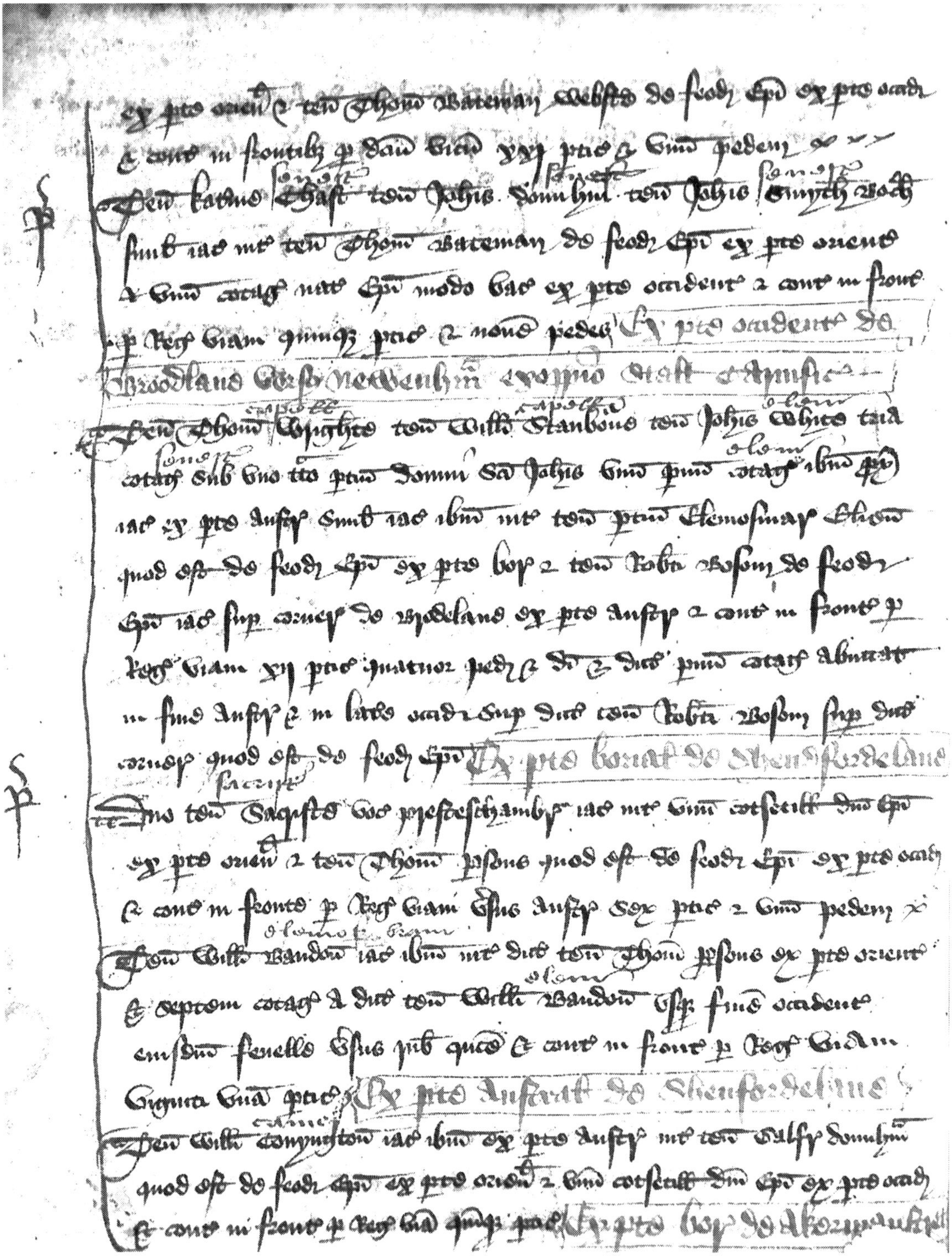

BL Harleian 329, fo. 28v

of 1417; this provides evidence for the ownership of each manuscript. P had all three seals; it forms part of the Crown archive and is clearly a copy of the Crown's part of the indenture. H and V were sealed by the Crown arbitrators and by the bishop, indicating that they represent the priory's part of the indenture. C was sealed by the arbitrators and by the prior and convent and therefore reproduce the bishop's part of the agreement. J lacks the text of the arbitration, but the fact that it records the names of the obedientiaries who received rent from specific holdings suggests that it was a priory document; the features common to J, C and P, described above, suggest that J was the copy of the prior and convent's part of the indenture, a copy left unfinished. EDC 1/C/8 appears to be a copy of the arbitration in the bishop's part of this document.

The street-by-street survey begins at the High Bridge; sub-headings indicate the surveyors' itinerary (map 4). The surveyors crossed the stone bridge over Cawdle Fen stream and continued along Potters Lane and Back Hill to Barton Square; they then followed round the boundary of the monastic vineyard and garden up to the wall of the sacrist's department. They returned to the north-east corner of Broad Street and surveyed the area between Broad Street and the river in two sweeps, starting with the east side of the street, and continuing along Waterside and the river bank. If the postulated location of Sedgwick on the south side of the 'common gutter' is correct, the surveyors' selection of which lanes should be included in the first and which in the second sweep is more rational, the first including holdings on or near the east side of Broad Street, the second running to Broad Hithe and along the river, ending at the 'common gutter'. The street layout north of Waterside is not clear and the reconstruction of this area may well need to be modified in the light of future archaeological findings. The survey continues along the north side of Forehill, Market Street, then Newnham and Nutholt Lane. The surveyors then crossed over to the west side of Lynn Road, at the junction of which stood the red cross; they recorded tenements in Egremont Street, Chapel Street, along the north side of St Mary's Street and along both sides of West Fen Road. The itinerary between Mepsale's corner, at the junction of Downham Road and St Mary's Street, and St John's hospital is difficult to reconstruct; the majority of holdings there belonged to the bishop; there were no holdings in Cambridge Road. The survey continues along Church Lane and Silver Street and ends with the High Street; H and V list the north side then the south, while in C, J and P the headings are in reverse order.

The unit of measurement is stated in the first section of the survey; it is the perch of 16½ feet, as in 1250. The length of the street frontage of all priory holdings and of some bishop's holdings is indicated, but this usually refers to the whole group, and information about an individual holding within the block is rare (map 4). It cannot be assumed that all the tenements listed in a block abutted the street; some might be two or more deep; there might be two tenures within a single building, and examples include the tenements of R. Brame and J. Lyster forming two cottages under one roof on the west side of Broad Street; nearby, John Bugge had two tenements 'under one roof' according to C and P. Occasionally other dimensions are indicated such as depth, as is the case for certain holdings on the north side of Forehill and elsewhere. Tenements were not necessarily rectangular, an extreme case being John Barkere's on the east side of Liles Lane; it measured the equivalent of 6.25m along the lane, 22.25m in length, and 33.4m at the north head 'along the ditch'.

Besides providing dimensions of holdings, the survey records their condition and use. A total of nine ponds is recorded on tenements in the Potters Lane area; as these could serve for stocking fish, they were worthy of mention for their economic value; one of the ponds, on the south side of Back Hill was part of a tenement with a dovecot. At the south end of Potters Lane was the site of a former pottery kiln, appropriately situated on the Kimmeridge clay belt and next to the stream. Gardens are recorded in the Potters Lane area and in a number of places around the town, including a plot at the corner of Silver Street and Church Lane. Central Ely remained rural. On the north side of Market Street stood the almoner's oxhouse and barns, and opposite were the butchers'

Map 4

Ely in 1417.
Map showing holdings of the prior's fee, and the surveyors' route.

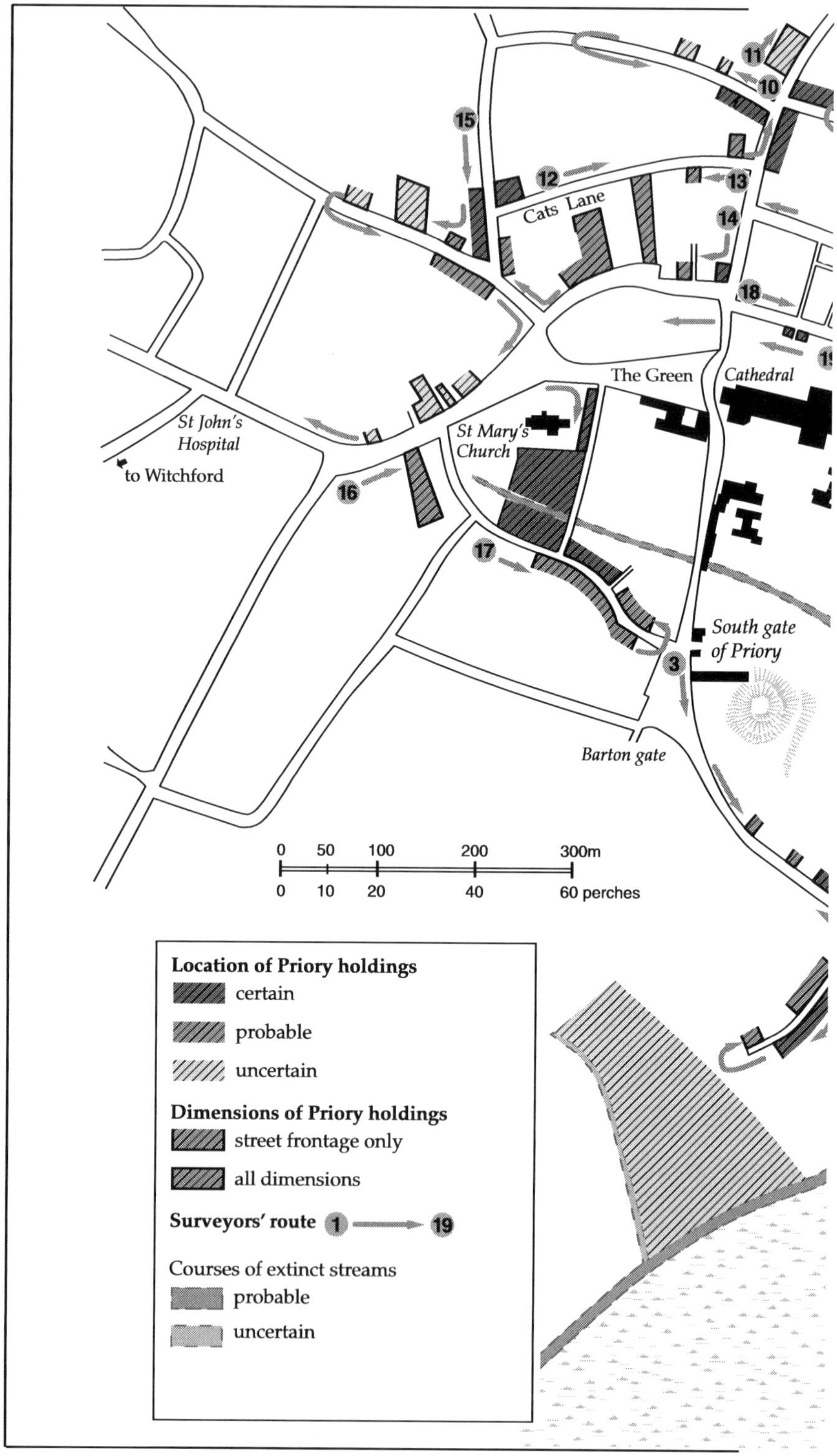

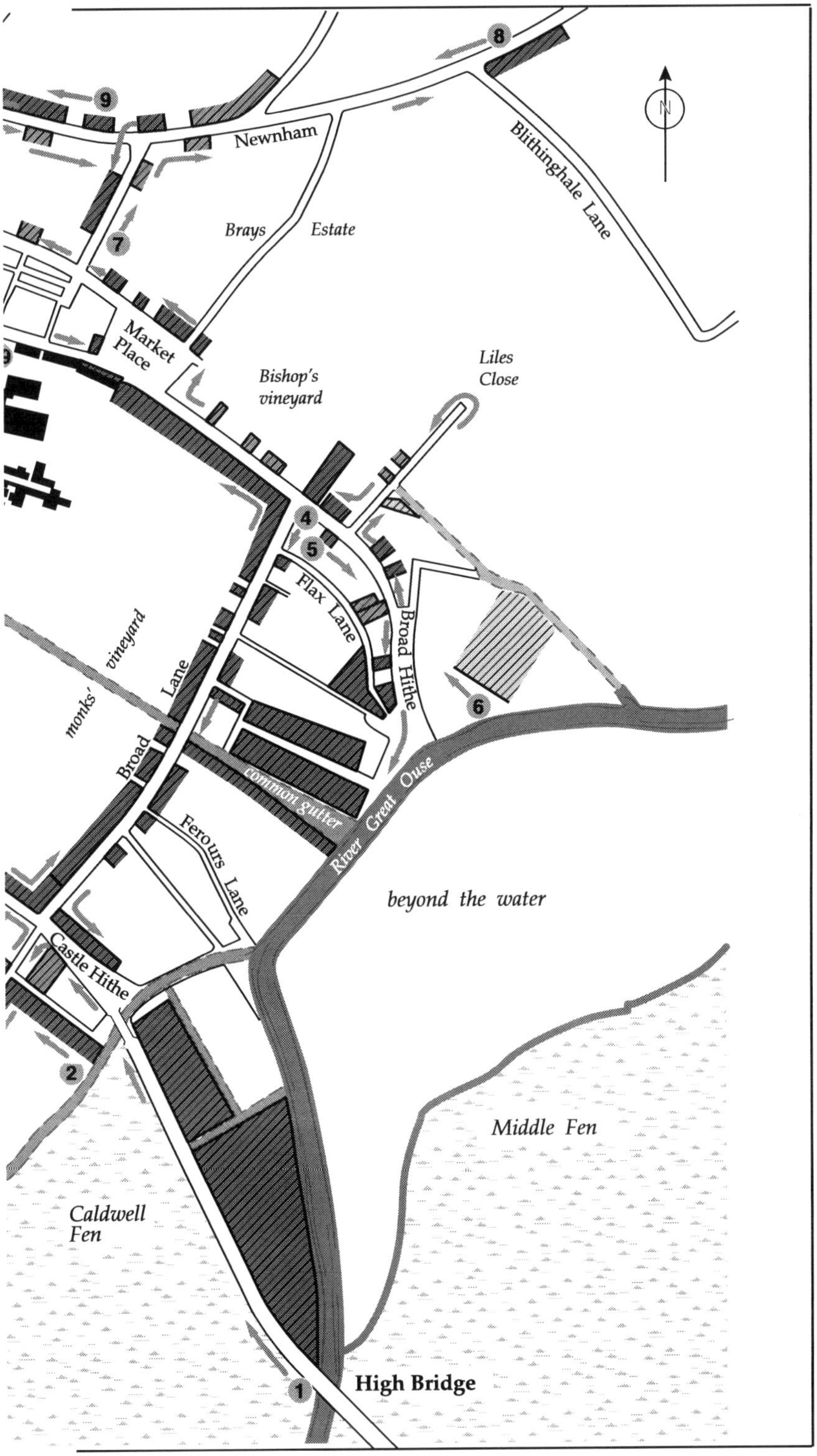

Newnham
Blithinghale Lane
Brays
Estate
Market Place
Bishop's vineyard
Liles Close
Flax Lane
Broad Hithe
monks' vineyard
Broad Lane
common gutter
River Great Ouse
Ferours Lane
beyond the water
Castle Hithe
Middle Fen
Caldwell Fen
High Bridge
1
2
4
5
6
7
8
9

stalls. To the east, the gates of Brays estate and those of the bishop's vineyard opened onto the market place. The sacrist's tithe barn stood west of St Mary's church. A horsemill with an associated barn stood near the Porta; it may well be the horsemill attached to the priory whose windmill stood nearby, on Cherry Hill. There were two mills in Newnham, the mound in the cemetery north of Prickwillow Road probably marking the site of the bishop's mill; *Drynstones* mill stood on or near Blithinghale Lane.

There are three named tenements in the survey, *Kyngstede* and *Spillecance* on the north side of Forehill, and *Aleynsyncook* on the corner between Market Street and Lynn Road, on the present site of the Ely Museum, a stone building of possible fourteenth-century origin.[159] All three were of the bishop's fee, and their position on a main thoroughfare suggests that they might have served as inns. Two tenements of the sacrist called *Pristeschambre*, in Nutholt Lane, may be the tenements occupied by the chaplains of both the parishes for which the sacrist was responsible, as recorded in the sacrist's account rolls of the first half of the fourteenth century. There is evidence for new construction on the west side of Lynn Road where the archdeacon had recently built a row of seven cottages, suggesting that opportunities for expansion were still being considered in early fifteenth-century Ely. Certain tenements were neglected and a number are recorded as vacant or in poor repair; many pertained to St John's hospital.[160]

The 1417 survey records whether a tenement was of the prior's or the bishop's fee. Three copies of the survey (H, J, V) also have a note in the margin next to many of the entries indicating which obedientiary should receive part or all of the rent; some holdings of the bishop's fee paid rent to an obedientiary, and some holdings paid to more than one recipient, probably explaining the discrepancies between the three copies in the names of recipient obedientiaries. The almoner and keeper of the Lady Chapel each received rent from more than sixty tenements in Ely, the steward of the household from some thirty-seven tenements, and the sacrist from some twenty-seven; additionally, each received rent jointly with another obedientiary from a small number of holdings. The cellarer received rent from fourteen tenements, and the remaining obedientiaries each had rent from fewer than ten holdings. The almoner's tenements can be correlated with those listed in the sixteenth-century priory rentals and in the almoner's account rolls of 1449–50 and 1473–4 where they are listed under 'Rent of the houses'.[161]

There are a few references to tenurial status. In the first section of the survey where Richard Masoun's two tenements are listed, an insertion specifies that one was held for a fixed rent of 4s, the other was copyhold. Ellen Brande's tenement near Potters Lane and John Bocher's at the north-east end of Broad Street were both freehold, as noted in the insertions. The status of some of the bishop's unfree tenements was also recorded; there were five cot-lands, in Potters Lane, Nutholt Lane, Downham Road, and Silver Street, two of which being described as 'lately subject to labour- service', while serf tenements were concentrated in the area between Downham Road and West End.

The insertions in H usually provide additional information, although a few are corrections. Most of the inserted material occurs in the sections on holdings around Waterside and along Forehill. Besides notes regarding the status of a tenure, there are notes about features of the holding, for instance a pond, or two cottages under one roof. Names of former holders are also inserted, some going back to the thirteenth century; these include Lucy wife of Stephen of Witchford and William the provisioner at Waterside, and Robert the merchant on the north side of Forehill. Occasionally an insertion gives the name of the present holder; on the north side of Forehill, J. Chaloner's tenement is 'now of Roger Cheyne', suggesting that the survey remained an active reference work.

159 K. Fearn, *Archaeological evaluation of the Old Gaol, Lynn Rd, Ely* (Historic Buildings Survey Group, 1994), p. 18.

160 Only five brethren and a master remained in 1379; documentary evidence for the period 1413–1443 is lost: Palmer, 'Hospitals at Ely', 86.

161 CUL EDC 1/F/1/13 and 14.

The sixteenth-century priory rentals

The priory rentals exist in a single copy, a volume of some 150 folios, of which all but the last four contain copies of rentals, or deal with manorial matters. The title of the volume 'Rentals of Chapter Estates 14 Henry VIII' occurs only on the cover and is in a modern hand. The date of this compilation of priory rentals, spanning the fifteen-year period preceding the Dissolution, is not clear, nor is its purpose. Folios 1–88v deal mainly with Ely holdings, but also include sources of income outside Ely deriving from both *temporalia* and *spiritualia*. These rentals, dating to the period between 1522–3 and 1524–5 are transcribed here, the material not relevant to Ely being summarised. The remainder of the volume (fos 93–143v) comprises rentals from nine villages on the Isle and in Cambridgeshire, and ranges in date from 1527–8 to 1537–8.[162]

The document is on paper, and the average size of the written page is 22½x17 cm. Fos 1–83 are in a generally regular hand, and written in black ink; from the penultimate entry on fo 83, the hand becomes gradually more irregular, and brown ink is also used for some sections; in the latter part of the volume, totals of income are frequently incomplete. Seven pages have been excised from the group of rentals dealing with Ely holdings; there is evidence for this in the gutter where the stub of one page is visible between fos 7 and 9, and the stubs of six pages between fos 87 and 94. There are several inserted folios: fos 88 and 93 with two blank pages between them, and fos 119 $^{2-10}$. The cover, and the flyleaf which may have formed the original cover, are parchment. On the reverse of the flyleaf is a list of kings since the Conquest, with the duration of each reign. The following page has a table of contents that has 'The Rental of the Sacrist in Ely' on fo 89, and 'Cottenham' on fo 93, suggesting that four of the six missing pages after fo 87 contained the rental for the sacrist's holdings in Ely.

The date and purpose of the compilation of this volume are not stated. The list of kings on the flyleaf ends with 'Henry VIII 14 years' (*Henricus viij – xiiij [annorum]*) which seems to have been taken as the date of the compilation, repeated on the spine of the volume as 'Rentals renewd 14 Henry 8^{vi}'. The earliest rentals date to the first year of Robert Wells' priorate, the latest to 1537–8; the volume was therefore completed and bound after 1537–8. The compilation may belong to the last years of the priory. Alternatively, it may date to the early years of the new foundation when Robert Wells had become first Dean; such a document would have been relevant at the time when Henry VIII was endowing his new foundation with former priory lands. Superscript emendations show that the rentals were updated, probably in the early decades of the new foundation, and a few superscript names can be traced to individuals active between the 1540s and 1560s. In 'A registre for the church of Ely', 'Thomas Goderik, gent.' occurs in the 1550s, and 'Robert Martche' in the 1560s, assuming that these are indeed the individuals recorded in the rentals and not their namesakes.[163] Further examination of sixteenth-century documents might shed light on this.

The headings for each of the rentals reflect the administrative subdivisions of the late medieval priory estate, and provide evidence for reorganisation in the period since 1417. The case of the cellarer's endowment is notable. His rental of 1523–4 records only two holdings, while in 1417 he received rent from at least fourteen holdings. The estates of 'Ketons', 'Hothams' and 'Stuntney' had formed part of his endowment in the fourteenth century; by the 1520s they were distinct units. The date of this subdivision cannot be traced, as the small number of fifteenth-century cellarer's account rolls that survive are fragile and were not examined; the infirmarer's account roll for 1458–9 indicates that the cellarer remained keeper of Ketons at that time.[164] Evidence for reorganisation

162 There are two blank pages between fos 88 and 93.

163 CUL EDC 2/2A/1, fos 18 and 20, and fo 27.

164 CUL EDC 1/F/14/1.

can also be seen in the transfer of assets formerly of the steward of the prior's household to the bailiff of Porta whose rental dates to 1522–3. These include a tenement in Broad Street held by John Wyssetre in 1417, and several tenements in Silver Street held by Andrew Botery and others in the same year. The transfer might have been recent, as suggested by two entries concerning a tenement on the east side of Broad Street, recorded as held of the steward of the prior's household in the almoner's rental (next to Mabel Palmer, fo 13v), and as a holding of the bailiff of the Porta in this bailiff's rental (John Rose's tenement, fo 31). The change may be connected with the visitation report of 1515 in which the prior was accused of maladministration and misuse of priory funds.[165]

The entries within each rental follow a roughly standard sequence: income from freehold (fixed rent) and copyhold (rent of houses) in Ely; rent from tenements, lands, fisheries, and other sources outside Ely; repayment of rent, including other outgoings. The rentals usually provide detailed information about holdings in Ely. The name of the tenant is usually followed by a description of the holding, including topographical information and, occasionally, dimensions; the entry then records the amount of rent owed and whether the holding is of the bishop's or the prior's fee; names of previous holders are often given.

Information provided by the rentals can complement that derived from the 1417 survey, and evidence from two entries in the rentals has been used for the reconstruction of priory holdings in Newnham and Waterside (map 4). On the north side of Newnham, the 1417 survey has a group of tenements with a total street frontage of 21 perches 1 foot (105.9 m). The rentals record a tenement 'in Newnham' lying on the west side of New Barns Road (Katherine Many, fo 38), suggesting that New Barns Road was considered part of Newnham at that date. It is assumed that this was also the case in 1417, suggesting that the holdings with a total street frontage of 21 perches 1 foot extended into New Barns Road, as shown on map 4. The second entry deals with a group of priory tenements north of Waterside. The 1417 survey gives the total frontage, recording that these holdings abut upon the 'ancient lode' to the north. The length of these tenements as reconstructed on map 4 derives from an entry in the rentals recording the length of a garden at the west end of the group abutting upon the 'common ditch' (Thomas Ruscell's garden, fo 10v), assuming that the 'common ditch' and the 'ancient lode' are the same feature. Other entries provide additional data for the layout of holdings listed in 1417. Those concerning the two blocks of land bounded by Egremont Street (Acreman Street), Chapel Street (Cats Lane) and St Mary's Street show that some tenements extended right across the block. Thomas Squery's tenement stretched from Egremont Street to Chapel Street (fo 52v), while John Davy and Robert Wryth had tenements extending from St Mary's Street to Chapel Street (fo 3v), the latter being traceable back to an entry in the 1417 survey. These examples also suggest, incidentally, that Chapel Street (Cats Lane) formed a sort of back lane between the streets to north and south.

A number of street and place names appear for the first time in the rentals. 'Benett Lane' in St Mary's parish (fo 4) may possibly be identified with Chiefs Street, off West Fen Road. 'The corner called Barkers Lane towards West Fen' (fo 3v) was 'Smale's corner' in 1417, and obviously distinct from Barkers Lane near Sedgwick. 'Sedgwick Lane' occurs for the first time, running along the southern boundary of the tenement called Sedgwick that had extended from Broad Street to the river in 1417, but which had been subdivided by the sixteenth century. 'Croyles corner' at the junction between Forehill and Broad Street was distinct from Croyles Lane near Castle Hithe.

165 Evans, *Ely Chapter ordinances*, pp. 65–6.

Named tenements, presumably inns, occur in various parts of the town. They include the Lamb, opposite Thomas Wright's tenement on Duke's corner, and on the site of the existing hotel of the same name, and the Angel, a public house opposite Castle Hithe until the late twentieth century, both retaining their late-medieval names into modern times. The Swan, opposite the Porta, and the Vine at Waterside had disappeared by the 1880s. The construction of new houses is recorded on Brays estate (fo 41), in Newnham (fo 53v) and in Silver Street, 'next to Ketons gate' (fo 78v). The Potters Lane area still had a number of ponds, one of which contained two fish tanks, and St Etheldreda's spring lay south-east of this lane. The descriptions of tenements show enclosure of land on Ketons estate south of Silver Street, and on the estates of Brays and Liles south of Newnham; there is also some evidence for enclosure of common land (fo 51v), a cause for grievance recorded in the 1548 inquiry.[166]

The priory rentals provide administrative information. The dates of previous leases on copyhold tenures and former levels of rent are often provided. The figures show a general reduction in rental income over the previous seventy years or so. In table 3, showing income and expenditure for each administrative unit, the rentals are grouped in chronological order.

Table 3. Total income and expenditure for the rentals transcribed in this volume. An asterisk denotes that the total is supplied.

		total income	*expenditure*
1522–3			
	Almoner	£56 0*s* 1*d**	£3 16*s* 8½*d*
	Bailiff of Porta	£11 6*s* 9*d*	£2 19*s* 2*d*
	Bailiff of Brays	£2 9*s* 2*d**	–
	Nornea	£6 6*s* 4*d*	–
	Bailiff of Caxtons	£10 7*s* 7*d*	£4 1*s* 6*d*
	Bailiff of Lady Chapel	£14 11*s* 11½*d*	–
	Infirmarer	£21 19*s* 3*d*	18*s*
1523–4			
	Precentor	£20 7*s* 6*d*	1*s* 4*d*
	Shrine-keeper	4*s* 3*d*	–
	Treasurer	£3 16*s*	2*s* 1*d*
	Cellarer	1*s* 2*d*	–
	Hothams	£20 14*s* 0*d*	>2*s* 4*d*[167]
	Stuntney	£26 0*s* 0½*d*	12*s* 4*d*
1524–5			
	Chamberlain	£23 0*s* 4*d*	£8 6*s* 11*d*
	Pittancer	£44 10*s* 11½*d*	3*s* 0¼*d*
	Ketons	£6 2*s* 9*d*	6*s* 2*d*

Outgoings, usually under the heading 'Repayment of rent', consisted mainly of payments to the bishop and other obedientiaries for holdings on which they had a financial claim. Some rentals included additional expenditure, such as the bailiff of Caxtons whose outgoings included pensions and wax, and those of the chamberlain that included funding for three parishes.

The rentals do not provide a complete picture of the late medieval holdings of the priory, nor can the total income and expenditure be calculated. Apart from lost entries on the missing folios, the latter part of this compilation is incomplete, lacking sums of money in several places. The rentals do, however, illustrate the varied nature of the priory endowment in Ely and beyond, on the eve of the Dissolution.

166 Palmer, *Enclosures*, p. 377.

167 Some figures are missing from entries in the section.

The Dissolution marked a break with the monastic past, but the abolition of the cathedral chapter between 1649 and 1660 was perhaps a more significant turning-point. In 1539 the priory estates had been seized by the Crown, but the prior and thirteen of the remaining monks were retained to maintain religious observance at Ely until the establishment of a new foundation. Henry VIII's new College, established in 1541, was headed by a dean and comprised a community of eight canons, eight minor canons, lay clerks and choir boys, as well as masters and scholars for the grammar school, almsmen and miscellaneous staff; it was endowed with former priory lands worth £995 annually, while the Crown retained priory assets valued at about £266.[168] Robert Steward, the last prior and first dean, remained in post until his death in 1557, despite the religious upheavals of the reigns of Edward VI and Queen Mary. His successor, Andrew Perne, was equally adaptable, his period of office (1557–89) falling mostly in the reign of Queen Elizabeth. Most of the senior members of the new foundation lived in Cambridge where they held important positions at the university, only staying in Ely during their periods of residence. The new foundation was, however, not entirely secure, as the concept of a cathedral within the protestant church was debatable, and in the 1580s the legality of Henry VIII's foundation charter was challenged, but confirmed in 1593.[169]

The episcopate of Thomas Goodrich, an active proponent of the Reformation, covered the final years of the priory and continued into the reign of Edward VI. Richard Cox, bishop of Ely 1559–1581, was an equally zealous reformer, but this did not prevent the compulsory purchase, by the Crown, of some of the best estates in the diocese. This bishop's death was followed by an eighteen-year vacancy of the see during which the Crown received all profits from the temporalities.[170] The Civil War had a major impact on the church in Ely. Bishop Wren was incarcerated in the Tower of London from 1642 to 1660, while the cathedral ceased to function normally from the autumn of 1643, and was closed down in 1649 when deans, chapters and cathedrals were abolished by Parliament. When they were restored in 1660, Bishop Wren was the only surviving senior ecclesiastical figure at Ely. The canons he appointed provided stability in the 1660s and 1670s in a period when the Chapter was concerned with the restoration of cathedral services, repair of the fabric and recovery of the estate.[171]

Dispersal of the priory archive had already begun in the 1530s when Robert Wells alias Steward appropriated a number of documents. Muniments were also removed by Canon Parker, subsequently archbishop of Canterbury, and by Dean Perne, and, in the years around 1600, they started to attract the interest of antiquaries. In 1649, documents that might serve as titles to property of the abolished cathedrals were taken to London. At the Restoration, Ely recovered much of this part of the archive, and in 1677, the Chapter ordered a review of record-keeping, providing an archive room in the cathedral.[172] Many of the priory documents that had been removed before the Civil War eventually found their way into public repositories. Archbishop Parker bequeathed his collection to Corpus Christi College, Cambridge, while the documents taken by Deans Steward and Perne came to form part of the Cotton Collection, now in the British Library. Robert Harley purchased many of the manuscripts collected by the seventeenth-century antiquarian, Sir Simonds

168 Atherton, 'Reformation to Restoration' in Meadows and Ramsay, *Ely Cathedral*, pp. 170, 179.

169 Atherton, 'Reformation to Restoration' in Meadows and Ramsay, *Ely Cathedral*, pp. 173–6, 182–3, 187.

170 Bentham, *History and antiquities of the Church of Ely*, pp. 189–95.

171 Bentham, *History and antiquities of the Church of Ely*, p. 201; Atherton, 'Reformation to Restoration' in Meadows and Ramsay, *Ely Cathedral*, p.191; P. Meadows, 'Dean and Chapter restored 1660–1836' in Meadows and Ramsay, *Ely Cathedral*, pp. 193–5.

172 N. Ramsay, 'The library and archives 1541–1836' in Meadows and Ramsay, *Ely Cathedral*, pp. 261–3, 266, 267–8, 269–71.

D'Ewes, and these are now part of the Harleian Collection at the British Library.[173] The archive of the bishopric has not been so well preserved. Most of the muniments were kept in Cambridge and appear to have been neglected in the eighteenth century, while the sale of Ely Place, Holborn, in 1772, led to further loss. The archive of the See was eventually brought together in Ely in the late nineteenth century.[174] Most of the archive of the Dean and Chapter and of the See is now deposited at the Cambridge University Library.

Post-Dissolution Ely remained a minor market centre, although the fairs were considered noteworthy.[175] The inhabitants continued paying rent to their, largely absentee, landlords, the Dean and Chapter, the Bishop and the Crown. Speed's map of Ely *c.*1610 is the earliest printed map of the town and provides a picture of the topography not long after the Dissolution, while the Parliamentary Surveys of 1649 describe Dean and Chapter holdings in the precinct, the town, and beyond, in the mid-seventeenth century. These documents record the town before the demolition of buildings in the precinct and in the bishop's palace complex, such as the demolition of the east wing of the bishop's palace that resulted in the creating of The Gallery as a thoroughfare. They also record the riverside area prior to the drainage of the South Level of the fens. The Old and New Bedford rivers, completed in 1631 and 1651 respectively, diverted some of the waters of the Ouse at Earith, reducing the volume of water flowing past Ely.[176] Archaeological evidence suggests that drainage was accompanied by attempts to dry out the ground in the area between Broad Street and the river, by extensive dumping of soil containing a quantity of seventeenth-century pottery.

The importance of Ely in the Middle Ages had been due in large part to the town's position within a large network of waterways extending from the Midlands to the North Sea. The range of waterborne communications was reduced following the creation of the Bedford rivers, but the arrival of the railway, in 1846, inserted Ely into a new system of communications. Ely railway station now forms a local hub whose range continues to expand in the twenty-first century.

[173] D. Owen, 'The Muniments of Ely Cathedral Priory' in C. N. L. Brooke *et al.*, eds, *Church and government in the middle ages* (Cambridge, 1976), pp. 171–2.

[174] Ramsay, 'Library and archives 1541–1836' in Meadows and Ramsay, *Ely Cathedral*, p. 276; D. M. Owen, *Ely Records: a handlist of the records of the bishop and archdeacon of Ely* (Cambridge, 1971), p. ix.

[175] *VCH*, 2, p. 87.

[176] *VCH*, 2, p. 78.

THE THIRTEENTH-CENTURY SURVEYS OF THE BISHOPS OF ELY

BL Cotton Tiberius B II, fos 86–93
and
CUL EDR G3/27, fos 1–7v

[fo 86] Incipit liber de inquisicionibus maneriorum episcopatus Elyensis factis tempore Johannis episcopi anno consecrationis sue secundo, de dominicis, de pratis et pasturis, de piscariis, de feodis militum, de redditibus assisis liberorum hominum, de operibus et consuetudinibus villanorum.

Incipit inquisicio manerii Elyensis.
De dominico. Dominicum huius manerii ita distinguitur: in Gruntifen sunt ducente quadraginta quinque acre; in Brieneshoue sexdecim acre; in Alfoshoue et Wrangeland quaterviginti tres acre dimidia; in Cratendon sexaginta acre; in Gresloue quaterviginti quindecim acre; in Roueshil et Weld quadringente sexaginta acre; in Blithingal sexcies viginti undecim acre dimidia; in Waterden sexcies viginti decem acre et dimidia; in Crosaue sexaginta acre; in Chedesfeld ducente \et/ una acre et dimidia. Summa mille quadringente quaterviginti due acre et dimidia.

De prato. Ad idem pertinent in Gruntifen quindecim acre prati; in Gresloue quinquaginta acre; in Chedesfeld viginti quinque acre tres rode; in Pandenhal et Blithingale triginta novem acre; in Blacwensaerd et Blithingalemere viginti una acre et dimidia; in Crassewell et Brademede triginta una acre. Summa centum quaterviginti una acre et dimidia et tres rode prati.

[fo 86v] **De piscariis.** Ad idem pertinet Trottiwere cum laca de Culanig, et tempore Galfridi episcopi reddebat triamilia anguillarum et triginta sex stikos, et Alexander gubernator tenet istam piscariam et est inquirendum per quem. Ad idem pertinet Upwere cum pertinenciis scilicet tres gurgites et mara de Sauesmere, et solebat reddere triamilia triginta sex stikorum et modo reddit tresdecim solidos et quatuor denarios. Ad idem pertinet Bradewere cum pertinenciis, scilicet Midlestewere, Marewere, Beche et medietas de Haveringemere, tota Langemere, Fridaywere et medietas de Alwodingewere, et tota Nakewere et medietas de Grantewere, et reddit quatuordecim milia anguillarum et dimidium et decem solidos in denariis. Ad idem pertinet piscaria de Crechemere quam Henricus de Walpol tenet hereditarie per cartam et reddit inde quinque solidos per annum. Ad idem pertinet piscaria quinque batellorum et reddit per annum quindecim solidos scilicet pro quolibet batello tres solidos et solvitur equaliter; et incipit ista piscaria ad Prichwilyu et durat usque ad Haveringemere.

De militibus. Symon de Insula tenet unum mesagium quod pertinet ad feodum militis. Warinus de Saham tenet unum mesagium quod pertinet ad feodum militis. Henricus Pelrin tenet unum mesagium quod pertinet ad feodum militis. Stephanus de Marisco tenet unum mesagium quod pertinet ad feodum militis. Willelmus Muschet tenet unum mesagium quod pertinet ad feodum militis.

De libere tenentibus. Robertus de Insula tenet unum mesagium quod fuit Ricardi de Melkesham pro duodecim denariis equaliter ad quatuor terminos, idem dat de witepunt unum denarium, et sciendum quod witepunt solvitur ad festum Sancti Michaelis et ad Pascha, et fodit in vinea sine cibo; idem tenet unum mesagium quod fuit Sermonatoris pro duodecim denariis equaliter. Bartholomeus de Tiveteshale tenet unum mesagium pro duodecim denariis equaliter; idem tenet octodecim acras de wara pro duodecim denariis equaliter. Willelmus Muschet tenet unum mesagium pro duodecim denariis equaliter et dat unum denarium de witepunt; idem tenet unum mesagium pro duodecim denariis equaliter et fodit in vinea. Willelmus filius Elye tenet triginta sex acras de wara cum mesagio suo pro decem solidis equaliter, et inveniet carucam suam semel in anno [fo 87] ad precarias episcopi et habebit cibum suum, et carettam suam ad roscum eodem modo per unum diem et in autumpno per unum diem eodem modo; idem tenet unum mesagium Selede pro duodecim denariis equaliter et unum denarium de witepunt. Paganus filius Alexandri tenet octodecim acras pro quinque solidis equaliter; idem tenet unum toftum cum sex acris pro duodecim denariis; idem tenet unum mesagium pro octo denariis equaliter et de witepunt unum denarium et fodit in vinea; idem tenet unum mesagium quod fuit Aelsi coci pro duodecim denariis equaliter et de witepunt unum denarium;

[fo 86] **Here begins the book of inquiries of the manors of the bishopric of Ely made in the second year of Bishop John's episcopate [1222], concerning demesne, meadow and pasture, fisheries, knights' fees, the fixed rents of free men, and the serfs' labour-services and customary obligations.**

Here begins the inquiry of the manor of Ely.
Demesne. The demesne of this manor is disposed thus: in Grunty Fen there are 245 acres; in *Brieneshoue* 16 acres; in *Alfoshoue* and *Wrangeland* 83½ acres; in *Cratendon* 60 acres; in *Gresloue* 95 acres; in *Roueshil* and *Weld* 460 acres; in Blithinghale 131½ acres; in Waterden 120½ acres; in *Crosaue* 60 acres; in *Chedesfeld* 201½ acres. Total 1482½ acres.[1]

Meadow. To the same [manor] pertain 15 acres of meadow in Grunty Fen; in *Gresloue* 50 acres; in *Chedesfeld* 25 acres 3 roods; in Padnal and Blithinghale 39 acres; in *Blacwensaerd* and Blithinghale mere 21½ acres; in Cresswell and *Brademede* 31 acres. Total 181½ acres and 3 roods of meadow.

[fo 86v] **Fisheries.** To the same [manor] pertains *Trottiwere* with *Culanig* lake, and it rendered 3000 eels and thirty-six sticks of eels in Bishop Geoffrey's time, and Alexander the steersman holds this fishery and we must inquire through whom he holds it.[2] To the same [manor] pertains Upware with its appurtenances namely three weirs and *Sauesmere* mere, and it used to render 3036 sticks of eels and now it renders 13*s* 4*d*. To the same pertains *Bradewere* with its appurtenances, namely *Midlestewere*, *Marewere*, *Beche* and half of Harrimere, all of *Langemere*, *Fridaywere* and half of *Alwoldingewere*, and all of *Nakewere* and half of *Grantewere*, and it renders 14500 eels and 10s in money. To the same pertains the fishery of Crouch Mere that Henry of Walpole holds hereditarily by charter and it renders 5*s* annually. To the same pertains a fishery of five boats, and it renders 15*s* annually, namely 3*s* for each boat, and it is paid in equal instalments; and this fishery begins at Prickwillow and extends to Harrimere.[3]

Knights. Simon de Insula holds a messuage that pertains to a knight's fee.Warin of Soham holds a messuage that pertains to a knight's fee. Henry Pelrin holds a messuage that pertains to a knight's fee. Stephen de Marisco holds a messuage that pertains to a knight's fee. William Muschet holds a messuage that pertains to a knight's fee.

Free tenants. Robert de Insula holds a messuage formerly Richard of Melksham's for 12*d* in equal instalments at the four terms, the same pays 1*d* wite pound, and note that wite pound is paid at Michaelmas and at Easter; and he digs in the vineyard with no food allowance;[4] the same holds a messuage that was the *sermonator*'s for 12*d* in equal instalments. Bartholomew of Tivetshall holds a messuage for 12*d* in equal instalments; the same holds 18 ware acres[5] for 12*d* in equal instalments. William Muschet holds a messuage for 12*d* in equal instalments and pays 1*d* wite pound; the same holds a messuage for 12*d* in equal instalments, and digs in the vineyard. William, Ellis' son, holds 36 ware acres with his messuage for 10*s* in equal instalments, and he must provide his plough once annually [fo 87] for the bishop's boon-works and he will receive his food allowance, and he must provide his cart in the same manner for [transporting] rushes for one day, and in autumn likewise for one day; the same holds Seleda's messuage for 12*d* in equal instalments and pays 1*d* wite pound. Payne, Alexander's son, holds 18 acres for 5*s* in equal instalments; the same holds a toft with 6 acres for 12*d*; the same holds a messuage for 8*d* in equal instalments and pays 1*d* wite pound, and digs in the vineyard; the same holds a messuage formerly of Aelsus the cook for 12*d* in equal instalments and pays 1*d* wite pound;

idem tenet unum mesagium pro sexdecim denariis equaliter et de witepunt unum denarium; idem tenet quandam partem de tofta Gerebaldi pro duodecim denariis equaliter et de witepunt unum denarium; idem tenet mesagium in quo sedet pro sex denariis; idem tenet unum mesagium quod fuit Johannis Burgeis pro duodecim denariis equaliter et de witepunt unum denarium et fodit; idem tenet unum mesagium quod fuit Radulphi aurifabri pro duodecim denariis equaliter et de witepunt unum denarium; idem tenet unum mesagium pro sex denariis equaliter et de witepunt unum denarium; idem tenet ibidem de purprestura et reddit sex denarios; idem tenet unum mesagium quod fuit Samuelis clerici pro duodecim denariis equaliter et de witepunt unum denarium; idem tenet unum mesagium quod fuit antiquitus operabile pro duodecim denariis equaliter; idem tenet unum hulmum pro duodecim denariis equaliter; idem tenet mesagium Nicholai filii Elye pro duodecim denariis et de witepunt unum denarium; idem tenet mesagium Johannis de bedderne pro sex denariis. Johannes de Walpol tenet octodecim acras de wara cum mesagio pro quinque solidis equaliter et de witepunt quatuordecim denarios et debet easdem consuetudines sicut Willelmus filius Elye. Unfridus Sauke tenet octodecim acras cum mesagio et crufta pro duobus solidis equaliter, et debet ire contra iusticiarios et replegiare homines episcopi et facere saisinam et dissaisinam extra insulam Elyensem et facere easdem consuetudines. Ricardus de ecclesia et Johannes specer tenent triginta sex acras, et dant de witepunt septem denarios et arabunt per annum tres acras sine cibo et debent easdem consuetudines sicut Unfridus. Willelmus filius Philippi tenuit aliquando sex acras que pertinere debent ad ministerium rosci sed modo eas vendidit et terra illa debet duos denarios et obolum de witepunt. Gilebertus filius Azonis tenet sex acras et debet ire contra iusticiarios. Mabilia tenet unum mesagium ante Berthonam pro sex denariis equaliter. Petrus filius Mabilie tenet unum mesagium pro sex denariis. Osbertus de Stradeset tenet unum mesagium pro sex denariis equaliter. Symon pistor [fo 87v] tenet unum mesagium pro sex denariis equaliter et de witepunt unum denarium et fodit. Willelmus de Derham tenet unum mesagium pro sex denariis equaliter et de witepunt unum denarium et fodit. Symon et Adelyna tenent unum mesagium pro sex denariis equaliter et de witepunt unum denarium et fodiunt. Robertus le beverant tenet unum mesagium pro octo denariis equaliter et de witepunt unum denarium. Ricardus le beverand tenet duo mesagia pro duobus solidis equaliter et de witepunt unum denarium et fodit. Johannes de Pulham tenet unum mesagium pro octodecim denariis equaliter, et reddit pro una piscaria pertinente ad idem mesagium tres solidos equaliter. Alanus gardener tenet unum mesagium pro sexdecim denariis equaliter et de witepunt unum denarium. Mabillia tenet unam purpresturam pro quinque denariis equaliter. Tofta que fuit Galfridi petit solebat reddere duodecim denarios equaliter et de witepunt unum denarium, et nunc est in manu episcopi. Amabilia filia Johannis de Benden tenet duo mesagia pro duobus solidis equaliter et de witepunt unum denarium que fuerunt Walteri filii Hugonis.

Thomas tinctor[7] tenet unum mesagium pro sexdecim denariis equaliter et de witepunt unum denarium. Robertus filius Anand tenet unum mesagium pro sexdecim denariis equaliter et de witepunt unum denarium. Robertus Quintelune tenet unum mesagium pro duodecim denariis equaliter, de witepunt unum denarium, et fodit. Willelmus capellanus tenet dimidium mesagium pro octo denariis equaliter et de witepunt unum obolum. Laurentius cementarius tenet unum mesagium pro sex denariis equaliter, de witepunt unum denarium. Johannes le brazur tenet unum mesagium pro sex denariis equaliter, de witepunt unum denarium, et fodit. Henricus de Brandon tenet unum mesagium pro octo denariis equaliter, de witepunt unum denarium. Johannes et Nicholaus filii Willelmi tenent mesagium Pericie pro duodecim denariis equaliter, de witepunt unum denarium. Elemosinarius tenet unum mesagium quod fuit Galfridi buteller pro duodecim denariis equaliter, de witepunt unum denarium, et fodit. Matilda Muschet tenet duo mesagia pro duobus solidis equaliter, de witepunt unum denarium. Robertus filius Petit tenet unum mesagium Johannis le child pro duodecim denariis equaliter, de witepunt unum denarium, et fodit.

Eustachius de Eye tenet unum mesagium et reddit unam gruem per annum. Herebertus de Hadenham tenet unum mesagium pro duodecim denariis equaliter, de witepunt unum denarium, et fodit. Willelmus Rugevin tenet unum mesagium pro duodecim denariis equaliter, de witepunt unum denarium, et fodit. Alwinus Pudding tenet unum

the same holds a messuage for 16*d* in equal instalments and pays 1*d* wite pound; the same holds a part of Gerebald's toft for 12*d* in equal instalments and pays 1*d* wite pound; the same holds the messuage in which he dwells for 6*d*; the same holds a messuage that was John Burgeis' for 12*d* in equal instalments and pays 1*d* wite pound, and digs; the same holds a messuage formerly of Ralph the goldsmith for 12*d* in equal instalments and pays 1*d* wite pound; the same holds a messuage for 6*d* in equal instalments and pays 1*d* wite pound; the same holds there newly cleared land and renders 6*d*; the same holds a messuage formerly of Samuel the clerk for 12*d* in equal instalments and pays 1*d* wite pound; the same holds a messuage that of old was subject to labour-service for 12*d* in equal instalments; the same holds a river-meadow for 12*d* in equal instalments; the same holds a messuage of Nicholas, Ellis' son, for 12*d* and pays 1*d* wite pound; the same holds John *de bedderne*'s messuage for 6*d*. John of Walpole holds 18 ware acres with a messuage for 5*s* in equal instalments and pays 14*d* wite pound, and he owes the same customary obligations as William, Ellis' son. Humfrey Sauke holds 18 acres with a messuage and a croft for 2*s* in equal instalments, and he must attend the justices and replevy[6] the bishop's men and perform seisin and disseisin outside the Isle of Ely, and perform the same customary obligations [as William, Ellis' son]. Richard *de ecclesia* and John the spicer hold 36 acres, and pay 7*d* wite pound, and they must plough 3 acres annually with no food allowance, and they owe the same customary obligations as Humfrey. William, Philip's son, once held 6 acres that pertain to the office of the rushes, but he has now sold them and that land owes 2½*d* wite pound. Gilbert, Azo's son, holds 6 acres and must attend the justices. Mabel holds a messuage in front of Barton for 6*d* in equal instalments. Peter, Mabel's son, holds a messuage for 6*d*. Osbert of Stradsett holds a messuage for 6*d* in equal instalments. Simon the baker [fo 87v] holds a messuage for 6*d* in equal instalments and pays 1*d* wite pound, and digs. William of Dereham holds a messuage for 6*d* in equal instalments and pays 1*d* wite pound, and digs. Simon and Adeline hold a messuage for 6*d* in equal instalments and pay 1*d* wite pound, and dig. Robert *le beverant* holds a messuage for 8*d* in equal instalments and pays 1*d* wite pound. Richard *le beverand* holds two messuages for 2*s* in equal instalments and pays 1*d* wite pound, and digs. John of Pulham holds a messuage for 18*d* in equal instalments, and renders 3*s* in equal instalments for a fishery pertaining to the same messuage. Alan the gardener holds a messuage for 16*d* in equal instalments and pays 1*d* wite pound. Mabel holds newly cleared land for 5*d* in equal instalments. A toft that was Geoffrey the small's used to render 12*d* in equal instalments and 1*d* wite pound, and now it is in the bishop's hand. Mabel, John de Benden's daughter, holds two messuages formerly of Walter, Hugh's son, for 2*s* in equal instalments and pays 1*d* wite pound.

Thomas the dyer holds a messuage for 16*d* in equal instalments and pays 1*d* wite pound. Robert, Anand's son, holds a messuage for 16*d* in equal instalments and pays 1*d* wite pound. Robert Quintelune holds a messuage for 12*d* in equal instaments, he pays 1*d* wite pound, and digs. William the chaplain holds half a messuage for 8*d* in equal instaments and pays ½*d* wite pound. Lawrence the mason holds a messuage for 6*d* in equal instalments, he pays 1*d* wite pound. John the brewer holds a messuage for 6*d* in equal instalments, he pays 1*d* wite pound, and digs. Henry of Brandon holds a messuage for 8*d* in equal instalments, he pays 1*d* wite pound. John and Nicholas, William's sons, hold Pericia's messuage for 12*d* in equal instalments, they pay 1*d* wite pound. The almoner holds a messuage formerly Geoffrey *buteller*'s for 12*d* in equal instalments, he pays 1*d* wite pound, and digs. Matilda Muschet holds two messuages for 2*s* in equal instalments, she pays 1*d* wite pound. Robert, Petit's son, holds a messuage of John *le child* for 12*d* in equal instalments, he pays 1*d* wite pound, and digs.

Eustace of Eye holds a messuage and renders one crane annually.[8] Herbert of Haddenham holds a messuage for 12*d* in equal instaments, he pays 1*d* wite pound, and digs. William Rugevin holds a messuage for 12*d* in equal instalments, he pays 1*d* wite pound, and digs. Aylwin Pudding holds a messuage

mesagium [fo 88] pro duodecim denariis equaliter et de witepunt unum denarium, et fodit. Ricardus de Manston tenet unum mesagium pro duodecim denariis equaliter et de witepunt unum denarium; idem tenet unum mesagium pro duodecim denariis equaliter et de witepunt unum denarium. Walterus Trubuille tenet unum mesagium pro viginti denariis equaliter et de witepunt unum denarium, et fodit. Robertus filius Goscelini tenet unum mesagium pro sexdecim denariis equaliter et de witepunt unum denarium, et fodit. Robertus filius Hugonis tenet unum mesagium pro sexdecim denariis et de witepunt unum denarium. Stephanus Druerie tenet unum mesagium pro sexdecim denariis equaliter et de witepunt unum denarium. Matilda Muschet tenet mesagium Rogeri Blake pro duodecim denariis equaliter. Alexander talliur tenet unum mesagium pro duodecim denariis equaliter et de witepunt unum denarium, et fodit. Serlo de Haukestun tenet unum mesagium pro duodecim denariis equaliter et de witepunt unum denarium. Ricardus de hospitio tenet unum mesagium pro sex denariis equaliter. Nicholaus palmer tenet unum mesagium pro duodecim denariis equaliter et de witepunt unum denarium. Granatarius tenet mesagium Godwini Boldiro pro octo denariis equaliter et de witepunt unum denarium. Alexander gubernator tenet unum mesagium pro sex denariis equaliter. Margeria filia Thome tenet unum mesagium pro octo denariis equaliter et de witepunt unum denarium. Petrus chien tenet unum mesagium pro duodecim denariis equaliter. Fulco de Dunham tenet unum mesagium pro sexdecim denariis equaliter et de witepunt unum denarium. Willelmus Makerel tenet unum mesagium pro duodecim denariis equaliter et de witepunt unum denarium. Johannes filius pistoris tenet unum mesagium pro sexdecim denariis equaliter et de witepunt unum denarium. Willelmus filius Gervasii tenet unum mesagium pro octo denariis equaliter et de witepunt unum denarium. Willelmus brakener tenet unum mesagium pro octo denariis equaliter et de witepunt unum denarium, et fodit. Malgerus Kayly tenet unum mesagium pro octo denariis equaliter. Alexander gubernator tenet unum mesagium quod pertinet ad ministerium navigandi episcopum. Reynerus de Ulmo tenet unum mesagium pro duodecim denariis equaliter et de witepunt unum denarium, et fodit. Rogerus Deth tenet unum mesagium pro duodecim denariis equaliter et de witepunt unum denarium. Henricus Muscerun tenet unum mesagium pro sex denariis equaliter et de witepunt unum denarium. Walterus tayllur tenet unum mesagium pro sex denariis equaliter et de witepunt unum denarium. Gerardus molendinarius tenet unum mesagium pro sex denariis et de witepunt unum denarium. [fo 88v] Johannes de refectorio tenet unum mesagium pro sex denariis equaliter et de witepunt unum denarium. Johannes cocus tenet unum mesagium pro sex denariis equaliter et de witepunt unum denarium. Robertus Sorgard tenet unum mesagium pro duodecim denariis equaliter. Rogerus pistor tenet unum mesagium pro duodecim denariis equaliter et de witepunt unum denarium. Henricus Tote tenet unum mesagium pro duodecim denariis equaliter. Galfridus verrarius tenet unum mesagium pro duodecim denariis et de witepunt unum denarium. Ranulfus clericus tenet unum mesagium pro octo denariis equaliter et de witepunt unum denarium. Robertus Niker tenet unum mesagium pro sex denariis equaliter et de witepunt unum denarium. Robertus mercator tenet unum mesagium pro octo denariis et de witepunt unum denarium. Godardus tallur tenet unum mesagium pro octo denariis equaliter et de witepunt unum denarium. Robertus diaconus tenet unum mesagium pro duodecim denariis equaliter et de witepunt unum denarium. Jordanus ferrun tenet unum mesagium pro duodecim denariis equaliter et de witepunt unum denarium. Johannes spicer tenet unum mesagium pro octo denariis equaliter et de witepunt unum denarium. Henricus Pudding tenet quandam partem vinee pro duobus denariis equaliter. Ricardus de Len tenet quandam partem pro quatuor denariis equaliter. Omnes hii predicti claudunt murum inter curias eorum et vineam.

Salomon aurifaber tenet unum mesagium pro sex denariis. Mauricius janitor tenet unum mesagium pro duodecim denariis equaliter et de witepunt unum denarium. Stephanus filius Unfridi tenet toftum Geremundi et debet de witepunt unum denarium, et fodit. Nicholaus Turfat tenet unum mesagium pro sex denariis equaliter et de witepunt unum denarium. Ranulfus tenet unum mesagium pro sex denariis equaliter et de witepunt unum denarium. Salomon aurifaber tenet unum mesagium pro viginti denariis equaliter et de witepunt unum denarium. Johannes culcitrarius tenet unum mesagium pro octo denariis et de witepunt unum denarium. Radulfus prestre tenet unum mesagium pro sex

[fo 88] for 12*d* in equal instalments and pays 1*d* wite pound, and digs. Richard de Manston holds a messuage for 12*d* in equal instalments and pays 1*d* wite pound; the same holds a messuage for 12*d* in equal instalments and pays 1*d* wite pound. Walter Trubuille holds a messuage for 20*d* in equal instalments and pays 1*d* wite pound, and digs. Robert, Jocelin's son, holds a messuage for 16*d* in equal instalments and pays 1*d* wite pound, and digs. Robert, Hugh's son, holds a messuage for 16*d* and pays 1*d* wite pound. Stephen Druerie holds a messuage for 16*d* in equal instalments and pays 1*d* wite pound. Matilda Muschet holds Roger Blake's messuage for 12*d* in equal instalments. Alexander the tailor holds a messuage for 12*d* in equal instalments and pays 1*d* wite pound, and digs. Serle of Hauxton holds a messuage for 12*d* in equal instalments and pays 1*d* wite pound. Richard *de hospitio* holds a messuage for 6*d* in equal instalments. Nicholas the pilgrim holds a messuage for 12*d* in equal instalments and pays 1*d* wite pound. The granary-keeper holds Godwin Boldiro's messuage for 8*d* in equal instalments and pays 1*d* wite pound. Alexander the steersman holds a messuage for 6*d* in equal instalments. Margery, Thomas' daughter, holds a messuage for 8*d* in equal instalments and pays 1*d* wite pound. Peter the dog holds a messuage for 12*d* in equal instalments. Fulk of Little Downham holds a messuage for 16*d* in equal instalments and pays 1*d* wite pound. William Makerel holds a messuage for 12*d* in equal instalments and pays 1*d* wite pound. John, the baker's son, holds a messuage for 16*d* in equal instalments and pays 1*d* wite pound. William, Gervase's son, holds a messuage for 8*d* in equal instalments and pays 1*d* wite pound. William the huntsman holds a messuage for 8*d* in equal instalments and pays 1*d* wite pound, and digs. Malgerus Kayly holds a messuage for 8*d* in equal instalments. Alexander the steersman holds a messuage that pertains to the office of transporting the bishop by boat. Rayner de Ulmo holds a messuage for 12*d* in equal instalments and pays 1*d* wite pound, and digs. Roger Deth holds a messuage for 12*d* in equal instalments and pays 1*d* wite pound. Henry Muscerun holds a messuage for 6*d* in equal instalments and pays 1*d* wite pound. Walter the tailor holds a messuage for 6*d* in equal instalments and pays 1*d* wite pound. Gerard the miller holds a messuage for 6*d* and pays 1*d* wite pound. [fo 88v] John *de refectorio* holds a messuage for 6*d* in equal instalments and pays 1*d* wite pound. John the cook holds a messuage for 6*d* in equal instalments and pays 1*d* wite pound. Robert Sorgard holds a messuage for 12*d* in equal instalments. Roger the baker holds a messuage for 12*d* in equal instalments and pays 1*d* wite pound. Henry Tote holds a messuage for 12*d* in equal instalments. Geoffrey the glazier holds a messuage for 12*d* and pays 1*d* wite pound. Ranulf the clerk holds a messuage for 8*d* in equal instalments and pays 1*d* wite pound. Robert Niker holds a messuage for 6*d* in equal instalments and pays 1*d* wite pound. Robert the merchant holds a messuage for 8*d* and pays 1*d* wite pound. Godard the tailor holds a messuage for 8*d* in equal instalments and pays 1*d* wite pound. Robert the deacon holds a messuage for 12*d* in equal instalments and pays 1*d* wite pound. Jordan the farrier holds a messuage for 12*d* in equal instalments and pays 1*d* wite pound. John the spicer holds a messuage for 8*d* in equal instalments and pays 1*d* wite pound. Henry Pudding holds a part of the vineyard for 2*d* in equal instalments. Richard of Lynn holds a part [of the vineyard] for 4*d* in equal instalments. All these aforesaid tenants [must] close the wall between their yards and the vineyard.

Solomon the goldsmith holds a messuage for 6*d*. Maurice the door-keeper holds a messuage for 12*d* in equal instalments and pays 1*d* wite pound. Stephen, Humfrey's son, holds Geremund's toft and owes 1*d* wite pound, and digs. Nicholas Turfat holds a messuage for 6*d* in equal instalments and pays 1*d* wite pound. Ranulf holds a messuage for 6*d* in equal instalments and pays 1*d* wite pound. Solomon the goldsmith holds a messuage for 20*d* in equal instalments and pays 1*d* wite pound. John the quilt-maker holds a messuage for 8*d* and pays 1*d* wite pound. Ralph the priest holds a messuage for 6*d*

denariis equaliter et de witepunt unum denarium. Willelmus mercator tenet unum mesagium pro sex denariis equaliter. Johannes filius Margarete tenet unum mesagium pro duodecim denariis equaliter et de witepunt unum denarium. Johannes de refectorio tenet unum mesagium pro duodecim denariis equaliter et de witepunt unum denarium. Alanus mercator tenet unum mesagium pro duodecim denariis equaliter et de witepunt unum denarium. Henricus faber tenet unum mesagium pro duodecim denariis equaliter et de witepunt unum denarium; [fo 89] idem reddit per annum quatuor denarios equaliter pro quadam particula terre. Philippus filius Willelmi tenet unum mesagium pro duodecim denariis equaliter et de witepunt unum denarium. Johannes de ecclesia tenet unum mesagium pro duodecim denariis equaliter et de witepunt unum denarium. Mauricius janitor tenet unum mesagium pro duodecim denariis equaliter, de witepunt unum denarium. Nicholaus de Hecham tenet unum mesagium pro duodecim denariis equaliter, de witepunt unum denarium. Galfridus beverand tenet unum mesagium pro octo denariis equaliter. Henricus Dammavill tenet unum mesagium pro duodecim denariis equaliter. Johannes culcitrarius tenet unum mesagium pro duodecim denariis equaliter, de witepunt unum denarium. Stephanus et Johannes culcitrarius tenent unum mesagium pro quatuor denariis equaliter et de witepunt unum denarium. Galfridus janitor tenet unum mesagium pro octo denariis equaliter et de witepunt unum denarium. Robertus messager tenet unum mesagium pro quatuor denariis equaliter et de witepunt unum denarium. Everard filius Ingeram tenet tria mesagia pro decem denariis et de witepunt unum denarium. Willelmus de Wintewrthe tenet unum mesagium pro octo denariis equaliter et de witepunt unum denarium. Rogerus filius Herberti tenet unum mesagium pro octo denariis et de witepunt unum denarium. Ailbern Scinhose tenet unum mesagium pro octo denariis equaliter et de witepunt unum denarium. Ricardus mercator tenet unum mesagium pro octo denariis equaliter et de witepunt unum denarium; idem tenet unum mesagium pro duodecim denariis equaliter et de witepunt unum denarium. Johannes le tanur tenet unum mesagium pro duodecim denariis equaliter et de witepunt unum denarium. Willelmus Puteman tenet unum mesagium pro octo denariis equaliter et de witepunt unum denarium. Ricardus tanur tenet unum mesagium pro duodecim denariis equaliter et de witepunt unum denarium. Hugo Nodinay tenet unum mesagium pro octo denariis equaliter et de witepunt unum denarium. Petrus Gernun tenet unum mesagium pro duodecim denariis equaliter. \Godefridus de Fulmer tenet unum mesagium pro duodecim denariis./ Ricardus de Sancto Albano tenet unum mesagium pro quatuordecim denariis equaliter. Godardus tenet unum mesagium pro viginti denariis equaliter et de witepunt unum denarium. Galfridus Fecard tenet unum mesagium pro sex denariis equaliter et de witepunt unum denarium; idem tenet de novo et reddit sexdecim denarios equaliter. Hugo clericus tenet unum mesagium pro sex denariis. Johannes culcitrarius tenet unum mesagium pro duodecim denariis et de witepunt unum denarium. Hugo Kipping tenet unum mesagium pro duodecim denariis [fo 89v] equaliter et de witepunt unum denarium. Willelmus filius Ricardi tenet duo mesagia pro duodecim denariis equaliter. Henricus Frechild tenet unum mesagium pro quatuor denariis et de witepunt unum denarium. Henricus Buc tenet unum mesagium pro duodecim denariis equaliter et de witepunt unum denarium. Robertus ruffus tenet mesagium quod fuit Alani pro quatuor denariis. Radulfus Poppe tenet unum mesagium pro duodecim denariis equaliter. Dauscin tenet unum mesagium pro quatuor denariis equaliter. Robertus Gernun tenet unum mesagium pro sex denariis de novo. Johannes pistor tenet unum mesagium pro sex denariis equaliter. Stephanus filius Unfridi tenet unum mesagium pro quatuor denariis et de witepunt unum obolum. Hugo carpentarius tenet unum mesagium pro duodecim denariis et de witepunt unum denarium. Hugo Kippint tenet unum mesagium pro duodecim denariis et de witepunt unum denarium. Philippus mercator tenet unum mesagium pro duodecim denariis equaliter et de witepunt unum denarium. Hugo filius Alani tenet unum mesagium pro duodecim denariis et de witepunt unum denarium. Robertus capellanus tenet unum mesagium pro duodecim denariis equaliter. Alexander brevetur tenet unum mesagium pro duodecim denariis. Mabilia tenet duo mesagia pro duobus solidis; eadem tenet quandam partem pro duobus denariis. Arnaldus Winter tenet unum mesagium pro octo denariis equaliter. Angerus tenet unum mesagium pro duodecim denariis equaliter et de witepunt unum

in equal instalments and pays 1*d* wite pound. William the merchant holds a messuage for 6*d* in equal instalments. John, Margaret's son, holds a messuage for 12*d* in equal instalments and pays 1*d* wite pound. John *de refectorio* holds a messuage for 12*d* in equal instalments and pays 1*d* wite pound. Alan the merchant holds a messuage for 12*d* in equal instalments and pays 1*d* wite pound. Henry the smith holds a messuage for 12*d* in equal instalments and pays 1*d* wite pound; [fo 89] the same renders 4*d* annually in equal instalments for a piece of land. Philip, William's son, holds a messuage for 12*d* in equal instalments and pays 1*d* wite pound. John *de ecclesia* holds a messuage for 12*d* in equal instalments and pays 1*d* wite pound. Maurice the door-keeper holds a messuage for 12*d* in equal instalments, he pays 1*d* wite pound. Nicholas of Hitcham holds a messuage for 12*d* in equal instalments, he pays 1*d* wite pound. Geoffrey *beverand* holds a messuage for 8*d* in equal instalments. Henry Dammavill holds a messuage for 12*d* in equal instalments. John the quilt-maker holds a messuage for 12*d* in equal instalments, he pays 1*d* wite pound. Stephen and John the quilt-maker hold a messuage for 4*d* in equal instalments and pay 1*d* wite pound. Geoffrey the door-keeper holds a messuage for 8*d* in equal instalments and pays 1*d* wite pound. Robert the messenger holds a messuage for 4*d* in equal instalments and pays 1*d* wite pound. Everard, Ingram's son, holds three messuages for 10*d* and pays 1*d* wite pound. William of Wentworth holds a messuage for 8*d* in equal instalments and pays 1*d* wite pound. Roger, Herbert's son, holds a messuage for 8*d* and pays 1*d* wite pound. Ailbern Scinhose holds a messuage for 8*d* in equal instalments and pays 1*d* wite pound. Richard the merchant holds a messuage for 8*d* in equal instalments and pays 1*d* wite pound; the same holds a messuage for 12*d* in equal instalments and pays 1*d* wite pound. John the tanner holds a messuage for 12*d* in equal instalments and pays 1*d* wite pound. William Puteman holds a messuage for 8*d* in equal instalments and pays 1*d* wite pound. Richard the tanner holds a messuage for 12*d* in equal instalments and pays 1*d* wite pound. Hugh Nodinay holds a messuage for 8*d* in equal instalments and pays 1*d* wite pound. Peter Gernun holds a messuage for 12*d* in equal instalments. \Godfrey of Fowlmere holds a messuage for 12*d*./ Richard of St Albans holds a messuage for 14*d* in equal instalments. Godard holds a messuage for 20*d* in equal instalments and pays 1*d* wite pound. Geoffrey Fecard holds a messuage for 6*d* in equal instalments and pays 1*d* wite pound; the same holds a newly created messuage and renders 16*d* in equal instalments. Hugh the clerk holds a messuage for 6*d*. John the quilt-maker holds a messuage for 12*d* and pays 1*d* wite pound. Hugh Kipping holds a messuage for 12*d* [fo 89v] in equal instalments and pays 1*d* wite pound. William, Richard's son, holds two messuages for 12*d* in equal instalments. Henry Frechild holds a messuage for 4*d* and pays 1*d* wite pound. Henry Buc holds a messuage for 12*d* in equal instalments and pays 1*d* wite pound. Robert the redhead holds a messuage formerly Alan's for 4*d*. Ralph Poppe holds a messuage for 12*d* in equal instalments. Dauscin holds a messuage for 4*d* in equal instalments. Robert Gernun holds a newly created messuage for 6*d*. John the baker holds a messuage for 6*d* in equal instalments. Stephen, Humfrey's son, holds a messuage for 4*d* and pays ½*d* wite pound. Hugh the carpenter holds a messuage for 12*d* and pays 1*d* wite pound. Hugh Kippint holds a messuage for 12*d* and pays 1*d* wite pound. Philip the merchant holds a messuage for 12*d* in equal instalments and pays 1*d* wite pound. Hugh, Alan's son, holds a messuage for 12*d* and pays 1*d* wite pound. Robert the chaplain holds a messuage for 12*d* in equal instalments. Alexander the scribe holds a messuage for 12*d*. Mabel holds two messuages for 2*s*; the same holds a piece of land for 2*d*. Arnald Winter holds a messuage for 8*d* in equal instalments. Angerus holds a messuage for 12*d* in equal instalments and pays 1*d* wite pound.

denarium. Henricus Pin tenet unum mesagium pro duodecim denariis et de witepunt unum denarium. Robertus venator tenet unum mesagium pro sex denariis equaliter et de witepunt unum denarium. Ricardus carec[tar]ius tenet unum mesagium pro duodecim denariis equaliter. Radulfus Tylly tenet unum mesagium pro sex denariis. Stephanus carpentarius tenet unum mesagium pro sex denariis. Alina Noble tenet unum mesagium pro tresdecim denariis equaliter. Robertus nuntius tenet unam croftam pro duodecim denariis. Galfridus janitor tenet unam croftam pro duodecim denariis. Gilbertus tallur tenet unum mesagium pro sex denariis; idem tenet quinque acras pro duodecim denariis equaliter. Petrus filius Azonis tenet duodecim acras pro octo solidis equaliter.

De consuetudinibus operariis. Philippus de Chedesham tenet unam plenam terram scilicet octodecim acras de wara et dat de witepunt ad Annunciationem tres denarios et obolum et ad festum Sancti Michaelis tres denarios et obolum, et dat tres gallinas et triginta ova; et debet qualibet ebdomada [fo 90] a festo Sancti Michaelis usque ad Pentecostem tres operaciones …

[fo 90v] **De plenis terris.** Godefridus de Chedesham tenet unam plenam terram eodem modo. Stephanus de Chedesham tenet unam plenam terram eodem modo. Hugo Butr’ tenet unam plenam terram eodem modo. Johannes filius Henrici tenet unam plenam terram eodem modo. Petrus Pinnac tenet unam plenam terram eodem modo. Eborardus de Neuenham tenet unam plenam terram eodem modo. Johannes Wlfrun tenet unam plenam terram eodem modo. Willelmus Wdeman tenet unam plenam terram eodem modo. Philippus Herbert tenet unam plenam terram eodem modo. Johannes Caperun tenet unam plenam terram eodem modo. Leviva vidua tenet unam plenam terram eodem modo. Stephanus Caperun tenet unam plenam terram eodem modo. Augustinus Cat tenet unam plenam terram eodem modo. Theobaldus filius Symonis tenet unam plenam terram eodem modo. Alanus filius Henrici tenet unam plenam terram eodem modo. Martinus bedellus tenet unam plenam terram eodem modo. Albertus de hospitali tenet unam plenam terram eodem modo. Albrictus tenet unam plenam terram eodem modo. Walkelinus prepositus tenet unam plenam terram eodem modo. Hugo bedellus tenet unam plenam terram eodem modo. Ricardus de Bluntesham tenet unam plenam terram eodem modo. Yvo Musepese tenet unam plenam terram eodem modo. Willelmus filius Alfredi tenet unam plenam terram eodem modo. Johannes Herbert tenet unam plenam terram eodem modo. Ricardus Pyc tenet unam plenam terram eodem modo. Aileva vidua tenet unam plenam terram eodem modo. \Aileva uxor Alani tenet unam plenam terram eodem modo./ Robertus ruffus tenet unam plenam terram eodem modo. Johannes del fen tenet unam plenam terram eodem modo. Henricus Athelard tenet unam plenam terram eodem modo. Margareta del fen tenet unam plenam terram eodem modo. Azo de Chedesham tenet unam plenam terram eodem modo, vel custodiet vaccas domini et totum exitum; idem tenuit predictam plenam terram tempore huius inquisicionis pro quatuor solidis equaliter et de witepunt septem denarios, et arabit quantum ipse qui tenet plenam terram.

De dimidiis terris. Thomas cupere tenet dimidiam terram scilicet duodecim acras et dat de witepunt quatuor denarios et obolum et terciam partem unius oboli [fo 91] ita scilicet quod tres huiusmodi tenentes dant quatuordecim denarios, et dat duas gallinas et viginti ova, et debet qualibet ebdomada a festo Sancti Michaelis usque ad Pentecostem duas operaciones…

Elyas filius Willelmi tenet duodecim acras eodem modo. Godardus tenet duodecim acras eodem modo. Agnes vidua tenet duodecim acras eodem modo. Willelmus de Lindon tenet duodecim acras eodem modo. Ingeram de Bele tenet duodecim acras eodem modo. Martinus filius Ingeram tenet duodecim acras eodem modo. David de Dunham tenet duodecim acras eodem modo. Symon Daggeto tenet duodecim acras eodem modo. Hugo de Dunham tenet duodecim acras eodem modo. Johannes filius Osberti tenet duodecim acras eodem modo. Emma del fen tenet duodecim acras eodem modo.

Henry Pin holds a messuage for 12*d* and pays 1*d* wite pound. Robert the huntsman holds a messuage for 6*d* in equal instalments and pays 1*d* wite pound. Richard the carter holds a messuage for 12*d* in equal instalments. Ralph Tylly holds a messuage for 6*d*. Stephen the carpenter holds a messuage for 6*d*. Aline Noble holds a messuage for 13*d* in equal instalments. Robert the messenger holds a croft for 12*d*. Geoffrey the door-keeper holds a croft for 12*d*. Gilbert the tailor holds a messuage for 6*d*; the same holds 5 acres for 12*d* in equal instalments. Peter son of Azo holds 12 acres for 8*s* in equal instalments.

Customary obligations and labour-services. Philip of Chettisham holds a full land, namely 18 ware acres, and pays 3½*d* wite pound at the Annunciation and 3½*d* at Michaelmas, and gives three hens and thirty eggs, and owes weekly [fo 90] from Michaelmas to Whitsun three days of labour- service...[9]

[fo 90v] **Full lands.** Godfrey of Chettisham holds a full land in the same manner. Stephen of Chettisham holds a full land in the same manner. Hugh Butr' holds a full land in the same manner. John, Henry's son, holds a full land in the same manner. Peter Pinnac holds a full land in the same manner. Eborard of Newnham holds a full land in the same manner. John Wlfrun holds a full land in the same manner. William Wdeman holds a full land in the same manner. Philip Herbert holds a full land in the same manner. John Caperun holds a full land in the same manner. Widow Leviva holds a full land in the same manner. Stephen Caperun holds a full land in the same manner. Augustine Cat holds a full land in the same manner. Theobald, Simon's son, holds a full land in the same manner. Alan, Henry's son, holds a full land in the same manner. Martin the beadle holds a full land in the same manner. Albert *de hospitali* holds a full land in the same manner. Albrictus holds a full land in the same manner. Walkelin the reeve holds a full land in the same manner. Hugh the beadle holds a full land in the same manner. Richard of Bluntisham holds a full land in the same manner. Ives Musepese holds a full land in the same manner. William, Alfred's son, holds a full land in the same manner. John Herbert holds a full land in the same manner. Richard Pyc holds a full land in the same manner. Widow Aileva holds a full land in the same manner. \Aileva, Alan's wife, holds a full land in the same manner./ Robert the redhead holds a full land in the same manner. John *del fen* holds a full land in the same manner. Henry Athelard holds a full land in the same manner. Margaret *del fen* holds a full land in the same manner. Azo of Chettisham holds a full land in the same manner, or else he must keep the lord's cows and all the calves; the same held the aforesaid full land at the time of this inquiry, for 4*s* in equal instalments and paid 7*d* wite pound, and he must plough as much as a full-land holder.

Half lands. Thomas *cupere* holds a half land, namely 12 acres and pays 4½*d* and one third of a halfpenny wite pound [fo 91] so that three holders in this category pay 14*d*, and he gives two hens and twenty eggs, and owes weekly from Michaelmas to Whitsun two days of labour-service ...

Ellis, William's son holds 12 acres in the same manner. Godard holds 12 acres in the same manner. Widow Agnes holds 12 acres in the same manner. William of Linden holds 12 acres in the same manner. Ingram of *Bele* holds 12 acres in the same manner. Martin, Ingram's son, holds 12 acres in the same manner. David of Little Downham holds 12 acres in the same manner. Simon Daggeto holds 12 acres in the same manner. Hugh of Little Downham holds 12 acres in the same manner. John, Osbert's son, holds 12 acres in the same manner. Emma *del fen* holds 12 acres in the same manner.[10]

Henricus filius Ricardi tenet duodecim acras eodem modo. Ailmund filius Henrici tenet duodecim acras eodem modo. Willelmus filius Almar' tenet duodecim acras eodem modo. Margareta del fen tenet sex acras et dat de witepunt duos denarios et obolum et debet medietatem aliarum operacionum et consuetudinum. Willelmus porcarius tenet sex acras et debet easdem consuetudines quas Margareta facit, vel debet custodire porcos domini ...
Henricus carectarius tenet quinque acras et ibit ad carucam domini; preterea debet unam operacionem qualibet ebdomada a Pentecoste usque ad festum Sancti Michaelis ... [fo 91v] ...
Thomas de Straham tenet quinque acras eodem modo.

De cothariis. Johannes de Chedesham tenet unam coteriam et dat de witepunt unum denarium, et debet qualibet ebdomada per totum annum unam operacionem, preterea metet de daywine dimidiam acram et ligabit. Alicia vidua tenet unam coteriam eodem modo. Alexander Dolitel tenet unam coteriam eodem modo. Walterus ad barram tenet unam coteriam eodem modo. Willelmus Flie tenet unam coteriam eodem modo. Elyas molendinarius tenet unam coteriam eodem modo. Ingeram Vinbel tenet unam coteriam eodem modo. Fulco Strange tenet unam coteriam eodem modo. Alexander molendinarius tenet unam coteriam eodem modo. Symon textor tenet unam coteriam eodem modo. Rogerus Fas tenet unam coteriam eodem modo. Willelmus Neuman tenet unam coteriam eodem modo. Petrus faber tenet unam coteriam eodem modo. Osbertus Brocorn tenet unam coteriam eodem modo. Alicia vidua tenet unam coteriam eodem modo. Reynerus carnifex tenet unam coteriam eodem modo. Alanus Tail tenet unam coteriam eodem modo. Saleman Coch' tenet unam coteriam eodem modo. Radulfus Payn tenet unam coteriam eodem modo. Gunnilda vidua tenet unam coteriam eodem modo. Robertus Caperun tenet unam coteriam eodem modo. Thurstannus Akermam tenet unam coteriam eodem modo. Radulfus de Wicheford tenet unam coteriam eodem modo. Hugo filius Azonis tenet unam coteriam eodem modo. Ediva vidua tenet unam coteriam eodem modo. Robertus filius Benedicti tenet unam coteriam eodem modo. Wimarca vidua tenet unam coteriam eodem modo. Alexander Sturd' tenet unam coteriam eodem modo. Willelmus Pecoc tenet unam coteriam eodem modo. Luvechild vidua tenet unam coteriam eodem modo. Nicholaus Drake tenet unam coteriam eodem modo. Willelmus filius Pagani tenet unam coteriam eodem modo. Alicia vidua tenet unam coteriam eodem modo. Robertus Cat tenet unam coteriam eodem modo. Gummer tenet unam coteriam eodem modo. Alanus textor tenet unam coteriam eodem modo. Alwinus Botild tenet unam coteriam eodem modo. Osbertus Multon tenet unam coteriam eodem modo. Ricardus Strud' tenet unam coteriam eodem modo. Dayman Bunting tenet unam coteriam eodem modo. Wimarca vidua tenet unam coteriam eodem modo. Radulfus Flye tenet unam coteriam eodem modo. Agnes vidua tenet unam coteriam eodem modo. Matilda Smale tenet unam coteriam eodem modo. [fo 92] Willelmus Smale tenet unam coteriam eodem modo. Rogerus Gerebold tenet unam coteriam eodem modo. Tony filius Aelsi tenet unam coteriam eodem modo. Alanus Obene tenet unam coteriam eodem modo. Nicholaus Galien tenet unam coteriam eodem modo. Henricus Pic tenet unam coteriam eodem modo. Ricardus Lof tenet unam coteriam eodem modo. Willelmus Cley tenet unam coteriam eodem modo. Lefchild filius Johannis tenet unam coteriam eodem modo. Jurdanus Pultorn tenet unam coteriam eodem modo. Azo filius Johannis tenet unam coteriam eodem modo. Quenilda vidua tenet unam coteriam eodem modo. Symon faber tenet unam coteriam eodem modo. Rogerus Sineker tenet unam coteriam eodem modo. Henricus Pulein tenet unam coteriam eodem modo. Agnes Raven tenet unam coteriam eodem modo. Matilda Buc tenet unam coteriam eodem modo. Cecilia Neuman tenet unam coteriam eodem modo. Johannes cuverur tenet unam coteriam eodem modo. Alanus Patun tenet unam coteriam eodem modo. Philippus Pas tenet unam coteriam eodem modo. Wimarca vidua tenet unam coteriam eodem modo. Ailwardus Sley tenet unam coteriam eodem modo. Johannes cutelere tenet unam coteriam eodem modo. Radulfus Bule tenet unam coteriam eodem modo. Robertus Athelard tenet unam coteriam eodem modo. Athelina tenet unam coteriam eodem modo. Emma Dodus tenet unam coteriam eodem modo. Edwinus Bunting tenet unam coteriam eodem modo. Alanus Fitun tenet unam coteriam eodem modo.

Henry, Richard's son, holds 12 acres in the same manner. Ailmund, Henry's son, holds 12 acres in the same manner. William, son of Almar, holds 12 acres in the same manner. Margaret *del fen* holds 6 acres and pays 2½*d* wite pound and owes a half of the other labour-services and customary obligations. William the swineherd holds 6 acres and owes the same customary obligations as Margaret performs, or he must keep the lord's swine ...
Henry the carter holds 5 acres and he must drive the lord's plough; besides he owes one day of labour-service weekly from Whitsun to Michaelmas ... [fo 91v] ...
Thomas of Stretham holds 5 acres in the same manner.

Cottars. John of Chettisham holds a cot-land and pays 1*d* wite pound, and owes one day of labour-service weekly throughout the year, besides he must reap ½ acre and bind the sheaves for a day's pay. Widow Alice holds a cot-land in the same manner. Alexander Dolitel holds a cot-land in the same manner. Walter *ad barram* holds a cot-land in the same manner. William Flie holds a cot-land in the same manner. Ellis the miller holds a cot-land in the same manner. Ingram Vinbel holds a cot-land in the same manner. Fulk Strange holds a cot-land in the same manner. Alexander the miller holds a cot-land in the same manner. Simon the weaver holds a cot-land in the same manner. Roger Fas holds a cot-land in the same manner. William Neuman holds a cot-land in the same manner. Peter the smith holds a cot-land in the same manner. Osbert Brocorn holds a cot-land in the same manner. Widow Alice holds a cot-land in the same manner. Rayner the butcher holds a cot-land in the same manner. Alan Tail holds a cot-land in the same manner. Solomon Coch' holds a cot-land in the same manner. Ralph Payn holds a cot-land in the same manner. Widow Gunhild holds a cot-land in the same manner. Robert Caperun holds a cot-land in the same manner. Thurstan Akermam holds a cot-land in the same manner. Ralph of Witchford holds a cot-land in the same manner. Hugh, Azo's son, holds a cot-land in the same manner. Widow Ediva holds a cot-land in the same manner. Robert, Bennet's son, holds a cot-land in the same manner. Widow Wymark holds a cot-land in the same manner. Alexander Sturd' holds a cot-land in the same manner. William Pecoc holds a cot-land in the same manner. Widow Luvechild holds a cot-land in the same manner. Nicholas Drake holds a cot-land in the same manner. William, Payne's son, holds a cot-land in the same manner. Widow Alice holds a cot-land in the same manner. Robert Cat holds a cot-land in the same manner. Gummer holds a cot-land in the same manner. Alan the weaver holds a cot-land in the same manner. Alwin Botild holds a cot-land in the same manner. Osbert Multon holds a cot-land in the same manner. Richard Strud' holds a cot-land in the same manner. Dayman Bunting holds a cot-land in the same manner. Widow Wymark holds a cot-land in the same manner. Ralph Flye holds a cot-land in the same manner. Widow Agnes holds a cot-land in the same manner. Matilda Smale holds a cot-land in the same manner. [fo 92] William Smale holds a cot-land in the same manner. Roger Gerebold holds a cot-land in the same manner. Tony, Aelsus' son, holds a cot-land in the same manner. Alan Obene holds a cot-land in the same manner. Nicholas Galien holds a cot-land in the same manner. Henry Pic holds a cot-land in the same manner. Richard Lof holds a cot-land in the same manner. William Cley holds a cot-land in the same manner. Lefchild, John's son, holds a cot-land in the same manner. Jordan Pultorn holds a cot-land in the same manner. Azo, John's son, holds a cot-land in the same manner. Widow Quenilda holds a cot-land in the same manner. Simon the smith holds a cot-land in the same manner. Roger Sineker holds a cot-land in the same manner. Henry Pulein holds a cot-land in the same manner. Agnes Raven holds a cot-land in the same manner. Matilda Buc holds a cot-land in the same manner. Cecily Neuman holds a cot-land in the same manner. John the roofer holds a cot-land in the same manner. Alan Patun holds a cot-land in the same manner. Philip Pas holds a cot-land in the same manner. Widow Wymark holds a cot-land in the same manner. Ailward Sley holds a cot-land in the same manner. John the cutler holds a cot-land in the same manner. Ralph Bule holds a cot-land in the same manner. Robert Athelard holds a cot-land in the same manner. Adeline holds a cot-land in the same manner. Emma Dodus holds a cot-land in the same manner. Edwin Bunting holds a cot-land in the same manner. Alan Fitun holds a cot-land in the same manner.

David de Dunham tenet unam coteriam eodem modo. Radulfus porcarius tenet unam coteriam eodem modo. Milisent vidua tenet unam coteriam eodem modo. Henricus filius Johannis tenet unam coteriam eodem modo. Willelmus Samke tenet unam coteriam eodem modo. Willelmus Gerebald tenet unam coteriam eodem modo. Radulfus Tote tenet unam coteriam eodem modo. Robertus Tote tenet unam coteriam eodem modo. Miriel relicta fabri tenet unam coteriam eodem modo. Johannes carectarius tenet unam coteriam eodem modo. Nicholaus Dammany tenet unam coteriam eodem modo. Emma ruffa tenet unam coteriam eodem modo. Henricus filius Lec' tenet unam coteriam eodem modo. Frethesent Cherl tenet unam coteriam eodem modo. Hugo de Chedesham tenet unam coteriam eodem modo. Ricardus Smale tenet unam coteriam eodem modo. Frethesent Oki tenet unam coteriam eodem modo.Ailredus Coc tenet unam coteriam eodem modo. Galfridus Akermam tenet unam coteriam eodem modo. Gervasius Spitman tenet unam coteriam eodem modo. Matilda Selide tenet unam coteriam eodem modo. Eborardus de Chedesham tenet unam coteriam eodem modo. Richolda vidua tenet unam coteriam eodem modo. [fo 92v] Philippus Kuermud tenet unum mesagium et dat de witepunt unum denarium et debet qualibet ebdomada a gula Augusti usque ad festum Sancti Michaelis unam operacionem; preterea metet dimidiam acram de daywine et fodit in vinea.

De liberis hominibus ultra aquam. Willelmus faber tenet unum mesagium pro duodecim denariis equaliter. Stephanus faber tenet unum mesagium pro quatuor denariis. Walterus faber tenet unum mesagium pro octo denariis. Nicholaus Disel tenet unum mesagium pro sex denariis. Willelmus Bunce tenet unum mesagium pro octo denariis. Alexander spicer tenet unum mesagium pro duodecim denariis. Johannes Revel tenet unum mesagium pro octo denariis. Henricus de Thornes tenet quandam terram in campis de Saham pro quinque solidis equaliter et debet navigare harnasium episcopi de Saham usque in Ely. Nicholaus Wdeking tenet unum mesagium ultra aquam pro quatuor denariis equaliter. Alanus mercator tenet unum mesagium pro quatuor denariis. Henricus de Riburg tenet unum mesagium pro quatuor denariis. Richolda vidua tenet unum mesagium pro quatuor denariis. Willelmus tanur tenet unum mesagium pro quatuor denariis. Elemosinarius tenet unum mesagium pro quatuor denariis. Johannes capellanus tenet unum mesagium pro quatuor denariis. Ricardus de Crauden tenet unum mesagium pro quatuor denariis. Matthaeus de Kent tenet unum mesagium pro quatuor denariis. Radulfus granarius tenet unum mesagium pro duobus denariis. Hugo Mud tenet unum mesagium pro duobus denariis. Eudo rosarius tenet unum mesagium pro duobus denariis. Goscelinus filius Alfredi tenet unum mesagium pro duobus denariis. Henricus frater prioris tenet unum mesagium pro duobus denariis. Jocelinus carpentarius tenet unum mesagium pro duobus denariis. Rogerus Gokay tenet unum mesagium pro duobus denariis. Walterus de Cotenham tenet unum mesagium pro duobus denariis. Nicholaus filius Cecilie tenet unum mesagium pro duobus denariis. Olivia de Bech tenet unum mesagium pro duobus denariis. Robertus clericus tenet unum mesagium pro duobus denariis.

De seldis carnificum. Robertus Cat tenet unam seldam carnificum pro sex denariis ad festum Omnium Sanctorum. Henricus Pudding tenet unam seldam pro sex denariis ad eundem terminum. Rogerus Pudding tenet unam seldam pro sex denariis. Radulfus Cat tenet unam seldam pro sex denariis. Robertus filius Benedicti tenet unam seldam pro sex denariis. [fo 93] Henricus de Coln tenet unam seldam pro sex denariis. Reynerus tenet unam seldam pro sex denariis. Willelmus tanur tenet unam seldam pro sex denariis. Johannes culcitrarius tenet unam seldam pro sex denariis. Henricus Pudding tenet unam seldam pro quatuor denariis et obolo. Stephanus filius Unfridi tenet unam seldam pro quinque denariis; idem tenet duas alteras seldas pro decem denariis. Johannes culcitrarius tenet duas seldas pro decem denariis. Petrus Gernun tenet unam seldam pro duodecim denariis. Sciendum quod totus redditus predictarum seldarum solvitur ad festum Omnium Sanctorum.

David of Little Downham holds a cot-land in the same manner. Ralph the swineherd holds a cot-land in the same manner. Widow Milicent holds a cot-land in the same manner. Henry, John's son, holds a cot-land in the same manner. William Samke holds a cot-land in the same manner. William Gerebald holds a cot-land in the same manner. Ralph Tote holds a cot-land in the same manner. Robert Tote holds a cot-land in the same manner. Muriel, the smith's widow holds a cot-land in the same manner. John the carter holds a cot-land in the same manner. Nicholas Dammany holds a cot-land in the same manner. Emma the redhead holds a cot-land in the same manner. Henry, son of Lec, holds a cot-land in the same manner. Frethesent Cherl holds a cot-land in the same manner. Hugh of Chettisham holds a cot-land in the same manner. Richard Smale holds a cot-land in the same manner. Frethesent Oki holds a cot-land in the same manner. Ailred Coc holds a cot-land in the same manner. Geoffrey Akermam holds a cot-land in the same manner. Gervase Spitman holds a cot-land in the same manner. Matilda Selide holds a cot-land in the same manner. Eborard of Chettisham holds a cot-land in the same manner. Widow Richolda holds a cot-land in the same manner. [fo 92v] Philip Kuermud holds a messuage and pays 1*d* wite pound, and owes one day of labour-service weekly from Lammas to Michaelmas; besides he must reap ½ acre for a day's pay, and he digs in the vineyard.

Free men beyond the water. William the smith holds a messuage for 12*d* in equal instalments. Stephen the smith holds a messuage for 4*d*. Walter the smith holds a messuage for 8*d*. Nicholas Disel holds a messuage for 6*d*. William Bunce holds a messuage for 8*d*. Alexander the spicer holds a messuage for 12*d*. John Revel holds a messuage for 8*d*. Henry de Thornes holds a piece of land in Soham fields for 5*s* in equal instalments, and he must carry the bishop's luggage by boat from Soham to Ely.[11] Nicholas Wdeking holds a messuage beyond the water for 4*d* in equal instalments. Alan the merchant holds a messuage for 4*d*. Henry de Riburg holds a messuage for 4*d*.[12] Widow Richolda holds a messuage for 4*d*. William the tanner holds a messuage for 4*d*. The almoner holds a messuage for 4*d*. John the chaplain holds a messuage for 4*d*. Richard of Croydon holds a messuage for 4*d*. Matthew of Kent holds a messuage for 4*d*. Ralph the granary-keeper holds a messuage for 2*d*. Hugh Mud holds a messuage for 2*d*.[13] Eudes *rosarius* holds a messuage for 2*d*. Jocelin, Alfred's son, holds a messuage for 2*d*. Henry, the prior's brother, holds a messuage for 2*d*. Jocelin the carpenter holds a messuage for 2*d*. Roger Gokay holds a messuage for 2*d*. Walter of Cottenham holds a messuage for 2*d*. Nicholas, Cecily's son, holds a messuage for 2*d*. Olive de Bech holds a messuage for 2*d*. Robert the clerk holds a messuage for 2*d*.

The butchers' stalls. Robert Cat holds a butcher's stall for 6*d* [payable] on All Saints' Day. Henry Pudding holds a stall for 6*d* at the same term. Roger Pudding holds a stall for 6*d*. Ralph Cat holds a stall for 6*d*. Robert, Bennet's son, holds a stall for 6*d*. [fo 93] Henry of Colne holds a stall for 6*d*. Rayner holds a stall for 6*d*. William the tanner holds a stall for 6*d*. John the quilt-maker holds a stall for 6*d*. Henry Pudding holds a stall for 4½*d*. Stephen, Humfrey's son, holds a stall for 5*d*; the same holds two other stalls for 10*d*. John the quilt-maker holds two stalls for 10*d*. Peter Gernun holds a stall for 12*d*. Note that all the rent of the aforesaid stalls is paid on All Saints' Day.

CUL EDR G3/27, fos 1–7v

[fo 1] **Incipit liber de inquisicionibus maneriorum episcopatus Elyensis factis tempore Hugonis Elyensis episcopi anno consecracionis sue vicesimo primo** per Rogerum de Abyton tunc senescallum, de advocationibus ecclesiarum, de dominicis, pratis, pasturis, boscis et mariscis et piscariis, de feodis militum.

De redditibus assisis liberorum hominum et aliorum, de operibus et consuetudinibus operariorum. Inquisicio facta per Willelmum filium Elye, Nicholaum fratrem eius, Salamonem aurifabrum, Philippum Manger, Martinum de Swafham, Nicholaum le coyltrer, Lucam Dolimer,[14] Adam pistorem, Hugonem filium Mabilie, Henricum piscatorem, Hugonem Wade, Moysem, Robertum Copin, Henricum le cuverur, Everardum le caruer, Aluredum Ruggele, Robertum ruffum, Willelmum filium Aluredi, Walterum Musepese, Ricardum de Bluntesham, Hugonem prepositum, Willelmum Godard, Philippum bedellum, Stephanum Vodeman, Johannem de Bele, Radulphum de Chetesham, Robertum Tubbe, Petrum Pinnok.

Dominicum huius manerii ita distinguitur scilicet in campo qui vocatur Gruntifen ducente et quadraginta et quatuor acre; in Cratendon sexaginta acre; in Alfoweshoue, Stonyhoue et Wrongelond cum chiselpettes quater viginti et quindecim acre; in Brieneshoure[15] quindecim acre et dimidia; in Grasseloue quater viginti et septemdecim acre; in Groshoue cum cunegera quinquaginta et due acre; in Roueshil cum stanpettes et cleypettes sex viginti acre; in Bandonhille quinquaginta et una acra; in Vaterslade scilicet inter Willelmum de Ely et dranam sex viginti et decem acre; in Weld septem viginti et una acra; in Waterden quinque viginti et quindecim acre; in Bliynghale[16] sex viginti et novemdecim acre; in Chedesfeld ducente et viginti novem acre et dimidia; in novo assarco de boscho de Chedesham triginta et quinque acre et dimidia. [col. 2] Summa tocius terre lucrabilis mille et quingente et viginti quatuor et dimidia acre per minorem centenam et per perticam sexdecim pedum et dimidii, que possunt lucrari per decem carucas unde quelibet sex carucarum de sex stottis et quelibet quatuor carucarum de sex bobus et duobus stottis cum consuetudine ville.

De prato falcabili scilicet in Gruntifen septemdecim acre; in Braslowe[17] et le Hay quaterviginti et una acra et tres rode; item ibidem viginti acre de novo hassaccate; in Blacwineserd cum mara viginti et due acre; in Craswelle, Brademede et Chinhale triginta et sex acre; in Chetesfeld viginti et quinque acre et dimidia; item ibidem circa novum assartum sex acre; in Pandenhale et Bliynghale quadraginta quatuor acre et dimidia; item ibidem septem acre de novo hassochate et una roda; item est ibidem quedam grava de spineto que continet sex acras; item est ibidem vinea novem acrarum et infra clausum eiusdem vinee octo acre de pastura. Summa acrarum tocius prati falcabilis ducente et sexaginta per minorem centenarium.

De marisco. Ad idem manerium pertinet quidam mariscus qui vocatur Caldewellefen qui durat a villa de Ely usque ad Brame, et a Brame usque ad Tethford ubi episcopus et prior et conventus, et villata de Ely et dominus Walterus de Ely et homines de Theford communicant tam in falcando quam pascendo vel piscando. Salomon tum aurifaber ibidem habet mariscum de Brame in separali sicut circumcingitur fossatis; et ex altera parte ripe est quedam languetta marisci inter Cloggeswere et magnum pontem et est communis sicut predictus mariscus et Caldewellefen. Item ex opposito de Brame est quidam mariscus qui vocatur Kyfen qui durat a Bramewere usque ad Tuyfolde et a Tuyfolde usque ad calcetum de Stunteney et est communis modo prenominato. Item ad idem pertinet quidam mariscus iuxta Kufen qui durat a Crowethornlode usque ad Biscopesdelf et a Biscopesdelf usque ad Sheldesstreng, et a Scheldestreng usque ad Antimere [fo 1v] polis et ab Antimere poles usque ad Bibelestal, et a Bibelestal usque ad maras de Undeleyefrith que est separale prioris de Ely;

[fo 1] **Here begins the book of inquiries of the manors of the bishopric of Ely made in the twenty-first year of the episcopate of Hugh bishop of Ely [1250]** by Roger of Abington then steward, concerning the advowson of churches, demesne, meadow, pasture, woodland and marsh and fisheries, concerning knights' fees.[18]

Concerning the fixed rents of free men and others, the serfs' labour-services and customary obligations The inquiry was made by William son of Ellis, his brother Nicholas, Solomon the goldsmith, Philip Manger, Martin of Swaffham, Nicholas the quilt-maker, Luke Dolimer, Adam the baker, Hugh son of Mabel, Henry the fisherman, Hugh Wade, Moses, Robert Copin, Henry the roofer, Everard the ploughman, Alfred Ruggele, Robert the redhead, William son of Alfred, Walter Musepese, Richard of Bluntisham, Hugh the reeve, William Godard, Philip the beadle, Stephen Vodeman, John de Bele, Ralph of Chettisham, Robert Tubbe, Peter Pinnok.

The demesne of this manor is disposed thus namely in the field called Grunty Fen 244 acres; in *Cratendon* 60 acres; in *Alfoweshoue*, *Stonyhoue* and *Wrongelond* with the gravel pits 95 acres; in *Brieneshoure* 15½ acres; in *Grasseloue* 97 acres; in *Groshoue* with the rabbit-warren 52 acres; in *Roueshil* with the stone pits and the clay pits 120 acres; in *Bandonhille* 51 acres; in *Vaterslade*, namely between William of Ely and the drain 130 acres; in *Weld* 141 acres; in Waterden 115 acres; in Blithinghale 139 acres; in *Chedesfeld* 229½ acres; in the new assart from Chettisham wood 35½ acres. [col. 2] Total sum of arable land 1524½ acres, by the short hundred and by the perch of 16½ feet,[19] that can be cultivated by ten ploughs, of which six ploughs of six stotts, and four of six oxen and two stotts, with the customary obligations owed by the township.

Hay meadow in Grunty Fen 17 acres; in *Braslowe* and *le Hay* 81 acres and 3 roods; also 20 acres of newly reclaimed land there; in *Blacwineserd* with the mere 22 acres; in Cresswell, *Brademede* and *Chinhale* 36 acres; in *Chetesfeld* 25½ acres; also around the new assart there 6 acres; in Padnal and Blithinghale 44½ acres; also 7 acres and 1 rood of newly reclaimed land there; there is also a thorn grove there that contains 6 acres; there is also a vineyard there of 9 acres, and within the enclosure of the same vineyard 8 acres of pasture. Total area of hay meadow: 260 acres, by the short hundred.

Marsh.[20] A marsh called Cawdle Fen pertains to the same manor, it extends from the township of Ely to Braham, and from Braham to Little Thetford where the bishop, the prior and convent, the township of Ely, Sir Walter de Ely and the men of Little Thetford exercise the right of common, in mowing as well as grazing or fishing. Solomon the goldsmith at the time holds in severalty there Braham marsh as it is enclosed with ditches; and on the other side of the bank is a tongue of marsh between *Cloggeswere* and the great bridge, and it is common just as the aforesaid marsh and Cawdle Fen. Opposite Braham there is a marsh called Cow Fen that extends from Braham weir to *Tuyfolde* and from *Tuyfolde* to Stuntney causeway, and it is common in the aforesaid manner. Also to the same manor pertains a marsh next to Cow Fen that extends from *Crowethornlode* to Bishop's delf and from Bishop's delf to *Sheldesstreng*, and from *Scheldestreng* to *Antimere* [fo 1v] pools and from *Antimere* pools to *Bibelestal*, and from *Bibelestal* to the meres of *Undeleyefrith* that is a private holding of the prior of Ely;

et ab Undeleyefrith usque ad Blakepol et a Blakepol usque ad Hukebechelode, et ab Hukebechelode usque ad Alwoldesdelf et ab Alwoldesdelf usque ad \baram/[21] de Redmere. Et ab illa bara usque ad Estfenwilyw; et ab Estfenwylyw usque ad Spanidelf et a Spanidelf per Wymdelf usque ad Guatteslodeshende, et a Guatteslodeshende usque ad Krechemer et a Krechemer usque ad Bollinges, et a Bollinges per Maydenelode usque Oldewellenhe. Et ex altera parte ripe de Oldewellenhe a Pralleswere usque Horningespolis, et ab Horningespolis per Derfordeshe usque Maneye, et a Maneye usque Fenegeyhe, et per Fenegeyehe usque Baldstaf, et a Baldstaf per Langereche et Danelode sub Hunneye quod est separale abbatis Ramensis usque Danelodeshende, et a Danelodeshende usque Gosepol, et a Gosepol usque ad Kirkelake, et a Kirkelake usque Menechenewode, et a Menechenewode usque Wenheye, et a Wenheye usque Wikhamhe et per Wichamhe et Dreibet et Chaterichlode usque Mephalehe, et a Mephalehe per Byhe et Wichamhe usque Wichamhythe, et a Wichamhiye per Wardeye et Lytleye usque Wichefordelond; et ex altera parte Wicheford est quidam mariscus qui vocatur Gruntifen ubi Stratham et villate que attingunt eidem marisco communicant cum villata de Ely. Sciendum tamen quod infra predictas metas est unus mariscus qui vocatur Bliyynghalefen qui durat ex una parte a Blyynghaledik usque Senelodes et ex altera a Padenhale Ord usque Halewerelak ubi non communicant aliqui cum domino episcopo in falcacione nisi tantum dominus prior de Ely, sed in pascendo est communis ut supra. Item infra easdem metas est quidam mariscus qui vocatur Middelfen ubi non communicat aliquis cum domino episcopo in falcacione nisi prior de Ely tantum, et tamen liberi homines de Ely ibidem possunt falcare cooperturam ad domos [col. 2] suas si voluerint sed in pascendo est communis ut supra. Item in Padenhal est quoddam separale episcopi ad fodiendum que durat a Pitemanesdik ex una parte, et a Wodegate ex altera usque Halewerelake et Senelowes. Item in Northfen est quoddam separale episcopi ad fodiendum quod durat a Nowedik[22] usque Bypert sed est commune ad falcandum et pascendum ut supra.

De stauro. Possunt ibi esse vacce viginti et duo tauri liberi, porci centum et duo verri liberi per minorem numerum, bidentes quingente cum bidentibus cotariorum suorum que debent iacere in falda domini per maiorem centum.

De molendinis. Sunt ibi duo molendina ventricia que nunc sunt ad firmam quorum unum pro quinque marcis et aliud pro sex marcis et est firma aliquando minor ad quem omnes censuarii et consuetudinarii debent sectam.

De piscariis ad idem pertinentibus scilicet Wpwere cum quatuor gurgitibus et Swanesmere, et solebat reddere tria milia et triginta sex stikos anguillarum sed modo reddit tresdecim solidos et quatuor denarios per annum ad duos terminos equaliter, scilicet ad festum Sancti Michaelis et ad Annunciacionem Beate Marie quam modo tenet Thomas de Theford. Item ad idem pertinet Bradewere cum pertinenciis scilicet Midlestwere, Marewere, Beche et medietas de Haveringmere et tota Langmere et Fridaywere [et medietas][23] de Alwoldingwere et tota Nakedwere et medietas de Grantewere et Belilake et Beryeilode, et reddit per annum quatuordecim milia et dimidium anguillarum prima Dominica Quadragesime et decem solidos equaliter ad quatuor terminos quam tenent hereditarie Henricus piscator, Thomas de Theford et Martinus de Swafham. Ad idem pertinet Yrithwere[26] cum Culdinglake quam sacrista tenet pro decem solidis equaliter, et tempore episcopi Galfridi Ridel solebat dicta piscaria reddere tria milia et triginta [sex][27] stikos anguillarum. Ad idem pertinet piscaria de Krechemere quam Henricus filius Oseberti de Walpol tenet hereditarie per cartam, et reddit quinque solidos[28] [fo 2] per annum ad scacariam. Ad idem pertinet piscaria sex batellorum que incipit ad Haveringmere et durat usque Prikewyley unde Hugo Wade tenet piscariam unius batelli et reddit per annum sex solidos ad quatuor terminos equaliter; item Henricus Daly tenet piscariam duorum badellorum pro sex solidis per annum equaliter; item Moyses piscator tenet piscariam unius batelli pro triginta et sex denariis ad quatuor terminos equaliter; item Rogerus Fot

and from *Undeleyefrith* to *Blakepol* and from *Blakepol* to *Hukebechelode*, and from *Hukebechelode* to *Alwoldesdelf* and from *Alwoldesdelf* to the barrier of *Redmere*; and from that barrier to *Estfenwylyw*; and from *Estfenwilyw* to *Spanidelf* and from *Spanidelf* through *Wymdelf* to *Guatteslodeshende*, and from *Guatteslodeshende* to Crouch Mere and from Crouch Mere to *Bollinges*, and from *Bollinges* through *Maydenelode* to *Oldwellenhe*. And on the other side of the bank of *Oldenwellenhe* from *Pralleswere* to *Horninges* pools, and from *Horninges* pools through *Derfordeshe* to Manea, and from Manea to *Fenegeyhe*, and through *Fenegeyehe* to *Baldstaf*, and from *Baldstaf* through *Langereche* and *Danelode*, below Honey Hill that is a private holding of the abbot of Ramsey, to *Danelodeshende*, and from *Danelodeshende* to *Gosepol* and from *Gosepol* to *Kirkelake*, and from *Kirkelake* to *Menechenewode*, and from *Menechenewode* to *Wenheye*, and from *Wenheye* to *Wikhamhe* and through *Wichamhe* and *Dreibet* and Chatteris lode to *Mephalehe*, and from *Mephalehe* through Byall Fen and *Wichamhe* to Witcham hithe and from Witcham hithe through Wardy Hill and Little Hill to Witchford land; and on the other side of Witchford is a marsh called Grunty Fen where Stretham and the townships adjoining the same marsh graze in common with the township of Ely. Note that within the aforesaid limits there is a marsh called Blithinghale Fen that extends from Blithinghale dike to *Senelodes* on one side, and from Padnal *Ord* to *Halewerelak* on the other where none have common rights of mowing with the lord bishop except for the lord prior of Ely, but it is common for grazing as above. Also within the same limits there is a marsh called Middle Fen where nobody has common rights of mowing with the lord bishop except for the prior of Ely only, but the free men of Ely may cut thatching for their houses [col. 2] if they wish, but it is common for grazing as above. Also in Padnal there is a private holding of the bishop for digging [turves] that extends from *Pitemanesdik* on one side, and from *Wodegate* on the other to *Halewerelake* and *Senelowes*. Also in North Fen is a private holding of the bishop for digging [turves] that extends from *Nowedik* to *Bypert* but it is common for mowing and grazing as above.

Livestock. There can be on the manor twenty cows and two free bulls, 100 pigs and two free boars, by the short hundred, 500 sheep together with the cottars' sheep that must lie in the lord's fold, by the long hundred.[24]

Mills. There are two windmills there that are now at farm, one for 5 marks and the other for 6 marks, and it is to the mill with the slightly lower rent that all the rent-paying and customary tenants owe suit.

Fisheries pertaining to the same manor namely Upware with four weirs[25] and *Swanesmere*, and it used to render 3036 sticks of eels but now it renders 13*s* 4*d* annually in equal instalments at two terms, namely at Michaelmas and at the Annunciation, Thomas of Little Thetford now holds it. To the same pertains *Bradewere* with appurtenances namely *Midlestwere*, *Marewere*, *Beche* and half of Harrimere and all of *Langmere* and *Fridaywere* [and half] of *Alwoldingwere* and all of *Nakedwere* and half of *Grantewere* and *Belilake* and *Beryeilode*, and renders 14500 eels annually on the first Sunday in Lent and 10*s* in equal instalments at the four terms; and Henry the fisherman, Thomas of Little Thetford and Martin of Swaffham hold these by inheritance. To the same [manor] pertains *Yrithwere* with *Culdinglake* that the sacrist holds for 10*s* in equal instalments, and the said fishery used to render three thousand and thirty[-six] sticks of eels in Bishop Geoffrey Ridel's time. To the same pertains the fishery of Crouch Mere that Henry, son of Osbert of Walpole holds hereditarily by charter, and it renders 5*s* [fo 2] annually at the exchequer. To the same pertains a fishery of six boats[29] that begins at Harrimere and extends to Prickwillow, whereof Hugh Wade holds a fishery of one boat and renders 6*s*[30] annually in equal instalments at the four terms; Henry Daly holds a fishery of two boats for 6*s* annually in equal instalments; Moses the fisherman holds a fishery of one boat for 36*d* in equal instalments at the four terms; Roger Fot

tenet piscariam unius batelli pro tribus solidis ad quatuor terminos equaliter; item Johannes gubernator tenet piscariam unius batelli pro tribus solidis ad quatuor terminos equaliter. Summa denariorum per annum quinquaginta sex solidi et quatuor denarii unde decem et octo solidi de piscaria batellorum et decem solidi de Bradewerefen allocantur infra redditum assisum, et quinque solidi de Crechemere super scacariam. Summa anguillarum xiiij milia et dimidium.

De militibus. Isti quinque debent wardam et debent sumonere alios milites de baronia episcopatus pro loco et tempore ad faciendum wardam in Ely et debent sectam ad curiam in Ely. Philippus de Insula tenet unum mesuagium quod pertinet ad feodum militis. Radulphus de Soham tenet unum mesuagium quod pertinet ad feodum militis. Henricus Pelerin tenet unum mesuagium quod pertinet ad feodum militis. Stephanus de Marisco tenet unum mesuagium quod pertinet ad feodum militis. Henricus Muschet tenuit unum mesuagium quod pertinebat ad feodum militis, quod mesuagium monachi tenent infra vineam suam ex dono episcopi qui nunc est, per escambium factum inter ipsum episcopum et Henricum Muschet de suo redditu apud Dittone.

De libere tenentibus. Robertus de Insula tenet unum mesuagium quod fuit Ricardi de Melkesham pro duodecim denariis per annum equaliter et dat de witepund ad duos terminos unum denarium scilicet ad festum Sancti Michaelis et ad Annunciacionem Beate Marie, et fodit in vinea per unum diem sine cibo; idem tenet unum mesuagium quod fuit sermonatoris pro duodecim denariis equaliter; et sciendum quod Johannes Maunsel, Johannes Pulein et Symon mercator nunc tenent illa duo mesuagia; idem [col. 2] tenuit unum mesuagium ubi vetus castellum fuit pro quo reddere solet duos solidos per annum equaliter sed nunc nihil inde reddit quia est in manu episcopi. Fratres hospitalis tenuerunt unum mesuagium pro duodecim denariis equaliter quod fuit Bartholomei de Tistishale quod nunc tenet sacrista Elyensis pro eodem redditu. Fratres hospitalis Sancte Marie Magdalene in Ely tenent octodecim acras de wara que fuerunt dicti Bartholomei pro duodecim denariis equaliter. Item Henricus Muschet tenuit quinque mesuagia pro quibus solet reddere quinque solidos per annum equaliter et duos denarios de witepund et fodere in vinea que mesuagia monachi de Ely tenent ex dono episcopi sine redditu per escambium factum inter ipsum episcopum et predictum Henricum de suo redditu apud Ditton. Willelmus filius Elye tenet triginta sex acras de wara cum mesuagio suo pro decem solidis equaliter, et inveniet carucam suam per unum diem in hyeme et per unum diem in Quadragesima ad precariam ad cibum domini; item inveniet similiter carettam suam per unum diem ad roscum cariandum in estate et carettam suam similiter per unum diem in autumpno ad bladum cariandum ad cibum domini; item debet esse unus custos messorum ad magnam precariam domini in autumpno ad cibum domini; et ibit cum senescallo domini et cum militibus apud Cantebregiam in adventu iusticiariorum ad postulandum ibidem libertates domini; et debet sectam ad halimot; idem tenet unum mesuagium quod fuit Selede pro duodecim denariis equaliter et dat unum denarium de witepund ad festum Sancti Michaelis et ad Annunciacionem Beate Marie equaliter. Agnes filia Johannis filii Pagani et due sorores tenent octodecim acras pro quinque solidis equaliter; eedem tenent unum mesuagium cum sex acris terre pro duodecim denariis equaliter; eedem tenent unum mesuagium pro octo denariis equaliter et dant de witepund unum denarium ad duos terminos ut supra, et fodere debent in vinea per unum diem a mane usque ad horam nonam sine cibo; eedem tenent unum mesuagium quod fuit Aelsi coci pro duodecim denariis equaliter et dant de witepund unum denarium ut supra; eedem tenent unum mesuagium pro sexdecim denariis equaliter et dant de witepund unum denarium ut supra; eedem tenent unam partem tofti Gereboldi pro duo [fo 2v] decim denariis equaliter et dant de witepund unum denarium ut supra; eedem tenent unum mesuagium in quo sedent pro sex denariis equaliter; eedem tenent unum mesuagium quod fuit Johannis Burgens pro duodecim denariis equaliter et dant de witepund unum denarium ut supra, et fodiunt in vinea ut supra; eedem tenent unum mesuagium quod fuit Radulphi aurifabri pro duodecim denariis equaliter et de witepund unum denarium ut supra; eedem tenent unum mesuagium pro sex denariis equaliter et de witepund unum denarium ut supra; eedem tenent quandam aream de purprestura pro sex

holds a fishery of one boat for 3*s* in equal instalments at the four terms; John the steersman holds a fishery of one boat for 3*s* in equal instalments at the four terms. Total money rents 56*s* 4*d* annually, of which 18*s* from the boat fishery and 10*s* from *Bradewerefen* are charged under the fixed rent, and 5s from Crouch Mere are charged at the exchequer. Total number of eels 14500.

Knights. These five owe guard duty and must summon the other knights of the bishop's barony telling them the place and the time for undertaking guard duty in Ely, and they owe suit to the court in Ely. Philip de Insula holds a message that pertains to a knight's fee. Ralph of Soham holds a message that pertains to a knight's fee. Henry Pelerin holds a message that pertains to a knight's fee. Stephen de Marisco holds a message that pertains to a knight's fee. Henry Muschet held a message that pertained to a knight's fee, the monks now hold it within their vineyard,[31] by the gift of the present bishop, by an exchange made between the bishop and Henry Muschet for his rent at Fen Ditton.[32]

Free tenants. Robert de Insula holds a message formerly Richard of Melksham's for 12*d* annually in equal instalments, and pays 1*d* wite pound at two terms namely at Michaelmas and at the Annunciation, and he digs in the vineyard for one day with no food allowance; the same holds a message formerly the *sermonator*'s for 12*d* in equal instalments; and note that John Maunsel, John Pulein and Simon the merchant now hold those two messages; the same [col. 2] held a message where the old castle stood for which he paid 2*s* annually in equal instalments but now it renders nothing because it is in the bishop's hand.[33] The brethren of the hospital[34] held a message formerly Bartholomew of Tivetshall's for 12*d* in equal instalments, the sacrist of Ely now holds it for the same rent. The brethren of the hospital of St Mary Magdalene in Ely hold 18 ware acres formerly the said Bartholomew's for 12*d* in equal instalments. Henry Muschet held five messages for which he used to render 5*s* annually in equal instalments and 2*d* wite pound, and dig in the vineyard,[35] the monks of Ely hold these messages rent-free by gift of the bishop by the exchange made between the bishop and the aforesaid Henry for his rent at Fen Ditton. William, Ellis' son,[36] holds 36 ware acres with his message for 10*s* in equal instalments, and he must provide his plough for one day in winter and one day in Lent as boon-work, with a food allowance from the bishop; likewise he must provide his cart for one day in the summer to carry rushes, and for one day in the autumn to carry corn, with a food allowance from the bishop; he must also be a supervisor of the reapers at the lord's great boon-work in the autumn with a food allowance from the bishop; and he must accompany the lord's steward and the knights to Cambridge to claim there the lord's liberties at the coming of the justices; and he owes suit of court at the halmote; the same holds a message formerly Seleda's for 12*d* in equal instalments and pays 1*d* wite pound in equal instalments at Michaelmas and at the Annunciation. Agnes, daughter of John, Payne's son, and her two sisters hold 18 acres for 5*s* in equal instalments;[37] the same hold a message with 6 acres of land for 12*d* in equal instalments; the same hold a message for 8*d* in equal instalments, and pay 1*d* wite pound at the two terms as above, and they must dig in the vineyard for one day from dawn to noon with no allowance of food; the same hold a message formerly of Aelsus the cook for 12*d* in equal instalments and they pay 1*d* wite pound as above; the same hold a message for 16*d* in equal instalments and pay 1*d* wite pound as above; the same hold a part of Gerebold's toft for [fo 2v] 12*d* in equal instalments and pay 1*d* wite pound as above; the same hold a message in which they dwell for 6*d* in equal instalments; the same hold a message formerly of John Burgens for 12*d* in equal instalments and they pay 1*d* wite pound as above, and dig in the vineyard as above; the same hold a message formerly of Ralph the goldsmith for 12*d* in equal instalments and pay 1*d* wite pound as above; the same hold a message for 6*d* in equal instalments and pay 1*d* wite pound as above; the same hold an area of newly reclaimed land for 6*d*

denariis equaliter; eedem tenet unum mesuagium quod fuit Samuelis clerici iuxta eandem purpresturam pro duodecim denariis equaliter et de witepund unum denarium ut supra; eedem tenent unum mesuagium quod antiquitus fuit operabile pro duodecim denariis \equaliter/; eedem tenent unum holmum pro duodecim denariis equaliter; eedem tenent unum mesuagium quod fuit Nicholai filii Elye cementarii pro duodecim denariis equaliter et de witepund unum denarium ut supra; eedem tenent unum mesuagium quod fuit Johannis de bederna pro sex denariis equaliter. Johannes de Walpol tenet octodecim acras de wara cum mesuagio pro quinque solidis equaliter et dat de witepund quatuordecim denarios ut supra, et inveniet carucam suam per unum diem in hyeme et per unum diem in Quadragesima ad cibum domini, et alias consuetudines facit sicut predictus Willelmus filius Elye. Nicholaus filius Elye et Willelmus de la Hale tenent octodecim acras de wara que fuerunt Petri Sauek cum mesuagio et crufta pro duobus solidis equaliter, et debent facere easdem consuetudines quas predictus Willelmus filius Elye; ad idem tenementum pertinet esse coronarium et replegiare homines episcopi, et debent ire contra iusticiarios et facere seisinas et disseisinas infra insulam et extra. Lodowycus et Alicia Barat uxor eius, et Radulphus le barbur et Agnes uxor eius tenent triginta sex acras de wara cum mesuagio et dant de witepund septem denarios ut supra, et arabunt tres acras per annum sine cibo, scilicet unam acram in hyeme et unam acram in Quadragesima et unam acram in estate, et debent esse coronatores et replegiare homines episcopi ut supra, et faciunt easdem consuetudines quas [col. 2] Willelmus filius Elye et Nicholaus predictus. Johannes aurifaber et elemosinarius et Petrus de Litleberi tenent sex acras cum mesuagio que fuerunt filii Philippi que pertinere solebant ad roseriam custodiendam, et dant [de] witepund duos denarios et obolum ut supra. Johannes de marisco tenet sex acras de wara et debet esse coronarius et erit coram iusticiariis sicut predictus Nicholaus. Petrus de Litlebery tenet unum mesuagium ante Bertonam quod fuit Mabilie pro sex denariis equaliter; idem Petrus tenet unum mesuagium ibidem pro sex denariis equaliter; item idem Petrus tenet unam purpresturam pro sex denariis equaliter; idem Petrus tenet duo mesuagia sub Bertonam pro duobus solidis equaliter; item tenet quandam partem iuxta eadem mesuagia pro duobus denariis equaliter. Rogerus de Fleg tenet unum mesuagium pro sex denariis equaliter. Johannes Kyld et Adam pistor tenent unum mesuagium pro sex denariis equaliter et de witepund unum denarium ut supra, et fodiunt in vinea ut supra. Willelmus de Derham tenet unum mesuagium pro octo denariis equaliter et de witepund unum denarium ut supra, et fodit in vinea ut supra. Matilda que fuit uxor Johannis le beverarunt et Thomas filius eius tenent unum mesuagium pro octo denariis equaliter et de witepund unum denarium ut supra; iidem tenent duo mesuagia pro duobus solidis equaliter et de witepund unum denarium, et fodiunt in vinea. Willelmus filius Barbote tenet unum mesuagium pro viginti denariis equaliter. Radulphus salsarius tenet unum mesuagium pro sex denariis equaliter et de witepund unum denarium. Toftum quod fuit Galfridi le petit solet reddere per annum duodecim denarios equaliter et unum denarium de witepund quod iacet iuxta placeam castri, et modo est in manu episcopi. Duo mesuagia que fuerunt Amabilie filie Johannis de Bendene solebant reddere duos solidos equaliter per annum et unum denarium de witepund que Willelmus de Furches modo tenet sine servicio, sed reddit per annum domino priori inde sexdecim denarios ut iuratores dicunt. Alanus ruffus de Horningesheia tenet unum mesuagium pro novem denariis equaliter et de witepund unum denarium ut supra quod mesuagium Reginaldus Huveles et Eva mater eius tenent de eo. Johannes de Rungeston tenet unum mesuagium quod fuit Thome le teynturer pro sexdecim denariis equaliter et de witepund unum denarium ut supra. Nicholaus le quilter [fo 3] tenet unum mesuagium quod fuit Roberti Anaunt pro sexdecim denariis equaliter et de witepund unum denarium ut supra, et fodit in vinea ut supra. Alicia relicta Roberti Coyntelowe et filius eius, et Ricardus de Lytlgate et Moyses piscator tenent unum mesuagium pro duodecim denariis equaliter et unum denarium de witepund, et fodiunt in vinea ut supra. Colinus ultra aquam tenet dimidium mesuagium quod fuit Willelmi capellani pro octo denariis et de witepund unum [denarium, et fodit ut supra. Alexander Skeppe de Yxninge tenet unum mesuagium quod fuit Laurentii cementarii pro sex denariis equaliter et de witepund unum denarium, et fodit ut supra. Johannes capellanus filius Hugonis clerici tenet unum mesuagium quod fuit Johannis le bracur pro

in equal instalments; the same hold a messuage formerly of Samuel the clerk next to the same reclaimed land for 12*d* in equal instalments and pay 1*d* wite pound as above; the same hold a messuage that of old was subject to labour-service for 12*d* \in equal instalments/; the same hold a river-meadow for 12*d* in equal instalments; the same hold a messuage formerly of Nicholas son of Ellis the mason for 12*d* in equal instalments and pay 1*d* wite pound as above; the same hold a messuage formerly of John *de bederna* for 6*d* in equal instalments. John of Walpole[38] holds 18 ware acres with a messuage for 5*s* in equal instalments and pays 14*d* wite pound as above, and he must provide his plough for one day in winter and one day in Lent, with an allowance of food from the bishop, and he performs the other services in the same way as the aforesaid William, Ellis' son. Nicholas, Ellis' son, and William de la Hale[39] hold 18 ware acres formerly of Peter Sauek with a messuage and a croft for 2*s* in equal instalments and they must perform the same services as the aforesaid William, Ellis' son; to the same tenement pertains the duty to serve as coroner and to replevy the bishop's tenants, and they must attend on the justices, and undertake seisin and disseisin within the Isle and outside. Lewis Barat and his wife Alice, and Ralph the barber and his wife Agnes hold 36 ware acres with a messuage and pay 7*d* wite pound as above, and they must plough three acres annually with no food allowance, namely one acre in winter, one acre in Lent and one acre in summer, and they must serve as coroners and replevy the bishop's tenants as above, and they must perform the same customary obligations as [col. 2] William, Ellis' son, and the aforesaid Nicholas. John the goldsmith and the almoner and Peter of Littlebury hold 6 acres with a messuage formerly of Philip's son that used to pertain to the office of keeper of the rushes, and they pay 2½*d* wite pound as above. John *de marisco* holds 6 ware acres, and he must serve as coroner and attend the justices as the aforesaid Nicholas. Peter of Littlebury[40] holds a messuage in front of Barton formerly Mabel's for 6*d* in equal instalments; the same Peter holds a messuage there for 6*d* in equal instalments; the same Peter[41] holds reclaimed land for 6*d* in equal instalments; the same Peter holds two messuages below Barton for 2*s* in equal instalments; the same holds a piece of land next to the same messuages for 2*d* in equal instalments. Roger de Fleg holds a messuage for 6*d* in equal instalments. John Kyld and Adam the baker hold a messuage for 6*d* in equal instalments and pay 1*d* wite pound as above, and they must dig in the vineyard as above. William of Dereham holds a messuage for 8*d* in equal instalments and pays 1*d* wite pound as above, and digs in the vineyard as above. Matilda formerly wife of John *le beverarunt* and her son Thomas hold a messuage for 8*d* in equal instalments and pay 1*d* wite pound as above; the same hold two messuages for 2*s* in equal instalments and pay 1*d* wite pound and dig in the vineyard. William, Barbota's son, holds a messuage for 20*d* in equal instalments. Ralph the sauce-maker holds a messuage for 6*d*[42] in equal instalments and pays 1*d* wite pound. A toft formerly of Geoffrey the small usually renders 12*d* annually in equal instalments and 1*d* wite pound, it lies next to the site of the castle and is now in the bishop's hand.[43] Two messuages formerly of Mabel, John de Bendene's daughter, used to render 2*s* annually in equal instalments and 1*d* wite pound, William de Furches now holds them without service but renders 16*d* annually to the lord prior, according to the jurors.[44] Alan the redhead of Horningsea holds a messuage for 9*d* in equal instalments and pays 1*d* wite pound as above, Reginald Huveles and his mother Eve hold it of him. John de Rungeston holds a messuage formerly of Thomas the dyer for 16*d* in equal instalments and he pays 1*d* wite pound as above. Nicholas the quilt-maker [fo 3] holds a messuage formerly Robert Anaunt's for 16*d* in equal instalments and pays 1*d* wite pound as above, and digs in the vineyard as above. Alice widow of Robert Coyntelowe and her son, and Richard de Lytlgate and Moses the fisherman hold a messuage for 12*d* in equal instalments and they pay 1*d* wite pound, and dig in the vineyard as above. Colin *ultra aquam* holds half a messuage formerly of William the chaplain for 8*d* and pays 1*d* wite pound, and digs as above. Alexander Skeppe of Exning[45] holds a messuage formerly of Lawrence the mason for 6*d* in equal instalments and pays 1*d* wite pound, and digs as above. John the chaplain, son of Hugh the clerk, holds a messuage formerly of John the brewer for

sex denariis equaliter et de witepund unum denarium, et fodit ut supra. Prior de Ely tenet unum mesuagium quod fuit Henrici de Braundon pro octo denariis equaliter et de witepund unum denarium. Item Johannes capellanus filius Hugonis clerici tenet unum mesuagium quod fuit Pericie pro duodecim denariis equaliter et de witepund unum denarium. Elemosinarius tenet unum mesuagium quod fuit Galfridi le butiler pro duodecim denariis equaliter et de witepund unum denarium, et fodit ut supra. Godwynus Boldiro et sacrista tenent unum mesuagium quod fuit Johannis le kild pro duodecim denariis equaliter et de witepund unum denarium, et fodiunt in vinea ut supra. Petrus de Eya miles tenet unum mesuagium et dat unam gruam per annum vel duos solidos. Bernardus de Hadenham tenet unum mesuagium quod fuit Herberti patris sui pro duodecim denariis equaliter et de witepund unum denarium, et fodit ut supra. Jervasius sutor et Henricus Fiket tenent unum mesuagium quod fuit Rugevin pro duodecim denariis equaliter et de witepund unum denarium, et fodiunt ut supra. Johannes Albin tenet unum mesuagium pro duodecim denariis equaliter et de witepund unum denarium, et fodit in vinea ut supra. Ricardus de Mannestone tenet duo mesuagia pro duobus solidis equaliter et dat de witepund duos denarios. Beatricia que fuit uxor Mathei Truboyle tenet unum mesuagium pro viginti denariis equaliter et de witepund unum denarium, et fodit ut supra. Johannes filius Roberti Gocelyni tenet unum mesuagium pro sexdecim denariis equaliter et de witepund unum denarium [col. 2] ut supra, et fodit in vinea ut supra. Rogerus Fot tenet unum mesuagium quod fuit Roberti filii Hugonis Bassat pro sexdecim denariis equaliter et de witepund unum denarium, et fodit ut supra. Martinus de Swafham tenet unum mesuagium quod fuit Stephani Drury pro sexdecim denariis equaliter et de witepund unum denarium, et fodit in vinea ut supra. Simon mercator et participes sui et Henricus filius Willelmi Cat tenent unum mesuagium quod fuit Alexandri cissoris pro duodecim denariis equaliter et de witepund unum denarium [et fodit][47] ut supra. Alicia relicta Aluredi coci tenet unum mesuagium quod fuit Sarlonis de Haueston pro duodecim denariis equaliter et de witepund unum denarium, et fodit ut supra. Ricardus de bedarda tenet unum mesuagium pro sex denariis equaliter. Magister Rogerus cementarius et Emma uxor eius, et Symon de Bereweye tenent unum mesuagium quod fuit Nicholai palmere pro duodecim denariis equaliter et de witepund unum denarium, et fodiunt ut supra. Elemosinarius tenet unum mesuagium quod fuit Godwini Boldiro pro octo denariis equaliter et de witepund unum denarium. Henricus Fiz tenet unum mesuagium equaliter pro sex denariis. Johannes filius Henrici Mansel tenet unum mesuagium pro octo denariis equaliter et de witepund unum denarium, et fodit in vinea ut supra. Johannes Dunham tenet unum mesuagium pro duodecim denariis equaliter quod fuit Petri le cheen. Item Albinus Tote tenet unam aream de mesuagio quod fuit Fulconis de Dunham pro duodecim denariis equaliter. Hugo filius Augustini tenet unam placeam de eodem mesuagio pro sexdecim denariis equaliter et de witepund unum denarium, et fodit ut supra. Willelmus Makerel tenet unum mesuagium pro duodecim denariis equaliter et de witepund unum denarium. Johannes filius Henrici Mansel tenet unum mesuagium quod fuit Willelmi Gervasi pro octo denariis equaliter et de witepund unum denarium, et fodit. Willelmus Heued tenet unum mesuagium pro sexdecim denariis equaliter et de witepund unum denarium. Amabilia relicta Oseberti brakener tenet unum mesuagium pro octo denariis equaliter et de witepund unum denarium, et fodit ut supra. Johannes de Staunford tenet unum mesuagium equaliter pro octo denariis quod fuit Margerie de Kayli. Johannes le steresman tenet unum mesuagium pro ministerio navigandi episcopum. Reynerus de Hulmo [fo 3v] tenet unum mesuagium pro duodecim denariis equaliter et de witepund unum denarium, et fodit ut supra. Johannes Dey[48] tenet unum mesuagium pro duodecim denariis equaliter et de witepund unum denarium, et fodit ut supra. Henricus Moyserun tenet unum mesuagium pro sex denariis equaliter et de witepund unum denarium, et fodit ut supra. Walterus cissor tenet unum mesuagium pro sex denariis equaliter et de witepund unum denarium, et fodit ut supra. Rogerus filius Gerardi tenet unum mesuagium pro sex denariis equaliter et de witepund unum denarium, et fodit in vinea. Ricardus de bederna tenet unum mesuagium pro sex denariis equaliter et de witepund unum denarium, et fodit. Ricardus filius Roberti Tede tenet unum mesuagium pro octodecim denariis equaliter et de witepund unum denarium, et fodit ut supra. Robertus Patin tenet unum mesuagium

6*d* in equal instalments and pays 1*d* wite pound, and digs as above. The prior of Ely holds a messuage formerly Henry of Brandon's for 8*d* in equal instalments and pays 1d wite pound. John the chaplain, son of Hugh the clerk, holds a messuage that was Pericia's for 12*d* in equal instalments and pays 1*d* wite pound. The almoner holds a messuage formerly of Geoffrey *le butiler* for 12*d* in equal instalments and pays 1*d* wite pound, and digs as above. Godwin Boldiro and the sacrist[46] hold a messuage formerly of John *le kild* for 12*d* in equal instalments and they pay 1*d* wite pound, and dig in the vineyard as above. Peter of Eye, knight, holds a messuage and renders one crane annually or 2*s*. Bernard of Haddenham holds a messuage, formerly of Herbert his father, for 12*d* in equal instalments and pays 1*d* wite pound and digs as above. Gervase the cobbler and Henry Fiket hold a messuage formerly Rugevin's for 12*d* in equal instalments and they pay 1*d* wite pound, and dig as above. John Albin holds a messuage for 12*d* in equal instalments and pays 1*d* wite pound, and digs in the vineyard as above. Richard de Mannestone holds two messuages for 2*s* in equal instalments and pays 2*d* wite pound. Beatrice, formerly Matthew Truboyle's wife, holds a messuage for 20*d* in equal instalments and pays 1*d* wite pound and digs as above. John, Robert Gocelyn's son, holds a messuage for 16*d* in equal instalments and pays 1*d* wite pound [col. 2] as above, and digs in the vineyard as above. Roger Fot holds a messuage formerly of Robert, Hugh Bassat's son, for 16*d* in equal instalments and pays 1*d* wite pound, and digs as above. Martin of Swaffham holds a messuage formerly Stephen Drury's for 16*d* in equal instalments and pays 1*d*d wite pound and digs in the vineyard as above. Simon the merchant and his associates, and Henry, William Cat's son, hold a messuage formerly of Alexander the tailor for 12*d* in equal instalments and pay 1*d* wite pound [and digs] as above. Alice, widow of Alfred the cook, holds a messuage formerly of Serle of Hauxton for 12*d* in equal instalments and pays 1*d* wite pound, and digs as above. Richard *de bedarda* holds a messuage for 6*d* in equal instalments. Master Roger the mason and his wife Emma, and Simon of Barway hold a messuage formerly of Nicholas the pilgrim for 12*d* in equal instalments and they pay 1*d* wite pound, and dig as above. The almoner[49] holds a messuage formerly Godwin Boldiro's for 8*d* in equal instalments and pays 1*d* wite pound. Henry Fiz holds a messuage for 6*d* in equal instalments. John, Henry Mansel's son, holds a messuage for 8*d* in equal instalments and pays 1*d* wite pound and digs in the vineyard as above. John Downham holds a messuage formerly of Peter the dog for 12*d* in equal instalments. Aubyn Tote holds one piece of a messuage formerly Fulk of Little Downham's for 12*d* in equal instalments. Hugh, son of Augustine, holds a plot of ground of the same messuage for 16*d* in equal instalments and pays 1*d* wite pound, and digs as above. William Makerel holds a messuage for 12*d* in equal instalments and pays 1*d* wite pound. John, Henry Mansel's son, holds a messuage formerly of William, son of Gervase, for 8*d* in equal instalments and pays 1*d* wite pound, and digs. William Heued holds a messuage for 16*d* in equal instalments and pays 1*d* wite pound. Mabel, widow of Osbert the huntsman, holds a messuage for 8*d* in equal instalments and pays 1*d* wite pound and digs as above.[50] John of Stamford holds a messuage formerly Margery de Kayli's for 8*d* in equal instalments. John the helmsman holds a messuage for the service of transporting the bishop by water. Rayner de Hulmo [fo 3v] holds a messuage for 12*d* in equal instalments and pays 1*d* wite pound, and digs as above. John Dey holds a messuage for 12*d* in equal instalments and pays 1*d* wite pound, and digs as above. Henry Moyserun[51] holds a messuage for 6*d* in equal instalments and pays 1*d* wite pound, and digs as above. Walter the tailor holds a messuage for 6*d* in equal instalments and pays 1*d* wite pound, and digs as above. Roger, Gerard's son, holds a messuage for 6*d* in equal instalments and pays 1*d* wite pound, and digs in the vineyard. Richard *de bederna* holds a messuage for 6*d* in equal instalments and pays 1*d* wite pound and digs. Richard, Robert Tede's son, holds a messuage for 18*d* in equal instalments and pays 1*d* wite pound, and digs as above. Robert Patin holds a messuage

pro duodecim denariis equaliter et de witepund unum denarium, et fodit ut supra. Elemosinarius tenet unum mesuagium quod fuit Henrici Tote pro duodecim denariis equaliter; item elemosinarius tenet unum mesuagium quod fuit Galfridi le verer pro duodecim denariis equaliter et de witepund unum denarium ut supra. Ranulfus clericus tenet unum mesuagium pro octo denariis equaliter et de witepund unum denarium, et fodit ut supra; idem tenet quandam partem terre versus vineam pro quatuor denariis equaliter. Henricus Niker tenet unum mesuagium pro sex denariis equaliter et de witepund unum denarium, et fodit ut supra; item idem tenet spissitudinem unius muri versus vineam pro duobus denariis equaliter. Walterus de Burewell tenet spissitudinem unius muri versus vineam pro uno denario per annum ad festum Sancti Andree et ad festum Sancti Johannis. Item elemosinarius tenet unum mesuagium quod fuit Roberti mercatoris pro octo denariis equaliter et dat de witepund unum denarium ut supra. Salomon aurifaber et Thomas Wrangsange tenent unum mesuagium quod fuit Godardi le taillur pro tresdecim denariis equaliter et de witepund unum denarium, et fodiunt ut supra. Item Willelmus le acatur tenet unum mesuagium quod fuit Roberti dyaconi pro duodecim denariis equaliter et de witepund unum denarium ut supra. Gundreda relicta Jurdani le ferour tenet unum mesuagium pro duodecim denariis equaliter et de witepund unum denarium, et fodit ut supra. Prior de Anglesheye tenet unum mesuagium quod fuit [col. 2] Albini clerici pro octo denariis equaliter et de witepund unum denarium. Henricus piscator tenet spissitudinem unius muri versus vineam pro duobus denariis equaliter. Heredes Ricardi de Len tenent quandam partem versus vineam pro quatuor denariis equaliter. Et sciendum quod Henricus Musserun ut omnes alii qui tangunt vineam usque ad portam vinee debent claudere murum inter curias eorum et predictam vineam.

Item Salomon aurifaber tenet unum mesuagium pro sex denariis equaliter. Mabilia de Lenna tenet unum mesuagium pro duodecim denariis equaliter et de witepund unum denarium ut supra. Ricardus filius Stephani tenet unum toftum quod fuit Geremundi pro quatuor denariis equaliter et de witepund unum denarium, et fodit in vinea. Hugo le fiz Willelmi le tanur tenet unum mesuagium pro sex denariis equaliter et de witepund unum denarium ut supra. Nicholaus filius Ranulfi de ecclesia tenet unum mesuagium pro sex denariis equaliter et de witepund unum denarium ut supra. Salomon aurifaber tenet unum mesuagium pro viginti denariis equaliter et de witepund unum denarium ut supra. Johannes filius Johannis le quilter tenet unum mesuagium pro octo denariis equaliter et de witepund unum denarium ut supra. Stephanus marscallus et Amisia uxor eius tenent unum mesuagium quod fuit Radulphi le prest pro sex denariis equaliter et de witepund unum denarium ut supra. Gilbertus filius Galfridi de camera et Radulphus de Harpele tenent unum mesuagium pro sex denariis equaliter quod fuit Willelmi mercatoris. Robertus de Hecham tenet unum mesuagium quod fuit Johannis filii Margarete pro duodecim denariis equaliter et de witepund unum denarium. Item Ricardus de bederna tenet unum mesuagium pro duodecim denariis equaliter et de witepund unum denarium ut supra quod fuit Johannis de refectorio. Item elemosinarius tenet unum mesuagium quod fuit Alani mercatoris pro duodecim denariis equaliter et de witepund unum denarium ut supra. Hugo capellanus filius Henrici fabri tenet unum mesuagium pro duodecim denariis equaliter et de witepund unum denarium ut supra; item tenet quandam placeam pro quatuor denariis equaliter. Johannes clericus frater ipsius Hugonis capellani tenet quandam placeam pro sex denariis equaliter. Philippus [fo 4] Mainger tenet unum mesuagium pro duodecim denariis equaliter et de witepund unum denarium, et fodit ut supra. Willelmus filius Johannis de ecclesia tenet unum mesuagium pro duodecim denariis equaliter et de witepund unum denarium, et fodit ut supra. Elemosinarius tenet mesuagium quod fuit Mauricii janitoris pro duodecim denariis equaliter et de witepund unum denarium ut supra. Item Robertus de Hecham tenet unum mesuagium pro duodecim denariis equaliter et de witepund unum denarium ut supra. Johannes filius Galfridi beveraunt tenet unum mesuagium pro octo denariis equaliter. Willelmus de Amavyl tenet unum mesuagium pro duodecim denariis equaliter. Salomon filius Alani aurifabri tenet unum mesuagium quod fuit Johannis culcitrarii et smalspon pro duodecim denariis equaliter et de witepund unum denarium ut supra.

for 12*d* in equal instalments and pays 1*d* wite pound and digs as above. The almoner[52] holds a messuage formerly Henry Tote's for 12*d* in equa;l instalments; the almoner[53] also holds a messuage formerly of Geoffrey the glazier for 12*d* in equal instalments and pays 1*d* wite pound as above. Ranulf the clerk[54] holds a messuage for 8*d* in equal instalments and pays 1*d* wite pound, and digs as above; the same holds a piece of land towards the vineyard for 4*d* in equal instalments. Henry Niker holds a messuage for 6d in equal instalments and pays 1*d* wite pound, and digs as above; the same holds the thickness of a wall towards the vineyard for 2*d* in equal instalments. Walter of Burwell holds the thickness of a wall towards the vineyard for 1*d* annually at the feast of St Andrew and at the feast of St John. The almoner[55] holds a messuage formerly of Robert the merchant for 8*d* in equal instalments and pays 1*d* wite pound as above. Solomon the goldsmith and Thomas Wrangsange hold a messuage formerly of Godard the tailor for 13*d* in equal instalments and they pay 1*d* wite pound, and dig as above. William the provisioner holds a messuage formerly of Robert the deacon for 12*d* in equal instalments and pays 1*d* wite pound as above. Gundreda, widow of Jordan the iron-worker, holds a messuage for 12*d* in equal instalments and pays 1*d* wite pound, and digs as above.[56] The prior of Anglesey Abbey holds a messuage formerly [col. 2] of Aubyn the clerk for 8*d* in equal instalments and pays 1*d* wite pound. Henry the fisherman holds the thickness of a wall towards the vineyard for 2*d* in equal instalments. The heirs of Richard of Lynn[57] hold a piece of land towards the vineyard for 4*d* in equal instalments. And note that Henry Musserun, like all the others whose land touches the vineyard as far as the vineyard gate, must close the wall between their yards and the aforesaid vineyard.

Solomon the goldsmith holds a messuage for 6*d* in equal instalments. Mabel of Lynn holds a messuage for 12*d* in equal instalments and pays 1*d* wite pound as above. Richard, Stephen's son,[58] holds a toft formerly Geremund's for 4*d* in equal instalments and pays 1*d* wite pound and digs in the vineyard. Hugh, William the tanner's son, holds a messuage for 6*d* in equal instalments and pays 1*d* wite pound as above. Nicholas, son of Ranulf *de ecclesia*, holds a messuage for 6*d* in equal instalments and pays 1*d* wite pound as above. Solomon the goldsmith holds a messuage for 20*d* in equal instalments and pays 1*d* wite pound as above. John, son of John the quilt-maker, holds a messuage for 8*d* in equal instalments and pays 1*d* wite pound as above. Stephen the farrier and his wife Amice hold a messuage formerly Ralph the priest's for 6*d* in equal instalments and they pay 1*d* wite pound as above. Gilbert, son of Geoffrey *de camera*, and Ralph de Harpele hold a messuage formerly of William the merchant for 6*d* in equal instalments. Robert of Hitcham holds a messuage formerly of John, Margaret's son, for 12*d* in equal instalments and he pays 1*d* wite pound. Richard *de bederna* holds a messuage formerly of John *de refectorio* for 12*d* in equal instalments and pays 1*d* wite pound as above. The almoner[59] holds a messuage formerly of Alan the merchant for 12*d* in equal instalments and pays 1*d* wite pound as above. Hugh the chaplain, son of Henry the smith, holds a messuage for 12*d* in equal instalments and pays 1*d* wite pound as above; he also holds a plot for 4*d* in equal instalments. John the clerk, brother of the same Hugh the chaplain, holds a plot for 6*d* in equal instalments. Philip [fo 4] Mainger holds a messuage for 12*d* in equal instalments and pays 1*d* wite pound, and digs as above. William, son of John *de ecclesia*, holds a messuage for 12*d* in equal instalments and pays 1*d* wite pound, and digs as above. The almoner[60] holds a messuage formerly of Maurice the door-keeper for 12*d* in equal instalments and pays 1*d* wite pound as above. Robert of Hitcham holds a messuage for 12*d* in equal instalments and pays 1*d* wite pound as above. John, son of Geoffrey *beveraunt*,[61] holds a messuage for 8*d* in equal instalments. William de Amavyl holds a messuage for 12*d* in equal instalments. Solomon, son of Alan the goldsmith, holds a messuage formerly of John the quilt-maker and *smalspon* for 12*d* in equal instalments and pays 1*d* wite pound as above.

Cecilia Bacston et Johannes culcitrarius tenent unum mesuagium pro quatuor denariis equaliter et de witepund unum denarium, et fodiunt ut supra. Rogerus filius Galfridi portarii tenet unum mesuagium pro octo denariis equaliter et dat de witepund unum denarium ut supra. Agnes relicta Roberti Stumpedogge tenet unum mesuagium pro quatuor denariis equaliter et de witepund unum denarium ut supra quod mesuagium fuit Roberti le messager. Henricus Fiz et Agnes uxor eius tenent unum mesuagium quod fuit Everardi filii Ingelrami pro duodecim denariis equaliter et de witepund unum denarium ut supra. Walterus Pintel tenet unum mesuagium pro novem denariis equaliter et dat de witepund unum denarium ut supra quod fuit Willelmi de Wynteworye. Rogerus filius Herberti tenet unum mesuagium pro novem denariis equaliter et de witepund unum denarium ut supra, et fodit ut supra. Johannes de Tid tenet unum mesuagium pro novem denariis equaliter et de witepund unum denarium, et fodit ut supra. Rogerus Fot et Beatricia de Stapele tenent duo mesuagia pro viginti denariis equaliter et de witepund duos denarios, et fodiunt. Petrus Pintil tenet unum mesuagium pro duodecim denariis equaliter et de witepund unum denarium, et fodit ut supra. Elemosinarius tenet unum mesuagium quod fuit Willelmi Putman pro octo denariis equaliter et de witepund unum denarium. Johannes filius Ricardi le tanur tenet unum mesuagium pro duodecim denariis equaliter et de witepund unum denarium, et fodit ut supra. Nicholaus Nodinay tenet unum mesuagium [col. 2] pro octo denariis equaliter et dat de witepund unum denarium ut supra. Emma relicta Gernun Petri tenet unum mesuagium pro duodecim denariis equaliter. Robertus de Sprouton tenet unum mesuagium quod fuit Godefridi de Fulmere pro duodecim denariis equaliter. Jacobus Kackenose filius Radulphi de Sancto Albano tenet unum mesuagium pro quatuor denariis equaliter. mesuagium pro duodecim denariis equaliter. Robertus de Sprouton tenet unum mesuagium quod fuit Godefridi de Fulmere pro duodecim denariis equaliter. Jacobus Kackenose filius Radulphi de Sancto Albano tenet unum mesuagium pro quatuor denariis equaliter. Simon filius Godardi tenet unum mesuagium pro viginti denariis equaliter et de witepund unum denarium, et fodit ut supra. Henricus Disel tenet unum mesuagium pro viginti duobus denariis equaliter et de witepund unum denarium, et fodit ut supra. Johannes capellanus filius Hugonis clerici et Emma Wortemuth tenent unum mesuagium pro sex denariis equaliter. Item elemosinarius tenet unum mesuagium quod fuit Johannis culcitrarii pro duodecim denariis equaliter et de witepund unum denarium. Walterus de hosteleria tenet unum mesuagium quod fuit Hugonis Kypping pro duodecim denariis equaliter et de witepund unum denarium. Item Ricardus de bederna tenet unum mesuagium pro duodecim denariis equaliter. Henricus plumbator tenet unum mesuagium pro quatuor denariis equaliter et dat de witepund unum denarium, et fodit ut supra. Item Philippus Mainger tenet unum mesuagium Henrici Buk pro duodecim denariis equaliter et de witepund unum denarium ut supra. Robertus ruffus tenet unum mesuagium pro quatuor denariis equaliter et de witepund unum denarium ut supra. Radulphus Poppe tenet unum mesuagium pro duodecim denariis equaliter. Josephus Doskyn tenet unum mesuagium pro quatuor denariis equaliter. Robertus Gernun tenet unum mesuagium pro sex denariis equaliter. Johannes de Hatfeld pistor episcopi tenet unum mesuagium pro sex denariis equaliter; idem tenet octodecim acras de wara pro ministerio custodiendi officium pistrine episcopi. Radulphus[63] filius Stephani Humfridi tenet unum mesuagium pro quatuor denariis equaliter et de witepund unum denarium. Gilbertus filius Hugonis carpentarii tenet unum mesuagium pro duodecim denariis equaliter et de witepund unum denarium, et fodit ut supra. Custancia filia Thome Fot tenet unum mesuagium quod fuit Hugonis Kipping pro duodecim denariis equaliter et de witepund unum denarium, et fodit ut supra. Henricus piscator et Agnes uxor eius tenent unum mesuagium pro duodecim denariis equaliter et de witepund unum denarium, et fodiunt ut supra. Robertus filius Albini le corveyser tenet unum mesuagium pro duodecim denariis equaliter et de wite [fo 4v] pund unum denarium, et fodit ut supra. Magister Alanus de Swafham tenet unum mesuagium pro duodecim denariis equaliter. Elemosinarius tenet unum mesuagium quod fuit Alexandri brevetur pro decem denariis equaliter. Sacrista tenet unum mesuagium quod fuit Arnaldi Wynter pro decem denariis equaliter. Caterina relicta Galfridi janitoris et Edelina soror eius tenent unum mesuagium quod fuit Angeri pro duodecim denariis equaliter et de witepund unum denarium, et fodiunt ut supra.

Cecily Bacston and John the quilt-maker hold a messuage for 4*d* in equal instalments and pay 1*d* wite pound, and dig as above. Roger, son of Geoffrey the door-keeper, holds a messuage for 8*d* in equal instalments and pays 1*d* wite pound as above. Agnes, widow of Robert Stumpedogge, holds a messuage formerly of Robert the messenger for 4*d* in equal instalments and pays 1*d* wite pound as above. Henry Fiz and his wife Agnes hold a messuage formerly of Everard, son of Ingram, for 12*d*[62] in equal instalments and pay 1*d* wite pound as above. Walter Pintel holds a messuage formerly William of Wentworth's for 9*d* in equal instalments and pays 1*d* wite pound as above. Roger, Herbert's son, holds a messuage for 9*d* in equal instalments and pays 1*d* wite pound as above, and digs as above. John of Tydd holds a messuage for 9*d* in equal instalments and pays 1*d* wite pound, and digs as above. Roger Fot and Beatrice de Stapele hold two messuages for 20*d* in equal instalments and they pay 2*d* wite pound, and dig. Peter Pintil holds a messuage for 12*d* in equal instalments and pays 1*d* wite pound, and digs as above. The almoner[64] holds a messuage formerly William Putman's for 8*d* in equal instalments and pays 1*d* wite pound. John, son of Richard the tanner, holds a messuage for 12*d* in equal instalments and pays 1*d* wite pound, and digs as above. Nicholas Nodinay holds a messuage [col. 2] for 8*d* in equal instalments and pays 1*d* wite pound as above. Emma, widow of Gernun Peter holds a messuage for 12*d* in equal instalments. Robert of Sproughton holds a messuage formerly Godfrey of Fowlmere's for 12*d* in equal instalments. James Kackenose, son of Ralph of St Albans, holds a messuage for 4*d*[65] in equal instalments. Simon, Godard's son, holds a messuage for 20*d* in equal instalments and pays 1*d* wite pound, and digs as above. Henry Disel holds a messuage for 22*d* in equal instalments and pays 1*d* wite pound, and digs as above. John the chaplain, son of Hugh the clerk, and Emma Wortemuth[66] hold a messuage for 6*d* in equal instalments. The almoner holds a messuage formerly of John the quilt-maker for 12*d* in equal instalments and pays 1*d* wite pound. Walter *de hosteleria* holds a messuage formerly Hugh Kypping's for 12*d* in equal instalments and pays 1*d* wite pound. Richard *de bederna* holds a messuage for 12*d* in equal instalments. Henry the lead-worker holds a messuage for 4*d* in equal instalments and pays 1*d* wite pound, and digs as above. Philip Mainger holds Henry Buk's messuage for 12*d* in equal instalments and pays 1*d* wite pound as above. Robert the redhead holds a messuage for 4*d* in equal instalments and pays 1*d* wite pound as above. Ralph Poppe holds a messuage for 12*d* in equal instalments. Joseph Doskyn holds a messuage for 4*d* in equal instalments. Robert Gernun holds a messuage for 6*d* in equal instalments. John of Hatfield, the bishop's baker, holds a messuage for 6*d* in equal instalments; the same holds 18 ware acres for the office of keeping the bishop's bakehouse.[67] Ralph, son of Stephen Humfrey's son, holds a messuage for 4*d* in equal instalments and pays 1*d* wite pound. Gilbert, son of Hugh the carpenter, holds a messuage for 12*d* in equal instalments and pays 1*d* wite pound, and digs as above. Custance, Thomas Fot's daughter, holds a messuage formerly Hugh Kipping's for 12*d* in equal instalments and pays 1*d* wite pound and digs as above. Henry the fisherman and Agnes his wife hold a messuage for 12*d* in equal instalments and pay 1*d* wite pound and dig as above. Robert, son of Aubyn the leather-worker, holds a messuage for 12*d* in equal instalments and pays [fo 4v] 1*d* wite pound, and digs as above. Master Alan of Swaffham holds a messuage for 12*d* in equal instalments. The almoner holds a messuage formerly of Alexander the scribe for 10*d* in equal instalments. The sacrist[68] holds a messuage formerly Arnald Wynter's for 10*d* in equal instalments. Catherine, widow of Geoffrey the door-keeper, and her sister Edeline hold a messuage formerly of Angerus for 12*d* in equal instalments and they pay 1*d* wite pound, and dig as above.

Henricus Tilly tenet unum mesuagium quod fuit Henrici Pyn pro duodecim denariis equaliter et de witepund unum denarium ut supra; idem Henricus et Emma Hunte tenent unum mesuagium pro sex denariis equaliter et de witepund unum denarium; idem Henricus tenet unum mesuagium pro sex denariis equaliter. Walterus palffreman tenet unum mesuagium quod fuit Ricardi carectarii pro duodecim denariis equaliter; idem Walterus tenet quinque acras de wara pro quatuor solidis equaliter. Rogerus Coder[69] tenet unum mesuagium quod fuit Stephani carpentarii pro sex denariis equaliter. Adam pistor tenet unum mesuagium quod fuit Aline le noble pro tresdecim denariis equaliter. Item Agnes relicta Roberti Stumpedogge tenet unum mesuagium pro duodecim denariis equaliter. Rogerus filius Galfridi janitoris tenet unum mesuagium pro duodecim denariis equaliter. Salomon filius Alani aurifabri tenet unum mesuagium et quinque acras de wara pro octodecim denariis equaliter. Gilbertus pistor de Chetesham tenet duodecim acras de wara pro octo solidis equaliter que fuerunt Petri filii Ace. Dominus episcopus tenet unum mesuagium quod fuit Roberti de camera ubi manent quatuor capellani ex provisione Hugonis episcopi ad celebrandum in perpetuum pro domino rege et pro domina regina et animabus omnium antecessorum suorum et pro episcopo et pro animabus omnium predecessorum et suorum successorum; quod quidem mesuagium solebat reddere duos solidos per annum equaliter et modo quietum est. Item Philippus Maynger tenet unum mesuagium pro sex denariis equaliter. Margeria Buccecake tenet unum mesuagium pro octo denariis equaliter. Due filie Alexandri le spicer tenent unum mesuagium pro duodecim denariis equaliter. Johannes Chateriz tenet unum mesuagium quod fuit Johannis Riuel pro octo denariis equaliter. Beatrix blodlatere tenet unam mansionem iuxta predictum mesuagium pro quatuor denariis equaliter. Eustachius de Tornes tenet quandam terram in campis de Saham pro quinque solidis equaliter, et debet navigare hernesium episcopi de Saham usque in Ely. Walterus de [col. 2] capella tenet octodecim acras terre et unum mesuagium cum pertinenciis pro sex solidis et octo denariis per annum equaliter ex dono episcopi Johannis et per confirmacionem episcopi qui nunc est. Stephanus Wodeman tenet dimidiam acram terre de novo feoffamento pro duodecim denariis per annum equaliter.

De liberis hominibus ultra aquam. Magister Rogerus cementarius tenet unum mesuagium quod fuit Rogeri Gokay pro duobus denariis equaliter. Mabilia de Lenna tenet unum mesuagium quod fuit Alani mercatoris pro quatuor denariis equaliter. Pitanciarius tenet unum mesuagium quod fuit Henrici de Riburg pro quatuor denariis equaliter. Nicholaus culcitrarius et Symon de Bereweye tenent unum mesuagium quod fuit Richolde vidue pro quatuor denariis equaliter. Hugo filius Willelmi le tanur tenet unum mesuagium pro quatuor denariis equaliter. Elemosinarius tenet unum mesuagium pro quatuor denariis equaliter. Rogerus Fot tenet unum mesuagium quod fuit Magistri Johannis capellani pro quatuor denariis equaliter. Willelmus le acatur tenet unum mesuagium quod fuit Ricardi de Crouden pro quatuor denariis equaliter. Nicholaus ultra aquam tenet unum mesuagium quod fuit Mathei de Kent pro quatuor denariis equaliter. Prior de Ely tenet unum mesuagium quod fuit Radulphi granatarii et Hugonis Muth pro quatuor denariis equaliter. Johannes filius Henrici Mansel tenet unum mesuagium quod fuit Eudonis rosarii pro duobus denariis equaliter. Everardus le paumer tenet mesuagium quod fuit Nicholai Wodekyng pro quatuor denariis equaliter. Ricardus filius Roberti Yede[70] tenet unum mesuagium quod fuit Goscelini filii Aluredi pro duobus denariis equaliter. Hugo filius Augustini tenet unam wyhtam scilicet unum mesuagium pro quatuor denariis equaliter. Willelmus de Derham tenet unum mesuagium quod fuit Henrici fratris prioris pro duobus denariis equaliter. Radulphus Knyttessanke tenet unum mesuagium quod fuit Gosselini carpentarii pro duobus denariis equaliter. Thomas de Cotenham tenet unum mesuagium quod fuit Walteri pro duobus denariis equaliter. Robertus filius Nicholai tenet unum mesuagium pro duobus denariis equaliter. Lucas Tholomen tenet unum mesuagium quod fuit Olive pro duobus [fo 5] denariis equaliter. Ace prest tenet unum mesuagium quod fuit Roberti clerici pro duobus denariis equaliter. Henricus piscator tenet unum mesuagium pro duobus denariis equaliter.

Henry Tilly holds a messuage formerly Henry Pyn's for 12*d* in equal instalments and pays 1*d* wite pound as above; the same Henry and Emma Hunte hold a messuage for 6*d* in equal instalments and pay 1*d* wite pound; the same Henry holds a messuage for 6*d* in equal instalments. Walter the groom holds a messuage formerly of Richard the carter for 12*d* in equal instalments; the same Walter holds 5 ware acres for 4*s* in equal instalments. Roger Coder holds a messuage formerly of Stephen the carpenter for 6*d* in equal instalments. Adam the baker holds a messuage formerly of Aline the noble for 13*d* in equal instalments. Agnes, widow of Robert Stumpedogge, holds a messuage for 12*d* in equal instalments. Roger, son of Geoffrey the door-keeper, holds a messuage for 12*d* in equal instalments. Solomon, son of Alan the goldsmith, holds a messuage and 5 ware acres for 18*d* in equal instalments. Gilbert the baker of Chettisham holds 12 ware acres formerly of Peter, Ace's son, for 8*s* in equal instalments. The lord bishop holds a messuage formerly Robert *de camera*'s in which four chaplains reside by Bishop Hugh's provision to celebrate [masses] in perpetuity for the lord king and the lady queen, and for the souls of all their ancestors, and for the bishop and for the souls of all his predecessors and successors; this messuage used to render 2*s* annually in equal instalments and now it is quit.[71] Philip Mayngér[72] holds a messuage for 6*d* in equal instalments. Margery Buccecake holds a messuage for 8*d* in equal instalments. Two daughters of Alexander the spicer hold a messuage for 12*d* in equal instalments. John Chatteris holds a messuage formerly John Riuel's for 8*d* in equal instalments. Beatrice the bloodletter holds a house next to the aforesaid messuage for 4*d* in equal instalments. Eustace de Tornes holds land in Soham for 5*s* in equal instalments, and he must carry the bishop's luggage by water from Soham to Ely. Walter *de* [col. 2] *capella* holds 18 acres of land and a messuage with appurtenances for 6*s* 8*d* annually in equal instalments, of the gift of Bishop John[73] and by confirmation of the present bishop. Stephen Wodeman holds ½ acre of land of the new feoffment for 12*d* annually in equal instalments.

Free men beyond the water. Master Roger the mason holds a messuage formerly Roger Gokay's for 2*d* in equal instalments. Mabel of Lynn holds a messuage formerly of Alan the merchant for 4*d* in equal instalments. The pittancer[74] holds a messuage formerly Henry de Riburg's for 4*d* in equal instalments. Nicholas the quilt-maker and Simon of Barway hold a messuage formerly of widow Richolda for 4*d* in equal instalments. Hugh, William the tanner's son, holds a messuage for 4*d* in equal instalments. The almoner[75] holds a messuage for 4*d* in equal instalments. Roger Fot holds a messuage formerly of Master John the chaplain for 4*d* in equal instalments. William the provisioner holds a messuage formerly Richard of Croydon's for 4*d* in equal instalments. Nicholas *ultra aquam* holds a messuage formerly Matthew of Kent's for 4*d* in equal instalments. The prior of Ely[76] holds a messuage formerly of Ralph the granary-keeper and Hugh Muth for 4*d* in equal instalments. John, son of Henry Mansel, holds a messuage formerly of Eudes *rosarius* for 2*d* in equal instalments. Everard the pilgrim holds a messuage formerly Nicholas Wodekyng's for 4*d* in equal instalments. Richard, Robert Yede's son, holds a messuage formerly of Jocelin, Alfred's son, for 2*d* in equal instalments. Hugh, son of Augustine, holds a *wyhta*, namely a messuage for 4*d* in equal instalments.[77] William of Dereham holds a messuage formerly of Henry, the prior's brother, for 2*d* in equal instalments. Ralph Knyttessanke holds a messuage formerly of Jocelin the carpenter for 2*d* in equal instalments. Thomas of Cottenham holds a messuage formerly Walter's for 2*d* in equal instalments. Robert, Nicholas' son, holds a messuage for 2*d* in equal instalments. Luke Tholomen holds a messuage formerly Olive's for 2*d* [fo 5] in equal instalments. Ace the priest holds a messuage formerly of Robert the clerk for 2*d* in equal instalments. Henry the fisherman holds a messuage for 2*d* in equal instalments.

De seldis carnificum. Symon Soyewombe[78] tenet unam seldam que fuit Roberti Cat pro sex denariis per annum ad festum Omnium Sanctorum; idem Symon Soyewombe tenet unam seldam que fuit Henrici Pudding pro sex denariis per annum eodem termino. Raude Godarde tenet unam seldam pro sex denariis per annum eodem modo. Henricus filius Willelmi Cat tenet unam seldam pro sex denariis per annum eodem termino que fuit Radulphi Cat. Nigellus Beneit tenet unam seldam pro sex denariis per annum eodem termino. \Robertus Benet tenet unam seldam pro sex denariis per annum eodem termino/ que fuit Henrici de Colne. Nicholaus filius Reineri tenet unam seldam pro sex denariis per annum eodem termino. Hugo Biscop tenet unam seldam pro sex denariis per annum eodem termino que fuit Willelmi le tanur. Fratres hospitalis Magdalene tenent unam seldam que fuit Johannis culcitrarii pro sex denariis per annum eodem termino. Willelmus Terdel tenet unam seldam que fuit Henrici Pudding pro quatuor denariis et obolo per annum eodem termino. Ricardus filius Stephani tenet tres seldas pro quindecim denariis per annum eodem termino. Robertus filius Nicholai clerici tenet duas seldas que fuerunt Johannis culcitrarii pro decem denariis per annum eodem termino. Emma relicta Petri Gernun tenet unam seldam pro duodecim denariis per annum eodem termino. Reginaldus de Lakyngehe le seler tenet unam placeam in foro pro duodecim denariis per annum equaliter.

De plenis terris. Petrus Pinnok tenet unam plenam terram que facit octodecim acras de wara et dat de witepund septem denarios scilicet ad Annunciacionem Beate Marie tres denarios et obolum, et ad festum Sancti Michaelis tres denarios et obolum, et tres gallinas ad Natale et triginta ova ad Pascha; et debet qualibet ebdomada a festo Sancti Michaelis usque ad Pentecostem tres operaciones...

[fo 5v, col. 2] Henricus Neweman tenet unam plenam terram scilicet octodecim acras de wara eodem modo. Willelmus de Bele tenet unam plenam terram scilicet octodecim acras de wara eodem modo. Holde Willam tenet octodecim acras de wara eodem modo. Dawe de Chetesham tenet octodecim acras de wara eodem modo. Nicholaus filius Johannis de Chetesham tenet octodecim acras eodem modo. Robertus filius Everardi ad baram tenet octodecim acras de wara eodem modo. Johannes Wlfrun tenet octodecim acras de wara eodem modo. \Stephanus Wodeman tenet octodecim acras de wara eodem modo./ Philippus Herberd tenet octodecim acras de wara eodem modo. \Philippus bedellus tenet xviij acras eodem modo./ Michael carectarius tenet octodecim acras de wara eodem modo. Radulphus le sumeter episcopi tenet octodecim acras de wara que fuerunt Ranulfi messarii eodem modo. Willelmus Gunnilde et Philippus Cat tenent octodecim acras de wara eodem modo. Walterus Pintel tenet octodecim acras de wara eodem modo. \Hugo filius Alani tenet xviij acras de wara eodem modo./ Henricus Pinnok tenet octodecim acras de wara eodem modo. Symon le wyche tenet unum mesuagium cum octodecim acris de wara eodem modo. Hamo ad hospitalem tenet octodecim acras de wara eodem modo. Hugo filius Waukelini tenet octodecim acras de wara [fo 6] eodem modo. Matilda relicta Hugonis tenet octodecim acras de wara eodem modo. \Ricardus de Bluntesham tenet xviij acras de wara eodem modo./ Walterus Musepese tenet octodecim acras de wara eodem modo. Willelmus filius Aluredi tenet octodecim acras de wara eodem modo. Symon Hereberd tenet octodecim acras de wara eodem modo. Aluredus Ruggele tenet octodecim acras de wara eodem modo. Everardus Childiring[79] tenet octodecim acras de wara eodem modo. Robertus filius Willelmi Aninory[80] tenet octodecim acras de wara eodem modo. \Robertus ruffus tenet xviij acras de wara eodem modo./ Johannes del fen tenet octodecim acras de wara eodem modo. Johannes Aedelard tenet octodecim acras de wara eodem modo. Ricardus Slypet tenet octodecim acras de wara eodem modo. Henricus ate fen tenet octodecim acras de wara eodem modo.

The butchers' stalls. Simon Soyewombe holds a stall formerly Robert Cat's for 6*d* annually on All Saints' Day; the same Simon Soyewombe holds a stall formerly Henry Pudding's for 6*d* annually at the same term. Raude Godarde holds a stall for 6*d* annually in the same manner. Henry, William Cat's son, holds a stall formerly Ralph Cat's for 6*d* annually at the same term. Nigel Beneit holds a stall for 6*d* annually at the same term. \Robert Benet holds a stall for 6*d* annually at the same term/ formerly Henry of Colne's. Nicholas, Rayner's son, holds a stall for 6*d* annually at the same term. Hugh Biscop holds a stall formerly William the tanner's for 6*d* annually at the same term. The brethren of the hospital of St Mary Magdalene hold a stall formerly of John the quilt-maker for 6*d* annually at the same term. William Terdel holds a stall formerly Henry Pudding's for 4½*d* annually at the same term. Richard, Stephen's son,[81] holds three stalls for 15*d* annually at the same term. Robert son of Nicholas the clerk holds two stalls formerly of John the quilt-maker for 10*d* annually at the same term. Emma, widow of Peter Gernun, holds a stall for 12*d* annually at the same term. Reginald of Lakenheath the saddler holds a site in the marketplace for 12*d* annually in equal instalments.

Full lands. Peter Pinnok holds a full land that comprises 18 ware acres, and pays 7*d* wite pound namely 3½*d* at the Annunciation, and 3½*d* at Michaelmas, and three hens at Christmas and thirty eggs at Easter; and owes weekly from Michaelmas to Whitsun three days of labour-service...

[fo 5v, col. 2] Henry Neweman holds a full land namely 18 ware acres in the same manner. William de Bele holds a full land namely 18 ware acres in the same manner. Holde Willam holds 18 ware acres in the same manner. Dawe of Chettisham holds 18 acres in the same manner. Nicholas, son of John of Chettisham, holds 18 acres in the same manner. Robert, son of Everard *ad baram*, holds 18 ware acres in the same manner. John Wlfrun holds 18 ware acres in the same manner. \Stephen Wodeman holds 18 ware acres in the same manner./ Philip Herberd holds 18 ware acres in the same manner. \Philip the beadle holds 18 acres in the same manner./ Michael the carter holds 18 ware acres in the same manner. Ralph, the bishop's pack-horse driver, holds 18 ware acres formerly of Ranulf the hayward in the same manner. William, Gunhild's [son], and Philip Cat hold 18 ware acres in the same manner. Walter Pintel holds 18 ware acres in the same manner. \Hugh, Alan's son, holds 18 ware acres in the same manner./ Henry Pinnok holds 18 ware acres in the same manner. Simon *le wyche* holds a messuage with 18 ware acres in the same manner. Hamon *ad hospitalem* holds 18 ware acres in the same manner. Hugh, Walkelin's son, holds 18 ware acres [fo 6] in the same manner. Matilda, Hugh's widow, holds 18 ware acres in the same manner. \Richard of Bluntisham holds 18 ware acres in the same manner./ Walter Musepese holds 18 ware acres in the same manner. William, Alfred's son, holds 18 ware acres in the same manner. Simon Hereberd holds 18 ware acres in the same manner. Alfred Ruggele holds 18 ware acres in the same manner. Everard Childiring holds 18 ware acres in the same manner. Robert, William Aninory's son, holds 18 ware acres in the same manner. \Robert the redhead holds 18 ware acres in the same manner./ John *del fen* holds 18 ware acres in the same manner. John Aedelard holds 18 ware acres in the same manner. Richard Slypet holds 18 ware acres in the same manner. Henry *ate fen* holds 18 ware acres in the same manner.

De dimidiis terris. Thomas le cupere tenet dimidiam terram scilicet duodecim acras de wara et dat de witepund quatuor denarios et obolum et terciam partem unius oboli ad duos terminos supradictos, ita scilicet quod tres huiusmodi tenentes dant quatuordecim denarios; et dat duas gallinas ad Natale et viginti ova ad Pascha, et debet qualibet ebdomada a festo Sancti Michaelis usque ad gulam Augusti duas operaciones ...

[fo 6v] Willelmus Starling tenet duodecim acras eodem modo. Willelmus Godard tenet duodecim acras eodem modo. Hugo le devel tenet duodecim acras eodem modo. Osebertus le lef tenet duodecim acras eodem modo. Johannes de Bele tenet duodecim acras eodem modo. Martinus le lord tenet duodecim acras eodem modo. Radulphus le newman et Stephanus Wodeman tenent duodecim acras eodem modo. Symon Daggeto tenet duodecim acras eodem modo. Robertus Fox tenet duodecim acras eodem modo. Philippus Albert tenet duodecim acras eodem modo. Matilda relicta Willelmi Aninori[82] tenet duodecim acras eodem modo. Willelmus Biscop tenet sex acras scilicet medietatem terre que fuit Aylmundi, et facit in denariis operacionibus et consuetudinibus medietatem omnium que facit predictus Thomas le cupere. Johannes Sygar tenet sex acras et unum mesuagium, et dat duos denarios et obolum per annum de witepund ad terminos supradictos, et \dat/ unam gallinam ad Natale et decem ova ad Pascha, et debet qualibet quindena per annum tres operaciones ... et in aruris et averagiis et omnibus aliis consuetudinibus faciet medietatem omnium que facit predictus Thomas le cupere. Preciosa relicta Thome de Straham tenet sex acras et unum mesuagium eodem modo sicut idem Johannes Sygar. Willelmus porcarius tenet sex acras et unum mesuagium eodem modo vel debet custodire porcos domini quotquot fuerint ... Et porcarius habebit unum markyngris et quietus erit de operacionibus suis et de averagiis suis. Nicholaus dabit duos denarios de witepund et obolum et facit araturam suam sicut predictus Johannes.

De cotariis in Ely. Henricus Fox de Chetesham tenet unam coteriam que continet unam acram, et dat de witepund unum denarium ad terminos supradictos, et debet qualibet ebdomada per totum annum unam operacionem ...

[col. 2] Johannes Baldewyn de Chetesham tenet unam coteriam que fuit Everardi eodem modo; idem Johannes tenet coteriam que fuit Ricolde vidue eodem modo. Johannes Balloc tenet unam coteriam eodem modo. Alexander Dolitel tenet unam coteriam eodem modo. Agnes relicta Ricardi de Bele tenet unam coteriam eodem modo. David Waleys tenet unam coteriam eodem modo. Ineta relicta Elye molendinarii tenet unam coteriam eodem modo. Mabilia Fareman tenet unam coteriam eodem modo. \Isabella Strug' tenet unam coteriam eodem modo./ Agneta Bordel tenet unam coteriam eodem modo. Simon le webstre tenet unam coteriam eodem modo. Ricardus de Coveneye tenet unam coteriam eodem modo. Willelmus le newman tenet unam coteriam eodem modo. \Nicholaus faber tenet j coteriam eodem modo./ Wymark filia Ranulfi le heyward tenet unum mesuagium eodem modo. Symon filius Radulphi tenet unam coteriam eodem modo. Nicholaus filius Reyneri tenet unam coteriam eodem modo. Alanus Ters tenet unam coteriam eodem modo. Nicholaus Pas tenet unam coteriam eodem modo. Galfridus Russel tenet unam coteriam eodem modo. Radulphus Payn tenet unam coteriam eodem modo. Alicia Dodus tenet unam coteriam eodem modo. Hugo Patin tenet unam coteriam eodem modo. Philippus filius Philippi[83] tenet unam coteriam eodem modo. Gilbertus Bulder tenet unam coteriam eodem modo. Hugo Wouth tenet unam coteriam eodem modo. Nigellus Beneit tenet unam coteriam eodem modo. David filius Wymark tenet unam coteriam eodem modo. \Henricus de Lopham tenet coteriam eodem modo./ Juliana Pecok tenet unam coteriam eodem modo. [fo 7] Thomas Dod tenet unam coteriam eodem modo. \Nicholaus Drak tenet unam coteriam eodem modo./ Martinus filius Willelmi Payn tenet unam coteriam. Johannes Aysbern[84] tenet unam coteriam eodem modo. Symon Sodwombe tenet unam coteriam eodem modo. Alanus le coverur et Symon textor tenent unam coteriam eodem modo. Symon Ruggele tenet unam coteriam eodem modo. Robertus Bor tenet unam coteriam eodem modo. Ricardus Hulle tenet unam coteriam eodem modo.

Half lands. Thomas *le cupere* holds a half land namely 12 ware acres and pays 4½*d* wite pound and one third of a halfpenny at the two terms, so that three holders in this category pay 14*d;* and he gives two hens at Christmas and twenty eggs at Easter, and owes weekly from Michaelmas to Lammas two days of labour-service …

[fo 6v] William Starling holds 12 acres in the same manner. William Godard holds 12 acres in the same manner. Hugh the devil holds 12 acres in the same manner. Osbert *le lef* holds 12 acres in the same manner. John de Bele holds 12 acres in the same manner. Martin *le lord* holds 12 acres in the same manner. Ralph the newman and Stephen Wodeman hold 12 acres in the same manner. Simon Daggeto holds 12 acres in the same manner. Robert Fox holds 12 acres in the same manner. Philip Albert holds 12 acres in the same manner. Matilda, widow of William Aninory, holds 12 acres in the same manner. William Biscop holds 6 acres namely half the land formerly Aylmund's, and provides in cash, labour-service and customary obligations half of all that the aforesaid Thomas *le cupere* provides. John Sygar holds 6 acres and a messuage, and pays 2½*d* wite pound annually at the aforesaid terms, and \gives/ a hen at Christmas and ten eggs at Easter, and owes three days of labour-service every fortnight in the year … and, in ploughing and carrying service and in all the other customary obligations, he must perform half of all the services that the aforesaid Thomas *le cupere* performs. Preciosa, widow of Thomas of Stretham, holds 6 acres and a messuage in the same manner as the same John Sygar. William the swineherd holds 6 acres and a messuage in the same manner, or else he must keep the lord's swine whatever their number … And the swineherd will receive a *markyngris*, and he will be quit of labour-services and carrying services. Nicholas must pay 2½*d* wite pound and plough as the aforesaid John.

Cottars in Ely. Henry Fox of Chettisham holds a cot-land that contains 1 acre, and pays 1*d* wite pound at the aforesaid terms, and owes one day of labour-service weekly throughout the year …

[col. 2] John Baldewyn of Chettisham holds a cot-land formerly Everard's in the same manner; the same John holds a cot-land formerly widow Ricolda's in the same manner. John Balloc holds a cot-land in the same manner. Alexander Dolitel holds a cot-land in the same manner. Agnes, widow of Richard de Bele, holds a cot-land in the same manner. David Waleys holds a cot-land in the same manner. Ineta, widow of Ellis the miller, holds a cot-land in the same manner. Mabel Fareman holds a cot-land in the same manner. \Isabel Strug' holds a cot-land in the same manner./ Agnes Bordel holds a cot-land in the same manner. Simon the weaver holds a cot-land in the same manner. Richard of Coveney holds a cot-land in the same manner. William the newman holds a cot-land in the same manner. \Nicholas the smith holds a cot-land in the same manner./ Wymark, daughter of Ranulf the hayward, holds a messuage in the same manner. Simon, Ralph's son, holds a cot-land in the same manner. Nicholas, Rayner's son, holds a cot-land in the same manner. Alan Ters holds a cot-land in the same manner. Nicholas Pas holds a cot-land in the same manner. Geoffrey Russel holds a cot-land in the same manner. Ralph Payn holds a cot-land in the same manner. Alice Dodus holds a cot-land in the same manner. Hugh Patin holds a cot-land in the same manner. Philip, Philip's son, holds a cot-land in the same manner. Gilbert Bulder holds a cot-land in the same manner. Hugh Wouth holds a cot-land in the same manner. Nigel Beneit holds a cot-land in the same manner. David, Wymark's son, holds a cot-land in the same manner. \Henry of Lopham holds a cot-land in the same manner./ Juliane Pecok holds a cot-land in the same manner. [fo 7] Thomas Dod holds a cot-land in the same manner. \Nicholas Drak holds a cot-land in the same manner./ Martin, William Payn's son, holds a cot-land. John Aysbern holds a cot-land in the same manner. Simon Sodwombe holds a cot-land in the same manner. Alan the roofer and Simon the weaver hold a cot-land in the same manner. Simon Ruggele holds a cot-land in the same manner. Robert Bor holds a cot-land in the same manner. Richard Hulle holds a cot-land in the same manner.

\Henricus Bole tenet unam coteriam eodem modo. Henricus le ledbed tenet unam coteriam eodem modo./ Wymark Pymme tenet unam coteriam eodem modo. \Agneta Houth tenet unam coteriam eodem modo./ Henricus le smale tenet unam coteriam eodem modo. Nicholaus Cakelard tenet unam coteriam eodem modo. Willelmus le smale tenet unam coteriam eodem modo. Johannes filius Agnete tenet unum mesuagium eodem modo. Guanilda Oubene tenet unam coteriam eodem modo. Galfridus Faukes tenet unam coteriam eodem modo. Stephanus Stephon tenet unam coteriam eodem modo. Robertus Clemme tenet unam coteriam eodem modo. Henricus Husebonde tenet unam coteriam eodem modo. Johannes Pimme tenet unum mesuagium eodem modo. Cecilia Pultehorn tenet unam coteriam eodem [modo]. Silvester Poleyn tenet unam coteriam eodem modo. Philippus Horecoppe tenet unam coteriam eodem modo. Gerardus de Straham tenet unam coteriam eodem [modo]. Petrus le syneke tenet unam coteriam eodem [modo]. Nicholaus Bunting tenet unam coteriam eodem modo. Radulphus Raven tenet unam coteriam eodem modo. Johannes Puleyn tenet unam coteriam eodem modo. Radulphus Pipernol tenet unam coteriam eodem modo. Thomas de Straham tenet unam coteriam eodem [modo]. Alanus Patin tenet unam coteriam eodem modo. Cristiana Pas tenet unam coteriam eodem modo. Stephanus Kynneday tenet unam coteriam eodem [modo]. \Ricardus Haybird[85] tenet unam coteriam eodem modo./ Eborardus plaureve tenet unam coteriam. Johannes Bule tenet unam coteriam eodem modo. Robertus Cakelard tenet unam coteriam eodem modo. Hugo cuteler tenet unam coteriam eodem modo. Osebertus Hunno tenet unam coteriam eodem modo. Hugo porcarius tenet unam coteriam eodem modo. Henricus Sok[86] tenet unam coteriam eodem modo. Cristiana de fenlond tenet unam coteriam eodem [modo]. Johannes porcarius tenet unam coteriam eodem modo. Dyonisius filius Johannis tenet unam coteriam eodem modo. Johannes le almoner tenet unam coteriam eodem modo. Ricardus Talpe tenet unam coteriam eodem modo. Adam de Pulham tenet unam coteriam eodem modo. Jurdanus faber tenet unam coteriam eodem modo. Agnes Tote tenet unam coteriam eodem modo. Henricus faber tenet unam coteriam eodem modo. Nicholaus Clamme tenet unam coteriam eodem [modo]. Stephanus schaluner tenet unam coteriam eodem modo. Willelmus Hund tenet unam coteriam eodem modo. Hugo Cherl tenet unam coteriam eodem modo. Stephanus Wodeman tenet unam coteriam eodem [modo]; idem tenet dimidiam acram pro duodecim denariis equaliter. Yvo de Burewell tenet unam coteriam eodem [modo]. [col. 2] Paganus le roper tenet unam coteriam eodem modo. Ace Cok tenet unam coteriam eodem modo. Hunfridus le cuverur tenet unam coteriam eodem modo. Adam Cok tenet unam coteriam eodem modo. Amabilia vidua tenet unam coteriam eodem modo. Henricus Buntyng tenet unam coteriam eodem modo. Willelmus Drie tenet unam coteriam, et facit omnia sicut predicti cotarii hoc excepto quod nullam facit operacionem inter festum Sancti Michaelis et gulam Augusti, sed inter gulam Augusti et festum Sancti Michaelis operabitur sicut alii, et fodit in vinea ut supra.

Et sciendum quod tota villata de Ely in communi, tam homagium prioris quam homagium domini episcopi, debent facere et sustinere duas quarentenas super calceta de Alderheye.[87]

\Henry Bole holds a cot-land in the same manner. Henry *le ledbed* holds a cot-land in the same manner./ Wymark Pymme holds a cot-land in the same manner. \Agnes Houth holds a cot-land in the same manner./ Henry *le smale* holds a cot-land in the same manner. Nicholas Cakelard holds a cot-land in the same manner. William *le smale* holds a cot-land in the same manner. John, son of Agnes, holds a messuage in the same manner. Guanild Oubene holds a cot-land in the same manner. Geoffrey Faukes holds a cot-land in the same manner. Stephen Stephon holds a cot-land in the same manner. Robert Clemme holds a cot-land in the same manner. Henry Husebonde holds a cot-land in the same manner. John Pimme holds a messuage in the same manner. Cecily Pultehorn holds a cot-land in the same [manner]. Silvester Poleyn holds a cot-land in the same manner. Philip Horecoppe holds a cot-land in the same manner. Gerard of Stretham holds a cot-land in the same [manner]. Peter *le syneke* holds a cot-land in the same [manner]. Nicholas Bunting holds a cot-land in the same manner. Ralph Raven holds a cot-land in the same manner. John Puleyn holds a cot-land in the same manner. Ralph Pipernol holds a cot-land in the same manner. Thomas of Stretham holds a cot-land in the same [manner]. Alan Patin holds a cot-land in the same manner. Christiana Pas holds a cot-land in the same manner. Stephen Kynneday holds a cot-land in the same [manner]. \Richard Haybird holds a cot-land in the same manner./ Eborard the plough reeve holds a cot-land. John Bule holds a cot-land in the same manner. Robert Cakelard holds a cot-land in the same manner. Hugh the cutler holds a cot-land in the same manner. Osbert Hunno holds a cot-land in the same manner. Hugh the swineherd holds a cot-land in the same manner. Henry Sok holds a cot-land in the same manner. Christiana de Fenlond holds a cot-land in the same [manner]. John the swineherd holds a cot-land in the same manner. Dennis, John's son, holds a cot-land in the same manner. John the almoner holds a cot-land in the same manner. Richard Talpe holds a cot-land in the same manner. Adam of Pulham holds a cot-land in the same manner. Jordan the smith holds a cot-land in the same manner. Agnes Tote holds a cot-land in the same manner. Henry the smith holds a cot-land in the same manner. Nicholas Clamme holds a cot-land in the same [manner]. Stephen the weaver holds a cot-land in the same manner. William Hund holds a cot-land in the same manner. Hugh Cherl holds a cot-land in the same manner. Stephen Wodeman holds a cot-land in the same [manner]; the same holds ½ acre for 12*d* in equal instalments. Ives of Burwell holds a cot-land in the same [manner]. [col. 2] Payne the rope-maker holds a cot-land in the same manner. Ace Cok holds a cot-land in the same manner. Humfrey the roofer holds a cot-land in the same manner. Adam Cok holds a cot-land in the same manner. Widow Mabel holds a cot-land in the same manner. Henry Buntyng holds a cot-land in the same manner. William Drie holds a cot-land, and performs all the same services as the aforesaid cottars except that he performs no labour-service between Michaelmas and Lammas, but between Lammas and Michaelmas he works like the others, and he digs in the vineyard as above.

And note that the whole township of Ely in common, both of the prior's homage and of the lord bishop's, must make and keep in repair two furlongs on Aldreth causeway.[89]

De prepositis et bedellis

Summa tocius redditus per annum cum piscaria sex batellorum et Bradewere Fen decem libre et octodecim solidi ad quatuor terminos scilicet termino Sancti Michaelis, termino Sancti Andree, termino Sancte Marie Annunciacionis, termino nativitatis Sancti Johannis.
Summa de witepund per annum quadraginta tres solidi quinque denarii et obolum ad duos terminos scilicet termino Sancti Michaelis, termino Annuciacionis.
Summa piscarie de Upwere per annum una marca ad duos terminos scilicet ad festum Sancti Michaelis et ad Annunciacionem Beate Marie.
Summa piscarie de Yrittiwere[88] decem solidi per annum ad quatuor predictos terminos usuales.
Summa piscarie de Krecchemere quinque solidi per annum qui pacantur super scacariam extra compotum manerii.
Summa anguillarum per annum quatuordecim milia et dimidium prima dominica Quadragesime.
Summa gallinarum per annum cum duobus prepositis et duobus bedellis et uno messario sexies viginti et septem scilicet termino Natalis.
Summa ovorum per annum mille et sexaginta per maiorem centenam preter porcarium, scilicet termino Pasche.
Summa operum per annum undecim milia quinque centene quinquaginta et quinque per minorem centenariam preter porcarium.

Reeves and beadles[90]

Grand total of rent annually, with the fishery of six boats and *Bradewere* Fen[91] £10 18*s* at the four terms namely at the terms of Michaelmas, St Andrew, the Annunciation, and the Nativity of St John.
Total wite pound annually: 43*s* 5½*d* at two terms, namely at the terms of Michaelmas and the Annunciation.
Total from the fishery of Upware annually: one mark at the two terms, namely at the terms of Michaelmas and the Annunciation.
Total of the fishery of *Yrittiwere*: 10*s* annually at the four aforesaid usual terms.
Total of the fishery of Crouch Mere: 5*s* annually that is paid at the exchequer, separate from the account of the manor.
Total eels annually: 14500, on the first Sunday of Lent.
Total hens annually, including those from the two reeves, the two beadles and one hayward: 120, at Christmas.
Total eggs annually: 1060 by the long hundred,[92] excluding the swineherd, at Easter.
Total days of labour-service annually: 11555, by the short hundred, excluding the swineherd.[93]

NOTES

[1] The correct total is 1473 acres.

[2] A 'stick' seems to have been synonymous with an 'eel'; the 1250 survey records that *Yrithwere* with *Culdinglake* used to render 3036 sticks of eels: R, fo 1v, col. 2; Geoffrey Ridel was bishop of Ely 1174–89; Bishop Nigel (1133–69) had granted *Throtingwere* fishery to Ingram (*Engelram*) the steersman and his heirs, for 2s annually: M, fos 158–9; the fishery is variously spelt *Trottiwere, Thrithwere, Thrittywere, Yrithwere.*

[3] Harrimere lay between Little Thetford and the confluence of the Old West river with the Cam, south of this village: G. Fowler, 'Fenland Waterways, Past and Present. South Level District. Part I', *PCAS*, 33 (1933), 112.

[4] The four terms, as specified in R fo 7 col. 2, are Michaelmas, St Andrew (30 November), the Annunciation, and the Nativity of St John (24 June); wite pound was a customary rent paid annually to the bishop, probably as an insurance against punishment for minor offences: N. Neilson, *Customary Rents* (Oxford, 1910), pp. 177, 184–5.

[5] The ware acre was probably equivalent to 1½ field acres and was a unit of fiscal responsibility: E. Miller, *The abbey and bishopric of Ely* (Cambridge, 1951), pp. 87, 118; the land consisted of individual strips distributed among the open fields of Ely.

[6] Release on bail.

[7] 'tentor' corrected to 'tinctor'.

[8] The crane was a high-status bird, probably hunted with hawks: N. Sykes, 'The Dynamics of Status Symbols: Wildfowl Exploitation in England AD 410–1550', *The Archaeological Journal*, 161 (2004), 98–9.

[9] The customary obligations are summarised in the Introduction.

[10] Alongside this entry, in the right margin: 'in the new roll, the lands of Emma and Henry are not listed here because they are listed elsewhere under full lands' (*terre Emme et Henrici non ponuntur in novo rotulo hic quia alibi ponuntur inter plenas terras*).

[11] Presumably along the medieval course of the Soham Lode that flows into the Great Ouse near Little Thetford; in the 1250 survey, this is the antepenultimate entry under 'Free tenants' ; the land was then held by Eustace de Tornes.

[12] 'pittancer' in the right margin alongside this and the following entry.

[13] 'prior' in the right margin alongside this and the following entry.

[14] 'Tolymer' C G.

[15] '*Brieneshowe*' C G.

[16] '*Blithinghale*' spelt with thorn C; this is the first of several instances where thorn is used in C; G occasionally uses this letter, but R uses 'y' indiscriminately, whether it stands for 'y' or for thorn.

[17] 'Graslowe' C G.

[18] 'During Hugh of Balsham's episcopate, AD 1277 and 1 Edward I' (*Tempore Hugonis de Balsham Episcopi Anno Domini 1277 et Edwardi primo*) C; this was inserted by Cole in the eighteenth century; G has a similar insertion: Miller, *Abbey and Bishopric*, pp. 5–6 n; the date of this survey is further discussed in the Introduction.

[19] The short hundred equals 100; the value of the perch varied from place to place in medieval England, so that it was necessary to define the value of the Ely perch, this is restated at the beginning of the 1417 Survey: H, fo 10v.

[20] The survey of marsh starts south of Ely and continues anti-clockwise towards the north, then west; some of the place-names are translated here, using D. Hall's identifications in *The Fenland Project, Number 6: The south-western Cambridgeshire fenlands* (EAA, 56, 1992), pp. 56–94, *passim*; and in *The Fenland Project, Number 10: Cambridgeshire survey, Isle of Ely and Wisbech* (EAA, 79, 1996), pp. 18–80, *passim*.

[21] In the left margin, replaces '*maram*' [deleted].

[22] 'Newedik' C G.

[23] C G.

[24] The long hundred equals 120, so the manor could sustain 600 sheep in addition to those of the cottagers.
[25] Three weirs in 1222.
[26] 'Thrithiwere' C.
[27] C G.
[28] '*bootgonges*' at the foot of col. 2; in the right margin C.
[29] Five boats in 1222, rendering a total of 15s annually.
[30] '3s' C G.
[31] 'pittancer' in the left margin.
[32] Bishop Hugh of Northwold had made this grant some twenty years previously when Ralph was prior (*c*.1229–38); Henry Muschet relinquished his claim on this messuage in exchange for release from the 12s annual rent that he owed the bishop for his tenement at Fen Ditton, a manor of the bishop of Ely where Henry occurs as a knight; the keeper of the priory vineyard had paid 54s for the purchase of this holding, and would pay 14s annually for it, at the bishop's exchequer: C, fo 16v; EDR G2/1, col. 189; R, fo 61v.
[33] The context suggests that the castle stood on relatively flat ground, and not on Cherry Hill; this castle may have formed part of the rebels' defences on the Isle of Ely during the civil war of King John's reign (see Introduction).
[34] 'sacrist' in the right margin; the hospital of St John the Baptist, at the west end of Ely, was amalgamated with that of St Mary Magdalene by Bishop Northwold, *c*.1240.
[35] 'monks' in the right margin.
[36] '*Dryngeston*' in the right margin.
[37] 'Brays' in the right margin; Agnes and her sisters were large land-holders in Ely, and grand-daughters of Payne, Alexander's son: T, fo 87; some of their holdings were to form Brays estate, mentioned in 1417 and 1522–3.
[38] 'prior' in the left margin.
[39] 'Brays' in the left margin.
[40] 'prior' in the right margin.
[41] 'cellarer' in the right margin.
[42] 'for 16d' (*pro sexdecim denariis*) C.
[43] Bishop Northwold appears to be taking back a compact block of land comprising both the former castle site (fo 2 col. 2) and adjoining land.
[44] '*Ditton, prior, dec*' written one below the other in the central margin.
[45] 'almoner' in the left margin.
[46] 'sacrist' in the left margin.
[47] C G.
[48] 'Deth' C.
[49] 'almoner' in the right margin.
[50] G has an additional entry: 'John of Stamford holds a messuage for 8d in equal instalments and pays 1d wite pound and digs as above' (*Johannes de Staunford tenet unum mesuagium pro octo denariis equaliter et de witepund unum denarium et fodit ut supra*).
[51] Henry Moyserun is the first of a group of tenants having a common boundary with the bishop's vineyard, as stated at the end of this section (col. 2) where the surname occurs as Musserun.
[52] 'chapel' in the left margin.
[53] 'almoner' in the left margin.
[54] 'almoner' in the left margin.
[55] 'almoner' in the left margin.
[56] 'keeper of the Lady Chapel' in the left margin.
[57] 'the heir…holds' (*heres…tenet*) C.
[58] 'cellarer' in the central margin, but it may refer to the following entry.
[59] 'almoner' in the central margin.

[60] 'almoner' in the left margin.
[61] 'almoner' in the left margin.
[62] 'for 10d' (*pro decem denariis*) C G.
[63] 'Ricardus' G.
[64] 'almoner' in the left margin.
[65] 'for 14d' (*pro quatuordecim denariis*) C G.
[66] 'sacrist' in the right margin.
[67] We must inquire who holds it and for what services' (*inquirendum quis tenet et pro qual'*) alongside this entry; the serjeanty of being the bishop's baker was created by Bishop Hervey and bought out by Bishop John de Ketene in 1310; Bishop Hervey's charter to Haldeyn, the first holder of this office, included the grant of a *mansura* and 18 acres of land: Miller, *Abbey and bishopric*, pp. 125, 283.
[68] 'sacrist' in the left margin.
[69] 'Codeyb' C, 'Coderb' G.
[70] 'Thede' C.
[71] This is the chantry on the Green established by Bishop Northwold; 'Cantaria de Ely Green' in the left margin alongside this entry, in a post-medieval hand.
[72] 'keeper of the Lady Chapel' in the left margin.
[73] John of Fountains, bishop 1220–25.
[74] 'pittancer' in the central margin.
[75] 'almoner' in the central margin.
[76] 'prior' in the central margin.
[77] This entry also occurs at the end of the previous section ('Free tenants') where it is deleted; C and G have this entry at the end of the previous section, after a blank space.
[78] 'Sothewombe' in this and the next entry C.
[79] 'Childyung' C.
[80] 'Aumory' C.
[81] 'almoner' in the left margin.
[82] 'Aumori' C.
[83] 'Philippi le bedel' C G.
[84] 'Aylbern' C.
[85] 'Aylward' C G.
[86] 'Shok' C.
[87] 'Alderhethe' C.
[88] 'Thrittywere' C.
[89] 'Note regarding Aldreth causeway' (*Memorandum de calceto de Alderhith*) in the right margin alongside this entry; the causeway ran from Aldreth, on the south-west edge of the Isle of Ely, to Willingham.
[90] This heading is followed by one or more blank lines in all three manuscripts.
[91] '19s' (*xixs*) superscript, over 'six boats' [this should be 18s], '10s' (*xs*) over '*Bradewere* Fen'.
[92] 1272 eggs.
[93] At the foot of fo 7, col. 2: 'Note that Henry Denver received from Bishop Robert [of Orford, bishop of Ely 1302–10] a plot of land out of the common between his messuage in Ely and the public waterway, next to the lode between the aforesaid plot and Castle Hithe, rendering to the bishop and his successors 3*d* annually at Michaelmas' (*Memorandum quod Henricus Denver cepit de Roberto episcopo eliensi quandam placeam terre de communi existenti a mesuagio suo in Ely usque ad altam ripam iuxta ladam inter placeam predictam et le Castelhyth, reddendo inde annuatim episcopo et suis successoribus iijd ad festum Michaelis*); also added in C.

THE 1417 SURVEY

BL Harleian 329, 10–24v

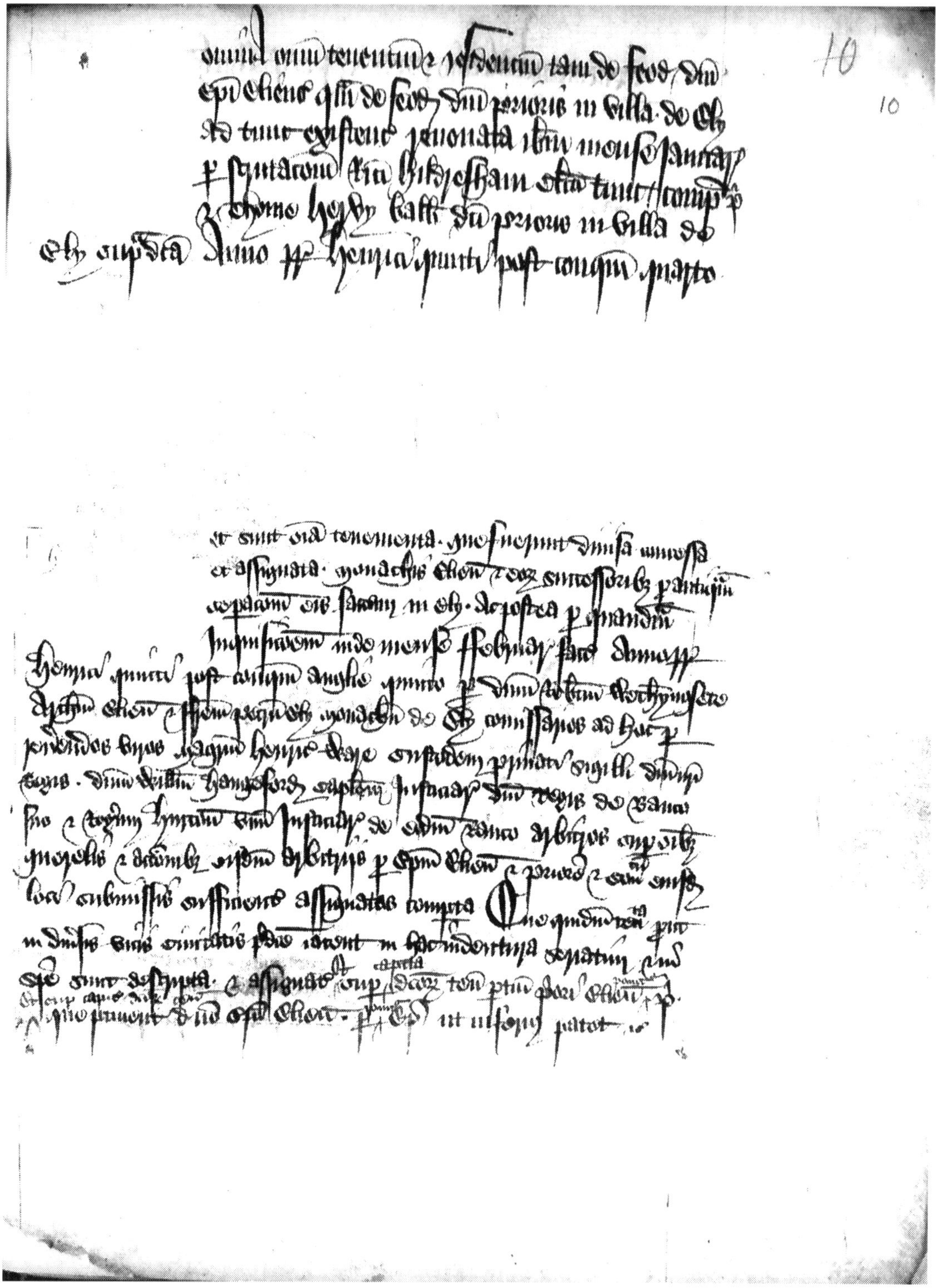

The names[1] of all the tenants and residents, both of the fee of the lord bishop of Ely and of the fee of the lord prior, then present in the town of Ely, compiled there by the scrutiny of Richard Hildresham clerk, accountant of the prior, and of Thomas Hervy, bailiff of the said prior, in Ely aforesaid, in January in 4 Henry V [January 1417].

These are all the tenements that were assigned to the monks of Ely and their successors by the ancient division[2] made for them in Ely; and afterwards found satisfactorily assigned, by an enquiry made in February in 5 Henry V [February 1418], by Sir Robert Wetheryngsete archdeacon of Ely, and brother Peter Ely monk of Ely, delegated for this purpose by the reverend men Master Henry Ware keeper of the privy seal of our lord king, Sir William Hangesford chief justice of the King's Bench and Roger Hinton[3] a justice of the same Bench, arbitrators in all the disputes and lawsuits that had been submitted to the same arbitration by the bishop of Ely and the prior and convent of the same place. These tenements are described and assigned in this indenture, in sequence and individually, as they lie in the various streets of the aforesaid town. \And/ at \the head/ of the said tenements pertaining to the prior of Ely \is written/ p[i]; \and at the head of the said tenements/ that pertain to the lord bishop of Ely \is written/ Ep as it appears below.[4]

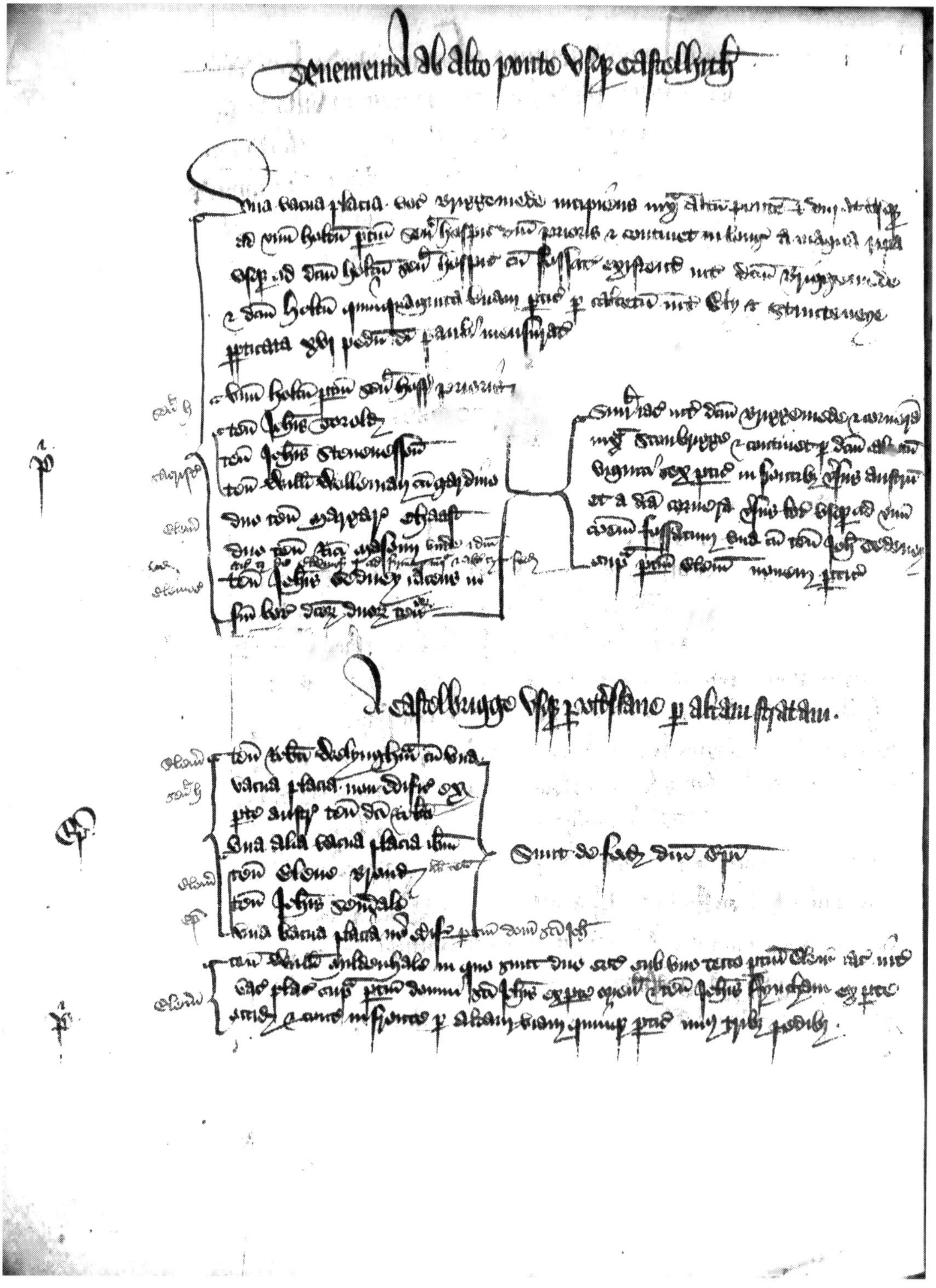

The tenements from the High Bridge to Castle Hithe

Prior
a vacant plot called Bridgemead beginning next to the High Bridge; and it extends to a holt pertaining to the steward of the lord prior's household, and contains in length, from the great bank to the said holt of the steward of the household, including the ditch between the said Bridgemead and the said holt, 51 perches along the causeway between Ely and Stuntney, measured by the perch of 16½ foot of St Paul.[5]

a holt pertaining to the steward of the prior's household [sh]
John Torold's tenement [s]
John Stevenesson's tenement [s]
William Wolleman's tenement with a garden [s]
two tenements of Margaret Chaast [e]
two tenements of Richard Masoun \whereof the same Richard holds one of the almoner for a rent of 4*s*, and the other he holds in fee/
John Gedney's tenement [e] lying at the north end of the said two tenements[6]

lying together between the said Bridgemead and the corner next to Stone Bridge, and they contain 26 perches[7] on the south frontage along the said causeway; and from the said corner towards the north up to a common ditch, including the above tenement of John Gedeney pertaining to the almoner, 9 perches.[8]

From Castle Bridge[9] to Potters Lane along the highway

Bishop
Robert Welyngham's tenement [e] with an unbuilt vacant plot [sh] south of the said Robert's tenement
another vacant plot there
Ellen Brande's tenement [e] \held freely/
John Sendale's tenement [e]
a vacant plot without buildings [e] \pertaining to St John's house/

they are of the lord bishop's fee.

Prior
William Mildenhale's tenement [e] in which are two cottages under one roof, pertaining to the almoner, lying between the above vacant plot pertaining to St John's house on the east and John Fincham's tenement[10] on the west, and it contains 5 perches less 3 feet in front along the highway.

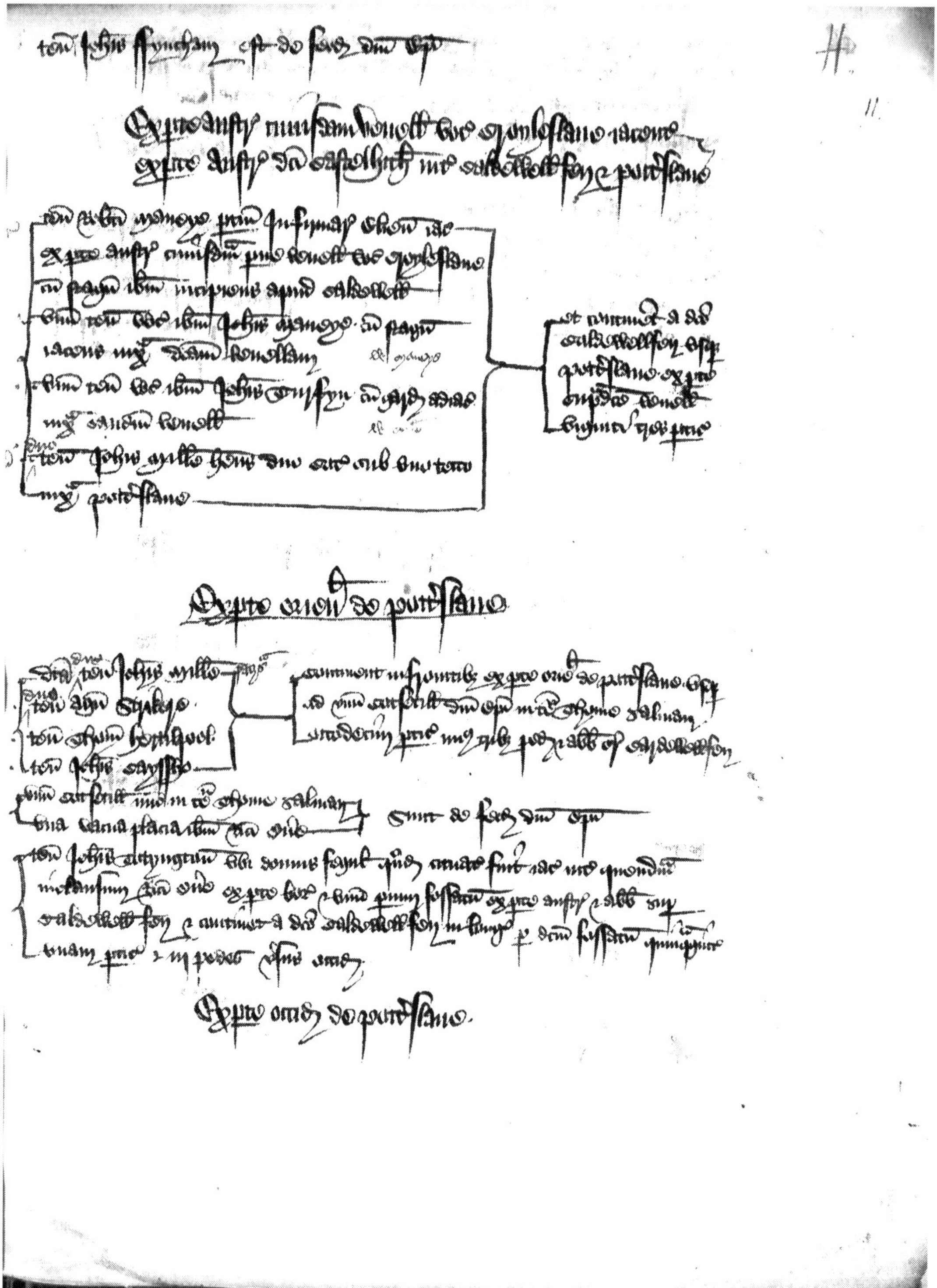

Bishop
John Fincham's tenement is of the lord bishop's fee.

On the south side of a lane called Croyles Lane, south of the said Castle Hithe between Caldwell Fen and Potters Lane[11]

Prior
Robert Maneye's tenement pertaining to the infirmarer of Ely with a pond there [i], beginning at Caldwell,[12] on the south side of a small lane called Croyles Lane
a vacant tenement of John Maneye there with a pond [h], lying next to the said lane \W. Maneys/
a vacant tenement of John Turfyn there with a garden adjoining [h], next to the same lane \W. Oulle/
\two/[13] tenement(s) of John Millere [i] having two cottages under one roof next to Potters Lane
and they contain 23 perches from the said Caldwell Fen to Potters Lane on the side of the aforesaid lane.

On the east side of Potters Lane

Prior
the said \two/ tenement(s) of John Millere \sacrist/
\two/ tenements[14] of Agnes Strikere
Thomas Hertilpool's tenement
John Cayssho's tenement
they contain in front on the east side of Potters Lane, to a cot-land of the lord bishop in Thomas Salman's tenure, 18 perches less 3 feet, and abutting upon Caldwell Fen.
Bishop
a cot-land now in the tenure of Thomas Salman
a vacant plot there of Richard Overe
they are of the bishop's fee.
Prior
John Totyngton's tenement [e] where a pottery was once situated, lying between an enclosure of Richard Overe on the north and a small ditch on the south, and abutting upon Caldwell Fen, and it contains in length along the said ditch 51 perches[15] and 3 feet from the said Caldwell Fen towards the west.

On the west side of Potters Lane

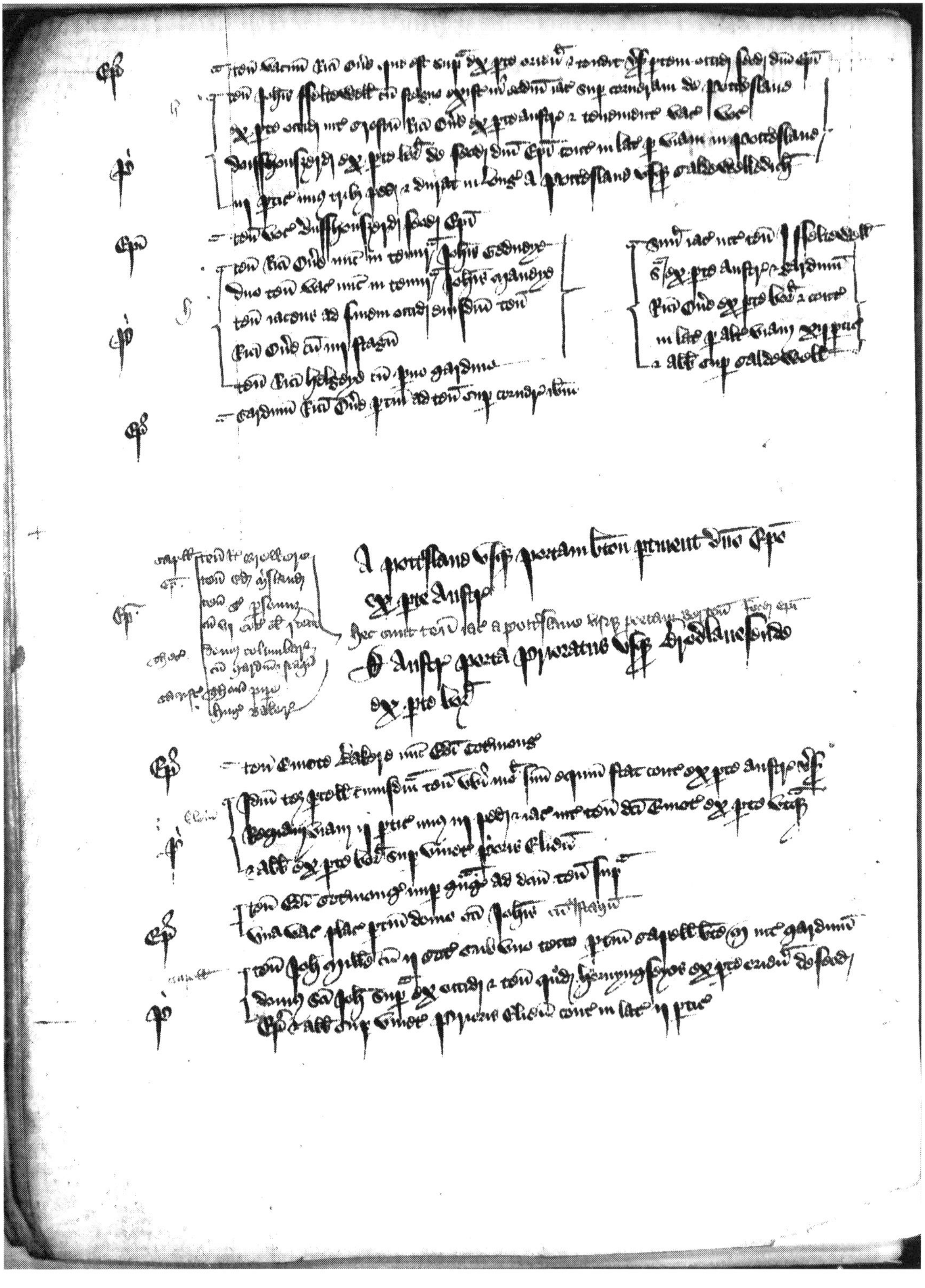

Bishop
Richard Overe's vacant tenement above, on the east, and it extends towards the west, of the lord bishop's fee.
Prior
John Feltewell's tenement [h] with a pond situated in the same, lying on the corner of Potters Lane on the west, between Richard Overe's croft on the south and a vacant tenement called Duffhousyerd on the north, of the lord bishop's fee. It contains in breadth along the road in Potters Lane[16] 3 perches less 3 feet, and extends in length from Potters Lane to Caldwell ditch.
Bishop
a tenement called Duffhousyerd, bishop's fee.
Prior
Richard Overe's tenement now in the tenure of John Gedneye[17]
two vacant tenements now in the tenure of John Maneye [h]
a tenement lying at the west end of the same tenement of Richard Overe with four ponds[18]
Richard[19] Helgeye's tenement with a small garden
lying together between John Feltewell's tenement above, on the south, and Richard Overe's garden on the north, and they contain in breadth along the highway[20] 12 perches, and abut upon Caldwell.[21]
Bishop
Richard Overe's garden pertaining to the tenement on the corner there.

From Potters Lane to Barton gate they pertain to the lord bishop, on the south side[22]

Bishop
R. Brewere's tenement [c]
Ed' Mersland's tenement
T. Persouns' tenement with seven cottages under one roof
a dovecot with a garden and a pond [t]
Thomas Pipere [s]
Hugh Baker
these are the tenements lying from Potters Lane to Barton gate, bishop's fee.

From the south gate of the Priory to Broad Lane's end[23] on the north side

Bishop
Emmotte Bakere's tenement now Edmund Cotermong's.
Prior
The same holds part of a tenement[24] where his horsemill stands [e], it contains on the south towards the king's highway 2 perches less 3 feet, and lies between tenements of the said Emmotte on either side and abuts upon the vineyard of the prior of Ely on the north.
Bishop
Edmund Cotermonge's tenement lately the barn for the abovesaid tenement
a vacant plot pertaining to St John's house\with a pond/
Prior
John Millere's tenement [c] with two cottages under one roof pertaining to the Lady Chapel between the garden of St John's house above on the west and a tenement formerly Hornyngseyes on the east, of the bishop's fee, and it abuts upon the vineyard of the prior of Ely, it contains in breadth 2 perches.[25]

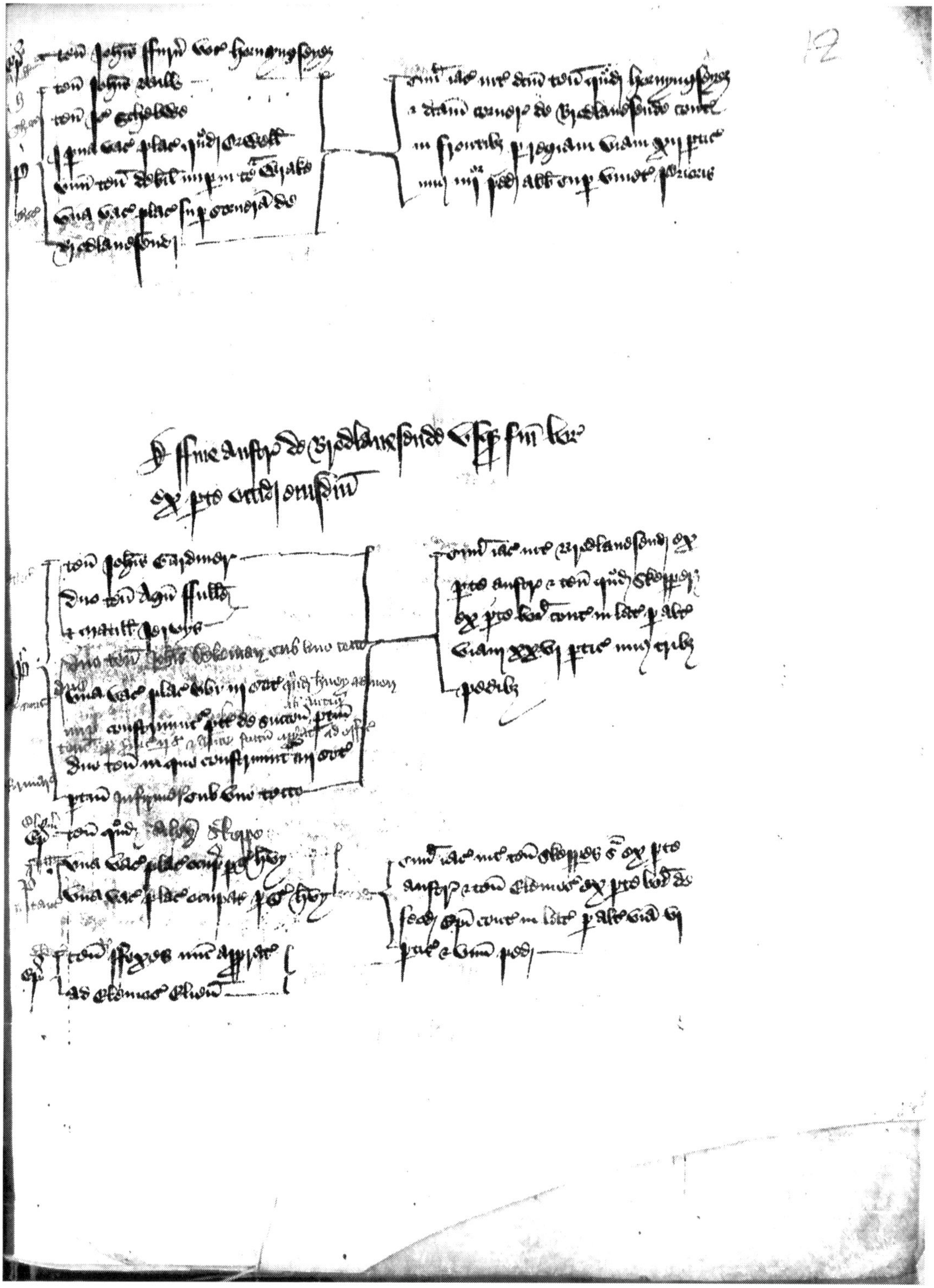

Bishop
a tenement of John Furner[26] called Hornyngseyes [c]
Prior
John Baille's tenement [h]
Isabel Schelwe's tenement [t][27]
a small vacant plot formerly Orwell's
a tenement in poor repair, lately in Wrake's[28] tenure
a vacant plot on the corner of Broad Lane's end [t]
lying together between the said tenement formerly Hornyngseyes and the said corner of Broad Lane's end, they contain 12 perches less 4 feet in front along the king's highway, they abut upon the prior's vineyard.

From the south end of Broad Lane's end to the north end, on the west side

Prior
John Gardiner's tenement [t]
two tenements of Agnes Fuller[29] and Matilda Jervys [t]
\two tenements of John Dekeman under one roof/[30]
one \two/ vacant plot(s) where three cottages \formerly Hervey Raven's/ recently stood pertaining to the pittancer of Sutton \from ancient times/ \held by service of 2*s* and appropriated to the office before *[illegible]*/[31]
two tenements in which stand four[32] cottages under one roof \pertaining to the infirmarer/ [i]
lying together between Broad Lane's end on the south and a tenement formerly Skepper's on the north, they contain 26 perches[33] less 3 feet in breadth along the highway.[34]
Bishop
a tenement formerly \of Alexander Skeppe/ [e]
Prior
a vacant plot occupied by Thomas Hervy [c]
a vacant plot occupied by T. Hervy [p]
lying together between the above Skeppere's tenement on the south and the almoner's tenement on the north, of the bishop's fee, they contain 6 perches and 1 foot in breadth along the highway.
Bishop
Foxe's tenement now appropriated to the almoner of Ely [e]

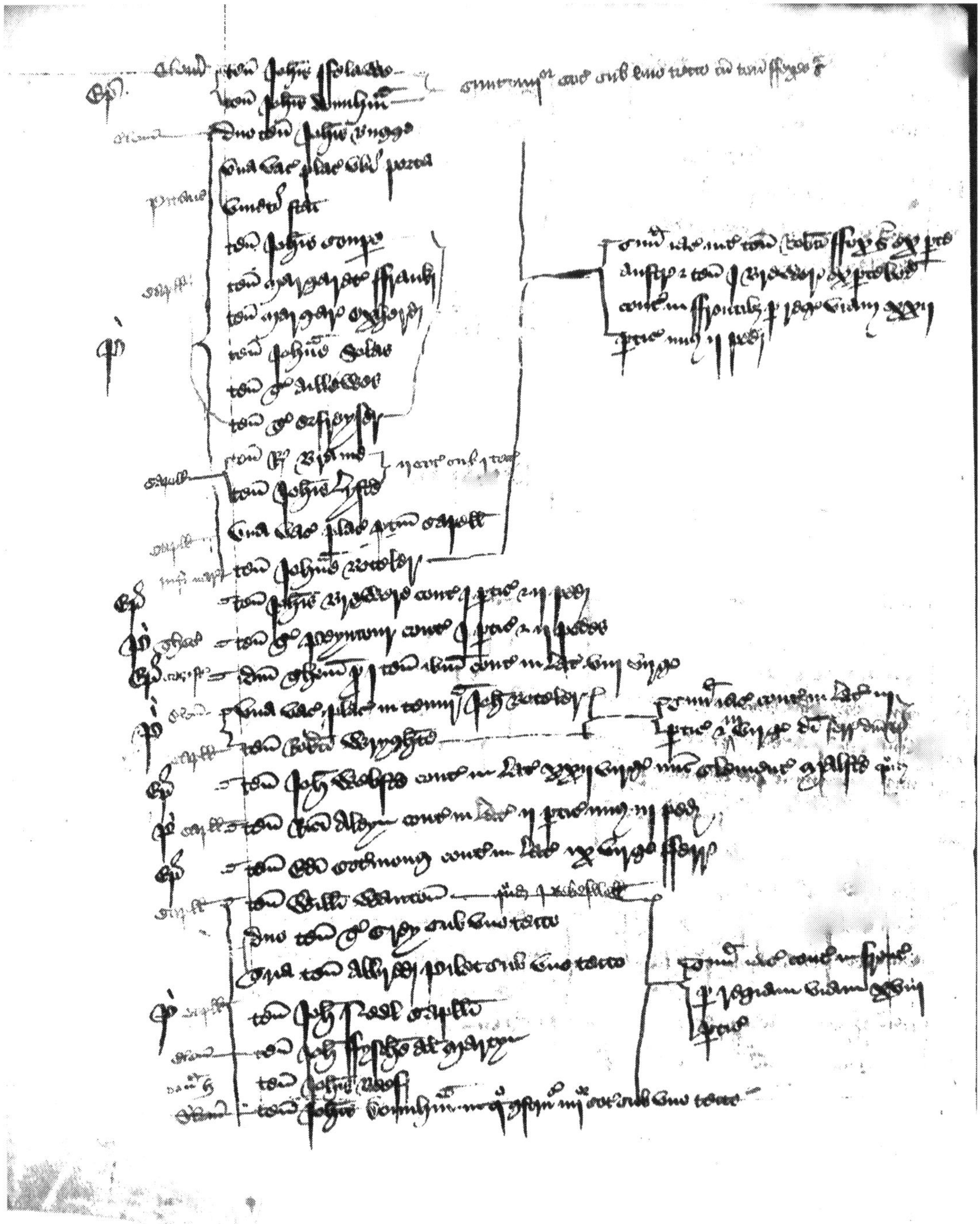

Bishop
John Felawe's tenement [e]
John Dounham's tenement
\they comprise four cottages under one roof together with the above Foxe's tenement/
Prior
two tenements of John Bugge [e][35]
a vacant plot[36] where the gate of the vineyard stands [p]
John Coupere's tenement [c]
Margaret Frank's tenement
Margaret Oxherd's tenement[37]
Joan Solas' tenement
T. Aillewes' tenement
T. Orfreyser's tenement [c]
R. Brame's tenement [c]
John Lystere's tenement [c] } \two cottages under one roof /
a vacant plot pertaining to the [Lady] Chapel [c]
Joan Boteler's tenement [i]
lying together between Robert Fox's tenement, above, on the south and John Brewer's tenement on the north, they contain 22 perches less 2 feet in front along the king's highway.
Bishop
John Brewere's tenement contains 1 perch and 2 feet.
Prior
T. Peyntour's tenement contains 1 perch and 2 feet [t][38]
Bishop
the same Thomas P. one tenement there contains in breadth 8 yards [s]
Prior
a vacant plot in the tenure of John Boteler [e]
Robert Wryghte's tenement [c]
lying together,[39] they contain in breadth 3 perches and \3/½ yards[40] of the lord king's iron.
Bishop
John Webstere's tenement contains in breadth 22 yards, now of Clement Malstere formerly *[blank]*
Prior
Richard Aleyn's tenement contains in breadth 2 perches less 3 feet [c]
Bishop
Edmund Cotermong's tenement contains in breadth 9 iron yards.
Prior
William Wauton's tenement \formerly J. Rebeswell's/ [c]
two tenements of T. Grey under one roof
three tenements of Albreda Pilet under one roof[41]
a tenement of John Neel chaplain [c]
a tenement of John Fyschere alias Martyn [e]
John Beef's tenement [sh]
John[42] Dounham's tenement in which stand four cottages under one roof [e][43]
lying together,[44] they contain 18 perches in front along the king's highway.

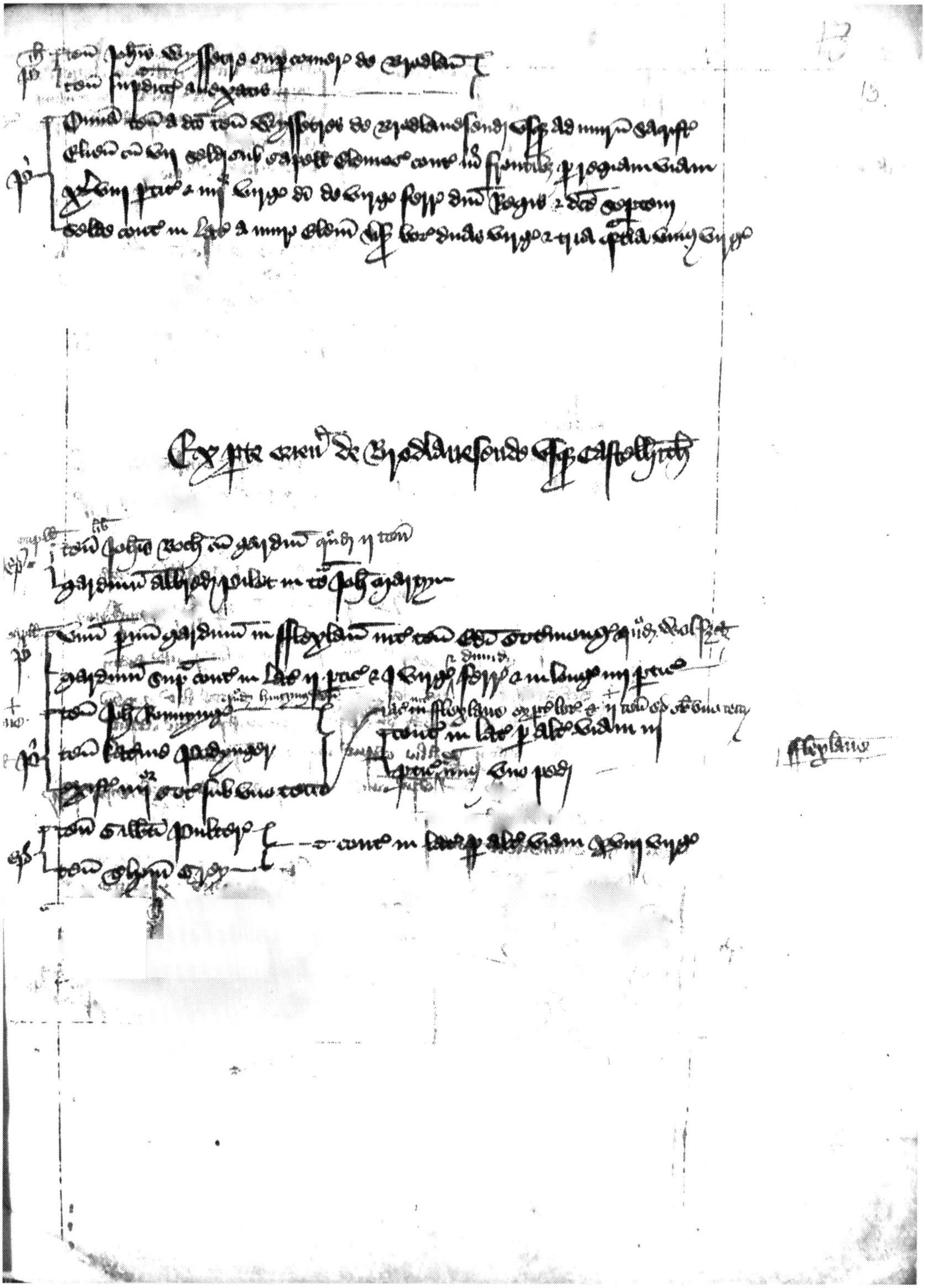

Prior
John Wyssetre's tenement on the corner of Broad Lane [sh][45]
the above tenements being attached to it.
Prior
all the tenements from the said tenement of Wyssetre, from Broad Lane's end to the wall of the sacristy of Ely,[46] together with seven stalls below the almonry chapel [e], they contain in front along the king's highway 48 perches and 4½ yards of the iron yard of the lord king; and the said seven stalls contain in breadth from the almonry wall towards the north 2¾ yards.

On the east side of Broad Lane's end to Castle Hithe

Bishop
John Bocher's \free/ tenement with a garden [c] \formerly two tenements/
Albreda Pilet's garden in the tenure of John Martyn.

Prior
Flax Lane
a small garden in Flax Lane between the tenement of Edmund Cotermong [c] \formerly Wolfz' and/ the above garden, it contains in breadth 2 perches and 1 \½/ iron yard, and in length 4 perches.[47]
John Rovnynge's tenement \formerly Huntyngdon's/[48]
Katherine Podynger's tenement comprising four cottages under one roof [c][49]
\lying between Flax Lane on the north, and two tenements of the bishop once a single tenure/ they contain in breadth along the highway 3 \½/ perches less 1 foot.[50]
Bishop
Gilbert Pultere's tenement
Thomas Grey's tenement
and they contain 18 yards in breadth along the highway.

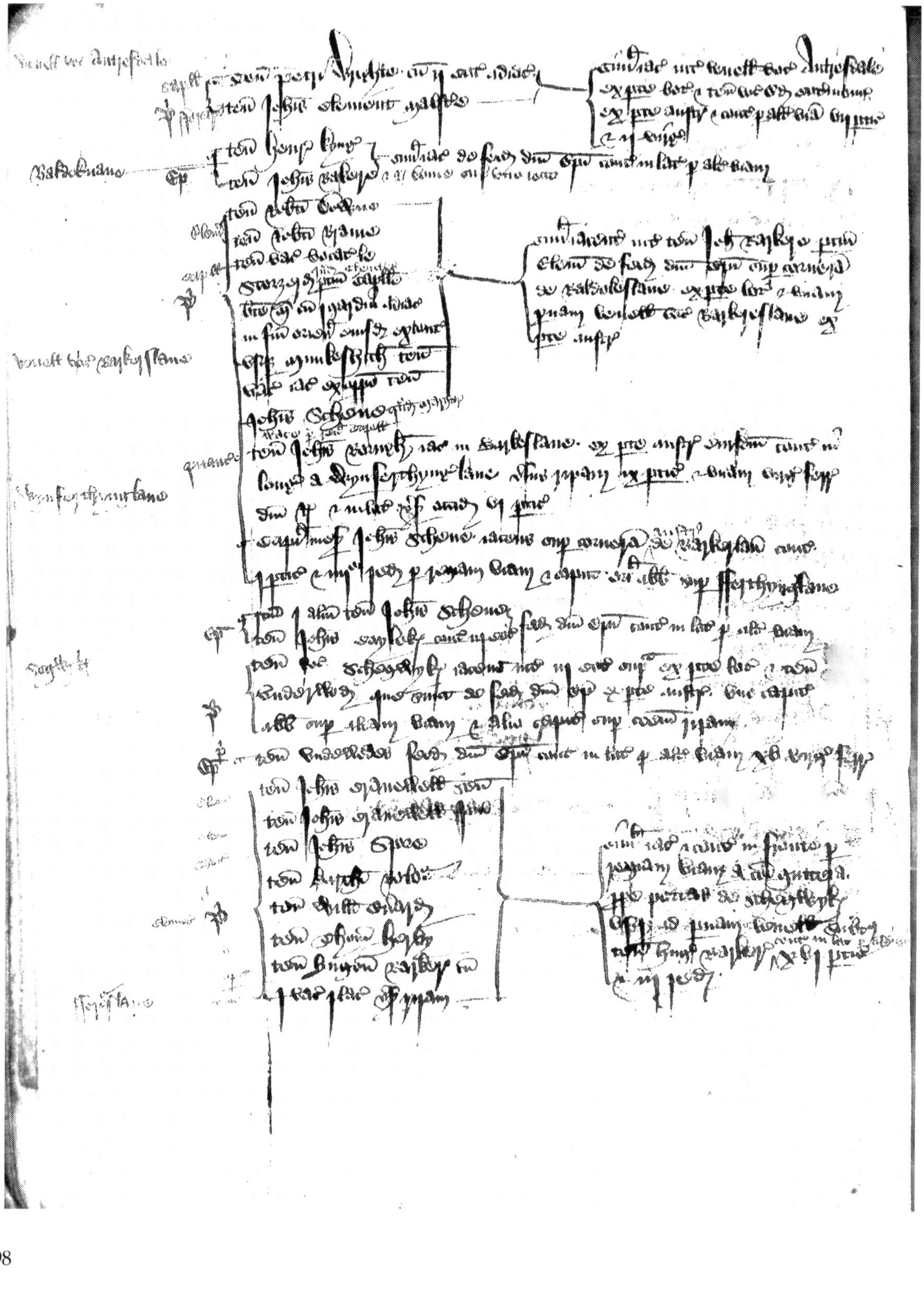

Lane called Antresdale
Prior
Peter Wrighte's tenement with two adjoining cottages [c]
a tenement of John Clement malt-maker [f][51]
lying together between a lane called Antresdale on the north and a vacant tenement of Edmund Cotermong on the south, and they contain 7 perches and 2 yards along the highway.
Baldocks Lane[52]
Bishop
Henry Kyng's tenement
a tenement of John Bakere \and R. Douce under one roof/[53]
lying together, of the lord bishop's fee, they contain in breadth along the highway *[blank]*
Prior
Robert Downe's tenement [e]
Robert Brame's tenement [e]
a vacant tenement called le Storyerd \formerly Chevlee/ pertaining to the Lady Chapel with a garden adjoining on its east boundary, extending to Monks' Hithe [c]; the vacant tenement lying opposite a tenement of John Schene[54] \formerly Margaret Wace's, according to the rental of the [Lady] Chapel/
lying together between John Barkere's tenement pertaining to the almoner of the lord bishop's fee on the corner of Baldocks Lane on the north, and a small lane called Barkers Lane on the south.
Lane called Barkers Lane
Winfarthing Lane
John Borugh's tenement lying in Barkers Lane on the south side [p], it contains in length from Winfarthing Lane towards the bank 9 perches and 1 iron yard of the lord king, and in breadth towards the west 6 perches.[55]
John Schene's principal messuage[56] lying on the \south/ corner of Barkers Lane, it contains 1 perch and 4 feet along the king's highway, and the east head abuts upon Farthing Lane.
Bishop
also another tenement of John Schene
John Cayloke's tenement comprising three cottages
of the lord bishop's fee, they contain in breadth along the highway *[blank]*
Sedgwick
Prior
a tenement called Sedgwicks lying between the above three cottages on the north, and Underwode's tenement on the south that are of the lord bishop's fee, one head abuts upon the highway the other upon the public bank.[57]
Bishop
Underwode's tenement of the lord bishop's fee [pri], contains 15 iron yards in breadth along the highway.
Prior
a tenement of John Cranewell senior [e]
a tenement of John Cranewell junior [e]
John Spore's tenement [t]
Bartholomew Bolour's tenement [sh]
William Everard's tenement [e]
Thomas Hervy's tenement [sh]
Hugh Barker's tenement [c] with a vacant plot towards the bank [e]
Ferours Lane
lying together, and they contain in front along the king's highway, from the common gutter near the gates of Sedgwick to a small lane under Hugh Barker's tenement \they contain in breadth along the highway/ 16 perches and 3 feet.

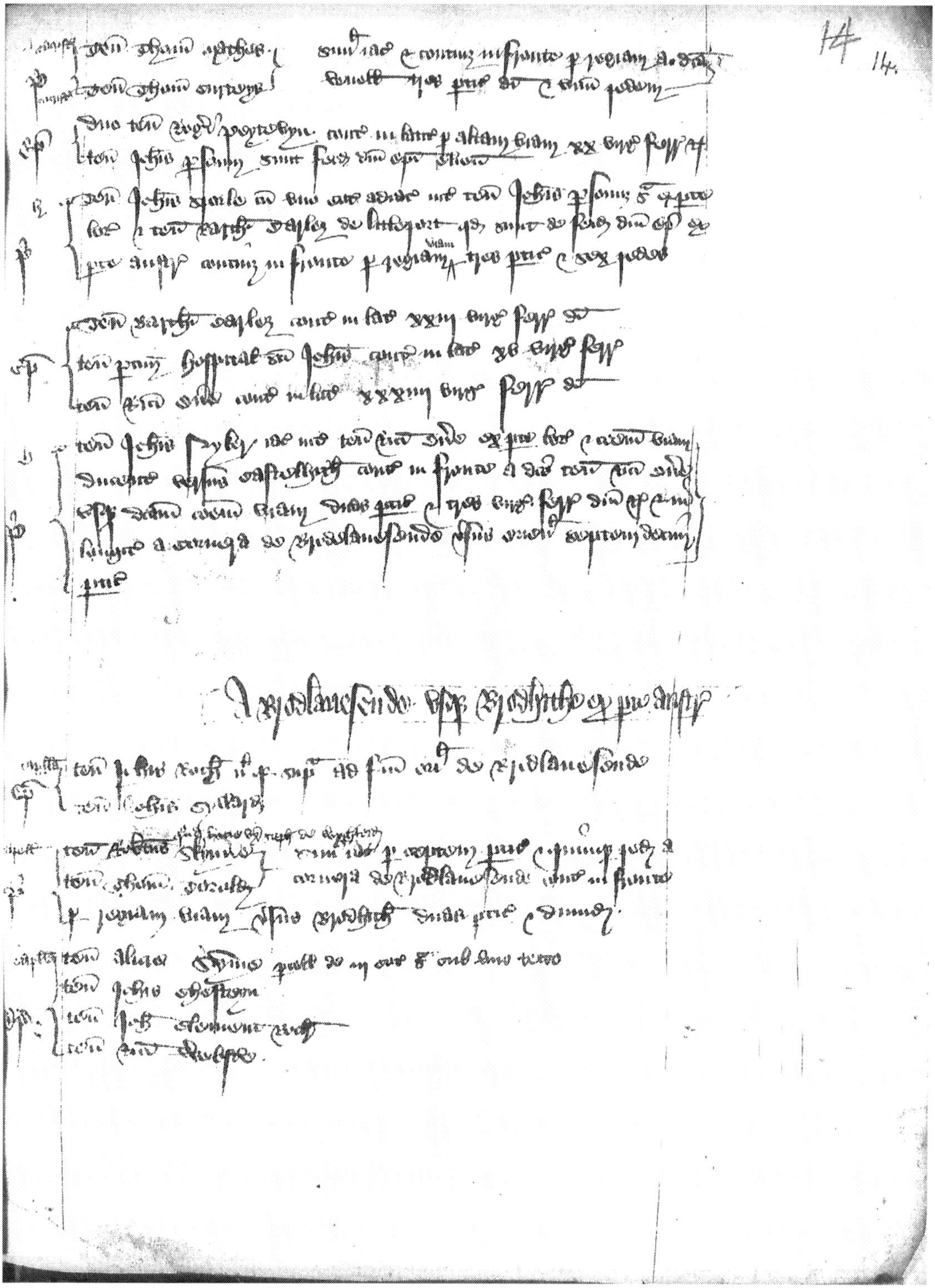

Prior
Thomas Mathes' tenement [s]
Thomas Curteys' tenement [s]
lying together, and they contain 3½ perches and 1 foot in front along the king's *[highway]* from the said lane.
Bishop
two tenements of Roger Peytevyn contain 20 iron yards of the king in breadth along the highway
John[58] Persouns' tenement; they are of the fee of the lord bishop of Ely.
Prior
John Sporle's tenement with an adjoining cottage [sh], between the above tenement of John Persounz on the north, and the tenement of Bartholomew Carlez of Littleport on the south, that are of the lord bishop's fee, they contain 3 perches and 6 feet in front along the king's highway.
Bishop
Bartholomew Carlez' tenement contains 23½ iron yards in breadth
a tenement pertaining to St John's hospital contains 15 iron yards in breadth
Richard Overe's tenement contains 34½ iron yards in breadth.
Prior
John Nyker's tenement [sh] lying between Richard Overe's tenement on the north and the public highway leading towards Castle Hithe, it contains in front 2 perches and 3 iron yards of the lord king from the said tenement of Richard Overe to the said public highway, and in length 17 perches from the corner of Broad Lane's end towards the east.

From Broad Lane's end to Broad Hithe on the south side

Bishop
John Bocher's tenement, nothing because [described] above at the east end of Broad Lane's end [c]
John Syward's tenement.
Prior
a tenement of Robert Skynnere[59] [c] \formerly of Lucy, wife of Stephen of Witchford/[60]
Thomas Torold's tenement[61]
lying together 7 perches and 5 feet from the corner of Broad Lane's end, they contain 2½ perches in front along the king's highway towards Broad Hithe.
Bishop
Alice Symme's tenement, part of the above three cottages under one roof [c]
John Chesteyn's tenement
a tenement of John Clement butcher
Richard Webstere's tenement.

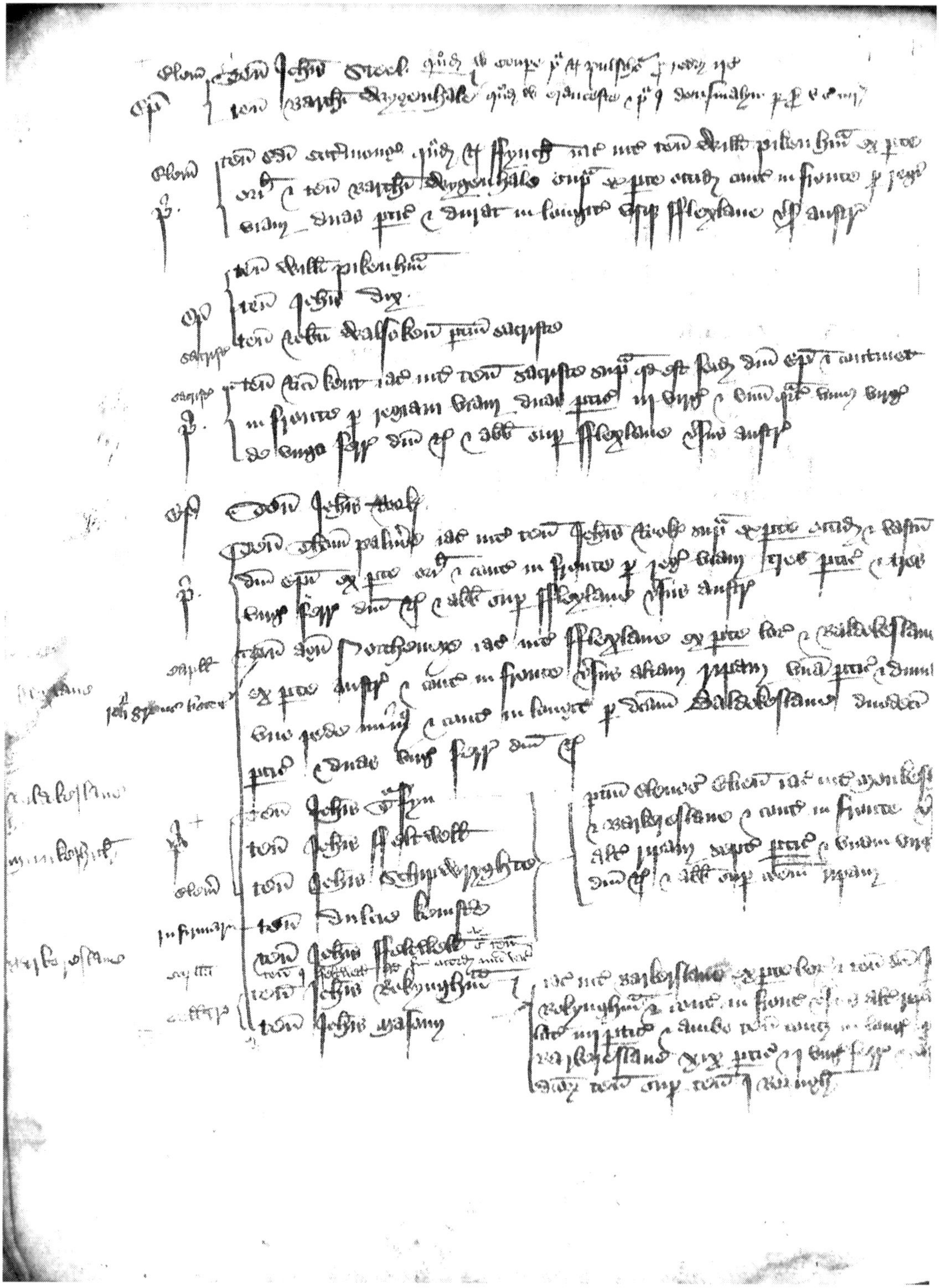

Bishop
John Steel's tenement [e] \formerly of W. Coupere then of R. Pulchour, for 2*s* rent/[62]
Bartholomew Wygenhale's tenement \formerly of W. Granceste and afterwards of J. Deusmalyn, by service of 5*s* 4*d*/
Prior
Edmund Cotermonge's tenement formerly of R.[63] Fynch [e], lying between William Pikenham's tenement on the east and the above tenement of Bartholomew Wygenhale on the west; it contains 2 perches in front along the king's highway, and extends in length up to Flax Lane towards the south.
Bishop
William Pikenham's tenement
John Dix's tenement
Robert Walsoken's tenement pertaining to the sacrist [s]
Prior
Richard Kent's tenement [s] lying between the above tenement of the sacrist that is of the lord bishop's fee;[64] and it contains in front along the king's highway 2 perches 3¼ yards of the iron yard of the lord king, and abuts upon Flax Lane towards the south.
Bishop
John Rooke's tenement.
Prior
Thomas Palmere's tenement[65] lying between the above tenement of John Rooke on the west, and the lord bishop's waste land on the east; and it contains in front along the king's highway 3 perches and 3 iron yards of the lord king, and abuts upon Flax Lane towards the south.
Flax Lane
Agnes Northeneye's tenement [c][66] lying between Flax Lane on the north and Baldocks Lane on the south, and it contains 1½ perches less 1 foot in front towards the public waterway, and it contains in length along the said Baldocks Lane 12 perches and 2 iron yards of the lord king.
Baldocks Lane
Monks' Hithe
John Turfyn's tenement [e]
John Feltwell's tenement [e]
John Schipwryghte's tenement [e]
Douce Kemstere's tenement [i]
Barkers Lane
John Feltwell's tenement [c] *[illegible]*/
\John Feltwell's tenement at the west boundary now vacant/[67]

pertaining to the almoner of Ely, lying between Monks' Hithe and Barkers Lane, and they contain in front towards the public waterway 7 perches and 1 yard of the lord king, and abut upon the public waterway.[68]

John Bokyngham's tenement [cel]
John Masoun's tenement [cel]

lying between Barkers Lane on the north and the said John Bokyngham's tenement,[69] and they contain 4 perches in breadth in front towards the public waterway, and both tenements contain 19 perches and 1 iron yard in length along the said Barkers Lane, and the west head of the said tenements [abuts] upon J. Borugh's tenement.

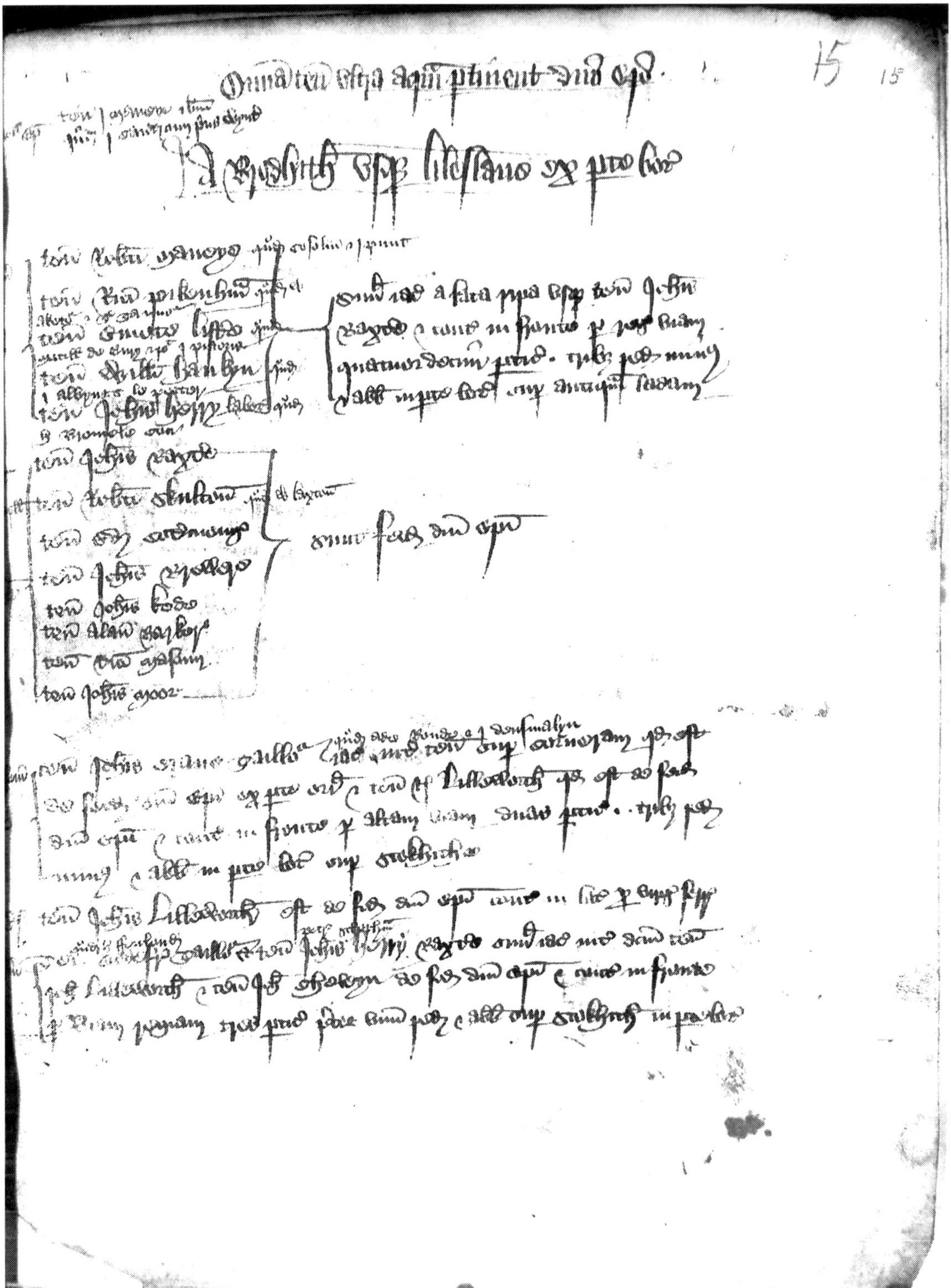

Omnia ten' ista aq[ue] p[er]tinent d[omi]no ep[iscop]o

15

ten' Joh[ann]is Sayre

ten' Joh[ann]is Bode

ten' Joh[ann]is Moor

All the tenements beyond the water pertain to the lord bishop[70]

Bishop
J. Maneye's tenement there [c], formerly J. Cantroun previously Wynter.[71]

From Broad Hithe to Liles Lane on the north side

Prior
Robert Maneye's tenement [e] \formerly Jocelin's and J. Punt's/
Richard Pikenham's tenement \formerly of W. the provisioner and T. the tanner/[72]
Emmotte Listere's tenement \formerly Matilda de Bury's, and afterwards J. the baker's/
William Haukyn's tenement \formerly of J. Albyne gatekeeper/
a tenement of John Herry[73] \labourer formerly of H. Bromele cook/
lying together from the broad bank to John Baxtere's tenement, and they contain 14 perches less 3 feet in front along the king's highway, and abut upon the ancient lode on the north.[74]

Bishop
John Baxtere's tenement[75]
Robert Skultoun's tenement [c] \formerly W. Laxtoun's/
Edmund Cotermong's tenement
John Brewere's tenement
John Kede's tenement
Alan Barker's tenement
Richard Masoun's tenement
John Moor's tenement
they are of the lord bishop's fee.

Prior
a tenement of John Crane tailor [e] \formerly of Adam Bonde and J. Deusmalyn/ lying between the tenement on the corner that is of the lord bishop's fee on the east, and a tenement of R. Lilleworth[76] that is of the lord bishop's fee, and it contains 2 perches less 3 feet in front along the highway, and abuts on the north upon Stock Hithe.

Bishop
John Lilleworth's tenement is of the lord bishop's fee, it contains in breadth 10 iron yards.

Prior
Godfrey Taillour's tenement [e]\formerly H. Fenlond's/ and John Herry baxter's tenement [e] \Peter Schopham's/ lying together between the said tenement of John Lilleworth and John Cheveyn's tenement of the lord bishop's fee, and they contain 3 perches less 1 foot in front along the king's highway, and abut upon Stock Hithe on the north.

Episcopi | tenens Johannes Skelyn
| tenens Henricus Allyne [illegible]
| tenens Alicia Porter | tenent de feodo domini episcopi Eliensis

Capite vii de Lillestane usque ad portam de Lilleshale

Episcopi | Mesuagium de tenente Alicie Porter [illegible]
| tenens Willelmi [illegible] | tenent de feodo domini episcopi

[illegible] | tenens Johannis [illegible] [illegible] [illegible] Johannis [illegible] ex parte [illegible] et tenens [illegible] Willelmi [illegible] ex parte [illegible] [illegible] [illegible] [illegible] [illegible] [illegible] [illegible] [illegible] [illegible] [illegible] [illegible] [illegible] [illegible] ad [illegible] [illegible] [illegible] [illegible] [illegible] [illegible] [illegible] [illegible] [illegible] domini episcopi

[illegible] | tenens [illegible] [illegible] [illegible] [illegible] [illegible]
Episcopi | tenens Johannis [illegible] | tenent de feodo domini episcopi
| tenens Johannis [illegible]
| [illegible] [illegible] [illegible] [illegible] de [illegible]

Capite orientali [illegible] Lillestane

Episcopi | [illegible] [illegible] [illegible] [illegible] [illegible] Johannis de feodo episcopi
[illegible] | [illegible] [illegible] [illegible] [illegible] [illegible] ex parte [illegible] de Lillestane [illegible] [illegible] [illegible] [illegible] [illegible] Johannis de feodo domini episcopi et tenens Johannis [illegible] ex parte [illegible] et [illegible] in [illegible] ex parte de Lillestane [illegible] [illegible] [illegible] [illegible] [illegible] domini episcopi.
Episcopi | [illegible] Johannis [illegible] est de feodo domini episcopi

Bishop
John Chevyn's tenement
Henry Albyn's tenement [c] \formerly *[illegible]*, covered with ivy, for 4½*d* pertaining to the bishop/[77]
Albreda Pilet's tenement
they are of the fee of the lord bishop of Ely.

On the east side of Liles Lane to the gate of Liles Close

Bishop
still Albreda Pilet's tenement with four cottages there under one roof
William Dounham's tenement
they are of the lord bishop's fee.
Prior
John Barkere's tenement [c] \formerly Agnes Grey's/ lying between a vacant plot of John Hunte on the east and a tenement lately William Dounham's on the west, it contains 1 perch 1 yard and 1 foot in front along the same lane, and it contains 4 perches and 2 iron yards and 1 foot in length towards the north, and in breadth at the north head along the ditch 6 perches 3½ yards of the lord king's iron yard.
Bishop
R.[78] Boston's tenement [c] \formerly Whithe's and afterwards Ralph Denver's formerly Richard Thede's/
John Eversholt's tenement
John Crane's tenement
two cottages there near the gate of Liles Holt
they are of the lord bishop's fee.

On the west side of the same Liles Lane

Bishop
a vacant plot pertaining to St John's house, of the bishop's fee.
Prior
two small cottages pertaining to the almoner [e] lying on the west side of Liles Lane between a vacant plot pertaining to St John's house of the lord bishop's fee and a tenement of John Plomer on the south, and they contain in front along Liles Lane 2 perches less ½ iron yard of the lord king.
Bishop
John Plomer's tenement [cel] is of the lord bishop's fee.

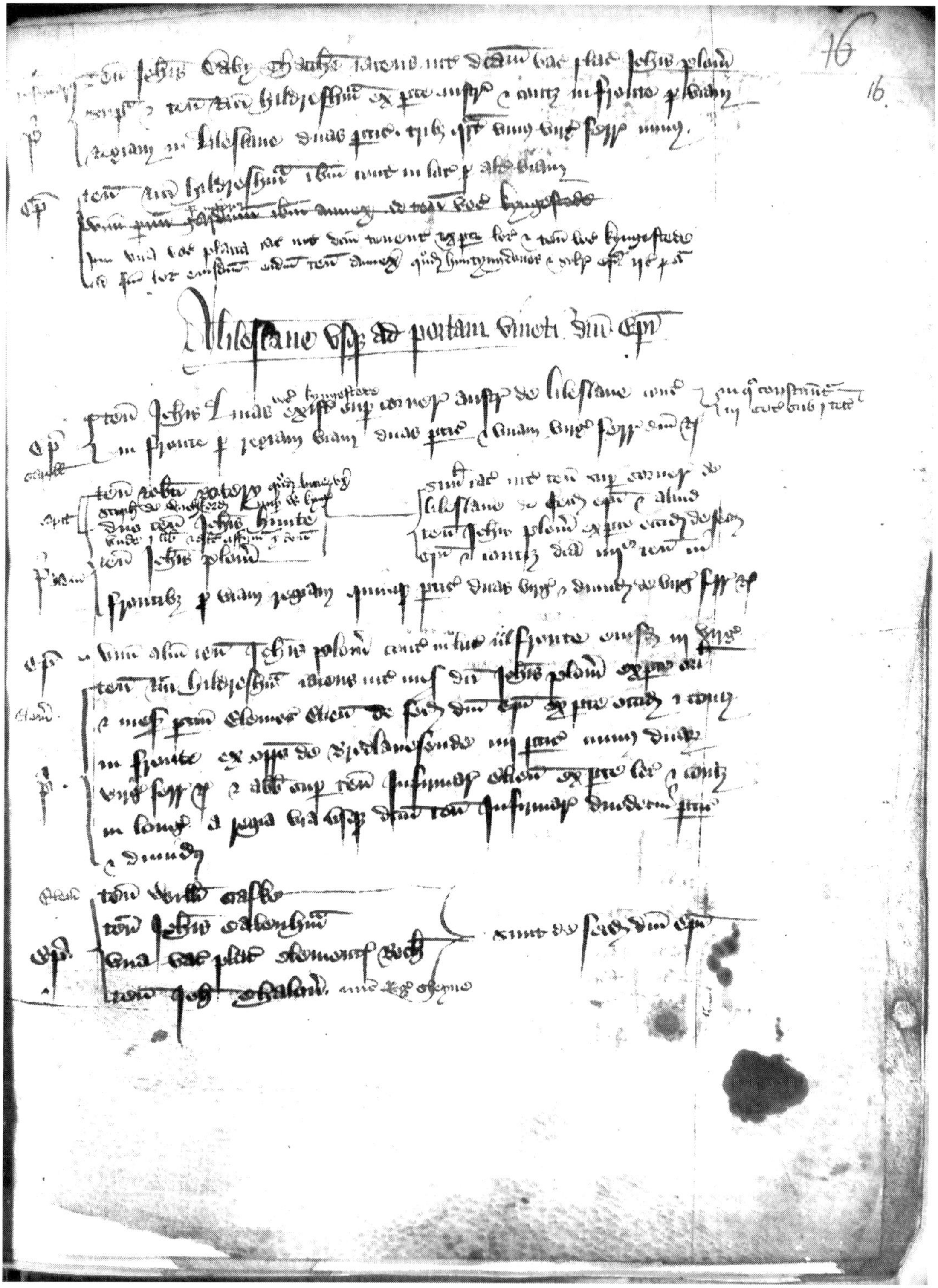

Prior
a tenement of John Davy thatcher [i] lying between the said vacant plot of John Plomer above and Richard Hildresham's tenement on the south, and it contains 2 perches less ¾ iron yard in front along the king's highway in Liles Lane.
Bishop
Richard Hildresham's tenement there contains in breadth along the highway *[blank]*
a small garden there annexed to a tenement called Kyngestede[79]
\also a vacant plot lying between the said tenement on the north and a tenement called Kyngestede, at the north boundary of the same, attached to the same tenement formerly Huntyngdone's, and it paid a rent of 2s annually to the bishop./

From Liles Lane to the gate of the lord bishop's vineyard

Bishop
John Lucas' tenement \called Kyngestede/ [c] situated on the south corner of Liles Lane, it contains in front along the king's highway 2 perches and 1 iron yard of the lord king
in which stand three cottages under one roof.

Prior
Robert Botery's tenement [c] \formerly of Lucy, wife of Stephen of Witchford, lately W. Kyng's/
two tenements of John Hunte [c] \one of which is free, the other owes 10*d* rent/
John Plomer's tenement [e]
lying together between the tenement on the corner of Liles Lane of the bishop's fee and another tenement of John Plomer on the west of the bishop's fee, and the said four tenements contain in front along the king's highway 5 perches 2½ yards of the king's iron yard.

Bishop
another tenement of John Plomer contains 3 yards in breadth in front.
Prior
Richard Hildresham's tenement [e], lying between a messuage of the said John Plomer on the east, and a messuage pertaining to the almoner of Ely of the lord bishop's fee on the west, and it contains in front opposite Broad Lane's end 4 perches less 2 iron yards of the king; and it abuts upon a tenement of the infirmarer of Ely on the north, and contains in length 12½ perches from the king's highway to the said tenement of the infirmarer.
Bishop
William Gaske's tenement [e]
John Cavenham's tenement
a vacant plot of Clement Bocher
John Chaloner's tenement \now of Roger Cheyne/
they are of the lord bishop's fee.

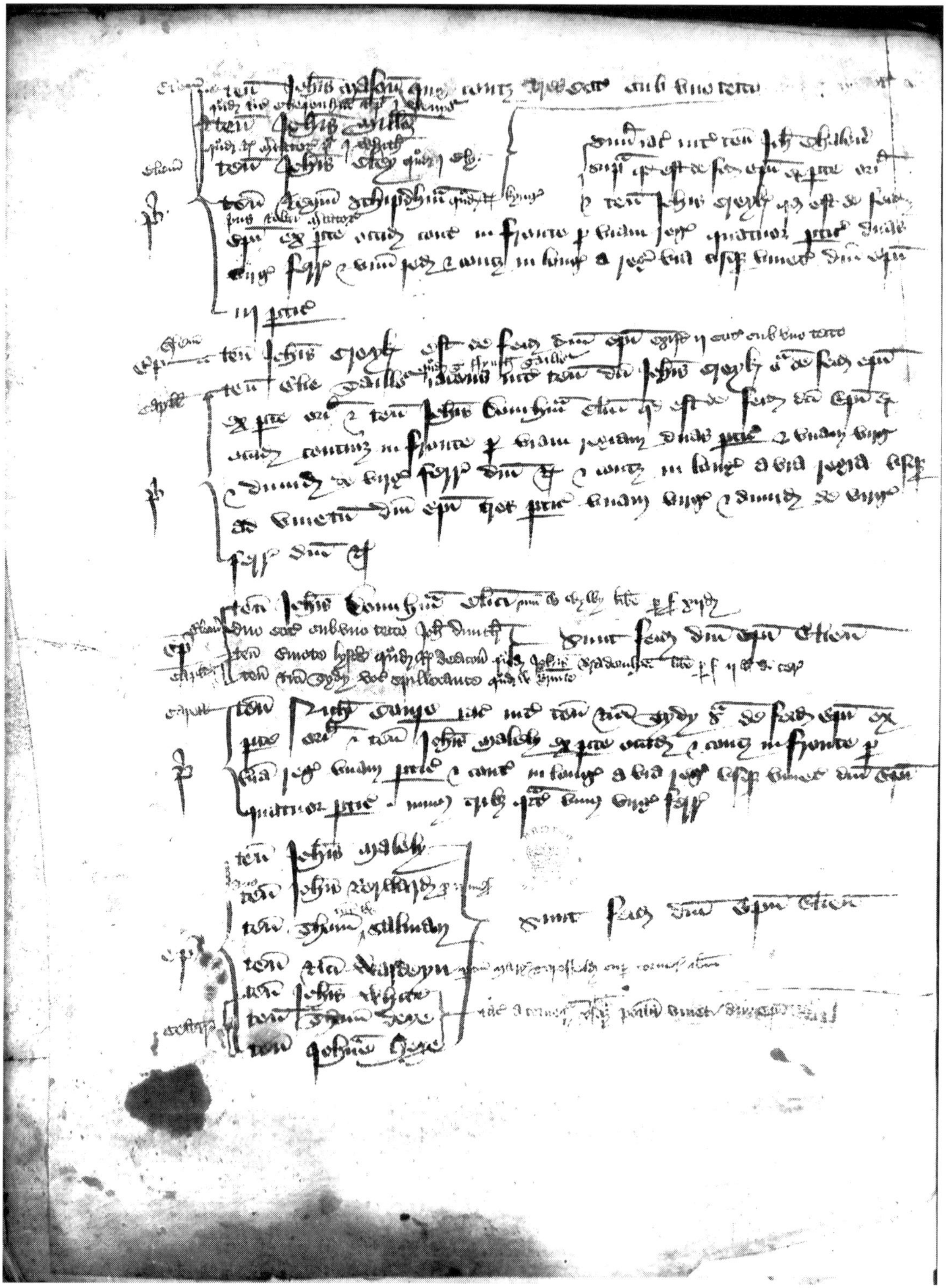

Prior
John Masoun's tenement [e] that contains three[80] cottages under one roof \formerly Richard Chepenham's and afterwards J. Wenyour's/
John Miller's tenement[81] \formerly of R. the merchant afterwards of J. Whith/[82]
John Cley's tenement \formerly J. Ely's/
Reginald Schipdham's tenement [e][83] \formerly R. Kyng's previously of Robert the merchant/
lying together between the above tenement of John Chaloner that is of the bishop's fee on the east and John Creyke's tenement that is of the bishop's fee on the west; they contain in front along the king's highway 4 perches 2 iron yards and 1 foot, and contain 3 perches in length from the king's highway to the lord bishop's vineyard.

Bishop
John Creyke's tenement [e] is of the lord bishop's fee \comprising two cottages under one roof/[84]

Prior
Elias Taillour's tenement [c] \formerly of T. Fynch tailor/ lying between the above tenement of the said John Creyke of the bishop's fee on the east and a tenement of John Dounham clerk that is of the said bishop's fee on the west; it contains in front along the king's highway 2 perches and 1½ yards of the lord king's iron yard, and contains in length from the king's highway to the lord bishop's vineyard 3 perches 1½ yards of the lord king's iron yard.

Bishop
a tenement of John Dounham clerk \now W. Wylby's freely by 12*d* service/
two cottages under one roof of J. Dunch [e]
Emmotte Lystere's tenement [c] formerly R. Deacon's \formerly John Bradenham's freely by service of two pounds of wax/
Richard Tydy's tenement [c] called Spillecance \formerly W. Brunne's/
they are of the lord bishop's fee.

Prior
Nicholas Coupere's tenement [c] lying between the above tenement of Richard Tydy of the bishop's fee on the east, and John Mabely's tenement on the west, and it contains 1 perch in front along the king's highway, and contains in length from the king's highway to the lord bishop's vineyard 4 perches less ¾ iron yard.

Bishop
John Mabely's tenement
\two/ tenement(s)[85] of John Berward \for two messuages/
a tenement of Thomas \now W./ Salman
Richard[86] Wardeyn's tenement \pertaining to Marg' Ropesfeld on the corner there/

John White's tenement [cel]
Thomas Deye's tenement [cel]
Joan Heye's tenement [cel]
\lying from the corner there to the gate of the bishop's vineyard/
they are of the fee of the lord bishop of Ely.

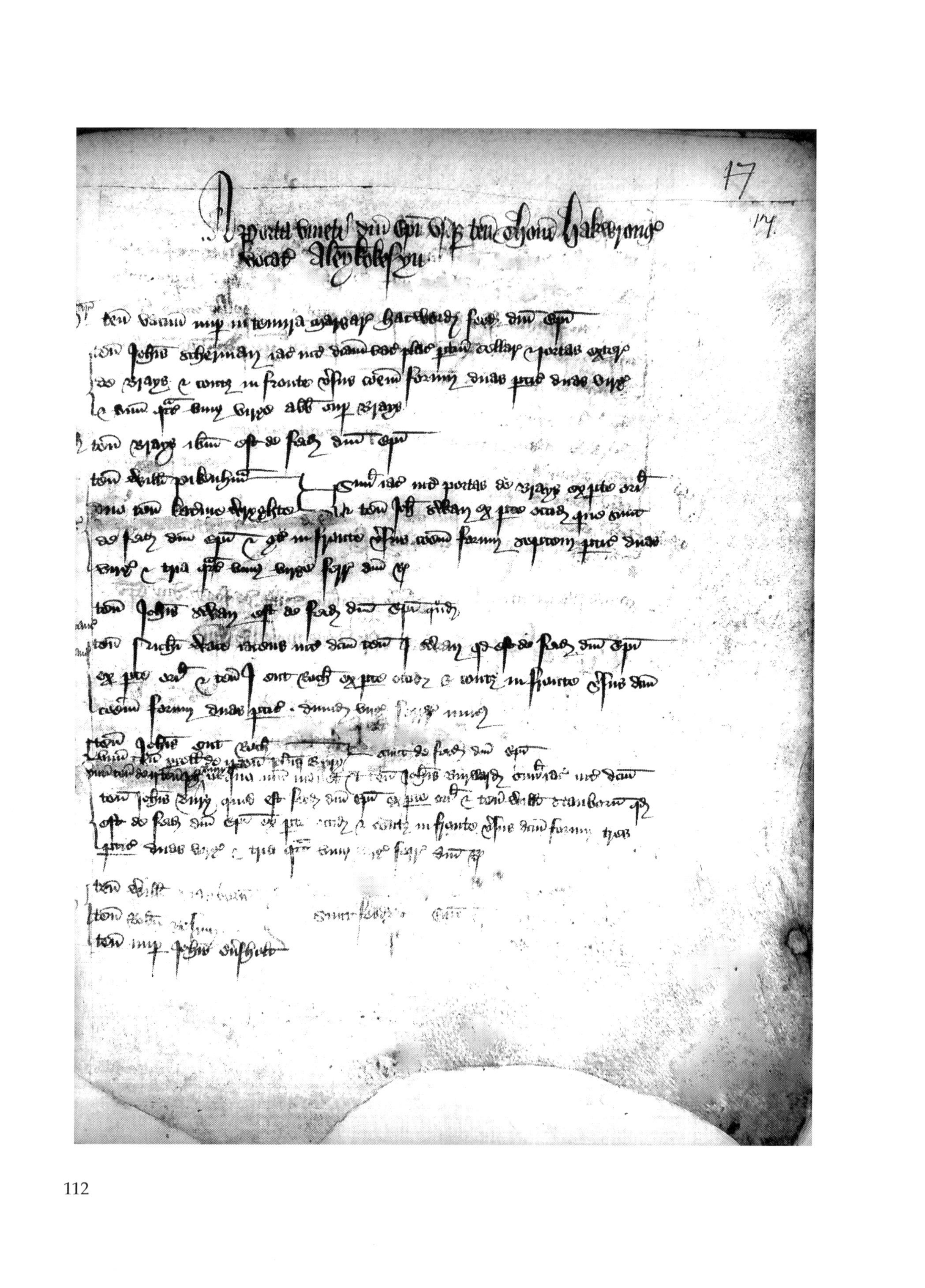

17

17

From the gate of the lord bishop's vineyard to a tenement of Thomas Hakwronge called Aleynkokesyn

Bishop

a vacant tenement [cel] lately in the tenure of Margaret Hacword, the lord bishop's fee.

Prior

John Scherman's tenement [sh] lying between the said vacant plot pertaining to the cellarer[87] and the outer gates of Brays, and it contains 2 perches 2¼ yards in front towards the common market, it abuts upon Brays.

Bishop

Brays tenement there [h] is of the lord bishop's fee.

Prior

William Pikenham's tenement[88]

two tenements of Katherine Wryghte [e][89]

lying together between the gates of Brays on the east, and John Swan's tenement on the west that are of the lord bishop's fee, and they contain in front towards the common market 7 perches 2¾ iron yards of the lord king.

Bishop

John Swan's tenement [p] is of the lord bishop's fee formerly *[blank]*[90]

[Prior]

Nicholas Wace's tenement [p][91] lying between the said tenement of J. Swan that is of the lord bishop's fee on the east and a tenement of John Cut butcher on the west, and it contains in front towards the said common market 2 perches less ½ iron yard.

Bishop

a tenement of John Cut butcher

one tenement, part of two tenements of John Bury

they are of the lord bishop's fee.

Prior

one tenement of the two tenements of John \Bury/ [s], in which he now resides,[92] and a tenement of John Burward,[93] lying together between the said tenement of John Bury that is of the lord bishop's fee on the east and the tenement of William Stanborum that is of the lord bishop's fee on the west, and they contain in front towards the said market 3 perches 2¾ iron yards of the lord king.

Bishop

William Stanborum's tenement

Robert Bosum's tenement

a tenement lately of John Eversholt

they are of the lord bishop's fee.

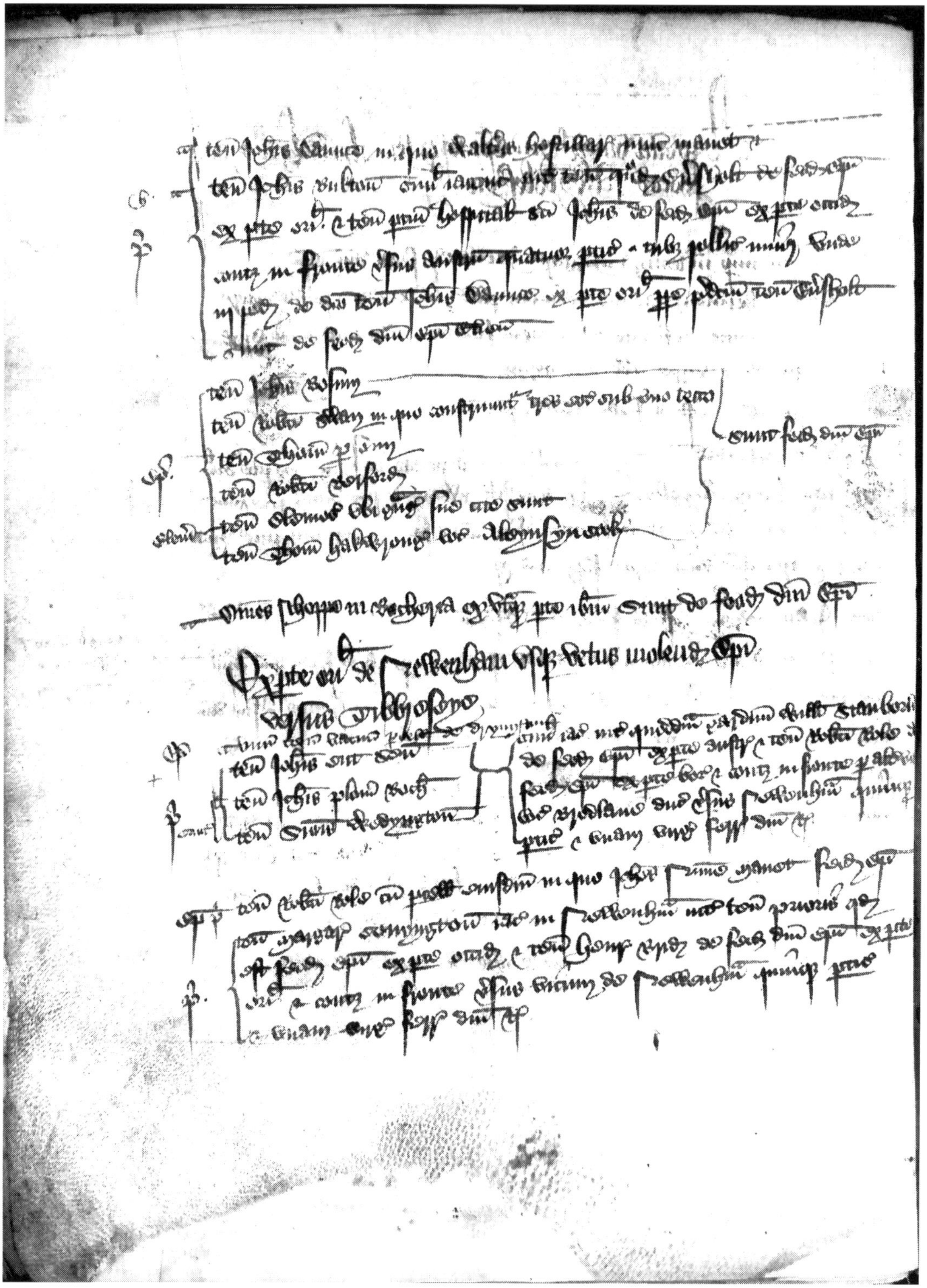

Prior
John Daunce's tenement[94] in which Walter the hosteler now resides and
John Bukton's tenement [sh] lying together between a tenement formerly Eversholt's of the bishop's fee on the east and a tenement pertaining to St John's hospital of the bishop's fee on the west, they contain in front towards the south 4 perches less 3 inches, of which 3 feet of John Daunce's said tenement on the east,[95] near the aforesaid tenement of Eversholt, are of the fee of the lord bishop of Ely.
Bishop
J. Bosum's tenement
a tenement of Robert Swan in which three[96] cottages are built under one roof
Thomas Persoun's tenement
Robert Berford's tenement
a tenement of the almoner where his barns lie [e]
a tenement of Thomas Hakwronge called Aleynsyncook
they are of the lord bishop's fee.

All the stalls in the butchery, on either side there, are of the lord bishop's fee.[97]

On the east side of Newnham to the bishop's old mill towards Turbutsey

\ *Bishop*
one vacant tenement part of Dryngstink/[98]
Prior
a tenement of John Cut senior[99]
a tenement of John Plomer butcher [can]
Simon Wedyngton's tenement [can]
lying together between a garden of William Stanborum of the bishop's fee on the south and Robert Bole's tenement of the bishop's fee on the north, and they contain in front along the highway called the broad lane leading towards Newnham 5 perches and 1 iron yard of the lord king.
Bishop
Robert Bole's tenement [pri] with a piece of the same in which John Nunne resides, of the bishop's fee.
Prior
Margaret Conyngton's tenement[100] lying in Newnham between the prior's tenement that is of the bishop's fee on the west and Henry Brid's tenement of the lord bishop's fee on the east, and it contains in front towards the street of Newnham 5 perches and 1 iron yard of the lord king.

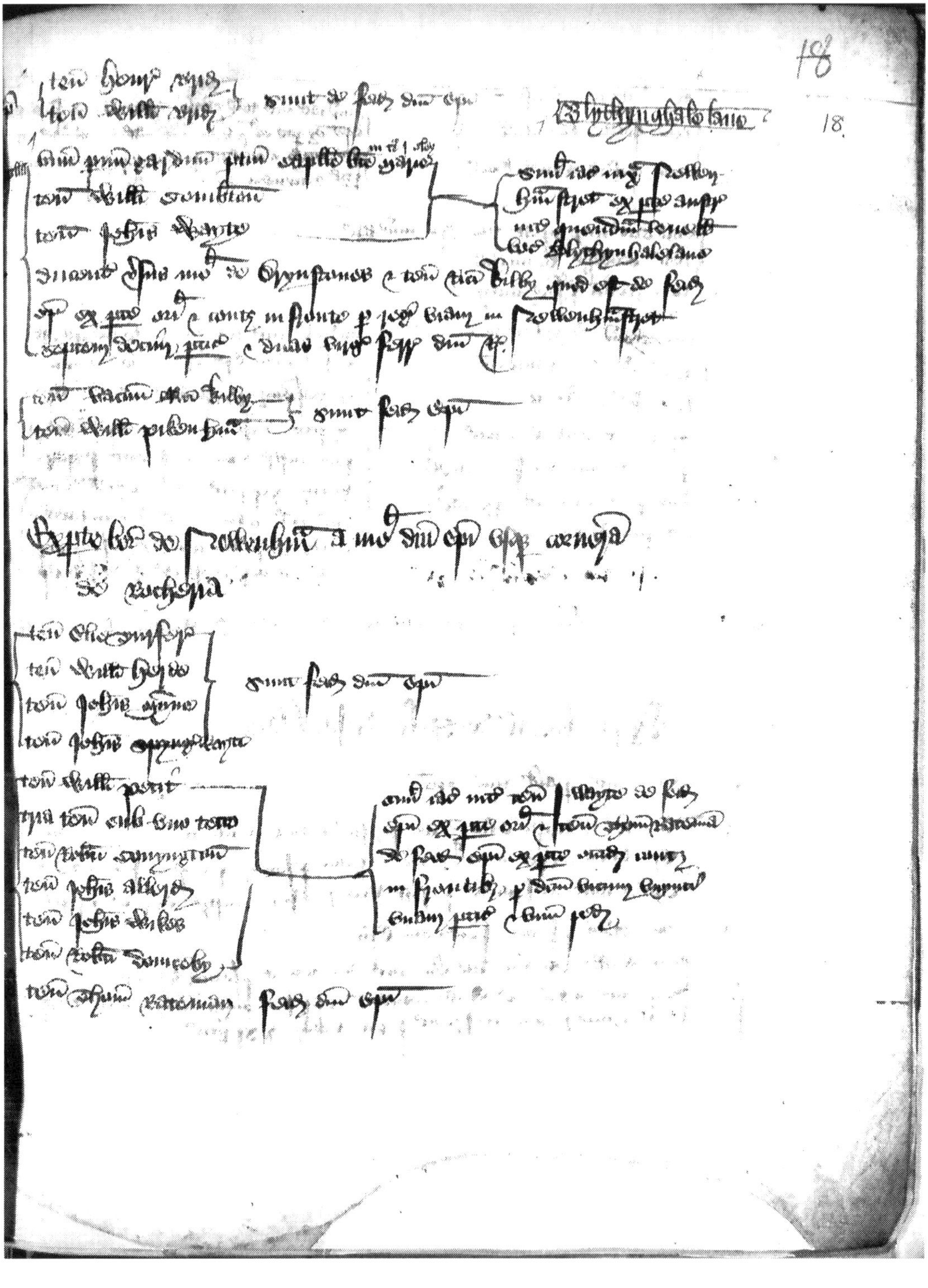

Bishop
Henry Brid's tenement
William Brid's tenement
they are of the lord bishop's fee.
Blithinghale Lane
Prior
a small garden pertaining to the Lady Chapel [c] \in the tenure of J. Cley/
William Comberton's tenement[101]
John Wayte's tenement
lying together next to Newnham Street on the south side between a lane called Blithinghale Lane leading towards Drynstones mill and Richard Kilby's tenement that is of the bishop's fee on the east, and they contain in front along the king's highway in Newnham Street 17 perches and 2 iron yards of the lord king.
Bishop
a vacant tenement of Richard Kilby
William Pikenham's tenement
they are of the bishop's fee.

On the north side of Newnham from the lord bishop's mill to the corner of the butchery
Bishop
Elias Turfer's tenement
William Herde's tenement
John Mynne's tenement
John Wayte's tenement
they are of the lord bishop's fee.
Prior
William Petit's tenement[102]
three tenements under one roof
Robert Conyngton's tenement
John Alberd's tenement
John Wikes' tenement[103]
Robert Domceby's tenement
lying together between J. Wayte's tenement of the bishop's fee on the east, and a tenement of Thomas Bateman[104] of the bishop's fee on the west, they contain in front along the said street 21 perches and 1 foot.
Bishop
Thomas Bateman's tenement, the lord bishop's fee.

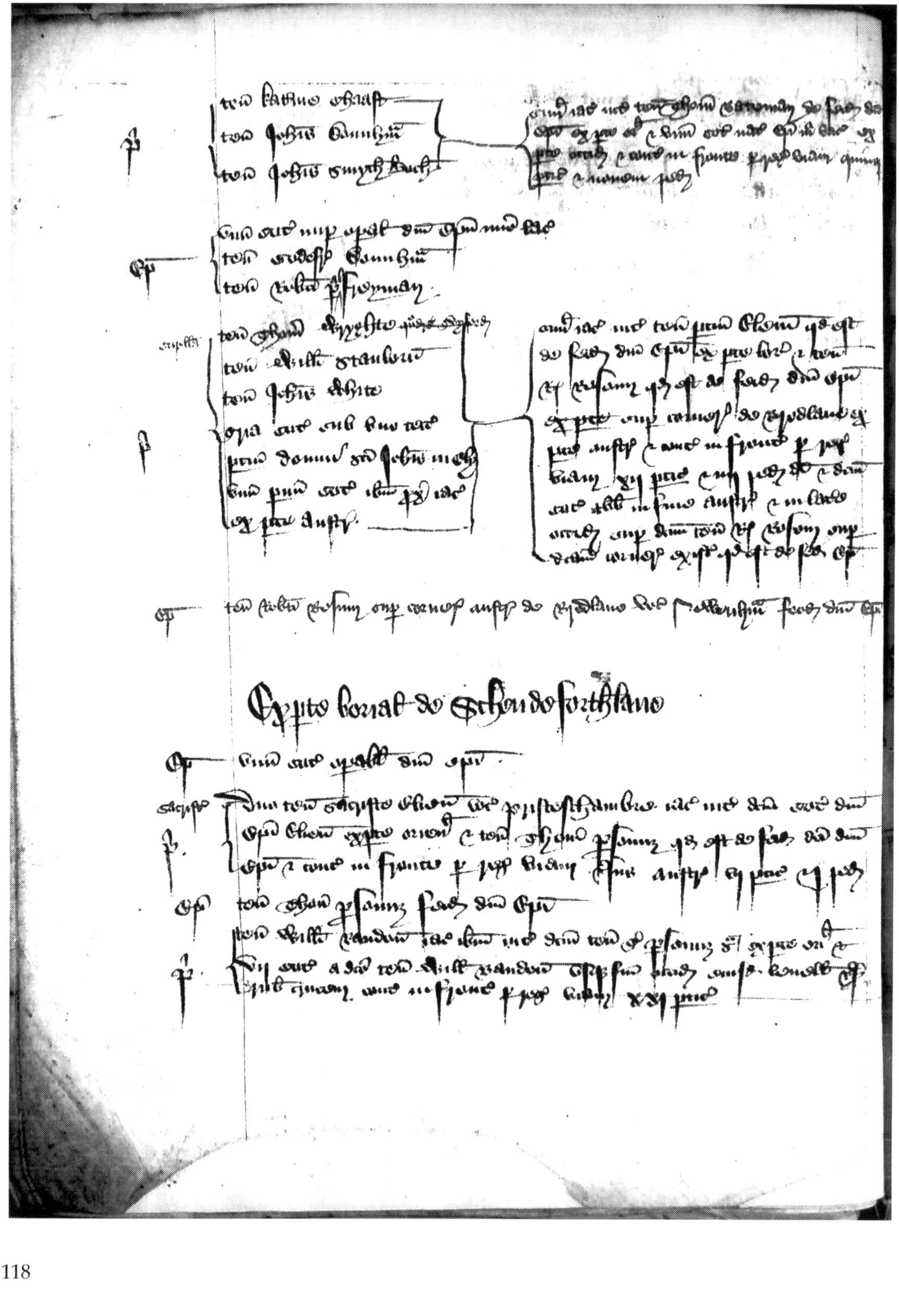

Prior
Katherine Chaast's tenement[105]
John Dounham's tenement
a tenement of John Smith butcher
\lying together between Thomas Bateman's tenement of the fee of the lord bishop on the east and a serf cot-land of the bishop now vacant on the west, and they contain 5 perches and 9 feet in front along the king's highway/[106]
Bishop
a cot-land of the lord bishop lately subject to labour-service, now vacant
Godfrey Dounham's tenement
Robert Palfreyman's tenement.
Prior
Thomas Wryghte's tenement [c] \formerly T. Syford/
William Stanborum's tenement[107]
John White's tenement[108]
three cottages under one roof pertaining to St John's house in Ely[109]
a small cottage nearest to it lying on the south side[110]
lying together between a tenement pertaining to the almoner that is of the lord bishop's fee on the north and a tenement of Robert Bosoun that is of the lord bishop's fee on the corner of the broad lane on the south, and they contain in front along the king's highway 12 perches and 4½ feet, and the said cottage abuts, on its south boundary and west side, upon the said tenement of Robert Bosom that is of the lord bishop's fee, situated on the said corner.
Bishop
Robert Bosum's tenement on the south corner of the broad lane called Newnham, the lord bishop's fee/

On the north side of Shendforth Lane

Bishop
a cot-land subject to labour-service, of the lord bishop.
Prior
two tenements of the sacrist of Ely called *Pristeschambre* [s], lying between the said cot-land of the lord bishop of Ely on the east and Thomas Persouns' tenement that is of the fee of the said lord bishop,[111] and they contain 6 perches and 1 foot in front along the king's highway towards the south.
Bishop
Thomas Persouns' tenement, the lord bishop's fee.
Prior
William Bandon's tenement[112] lying there between the said tenement of Thomas Persounz above, on the east and seven cottages from the said tenement of William Bandon to the west end of the same lane towards the red cross, they contain 21 perches in front along the king's highway.

19 19.

Ex parte austr' de Schendesforthlane

Unum cotsetill' dni Epi Elien'
tenet Willelmus ~~Comberton~~ Donyngton [illegible] [illegible] tenet Galfr' Dunham
quod est de feod' dni Epi ex parte occid' & unum cotsetill' dni Epi Elien'
ex parte orient' unde in fine [illegible] versus [illegible]
tenet Galfr' Dunham feod' dni Epi

Ex parte bor' de Agmondeshote

tenet Thomas Draper [illegible] in uno [illegible] terra feod' dni Epi
Unum [illegible] [illegible] [illegible] [illegible] tenet [illegible] [illegible] & [illegible] de
feod' dni Epi ex parte occid' & unam [illegible] placeam quod est de feod' dni
Epi ex parte orient' & unde in fine [illegible] [illegible] [illegible]
Una [illegible] placea ibidem est feod' dni Epi
Una tenet [illegible] [illegible] [illegible] [illegible] [illegible] placea [illegible] ex parte occid'
& unum tenet [illegible] dni Epi ex parte orient' & unde in fine [illegible]
[illegible] [illegible] [illegible] [illegible] [illegible] [illegible] [illegible].
tenet Willelmus [illegible]
tenet Johannes [illegible] } [illegible] de feod' dni Epi
tenet [illegible] [illegible]

Ex parte austr' de Agmondeshote.

On the south side of Shendforth Lane

Bishop
a cot-land of the lord bishop of Ely.
Prior
William Conyngton's tenement[113] lying there between a tenement of Geoffrey Dounham that is of the lord bishop's fee on the east, and a cot-land of the lord bishop of Ely on the west, it contains 5 perches in front along the king's highway.
Bishop
Geoffrey Dounham's tenement, the lord bishop's fee.

On the north side of Acreman Street

Bishop
Ellen Baret's tenement [c] comprising three cottages under one roof, the lord bishop's fee.
Prior
a cottage pertaining to the sacrist [s] lying between the above tenement formerly Barette's that is of the lord bishop's fee on the east, and a vacant plot that is of the lord bishop's fee on the west, and it contains 2 perches in front along the king's highway.
Bishop
a vacant plot there is of the lord bishop's fee.
Prior
two tenements[114] of Robert Brevetour [e] lying between the said vacant plot above on the east, and a serf tenement of the lord bishop on the west, and they contain 4 perches less ½ iron yard in front along the king's highway.
Bishop
William Ace's tenement
John Janyn's tenement
Ed' Schepherde's tenement
they are of the lord bishop's fee.

On the south side of Acreman Street

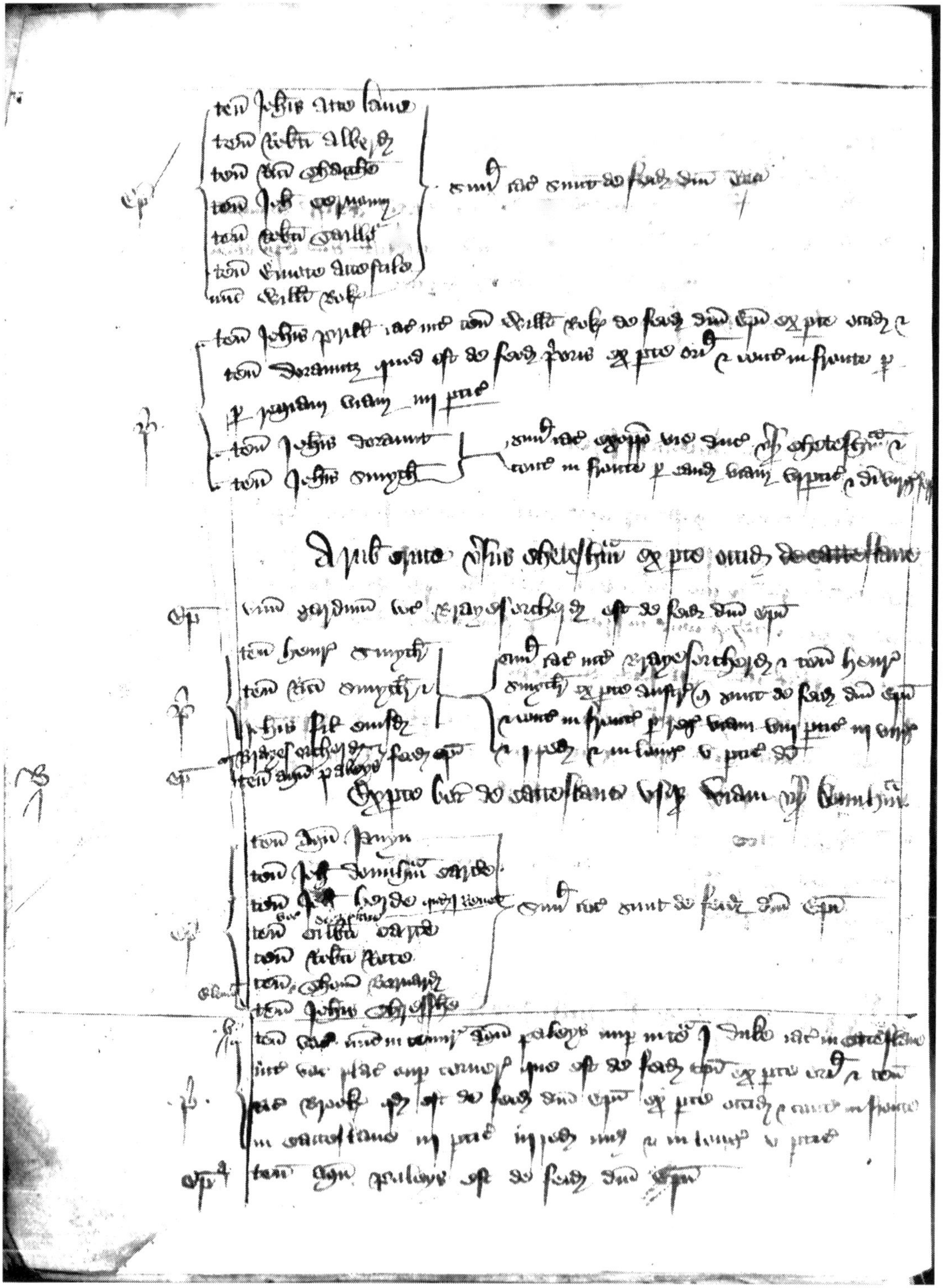

Bishop
John atte Lane's tenement
Robert Alberd's tenement
Richard Thacchere's tenement
John Gernoun's tenement
Robert Taillour's tenement
a tenement of Emmotte atte Stile now William Bok's
lying together, they are of the lord bishop's fee.
Prior
John Prill's tenement[115] lying between William Bok's tenement of the lord bishop's fee on the west, and Dorauntz' tenement that is of the prior's fee on the east, and it contains 4 perches in front along the king's highway.

John Doraunt's tenement[116]
John Smyth's tenement
lying together opposite the road leading towards Chettisham, and they contain 6 perches and ½ iron yard in front along the same road.

From the red cross towards Chettisham on the west side

Bishop
a garden called Brays orchard is of the lord bishop's fee.
Prior
Henry Smyth's tenement[117]
a tenement of Richard Smyth and of his son, John
lying together between Brays orchard[118] and Henry Smyth's tenement on the south that are of the lord bishop's fee, and they contain 8 perches 3 yards and 1 foot in front along the king's highway, and in length[119] 5½ perches.[120]
Bishop
Brays orchard[121]
Agnes Paleye's tenement
bishop's fee/

On the north side of Cats Lane to the road towards Little Downham

Bishop
Agnes Janyn's tenement
a tenement of John Dounham carter
John Herde's tenement \formerly J. Benet called Scotplace/
Gilbert Cartere's tenement
Robert Rote's tenement
Thomas[122] Bernard's tenement [e]
John Thresshere's tenement [e]
lying together, they are of the lord bishop's fee.
Prior[123]
a vacant tenement now in Agnes Paleys' tenure[124] lately in J. Duke's, lying in Cats Lane between a vacant plot on the corner that is of the bishop's fee on the east and Richard Brook's tenement that is of the lord bishop's fee on the west, and it contains 3 perches less 3 feet in front in Cats Lane, and 5 perches in length.[125]
Bishop[126]
Agnes Paleys' tenement is of the lord bishop's fee.[127]

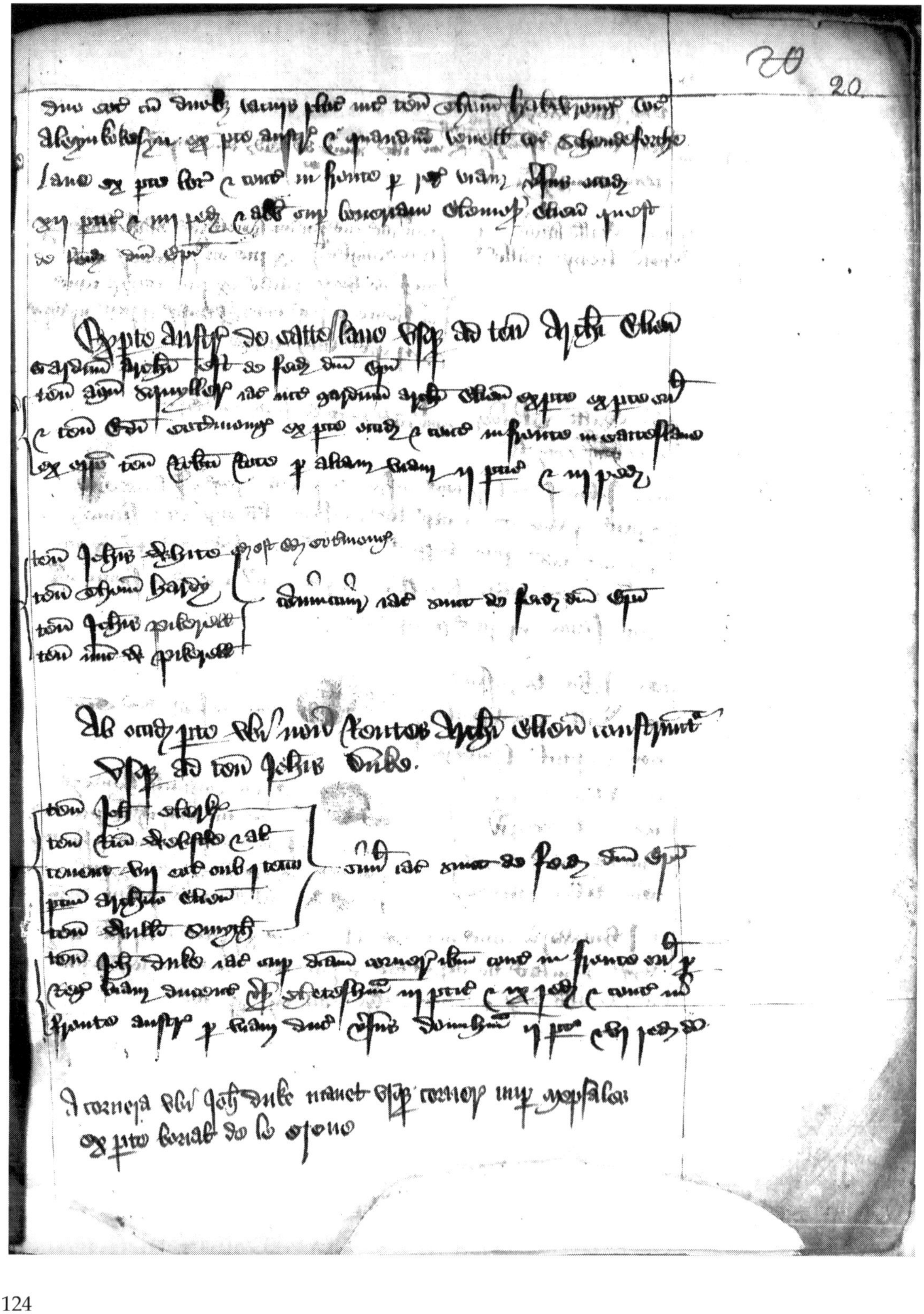

Prior[128]
two cottages with two vacant plots[129] [e] between the tenement of Thomas Hakwrong called Aleynkokesyn on the south, and a lane called Shendforth Lane on the north, and they contain 12 perches and 4 feet in front along the king's highway towards the west, and abut upon the almoner's ox-house that is of the lord bishop's fee.[130]

On the south side of Cats Lane to the tenement of the archdeacon of Ely

Bishop
the archdeacon's garden is of the lord bishop's fee.
Prior
Agnes Squyller's tenement [e][131] lying between the garden of the archdeacon of Ely on the east and Edmund Cotermong's tenement on the west, and it contains 2 perches and 3 feet along the highway in front in Cats Lane opposite Robert Rote's tenement.
Bishop
John White's tenement \that is of Edmund Cotermong/[132]
Thomas Hardy's tenement
John Pikerell's tenement
a tenement now of W. Pickerell
lying together, they are of the lord bishop's fee.

From the west side where the archdeacon of Ely's new rents are built to John Duke's tenement[133]

Bishop
John Clerk's tenement
a tenement of Richard Webster and other tenants, being seven cottages under one roof pertaining to the archdeacon of Ely[134]
William Smyth's tenement
lying together they are of the lord bishop's fee.
Prior
John Duke's tenement[135] lying on the said corner there, it contains 3 perches and 9 feet on the east frontage along the king's highway leading towards Chettisham, and it contains 2 perches and 6½ feet[136] on the south frontage along the road leading towards Little Downham.

From the corner where John Duke lives to the corner lately Mepsale's on the north side of the Green[137]

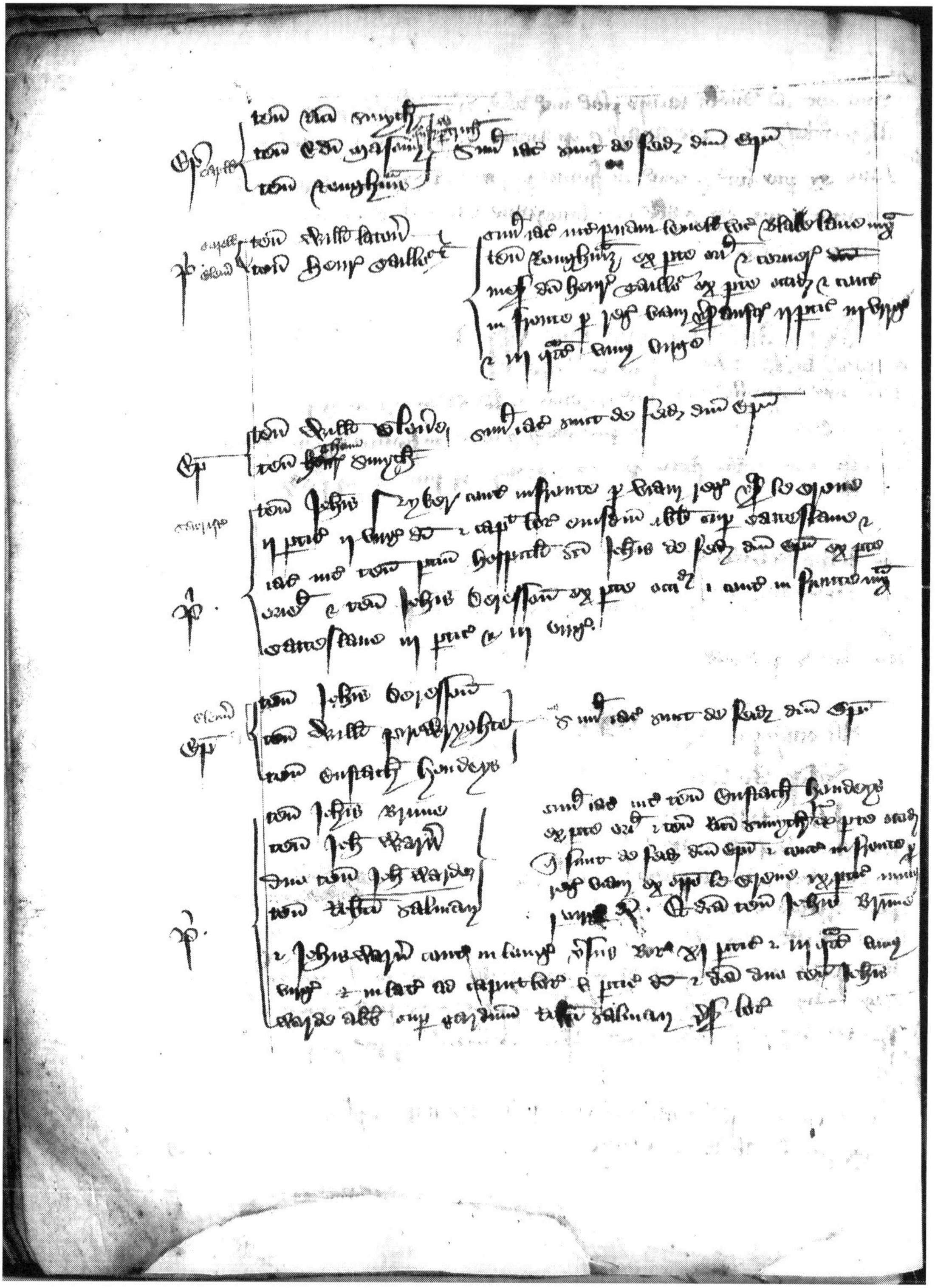

Bishop
Richard Smyth's tenement
Ed' Masoun's tenement [c] \formerly of W. Pertrich/
Rougham's tenement[138]
lying together, they are of the lord bishop's fee.
Prior
William Latoner's tenement [c][139]
Henry Taillour's tenement [e]
lying together between a small lane called Blake Lane next to Rougham's tenement on the east and the corner of the messuage of the said Henry Taillour on the west,[140] and they contain 2 perches 3¾ yards in front along the king's highway towards the south.
Bishop
William Glovere's tenement
Thomas Smyth's tenement
lying together, they are of the lord bishop's fee.
Prior
John Nyker's tenement [s] contains 2 perches 2½ yards in front along the king's highway towards the Green, and its north head abuts upon Cats Lane, and it lies between a tenement pertaining to St John's hospital of the lord bishop's fee on the east, and John Deresson's tenement on the west, and it contains 3 perches and 3 yards in front next to Cats Lane.

Bishop
John Deresson's tenement [e]
William Prowryghte's[141] tenement [e]
Eustace Hondey's tenement
lying together, they are of the lord bishop's fee.
Prior
John Brunne's tenement[142]
John Warner's tenement
two tenements of John Warde[143]
Robert Salman's tenement
lying together between Eustace Hondey's tenement on the east and a tenement of Richard Smyth \junior/ on the west that are of the lord bishop's fee, and they contain 9 perches less 1½ yards in front along the king's highway opposite the Green; and the said tenements of John Brunne and John Warner contain 11 perches and ¾ yard in length[144] towards the north, and 5½ perches in breadth at the north head, and the said two tenements of John Warde abut upon Robert Salman's garden towards the north.

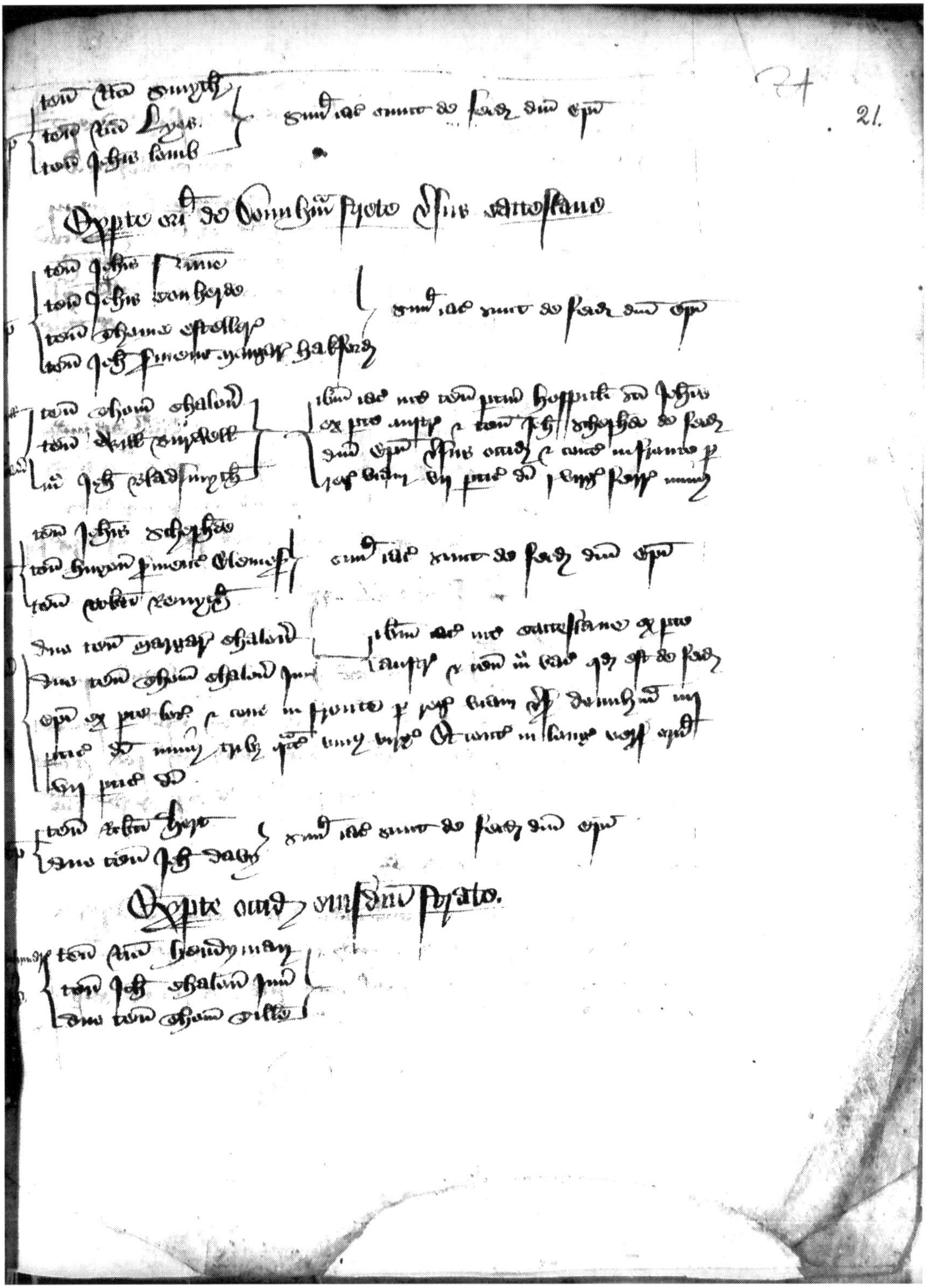
21.

Bishop
Richard Smyth's tenement
Richard Lye's tenement
John Lomb's tenement
lying together, they are of the lord bishop's fee.

On the east side of Downham Street towards Cats Lane

Bishop
John Nunne's tenement
John Couherde's tenement
Thomas Osteller's tenement
a tenement of John, servant of Margaret Hakford
lying together, they are of the lord bishop's fee.
Prior
a tenement of Thomas Chaloner [c][145]
William Burwell's tenement [e], now John Bladsmyth's
lying there between a tenement pertaining to St John's hospital on the south and John Scheperde's tenement[146] of the lord bishop's fee towards the west, and they contain 7½ perches less 1 iron yard in front along the king's highway.
Bishop
John Schepherde's tenement
a tenement of Hugh, a servant of the almoner
Robert Benyth's tenement
lying together, they are of the lord bishop's fee.
Prior
two tenements of Margaret Chaloner [e][147]
two tenements of Thomas Chaloner junior [e?][148]
lying there between Cats Lane on the south and a tenement now vacant that is of the bishop's fee on the north, and they contain 4½ perches less ¾ yard in front along the king's highway towards Little Downham; and they contain 7½ perches in length towards the east.
Bishop
Robert Hert's tenement
two tenements of John Davy
lying together, they are of the lord bishop's fee.

On the west side of the same street

Prior
Richard Hendyman's tenement [i][149]
a tenement of John Chaloner junior[150]
two tenements of Thomas Tillere[151]

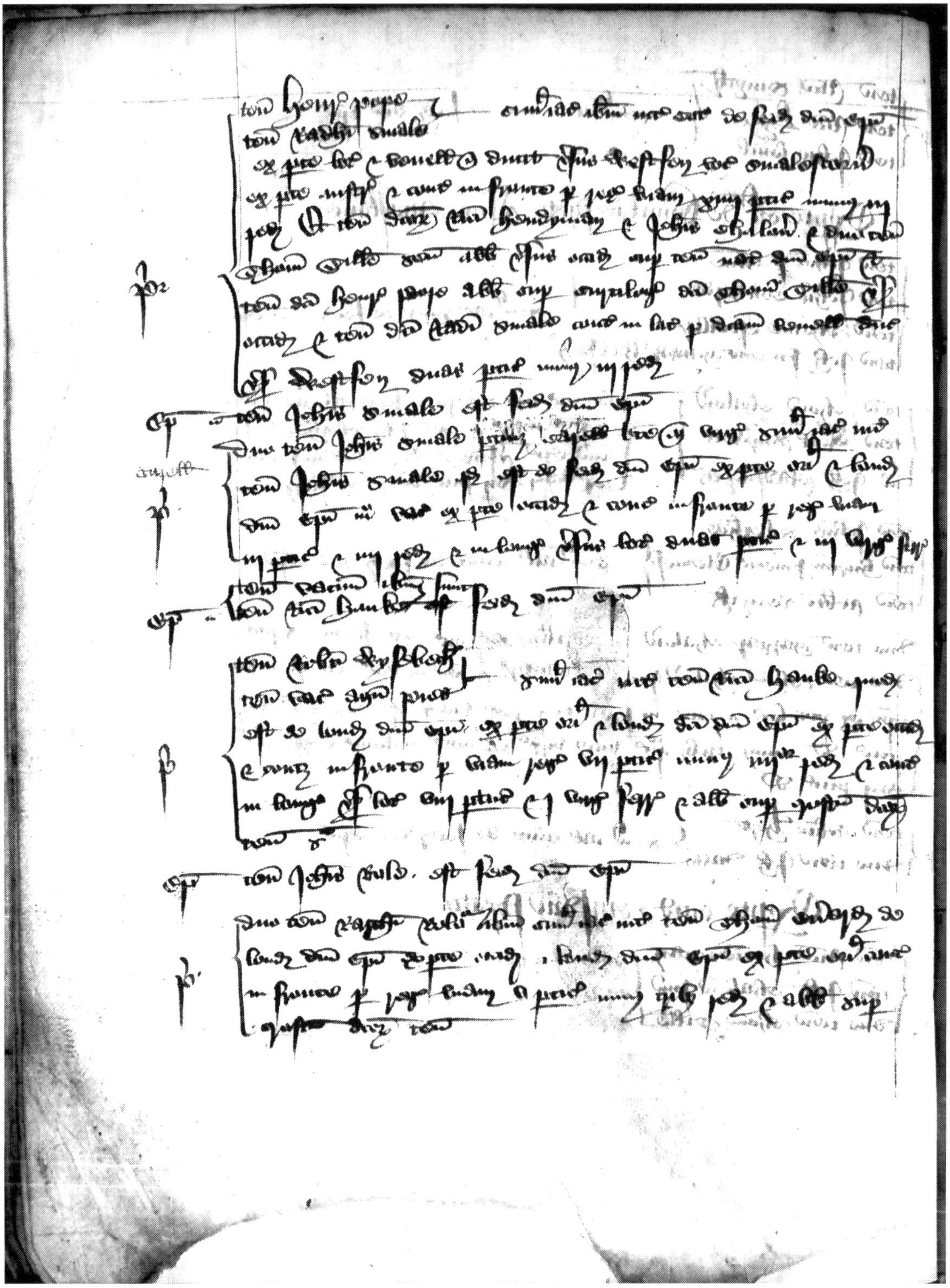

Prior
Henry Pope's tenement[152]
Ralph Smale's tenement[153]
lying together there between a cot-land of the lord bishop's fee on the north and a lane that leads towards West Fen called Smale's corner on the south, and they contain 14 perches less 3 feet in front along the king's highway; and the tenements of the said Richard Hendyman and John Chaloner and the two tenements of Thomas Tillere senior abut towards the west upon a serf tenement of the lord bishop, and the tenement of the said Henry Pope abuts upon the curtilage of the said Thomas Tillere towards the west; and the tenement of the said Ralph Smale contains in breadth 2 perches less 3 feet along the said lane leading towards West Fen.
Bishop
John Smale's tenement is of the lord bishop's fee.
Prior
two tenements of John Smale [c][154] pertaining to the Lady Chapel lying together between John Smale's tenement that is of the lord bishop's fee on the east and a holding of the lord bishop's bondage now vacant on the west, and they contain 3 perches and 4 feet in front along the king's highway, and 2 perches and 3 iron yards in length towards the north.
Bishop
a vacant tenement there
Richard Hauke's tenement
they are of the lord bishop's fee.
Prior
a tenement of Robert Wysebech[155]
a vacant tenement of Agnes Pie
lying together between Richard Hauke's tenement that is of the lord's bondage on the east, and a holding of the said lord bishop's bondage on the west; and they contain 7 perches less 4 feet in front along the king's highway, and they contain 8 perches and 1 iron yard in length towards the north and abut upon the croft of the said tenements above.
Bishop
John Bole's tenement is of the lord bishop's fee.
Prior
two tenements of Bartholomew Bolour[156] there lying together between Thomas Everard's tenement of the lord bishop's bondage on the west, and a holding of the lord bishop's bondage on the east; they contain 5 perches less 3 feet in front along the king's highway and abut upon the crofts of the said tenements.

88

22.

dom Thome [illegible] obiit de [illegible] dni epi

Capitulo [illegible] celebrato de West[illegible] mag Johis [illegible]

dom Johis [illegible]
dom [illegible]
dom Henr [illegible]
dom [illegible]
dom mag [illegible]
— sunt [illegible] de [illegible] dni epi

dom Johis Pikworth
Ricus [illegible]
dno dom [illegible]
— sunt isti [illegible] [illegible] obiit de [illegible] epi [illegible] [illegible] de [illegible] dni epi [illegible] in Francia [illegible]

[illegible] [illegible] [illegible] dni epi

dom Johis [illegible] obiit de [illegible] dni epi

Capitula [illegible] dom [illegible] de [illegible]

[illegible]

dom [illegible]
dom Johis [illegible]
dom Johis [illegible]
dom [illegible]
dom dom [illegible]
dom Johis [illegible]
dom [illegible]
dom Johis [illegible]
dom Joh [illegible]
dom [illegible]
dom [illegible]
dom Johis [illegible]
— sunt isti sunt de [illegible] dni epi

Bishop
Thomas Everard's tenement is of the lord bishop's fee.

On the south side of the same street of West Fen to the tenement lately John Mepsale's

Bishop
John Heyward's tenement
an unoccupied tenement
Henry Peddere's tenement
Ralph Spellere's tenement
a tenement lately John Clare's
lying together, they are of the lord bishop's fee.
Prior
John Pikworth's tenement formerly Russell[157]
two tenements of Christiana Snoryng [can]
lying together between David Llanlidan's tenement that is of the bishop's fee on the west and a cot-land that is of the lord bishop's bondage on the east, and they contain in front towards the said street 14 perches less 6 feet, and abut upon a holding of the lord bishop's bondage.
Bishop
John Bladsmyth's tenement is of the lord bishop's fee.

From the highway from Mepsale's tenement to the West Fen, on the north side

Bishop
Richard Massenger's tenement
John Bladsmyth's tenement
John Alderet's tenement
Robert Jakkesson's tenement
Ralph Smale's tenement
John Reyne's tenement
Maurice Taillour's tenement
John Pulham's tenement
John Skot's tenement
Robert Gyssyng's tenement
Robert Glovere's tenement
John Swyft's tenement
lying together, they are of the lord bishop's fee.

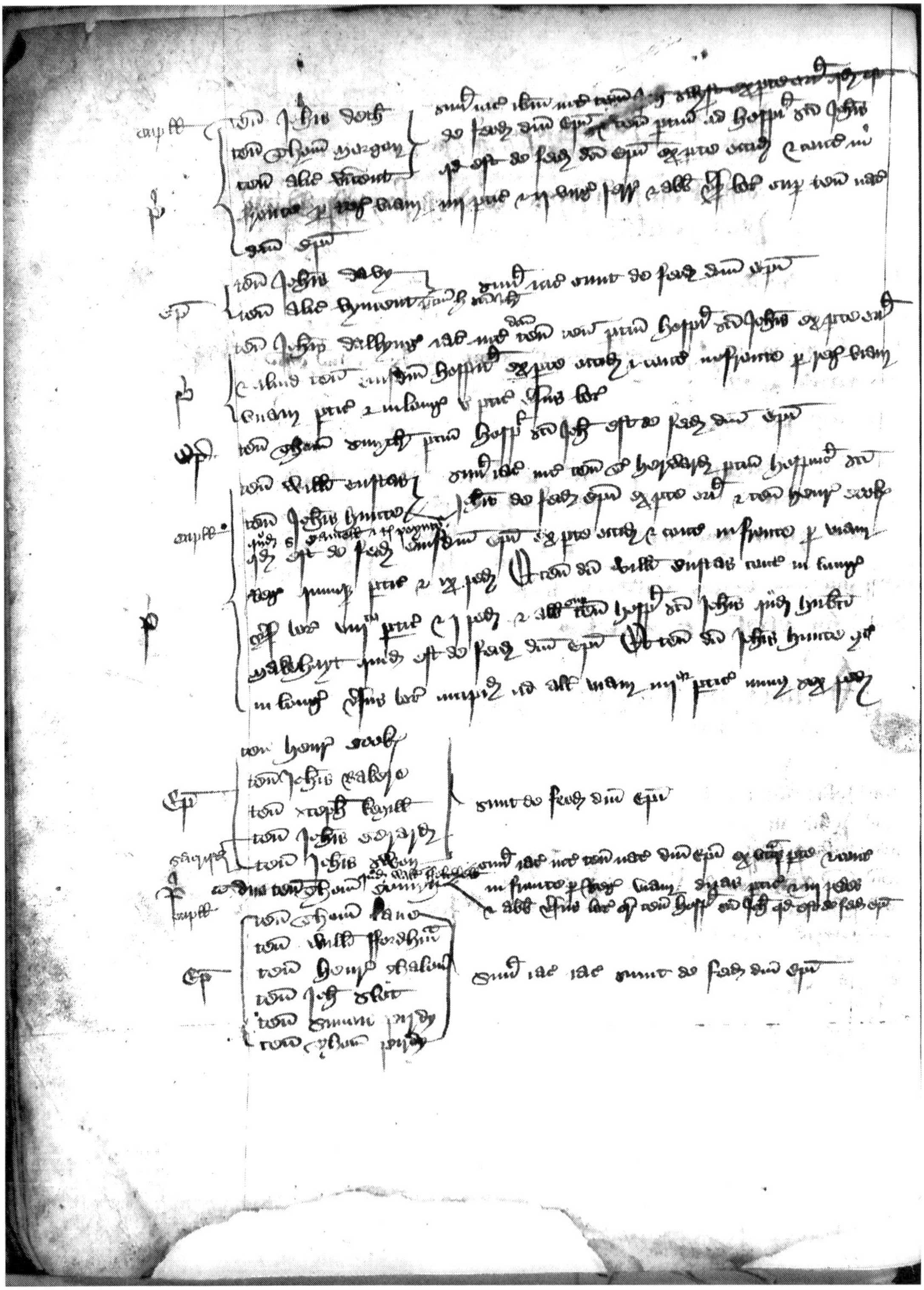

Prior
John Deth's tenement [c][158]
Thomas Morgan's tenement
Alice Vincent's tenement
lying together there between John Swyft's tenement on the east that is of the lord bishop's fee and a tenement pertaining to St John's hospital that is of the lord bishop's fee on the west, and they contain 4 perches and 2 iron yards in front along the king's highway, and abut towards the north upon a serf tenement of the lord bishop.
Bishop
John Davy's tenement
Alice Vyncent's tenement \pertaining to St John's hospital/[159]
lying together, they are of the lord bishop's fee.
Prior
John Dallyng's tenement[160] lying between the said tenement pertaining to St John's hospital on the east and another tenement of the same hospital on the west, and it contains 1 perch in front along the king's highway, and 5 perches in length towards the north.
Bishop
Thomas Smyth's tenement pertaining to St John's hospital is of the lord bishop's fee.
Prior
William Eustas' tenement[161]
John Hunte's tenement [c] \formerly S. Gamell's and R. Peyntour's/
lying together between T. Herward's tenement pertaining to St John's hospital of the bishop's fee on the east and Henry Cook's tenement that is of the same bishop's fee on the west, and they contain 5 perches and 9 feet in front along the king's highway; and the tenement of the said William Eustas contains 8 perches and 1 foot in length towards the north, and abuts upon a tenement of St John's hospital formerly Hubert Makehayt's that is of the lord bishop's fee; and the tenement of the said John Hunte contains 4 perches less 6 feet in length towards the north, beginning at the highway.
Bishop[162]
Henry Cook's tenement
John Bakere's tenement
Stephen Kegill's tenement
John Gerard's tenement [s]
John Swon's tenement [s]
they are of the lord bishop's fee.
Prior
two tenements of Thomas Comyn[163] [c] \formerly Walter Feltewell's/
lying together between serf tenements of the lord bishop on either side, and they contain 2 perches and 3 feet in front along the king's highway, and abut towards the north upon a tenement of St John's hospital that is of the bishop's fee.
Bishop
Thomas Lane's tenement [c]
William Fordham's tenement
Henry Chaloner's tenement
John Skot's tenement
Simon Pirdy's tenement
Thomas Pirdy's tenement
lying together, they are of the lord bishop's fee.

23

Ex p'te occ' cursus aque de Westh'm usq' ad fin' ville vocat' Est'e Wichford

ten' Kemersdon ten' Joh'is Horsnap ten' Joh'is Lufford ten' Joh'is Ashburn ten' Will'i Morgan ten' Thome Crane	sunt lib'e tenur' de feod' d'ni Ep'i

Ex p'te austr' cursus aque a hosp' [illegible] Joh'is usq' [illegible] Magistro

ten' Joh'is [illegible] ten' Will'i Waldeyn ten' Joh'is Dack ten' Ric' Payn ten' Thome Page	sunt lib'e tenur' de feod' [illegible] d'ni Ep'i

ten' Joh'is Hacker lib'e ten' [illegible] d'no Ep'o [illegible] [illegible] [illegible] in fronte [illegible] [illegible] [illegible] [illegible] [illegible] [illegible] aque [illegible] [illegible] [illegible] [illegible] [illegible] ad caput aque [illegible] [illegible] [illegible]

ten' Thome Lamleye est de feod' d'ni Ep'i

Ex p'te orient' cursus [illegible] [illegible]

ten' Jo' Lapford lib'e ten' ex p'te occ' [illegible] [illegible] in fronte [illegible] [illegible] [illegible] [illegible] [illegible] [illegible] [illegible] [illegible] [illegible] [illegible] [illegible] [illegible] [illegible] [illegible] [illegible] [illegible] [illegible] [illegible] ad caput aque [illegible]

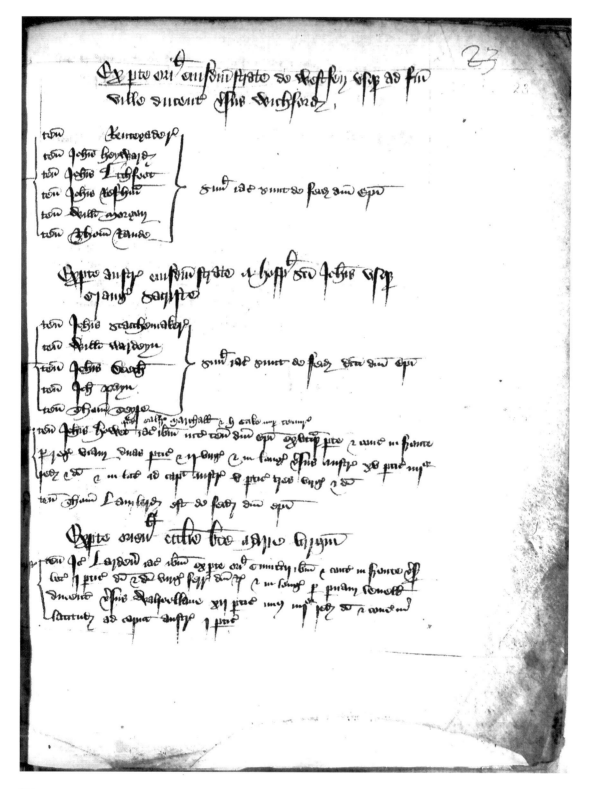

On the east side of the same street of West Fen to the limits of the town leading towards Witchford[164]

Bishop
a tenement of *[blank]* Rentegaderer
John Heyward's tenement
John Lithfoot's tenement
John Recham's tenement
William Morgon's tenement
Thomas Rande's tenement
lying together, they are of the lord bishop's fee.

On the south side of the same street from St John's hospital to the sacrist's barn[165]

Bishop
John Scacchemakerer's tenement
William Wardeyn's tenement
John Deeth's tenement
John Payn's tenement
Thomas Teype's tenement
lying together, they are of the lord bishop's fee.
Prior
John Howet's tenement [c] \formerly Geoffrey Marchall's and lately H. Cake's tenure/[166] lying there beween tenements of the lord bishop on either side, and it contains 2 perches and 2 yards in front along the king's highway, and 15 perches 4½ feet in length towards the south, and 5 perches 3½ yards in breadth at the south head.
Bishop
Thomas Lamberd's tenement is of the lord bishop's fee.

On the east side of St Mary's church

Prior
Isabel Lardener's tenement [s] lying there on the east side of the churchyard there, and it contains in front towards the north 1½ perches[167] and ½ iron yard of the lord king, and 12 perches less 4½ feet in length along the small lane leading towards Walpole Lane, and it contains 1 perch in breadth at the south head.

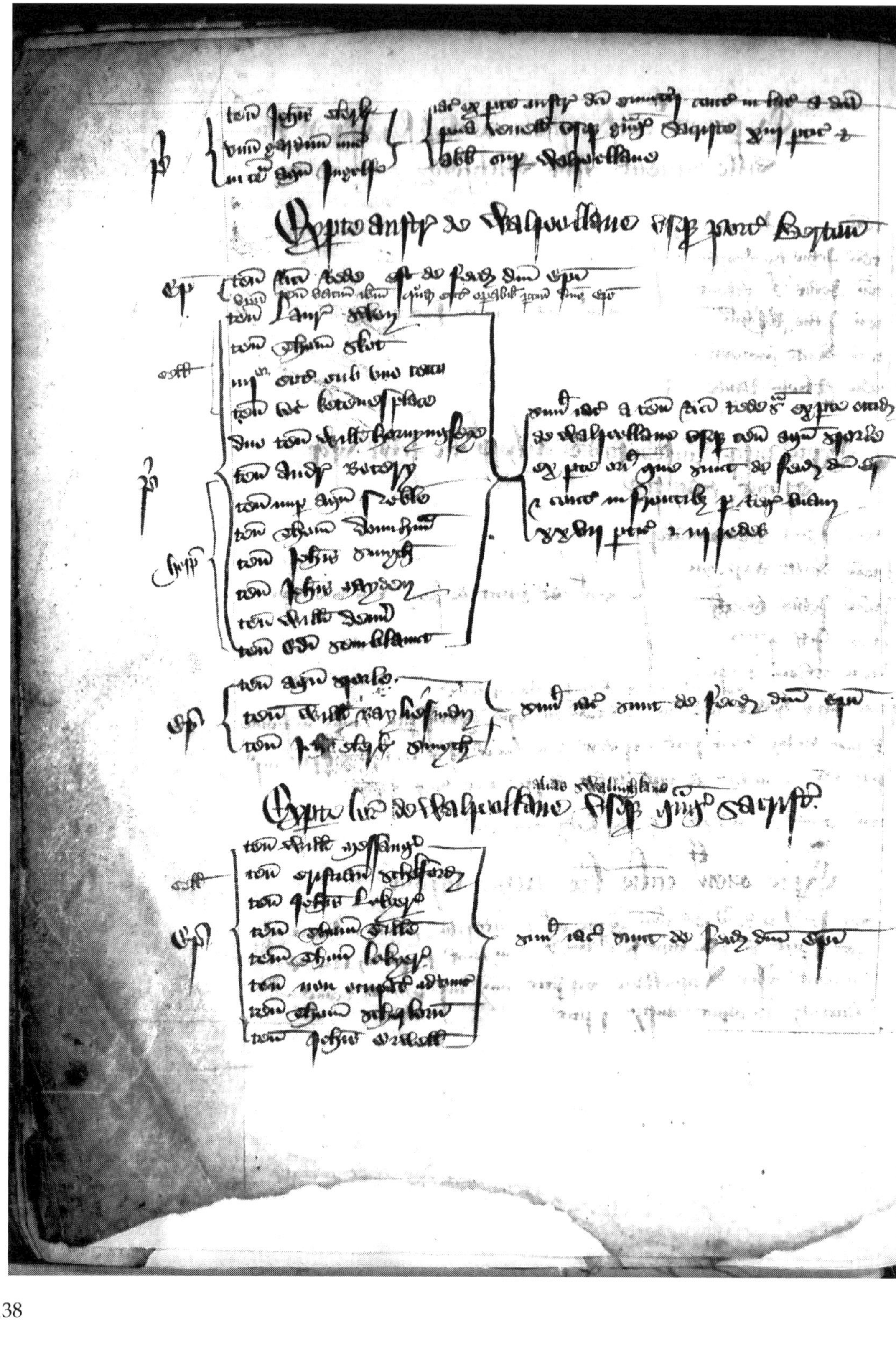

Prior
John Clerk's tenement
a garden now in the tenure of Agnes Ingolf[168]
lying on the south side of the said churchyard, they contain 13 perches in breadth from the said small lane to the sacrist's barn, and abut upon Walpole Lane.

On the south side of Walpole Lane to Barton gate

Bishop
Richard Rede's tenement is of the lord bishop's fee
\a vacant tenement there formerly a cot-land subject to labour-service pertaining to the lord bishop/
Prior
Laurence Swon's tenement [cel]
Thomas Skot's tenement [cel]
four cottages under one roof [cel]
a tenement called Ketenesplace [cel]
two tenements of William Hornyngseye[169]
Andrew Botery's tenement [sh]
a tenement lately Agnes Noble's [sh]
Thomas Dounham's tenement [sh]
John Smyth's tenement [sh]
John Mayden's tenement [sh]
William Denver's tenement [sh]
Ed' Semblaunt's tenement [sh][170]
lying together from the above tenement of Richard Rede on the west side of Walpole Lane to Agnes Sporle's tenement on the east that are of the lord bishop's fee, and they contain 27 perches and 3 feet in front along the king's highway.
Bishop
Agnes Sporle's tenement
William Bayliesman's tenement
a tenement of John Clerk smith
lying together, they are of the lord bishop's fee.

On the north side of Walpole Lane \alias Swallow Lane/ to the sacrist's barn

Bishop
William Messanger's tenement
Christiana Schelford's tenement [cel]
John Lokyer's tenement
Thomas Tillere's tenement
Thomas Lokyer's tenement
a tenement not occupied at the time
Thomas Scherborn's tenement
John Orwell's tenement
lying together, they are of the lord bishop's fee.

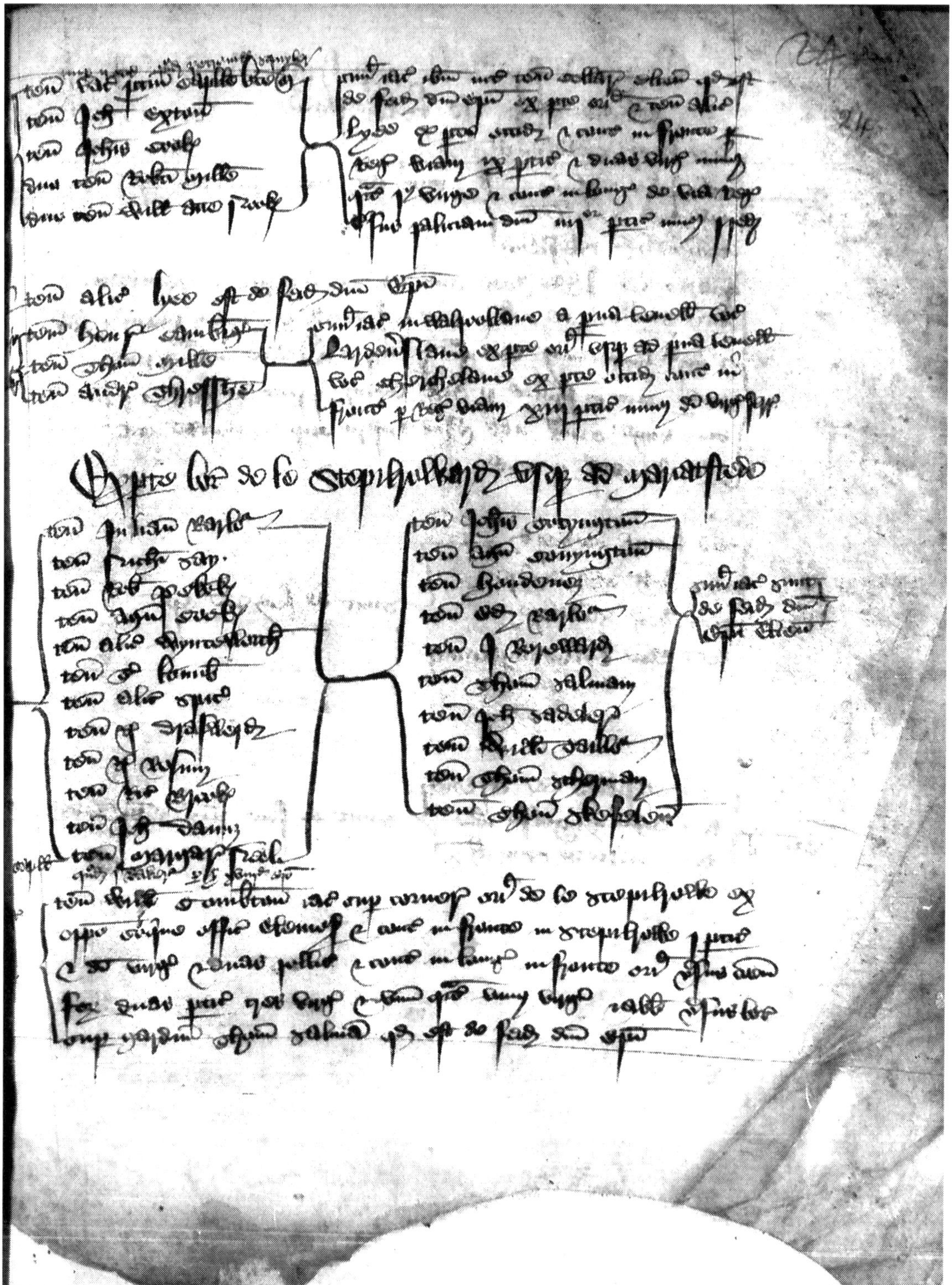

Prior
a vacant tenement [c] pertaining to the Lady Chapel \lately two cottages formerly Petronilla Squyler's/
John Extoun's tenement[171]
John Cook's tenement
two tenements of Robert Millere
two tenements of William atte Nooke [h][172]
lying together there between a tenement of the cellarer of Ely that is of the lord bishop's fee on the east and Alice Lyee's tenement on the west, and they contain 9 perches and 2 yards less ¼ yard in front along the king's highway, and they contain 4 perches less 1 foot in length from the king's highway towards the lord's palace.
Bishop
Alice Lyee's tenement is of the lord bishop's fee.
Prior
a tenement[173] of Henry Cambrige [s]
Thomas Millere's tenement[174]
Andrew Thresshere's tenement [i]
lying together in Walpole Lane, from a small lane called Lardeners Lane on the east to a small lane called Church Lane on the west, they contain 13 perches less ½ iron yard in front along the king's highway.

On the north side of the Steeple Row ward to the market place[175]

Bishop
Juliane Barbour's tenement
Nicholas Say's tenement
Robert Pekok's tenement
Agnes Cook's tenement
Alice Wynteworth's tenement
T. Lombe's tenement
Alice Spicer's tenement
R. Draswerd's tenement
R. Bosum's tenement
Richard Brook's tenement
John Daunz' tenement
Margaret Neel's tenement [c] \formerly J. Baker's by 18*d* service to the bishop/
John Totyngton's tenement
Agnes Conyngton's tenement
Houdenez' tenement
Ed' Barbour's tenement
J. Boreward's tenement
Thomas Salman's tenement
John Sadeler's tenement
William Taillour's tenement
Thomas Scherman's tenement
Thomas Skefelen's tenement
lying together, they are of the fee of the lord bishop of Ely.
Prior
William Comberton's tenement [s] lying on the east corner of the Steeple Row, opposite the kitchen of the almoner's department; and it contains 1 perch and ½ yard and 2 inches in front in Steeple Row, and it contains 2 perches 3¼ yards in length on the east frontage towards the common market, and abuts towards the north upon Thomas Salman's garden that is of the lord bishop's fee.[176]

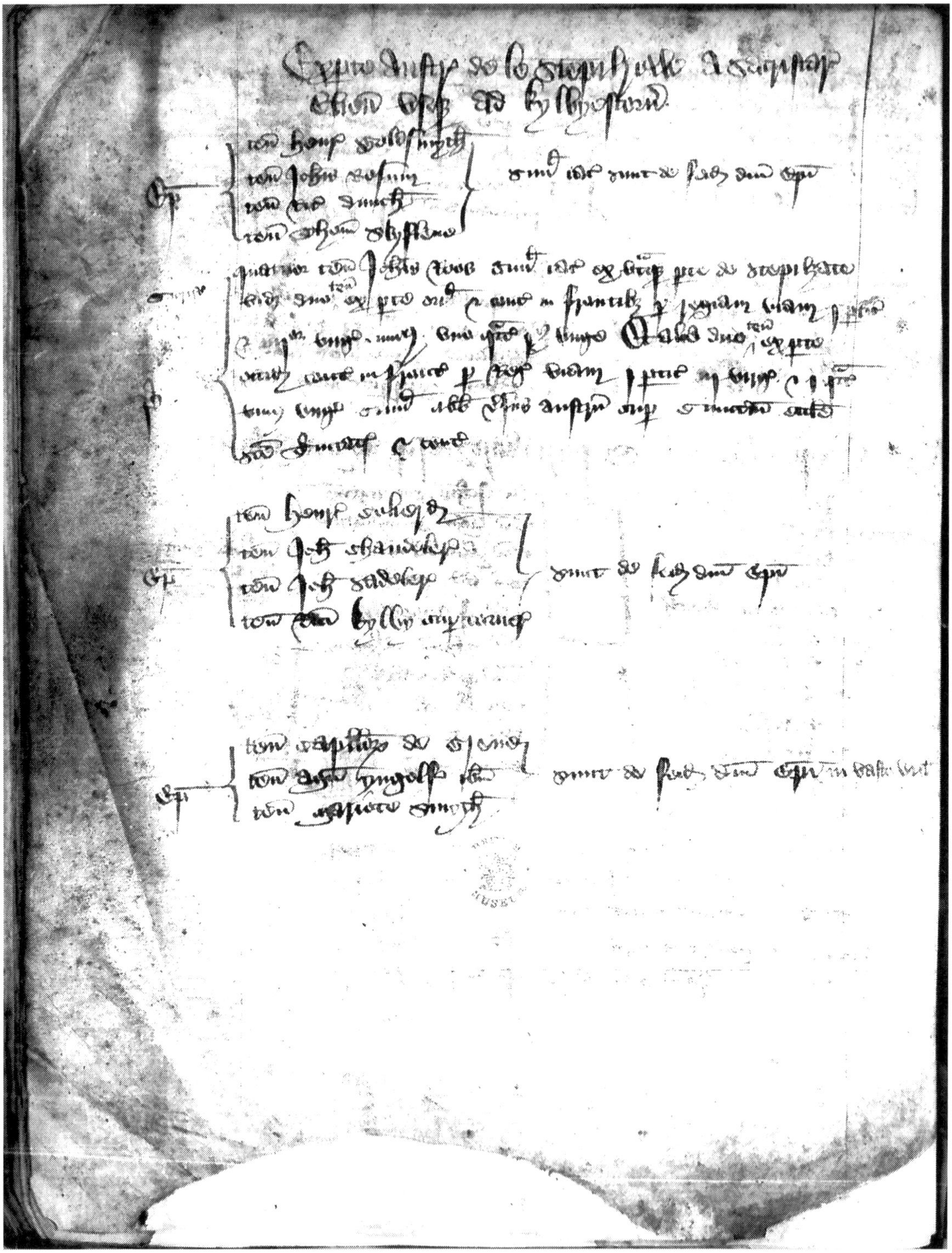

On the south side of the Steeple Row, from the department of the sacrist of Ely to Kylby's corner

Bishop
Henry Goldsmyth's tenement
John Bosum's tenement
Richard Dunch's tenement
Thomas Skyflene's tenement
lying together, they are of the lord bishop's fee.
Prior
four tenements of John Roos [s] lying together on either side of Steeple Gate, namely two tenements on the east side and they contain 1 perch and 4 yards less ¼ yard in front along the king's highway; and the other two \tenements/ on the west side contain 1 perch 3¼ yards in front along the king's highway, abutting together towards the south upon the churchyard of Holy Trinity church, and they contain *[blank]* [177]

Bishop
Henry Colierd's tenement
John Chandeler's tenement
John Sadeler's tenement
Richard Kylby's tenement on the corner
they are of the lord bishop's fee.

Bishop
the tenement of the chaplains of the Green[178]
Agnes Yngolf's tenement there
Mariota Smyth's tenement
they are of the lord bishop's fee in the town's waste land.

NOTES

[1] Initial N for 'Nomina' in the top left corner of the space, presumably intended for a large capital; likewise at the beginning of the second paragraph, initial H for 'Hec'.

[2] This was a piecemeal process (see Introduction).

[3] 'Horton' P V.

[4] Parts of this introductory section occur, in varied order, in the other copies of the survey.

[5] The 'foot of St Paul' was the standard twelve-inch foot; it is mentioned in late twelfth-century documents as being displayed on a column in St Paul's church; an iron rod provided the standard measure for the yard and the foot, and measurements by 'the king's iron yard' occur from the late twelfth century: R.D. Connor, *The Weights and Measures of England* (1987), pp. 85–6.

[6] P omits this entry; V has an additional entry after this: 'William Clere's tenement [c]'.

[7] '26½ perches' C P.

[8] C P add 'and all the aforesaid tenements abut upon the said common ditch on the north'.

[9] 'Castle Hithe' C P V.

[10] C P V add 'now Edmund Cotermong'.

[11] Heading omitted C P.

[12] 'Caldwell Fen' C P.

[13] 'a tenement' C P V; singular also in the first entry under the following heading C P V.

[14] 'a tenement' C; abbreviated P V, so uncertain whether singular or plural.

[15] '41 perches' C P.

[16] 'on the east head next to Potters Lane' C P.

[17] 'Richard Overe's tenement containing a pond, in which John Gedney resides' C P.

[18] C P add 'lately in the tenure of John Stumbill/Tumbyll' respectively.

[19] 'Robert' C P.

[20] 'along Potters Lane' C; P has 'at the head next to Potters Lane'.

[21] 'Caldwell ditch' C P V.

[22] The list of holdings is an insertion, omitted in V; C P have 'From Potters Lane to the gates of Barton none'.

[23] 'Broad Lane' C P.

[24] This entry begins 'Edmund Cotermong's tenement … ' C P; these two manuscripts refer to the tenements on either side as 'of the said Edmund, lately Emmotte Baker's'.

[25] C P add 'along the highway'.

[26] 'Furum' V.

[27] 'John Shelwe' V; C P have additionally after this entry 'Margaret Taillour's tenement'.

[28] 'Robert Wrake' C P.

[29] 'Fulke' V.

[30] 'tenement of Thomas Dekeman' in the left margin V.

[31] 'Pittancer of Sutton' in the left margin; instead of this entry, V has 'a vacant plot where three cottages formerly stood, pertaining to the pittancer of Sutton', and C P have 'two vacant tenements with a standing cottage where lately there were three cottages'; the title 'pittancer of Sutton' is discussed in the Introduction; Hervey Raven and his wife Agnes bought the tenement in the later thirteenth century, and for this they had to pay the pittancer an annual rent of 2s: BL Egerton 3047, fo 145 r and v.

[32] 'three' V.

[33] '25 perches' C P.

[34] All the priory holdings on the west side of Broad Lane are described as 'abutting upon the prior's vineyard' C P.

[35] C P add 'under one roof and a solar at the north end'.

[36] C P add 'with a pond'.
[37] Omitted C P.
[38] 'between the said tenement of John Brewere on the south and the lord bishop's tenement in the tenure of the same John on the north' C P.
[39] C P add 'between a tenement of the lord bishop now in the tenure of Thomas Peyntour on the south and a tenement of John Clement baker on the north'; but P has 'John Clement barker'.
[40] '3 perches and ½ yard' V.
[41] Albreda Pilet was the widow of John Pelet who bequeathed Liles Place to the prior and convent; an indenture of 12 August 1417 records the agreement with the latter and Albreda that she would retain Liles Place until her death: BL Egerton 3047, fos 118–9.
[42] 'Joan' C P.
[43] Manuscript J begins here with ' in which stand four cottages ...'
[44] C J P add 'between a tenement of the said Edmund Cotermong on the south and the corner of Broad Lane's end on the north'.
[45] C J P have 'John Wyncestre', pertaining to the steward of the household; this tenement is included in the street frontage measuring 18 perches; note that J has '*senesc*' to denote rents of the steward of the prior's household where H usually has '*h*'; from this entry to the end of the survey, a holding marked '*senesc*' in J and '*h*' in H will be considered a rent of the steward of the household, and marked [sh].
[46] C P add 'that is of the bishop's fee'.
[47] '... between Edmund Cotermong's tenement ... on the east and Albreda Pylet's garden on the west ... and abuts upon Flax Lane and contains there in breadth 2 perches and 1½ yards ... and in length towards the north 4 perches' C J P.
[48] Rent of the Lady Chapel J.
[49] 'four cottages under one roof' separate entry C J P V.
[50] C J P have 'lying between Flax Lane on the north and three tenements of the lord bishop under one roof on the south; which four cottages of the prior contain in front along the king's highway 3½ perches less 1 foot'. V has 'two tenements of the bishop under one roof'.
[51] Treasurer's rent J.
[52] The manuscript (H) has 'Baldoknane'.
[53] In the body of the text V; almoner's rent V.
[54] Sacrist's rent J.
[55] '7 perches' C.
[56] Rent of the steward of the household C P.
[57] '... abuts upon the broad bank towards the east and upon Broad Lane towards the west' C J P.
[58] 'Thomas' V.
[59] 'William Skynnere' C J P.
[60] In the body of the text V; Stephen of Witchford and his wife Lucy acquired this holding in the later thirteenth century, and Lucy, when widowed, granted it to the prior and convent: M, fos 457–8.
[61] Rent of the Lady Chapel C J P.
[62] In the body of the text, as is the insertion in the next entry V.
[63] 'Robert' C P.
[64] C J add 'on the west and John Rook's tenement on the east'.
[65] Rent of the Lady Chapel J.
[66] 'Joh' Grene Botel'' in the left margin.
[67] C J P have a single entry for John Feltwell.
[68] P adds 'and in length along Barkers Lane from the said bank towards the west 25 perches'.
[69] C J P have 'and the said John Bokyngham's tenement contains 4 perches in breadth in front towards the public waterway, and both tenements contain in length along the said Barkers Lane ...'
[70] Heading and section omitted C J P V.

[71] This entry is an insertion; V has 'all the tenements beyond the river pertain to the lord bishop, except for John Maney's tenement there' at the end of the previous section.

[72] This entry and the following two (E. Listere, W. Haukyn) are almoner's rents J; William the provisioner is mentioned in the 1250 survey, and in the priory cartulary where one of his holdings is a tenement 'at the great bank' extending to the river: M, p. 507.

[73] C J P add 'now of John Baxtere'; almoner's rent J.

[74] There are thirteenth-century references to this lode; Stock Hithe also mentioned on this folio was presumably the landing stage connected with this lode (see Introduction).

[75] 'T. Martyn' in the margin.

[76] 'Lilleford' C J P.

[77] Part of the insertion is barely legible; assuming that the reading is correct, the reference to ivy may be connected with the ritual use of this plant; the sacrist rolls record that the tenants from Wentworth brought ivy to the cathedral at Easter, and the Customs of Hereford Cathedral, listing required ornaments in the cathedral church for each season, includes ivy for Easter: F.R. Chapman, ed., *Sacrist Rolls of Ely* (2 vols, Cambridge, 1907), ii, pp. 69, etc.; H. Bradshaw and C. Wordsworth, eds, *Statutes of Lincoln Cathedral* (2 vols, Cambridge, 1892–7), ii, p. 70.

[78] 'Robert' V.

[79] Line deleted in H 'because below'; included in V.

[80] 'two' C J P.

[81] Almoner's rent J.

[82] There are references to two tenements formerly of Robert the merchant in this section; they may form part of a single larger holding of thirteenth-century date; Robert the merchant occurs as the holder of a messuage in the 1222 survey, and as the former holder in 1250; at the latter date, the almoner held this messuage which had been granted to him by Margaret, widow of Robert: M, pp. 516–7.

[83] Rent of the Lady Chapel J.

[84] This insertion is in the body of the text, as are those in the next entry and in the last entry on this folio, in V.

[85] Word abbreviated in H, 'a tenement' V.

[86] 'Thomas' V.

[87] J P add 'on the east'.

[88] 'Richard Pykenham' V; steward of the household's rent J.

[89] V adds 'one of which she had of the almoner for a rent'.

[90] Pittancer's rent V.

[91] Steward of the household's rent J.

[92] C J P have 'John Bury's tenement next to his tenement in which he resides'.

[93] 'John Burghard', sacrist's rent J.

[94] Rent of the Lady Chapel J.

[95] '... on the west' C P.

[96] 'four' V.

[97] Line omitted in C J P; in V, this forms the antepenultimate entry of the section, and is followed by 'The [Lady] Chapel holds two stalls lying on the south side of the butchers' stalls, formerly 6d; also one stall in the butchery in the tenure of R. Berford 6d'.

[98] In the body of the text V.

[99] Chamberlain's rent V; J has chamberlain's rent for this and the following two entries.

[100] Steward of the household's rent J.

[101] Steward of the household's rent for this and the following entry J.

[102] Steward of the household's rent for this and the following three entries J.

[103] Almoner's rent J.

[104] C J P add 'weaver' (*webstere*).

[105] Steward of the household's rent for this and the following two entries J.

[106] These entries are followed by the heading 'On the west side of the broad lane towards Newnham opposite the butchers' stalls' C J P; as the bishop's holdings are omitted in C J P, it is not clear whether the next three entries under *Bishop* should be included among the tenements on the west side of the lane.
[107] Rent of the Lady Chapel J.
[108] Almoner's rent J.
[109] Steward of the household's rent J.
[110] Almoner's rent J.
[111] J P add 'on the west'.
[112] Rent of the 'almoner Braham' J; 'Braham' occurs as the heading of a subsection in the almoner's rental, in the sixteenth-century priory rentals, fos 15–15v.
[113] Chamberlain's rent J.
[114] 'two cottages' C J P.
[115] Rent of the Lady Chapel J.
[116] Steward of the household's rent J.
[117] This and the following entry are combined into one C J P; J has 'a tenement of Henry Smyth and of his son John', steward of the household's rent; C P have 'a tenement of Henry Smyth, Richard Smyth and his son John'.
[118] 'now vacant' C J P.
[119] C J P add 'from the said king's highway towards the west'.
[120] C J add 'and 2 iron yards'; P has '5 perches and 2 iron yards'; C J P add 'and abut upon a bishop's fee'.
[121] V has these two holdings of the bishop's fee in reverse order, and in the body of the text.
[122] 'Robert' V.
[123] 'b' in the left margin; this entry is at the head of the section 'On the north side of Cats Lane' V.
[124] Steward of the household's rent J.
[125] C J P add 'towards the north'.
[126] 'a' in the left margin.
[127] Entry omitted in V.
[128] 'A1' in the left margin.
[129] 'two adjoining vacant plots' J P.
[130] J P V have this entry at the end of the section headed 'From the red cross towards Chettisham … '
[131] Rent of the 'almoner Braham' J.
[132] In the body of the text V.
[133] This heading is omitted in C J P V; V lists all the entries in this section under the heading 'From the corner where John Duke lives to the west street leading towards Little Downham', and this section is continuous up to the heading 'On the east side of Downham Street'.
[134] Two separate entries in V: 'Richard Webster's tenement', and 'seven cottages under one roof'.
[135] Granger's rent J; C J P have this entry at the beginning of the following section ('From the corner where John Duke lives …')
[136] '5½ feet' C J P.
[137] 'From the corner where John Duke lives to the west street leading towards Little Downham' C J P.
[138] Rent of the Lady Chapel V.
[139] Rent of the almoner J, but of the Lady Chapel V.
[140] 'The corner on the west side of the said Henry Taillour's tenement' C J P.
[141] 'Plowhwryght' V.
[142] Rent of the Black Hostelry, for this and the following entry J.
[143] 'two tenements of John Warde and William Webster' V; rent of the Lady Chapel, for this and the following entry J.
[144] C J P have 'in front' .
[145] 'tenements' P; 'Thomas Chaloner senior' C J P; V adds 'formerly of Ives the merchant'.

[146] Rent of the 'almoner Braham' J.
[147] 'Margaret Clares' C J P.
[148] Rent of the Lady Chapel J.
[149] Steward of the household's rent J.
[150] Infirmarer's rent J.
[151] 'Thomas Tilere senior' C J P.
[152] Cellarer's rent J.
[153] Almoner's rent J.
[154] V adds 'formerly N. Roswith'.
[155] Steward of the household's rent for this and the following entry J.
[156] Steward of the household's rent J.
[157] 'Sacrist, shrine-keeper' superscript over 'J. Pikworth', 'precentor' over 'Russell' J.
[158] Rent of the Lady Chapel for this and the following two entries J.
[159] In the body of the text V.
[160] Rent of the Lady Chapel J.
[161] Rent of the Lady Chapel J.
[162] This is preceded by the heading 'On the west side of the same street' V; C J P have the same heading as V, before the following set of prior's holdings.
[163] 'Thomas Belleman' C J P.
[164] Heading omitted V.
[165] 'On the east side of the same street from St John's hospital to the sacrist's barn' V.
[166] In the body of the text V.
[167] '1 perch' J.
[168] Sacrist's rent J.
[169] Cellarer's rent J.
[170] C J P add 'in which John Soham resides'.
[171] Rent of the Lady Chapel for this and the following two entries J.
[172] 'Robert atte Nooke' P; sacrist's rent J; hosteller's rent V.
[173] 'two tenements' V.
[174] Infirmarer's rent J V.
[175] This section is listed after that headed 'On the south side of Steeple Row' C J P.
[176] An unfinished entry follows in J 'Thomas Smyth's tenement ...', rent of the Lady Chapel and of the granger; J breaks off here.
[177] C J P have 'and contain 1 perch less ¾ iron yard in length'.
[178] Bishop Hugh of Northwold had established this chantry, served by four chaplains: R, fo 4v.

THE SIXTEENTH-CENTURY PRIORY RENTALS:

CUL EDC 1/C/7

fo 1

Rentale fratris Johannis Ely elemosinarii eliensis de omnibus terris et tenementis suis in Ely predicta renovatum anno regni Regis Henrici octavi quartodecimo

Item Johanne Feldyng armigero pro uno tenemento quondam Johannis pistoris nuper Roberti Savage et Edmundi Goturmong, pro molendino equino ibidem constructo; et continet ex parte australi versus regiam viam duas perticas minus tribus pedibus et iacet inter tenementa dicti Edmundi ex utraque parte et abuttat ex parte boriali super vinetum domini prioris et reddit per annum xijd. Quod est de feodo domini prioris.

Item Thoma Tyler <Johanne Cropley> pro uno tenemento; scituatur ad ripam castri quondam Thome Suttons postea Thome Weykys nuper Margarete Brond, iacet inter tenementum elemosinarii eliensis ex parte orientali et tenementum Roberti Willy ex parte occidentali, et caput australe [abuttat] super venellam vocatam Croyslane et caput boriale abuttat super regiam viam, ut in carta Radulfhi Chaterys patet et reddit per annum iiijs. De feodo domini episcopi.

Item Roberto Wylly <Johanne Cropley> pro una quadam parcella; iacet inferiori parte tenementi sui iuxta Potterslane ex parte occidentali, nuper in tenura Thome Heth quondam Rogeri Davy et postea Johanne Sendall, et reddit per annum iiijd. De feodo domini episcopi.

Item ballivo domini prioris eliensis <J. Ellis> pro uno gardino; iacet in Brodlane quondam Willelmi Watons, iuxta tenementum dicti Willelmi et postea Ade Thorny et nuper in tenura Roberti Wrygth, et reddit per annum xviijd. De feodo domini prioris.

fo 1v

Item infirmario eliensi pro uno tenemento; iacet ad latam ripam nuper in tenura Johannis Atkyn et postea in tenura Thome Newhows, ut in anno xij^{mo} Regis Henrici vj^{ti} patet et reddit per annum ijs vjd. De feodo domini prioris.

Item Thoma Palmer ffescher <Thoma Hodelom> pro tenemento suo quondam Johannis Feltwell nuper in tenura Thome Writh et postea in tenura Thome Martyn; et iacet ad latam ripam inter communes venellas ex utraque parte et abuttat super regiam viam, et reddit per annum xxd. De feodo domini prioris.

Item Willelmo Palmer mason <Baran> pro uno tenemento iuxta tenementum predictum, nuper in tenura Henrici Palmer patris sui quondam Thome Writh et postea Thome Martyn, quondam pertinente ad dictum tenementum Thome Palmer ffischer, et reddit per annum xvjd ut in carta Willelmi de Wellyngton patet. De feodo prioris.

Item Thoma Browne pro uno tenemento quondam Johannis Browod et Edmundi Coturmong; scituatur versus ad latam ripam inter tenementum Thome Aldered ex parte orientali et tenementum Thome Browne ex parte occidentali, unum caput abuttat super regiam viam et abuttat super austrum super Flexlane, ijs. De feodo domini prioris.

fo 2

Item Thoma Aldred pro uno tenemento iuxta tenementum predictum nuper Johannis Corbett; et iacet inter tenementum sacriste eliensis ex parte orientali et tenementum de Thoma Browne waturman ex parte occidentali, et abuttat super regiam viam et caput austrum super Flexlane, ut in carta Simonis le porter patet et reddit per annum xijd. De feodo domini prioris.

Item custode graciarum de Reddmans <Cattell> pro uno tenemento nuper Ricardi Bakers et quondam Alicie[1] Goturmong et postea Johannis Downham rectoris Norwold, nunc in tenura Willelmi Falgatt; et iacet versus ad latam ripam inter tenementum Thome Browne waturman ex parte orientali et tenementum Johannis Bekyls heyyerman ex parte occidentali, abuttat ex parte boriali super regiam viam, abuttat ex parte australi super Flexlane, et reddit per annum ijs. De feodo domini episcopi.

fo 1

The rental of brother John Ely, almoner of Ely, of all his lands and tenements in Ely aforesaid renewed in 14 Henry VIII [1522–3]

From John Feldyng esquire for a tenement formerly of John the baker lately of Robert Savage and Edmund Goturmong, for the horsemill built there; and it contains on the south side towards the king's highway 2 perches less 3 feet and lies between tenements of the said Edmund on either side, and abuts on the north side upon the vineyard of the lord prior and renders 12*d* annually. It is of the lord prior's fee.

From Thomas Tyler <John Cropley> for a tenement; it lies at the castle bank formerly of Thomas Sutton afterwards of Thomas Weykys lately of Margaret Brond, it lies between a tenement of the almoner of Ely on the east side and Robert Willy's tenement on the west side, and the south head [abuts] upon a lane called Croyles Lane and the north head abuts upon the king's highway, as it appears in Ralph Chaterys' charter and renders 4*s* annually. Of the lord bishop's fee.

From Robert Wylly <John Cropley> for a piece of land; it lies at the lower end of his tenement next to Potters Lane on the west side, lately in the tenure of Thomas Heth formerly of Roger Davy and afterwards of Joan Sendall, and renders 4*d* annually. Of the lord bishop's fee.

From the bailiff of the lord prior of Ely <J. Ellis> for a garden; it lies in Broad Lane formerly William Waton's, next to the said William's tenement, and afterwards of Adam Thorny, and lately in the tenure of Robert Wrygth, and renders 18*d* annually. Of the lord prior's fee.

fo 1v

From the infirmarer of Ely for a tenement; it lies at the broad bank lately in John Atkyn's tenure and afterwards in the tenure of Thomas Newhows, as it appears in 12 Henry VI [1433–4] and renders 2*s* 6*d* annually. Of the lord prior's fee.

From Thomas Palmer fisherman <Thomas Hodelom> for his tenement formerly John Feltwell's lately in Thomas Writh's tenure and afterwards in Thomas Martyn's tenure; and it lies at the broad bank between a common lane on either side and abuts upon the king's highway, and renders 20*d* annually. Of the lord prior's fee.

From William Palmer mason <Baran> for a tenement next to the aforesaid tenement, lately in the tenure of Henry Palmer his father, formerly Thomas Writh's and afterwards Thomas Martyn's, formerly pertaining to the said tenement of Thomas Palmer fisherman, and renders 16*d* annually as it appears in William de Wellyngton's charter. Of the prior's fee.

From Thomas Browne for a tenement formerly of John Browod and Edmund Coturmong; it lies towards the broad bank between Thomas Aldered's tenement on the east side and Thomas Browne's tenement on the west side, one head abuts upon the king's highway, and it abuts on the south upon Flax Lane, 2*s*. Of the lord prior's fee.

fo 2

From Thomas Aldred for a tenement next to the aforesaid tenement, lately John Corbett's; and it lies between a tenement of the sacrist of Ely on the east side and a tenement of Thomas Browne waterman on the west side, and it abuts upon the king's highway, and the south head upon Flax Lane, as it appears in the charter of Simon the gatekeeper and renders 12*d* annually. Of the lord prior's fee.

From the keeper of Redman's charity[3] <Cattell> for a tenement lately Richard Baker's and formerly Alice Coturmong's and afterwards of John Downham rector of Northwold, now in William Falgatt's tenure; and it lies towards the broad hithe between a tenement of Thomas Browne waterman on the east side and a tenement of John Bekyls *heyyerman* on the west side, it abuts on the north side upon the king's highway, it abuts on the south side upon Flax Lane, and renders 2*s* annually. Of the lord bishop's fee.

Item custode graciarum Reddmans pro alio tenemento nuper Ricardi Bakers nuper Johannis Lesters quondam Johannis Sturmyng; iacet versus Broydhyt inter tenementum Edwardi Burd nuper Ricardi Hilderham ex parte occidentali et mesuagium capelle Beate Marie et grangium Edmundi Burd ex parte orientali, nuper in tenura Ricardi Heldersham, ut in anno vij^{o} Henrici vj^{ti} patet, et reddit per annum xvijd obolum. De feodo dominis prioris.
Item Edwardo Burde pro quadam parcella tenementi nuper Ricardi Eldersham quondam Sturmyng et postea Baxtard; iacet versus Brodheyth in longitudine iuxta clausum[2] infirmarii ex parte boriali, iacet \inter/ tenementum Edwardi Burd ex parte occidentali et tenementum Johannis Lysters ex parte boriali, ut in anno Henrici vj^{ti} vij^{mo} patet, et reddit vijd obolum. De feodo prioris.
fo 2v
Item Edwardo Burd pro tenemento suo quondam Thome Heldersham postea Stephani Johye et Willelmi Roxham; iacet ex opposito le spore ad le Broydlaynesende, scituatum inter tenementa dicti Edwardi Burde ex utraque parte versus ad latam ripam, et reddit per annum xijd. De feodo prioris.
Item magistro capelle Beate Marie Virginis pro uno tenemento quondam Thome Witriche nuper Roberti Barburs ex opposito le arche, inter tenementum capelle Beate Marie ex parte orientali et tenementum elemosinarii eliensis ex parte occidentali et abuttat super regiam viam et aliud caput super vinetum domini episcopi, et reddit per annum xijd. De feodo episcopi.
Item Willelmo Hardyng <now Bowll> pro uno tenemento; scituatur in Newnam nuper in tenura Johanne Brewoyd et postea Ricardi Pikenham quondam Willelmi Brewoyd, et reddit per annum vjd, ut in carta Gilberti de le Taillour patet, et reddit per annum vjd. De feodo prioris.
Item Willelmo Hardyng pro uno tenemento suo, quondam Johannis Browod et Willelmi Othorpis et postea Johannis Marion nuper Willelmi Browod, ut patet in carta Ricardi filii Stephani de Ely et reddit per annum iiijs iiijd. De feodo episcopi.
fo 3
Item domino Roberto Burne capellano pro uno tenemento; scituatur in Newnam quondam Ricardi Banke et postea in tenura Nicholai Chandeler, et reddit per annum vjd. De feodo prioris.
Item magistro hospitalis Sancti Johannis pro uno tenemento quondam Petri Fedelers; et iacet in Newnam inter tenementa elemosinarii ex utraque parte, unum caput abuttat super regiam viam ex parte orientali et abuttat ex parte occidentali super gardinum Johannis Longys, et reddit per annum ijs. De feodo prioris.
Item Thoma Gallant pro uno tenemento nuper Ricardi Watkyn quondam Willelmi Harman et postea Andree Bolle; iacet inter tenementum Johannis Wellys capellani ex parte orientali et tenementum magistri Sancti Johannis ex parte occidentali, et abuttat super regiam viam ex parte australi, ut indentura Willelmi Herman patet et reddit per annum xiijd. De feodo prioris.
Item Willelmo Sempull <Wedon Sybley> pro uno tenemento suo nuper Ricardi Cooke quondam Roberti Berforh et postea Johannis Eklyngton; iacet inter tenementum vocatum Ambryberns ex parte occidentali et tenementum Thome Sebbley ex parte orientali, et abuttat super regiam viam ex parte australi, abuttat ex parte boriali super terram elemosinarii eliensis in tenura dicti Willelmi Sempull, et reddit ijd. De feodo episcopi.
fo 3v
Item Johanne Davy pro tenemento suo nuper in tenura Willelmi Plowewryght; iacet in parochia Beate Marie inter tenementum Thome Sloowe ex parte occidentali et tenementum Roberti Wryth ex parte orientali, et abuttat super regiam viam ex parte australi, abuttat ex parte boriali super Cattyslane, ut in anno *[blank]* Henrici vj^{ti} patet, et reddit per annum iijd obolum. De feodo episcopi.
Item Roberto Wryth <Mr Twiford> pro tenemento suo nuper in tenura Johannis Smyth; iacet iuxta tenementum Johannis Davy ex parte occidentali et tenementum sacriste eliensis in tenura Roberti Corford ex parte orientali, et unum caput abuttat super regiam viam ex parte australi et abuttat ex parte boriali super venellam vocatam Catyslane, ut in anno xj^{mo} Regis Henrici vj^{ti} patet, et postea in tenura Gyssyns ut in anno xvj^{o} patet, et reddit per annum jd obolum. De feodo prioris.

From the keeper of Redman's charity for another tenement lately Richard Baker's lately John Lester's formerly John Sturmyng's; it lies towards Broad Hithe between a tenement of Edward Burd lately Richard Hilderham's on the west side and a messuage of the Lady Chapel and Edmund Burd's barn on the east side, lately in Richard Heldersham's tenure, as it appears in 7 Henry VI [1428–9] and renders 17½*d* annually. Of the lord prior's fee.[4]
From Edward Burde for part of a tenement lately Richard Eldersham's formerly Sturmyng and afterwards Baxtard; it lies towards Broad Hithe in length next to the infirmarer's enclosure[5] on the north side, it lies \between/ Edward Burd's tenement on the west side and John Lyster's tenement on the north side, as it appears in 7 Henry VI [1428–9] and renders 8½*d*. Of the prior's fee.
fo 2v
From Edward Burd for his tenement formerly of Thomas Heldersham afterwards of Stephen Johye and William Roxham; it lies opposite *le spore* at the Broad Lane's end, situated between tenements of the said Edward Burde on either side towards the broad bank, and renders 12*d* annually. Of the prior's fee.
From the master of the Lady Chapel for a tenement formerly of Thomas Witriche lately Robert Barbur's opposite the arch, between a tenement of the Lady Chapel on the east side and a tenement of the almoner of Ely on the west side, and it abuts upon the king's highway, and the other head upon the lord bishop's vineyard, and renders 12*d* annually. Of the bishop's fee.
From William Hardyng <now Bowll> for a tenement; it lies in Newnham, lately in the tenure of Joan Brewoyd and afterwards of Richard Pikenham formerly of William Brewoyd, and renders 6*d* annually as it appears in Gilbert de le Taillour's charter, and renders 6*d* annually. Of the prior's fee.[6]
From William Hardyng for his tenement formerly of John Browod and William Othorpis and afterwards of John Marion lately William Browod, as it appears in the charter of Richard, son of Stephen de Ely, and renders 4*s* 4*d* annually. Of the bishop's fee.[7]
fo 3
From master Robert Burne chaplain for a tenement; it lies in Newnham formerly Richard Banke's and afterwards in Nicholas Chandeler's tenure, and renders 6*d* annually. Of the prior's fee.
From the master of St John's hospital for a tenement formerly Peter Fedeler's; and it lies in Newnham between tenements of the almoner on either side, one head abuts upon the king's highway on the east side, and it abuts on the west side upon John Longys' garden, and renders 2*s* annually. Of the prior's fee.
From Thomas Gallant for a tenement lately Richard Watkyn's formerly William Harman's and afterwards Andrew Bolle's; it lies between a tenement of John Wellys chaplain on the east side and a tenement of the master of St John on the west side, and it abuts upon the king's highway on the south side, as it appears in William Herman's indenture and renders 13*d* annually. Of the prior's fee.
From William Sempull <Wedon Sybley> for his tenement lately Richard Cooke's formerly Robert Berforh's and afterwards John Eklyngton's; it lies between a tenement called Ambry Barns on the west side and Thomas Sebbley's tenement on the east side, and it abuts upon the king's highway on the south side, it abuts on the north side upon land of the almoner of Ely in the said William Sempull's tenure, and renders 2*d*. Of the bishop's fee.
fo 3v
From John Davy for his tenement lately in William Plowewryght's tenure; it lies in St Mary's parish between Thomas Sloowe's tenement on the west side and Robert Wryth's tenement on the east side, and it abuts upon the king's highway on the south side, it abuts on the north side upon Cats Lane, as it appears in *[blank]* Henry VI, and renders 3½*d* annually. Of the bishop's fee.
From Robert Wryth <Mr Twyford> for his tenement lately in John Smyth's tenure; it lies next to John Davy's tenement on the west side, and a tenement of the sacrist of Ely in Robert Corford's tenure on the east side, and one head abuts upon the king's highway on the south side, and it abuts on the north side upon a lane called Cats Lane, as it appears in 11 Henry VI [1432–3] and afterwards in Gyssyn's tenure as it appears in the sixteenth year, and renders 1½*d* annually. Of the prior's fee.

Item Willelmo Schelford <Lane> pro uno tenemento suo; scituatur in parochia Beate Marie super corneram vocatam Barkers Lane versus Westffene quondam in tenura Ricardi Smale nuper in tenura Johannis Newtone et postea Johannis Fynche, et soleb' redd' ad festum Sancte Etheldrede Virginis unam libram et dimidiam cimini per annum, j libram dimidiam. De feodo prioris.
fo 4
Item Johanne \Gylberd/ pro uno tenemento ibidem nuper in tenura Johanne Newton; scituatur ex opposito Berkerslane versus Westffene, iacet inter tenementum magistri Sancti Johannis ex parte australi et terram Johannis Gilbard ex parte boriali nuper in tenura Thome Hadnam, et unum caput abuttat super regiam viam ex parte occidentali, ut in carta Nicholai Brite patet, ijs ijd. De feodo prioris.
Item magistro capelle Beate Marie Virginis pro uno tenemento nuper in tenura Thome Perkyn quondam in tenura Willelmi Twyforth <nuper Edwardi Hale modo Thome Smithe>; iacet in parochia Beate Marie Virginis, et reddit per annum ijs ijd. De feodo prioris.
Item eodem magistro capelle Beate Marie Virginis pro uno tenemento; scituatur in parochia Beate Marie in venella vocata Benettlane ex opposito tenementi Johannis Smale iuxta tenementum Willelmi Cowper, et reddit per annum xijd. De feodo prioris.

Summa xxxvs vjd

fo 4v
Firma domorum. Item Johanne Perker <Thomas Sawyer> pro uno tenemento; scituatur ultra pontem lapideum nuper in tenura Johannis Halpeny et postea Ricardi Bartlet, iacet inter tenementum Thome Aldered ex parte orientali et tenementum nuper Garret ex parte occidentali, abuttat super commune fossatum ex parte boriali et caput australe abuttat super calcetum versus Stunteney, per copiam ut in anno xij^{mo} Henrici viij^{vi} patet et reddit vjs. De feodo prioris.
Item Edmund Humfry <Robert Bosley> pro uno tenemento suo nuper Willelmi Wattons et postea Johannis Degrene ut in anno xv Regis Edwardi iiij^{ti} patet; iacet apud Castelhyt ultra pontem inter tenementum Ricardi Plomers ex parte australi et tenementum elemosinarii eliensis ex altera parte, et abuttat super communem fossatum, per copiam ut in anno *[blank]* Henrici vij^{mi} patet, ijs iiijd. De feodo prioris.
Item Petro Coke <W. Long> pro uno tenemento; scituatur iuxta pontem lapideum inter tenementum Roberti Orton ex parte occidentali et abuttat ex parte boriali super regiam viam, et abuttat ex parte australi super communem venellam vocatam Croyslane, per copiam ut in anno tercio Henrici viij^{vi} patet, et reddit iiijs. De feodo episcopi.
Item Roberto Orton <J. Andderson> pro uno tenemento iuxta tenementum predictum vocatum Le Angell, nuper in tenura Petri Coke, inter tenementum Thome Tiler ex parte occidentali, unum caput abuttat super regiam viam et abuttat ex parte australi super venellam vocatam Croyslane, per copiam ut in anno Henrici viij terciodecimo patet et reddit iiijs. De feodo episcopi.
fo 5
Item Roberto Wylly pro ij^{bus} tenementis sub uno tecto quondam in tenura Henrici Wycham et postea in tenura Roberti Tomson; scituantur apud Stonbryge inter hortum pertinentem domui Sancti Johannis in Ely ex parte occidentali et tenementum Roberti Wylly ex parte orientali, et continent in fronte per altam viam quinque perticas tribus pedibus minus, per copiam ad terminum vite sue ut in anno vij^{mo} Regis Henrici viij^{vi} patet, et reddit per annum iiijs. De feodo prioris.
Item Roberto Orton pro uno clauso[9] nuper Willelmi Bowyer ut in anno xxj Regis Henrici vij^{mi} patet; iacet prope Potterslane ex parte australi et terram domini episcopi eliensis ex parte boriali, et ex parte occidentali clausum[10] nuper Pullam, per copiam ad terminum vite sue ut in anno septimo Regis Henrici viij^{vi} patet, et reddit per annum iijs iiijd. De feodo prioris.

From William Schelford <Lane> for his tenement; it lies in St Mary's parish on the corner called Barkers Lane towards West Fen,[8] formerly in Richard Smale's tenure lately in the tenure of John Newtone and afterwards of John Fynche, and it used to render 1½ pounds of cumin annually at the feast of St Etheldreda, the Virgin, 1½ pounds. Of the prior's fee.
fo 4
From John \Gylberd/ for a tenement there lately in Joan Newton's tenure; it lies opposite Barkers Lane towards West Fen, it lies between a tenement of the master of St John on the south side and John Gilbard's land on the north side lately in Thomas Hadnam's tenure, and one head abuts upon the king's highway on the west side, as it appears in Nicholas Brite's charter, 2*s* 2*d*. Of the prior's fee.
From the master of the Lady Chapel for a tenement lately in Thomas Perkyn's tenure formerly in William Twyforth's tenure <lately Edward Hale's now Thomas Smithe's>; it lies in St Mary's parish and renders 2*s* 2*d* annually. Of the prior's fee.
From the same master of the Lady Chapel for a tenement; it lies in St Mary's parish in a lane called Benett Lane, opposite John Smale's tenement next to William Cowper's tenement , and renders 12*d* annually. Of the prior's fee.

Total 35s 6d

fo 4v
Rent of the houses. From John Perker <Thomas Sawyer> for a tenement; it lies beyond the stone bridge lately in the tenure of John Halpeny and afterwards of Richard Bartlet, it lies between Thomas Aldered's tenement on the east side and a tenement lately Garret's on the west side, it abuts upon the common ditch on the north side and the south head abuts upon the causeway towards Stuntney, by copy as it appears in 12 Henry VIII [1520–21] and renders 6*s*. Of the prior's fee.
From Edmund Humfry <Robert Bosley> for his tenement lately William Watton's and afterwards John Degrene's as it appears in 15 Edward IV [1475–6]; it lies at Castle Hithe beyond the bridge between Richard Plomer's tenement on the south side and a tenement of the almoner of Ely on the other side, and it abuts upon the common ditch, by copy as it appears in *[blank]* Henry VII, 2*s* 4*d*. Of the prior's fee.
From Peter Coke <W. Long> for a tenement; it lies next to the stone bridge between Robert Orton's tenement on the west side, and it abuts on the north side upon the king's highway, and it abuts on the south side upon a common lane called Croyles Lane, by copy as it appears in 3 Henry VIII [1511–12] and renders 4*s*. Of the bishop's fee.
From Robert Orton <J. Andderson> for a tenement next to the aforesaid tenement called The Angel, lately in Peter Coke's tenure, between Thomas Tiler's tenement on the west side, one head abuts upon the king's highway and it abuts on the south side upon a lane called Croyles Lane, by copy as it appears in 13 Henry VIII [1521–2] and renders 4*s*. Of the bishop's fee.
fo 5
From Robert Wylly for two tenements under one roof formerly in Henry Wycham's tenure and afterwards in Robert Tomson's tenure; they lie at Stone Bridge between a yard pertaining to the house of St John in Ely on the west side and Robert Wylly's tenement on the east side, and they contain in front along the highway 5 perches less 3 feet, by copy for his lifetime as it appears in 7 Henry VIII [1515–16] and renders 4*s* annually. Of the prior's fee.
From Robert Orton for an enclosure lately William Bowyer's as it appears in 21 Henry VII [1505–06]; it lies near Potters Lane on the south side and land of the lord bishop of Ely on the north side, and on the west side near an enclosure lately Pullam's, by copy for the term of his life, as it appears in 7 Henry VIII [1515–16] and renders 3*s* 4*d* annually. Of the prior's fee.

Item Margareta Pullam <Mr Goodryg> pro uno inclauso prati continenti iiij^{or} acras quondam Johannis Eriswell ut in anno xiiij^{o} Regis Edwardi iiij^{ti} patet, nuper Rogeri Bowtor ut in anno xviij^{o} Henrici vij patet, et iacet in quodam clauso nuper Thome Persons, caput orientale et caput occidentale abuttant super aquam versus a fonte Sancte Etheldrede, abuttat ex parte australi super le tylekylleclaus, per copiam ad terminum annorum ut in anno Regis Henrici vij^{i} xx^{o} patet et reddit per annum iiijs. De feodo prioris.

Item magistro capelle Beate Marie pro uno cotagio scituato in Brodlane ex parte occidentali; \iacet/ iuxta tenementum pitanciarii eliensis nuper in tenura Johannis Davel ex parte australi, unum caput abuttat super regiam viam ex parte orientali et caput occidentale abuttat super vinetum domini prioris, et reddit per annum xd. De feodo prioris.

fo 5v

Item Ricardo Fote pro uno tenemento cum gardino adiacente; scituatur in Brodelane ex parte occidentali inter tenementum elemosinarii eliensis ex parte boriali in tenura Johannis Miller et gardinum Ricardi Dodson ex parte australi, unum caput abuttat super regiam viam ex parte orientali et abuttat super vinetum domini prioris ex parte occidentali, nunc in tenura Roberti Yngram, per annum et reddit xiiijd ut in anno xx^{o} Henrici vij^{mi} patet. De feodo prioris.

Item Ricardo Wesenam pro uno tenemento iuxta tenementum predictum nuper in tenura Johannis Glover; iacet inter tenementum Roberti Yngram ex parte australi et tenementum elemosinarii eliensis ex parte boriali, unum caput abuttat super regiam viam ex parte orientali et abuttat super vinetum domini prioris ex parte occidentali, et reddit iiijs. De feodo prioris.

Item Johanne Shepard pro uno tenemento iuxta tenementum predictum nuper in tenura Johannis Haltam; iacet inter tenementum Ricardi Wesenam ex parte australi et tenementum pitanciarii eliensis ex parte boriali, unum caput abuttat super regiam viam ex parte orientali et caput occidentale abuttat super vinetum domini prioris, et reddit per annum vs. De feodo prioris.

Item Waltero Larlyng pro \uno/ tenemento; situatur in Brodelane nuper in tenura Johannis Mower inter tenementum magistri capelle Beate Marie ex parte australi et tenementum Willelmi Salmon ex parte boriali, unum caput abuttat super vinetum domini prioris et abuttat ex parte boriali super regiam viam, et reddit per annum iiijs. De feodo prioris.

fo 6

Item Ricardo Rechisson pro uno tenemento iuxta tenementum predictum nuper in tenura Johannis Collys; iacet inter tenementum elemosinarii eliensis ex parte australi, et unum caput abuttat super regiam viam et ex parte occidentali abuttat super vinetum domini prioris, et reddit per annum ad quatuor terminos anni iiijs. De feodo prioris.

Item Johanne Estlyn pro uno tenemento; scituatur in Brodlane, nuper in tenura Johannis Tucke et iacet inter tenementum senescalli hospicii ex parte boriali, et abuttat super regiam viam ex parte orientali et unum caput abuttat super vinetum domini prioris ex parte occidentali, et reddit per annum iijs iiijd. De feodo prioris.

Item Gilbarto Herrys pro uno tenemento nuper in tenura Alani Moll; scituatur in Brodelane inter tenementum elemosinarii eliensis ex parte boriali in tenura Henrici Holiet, unum caput abuttat super regiam viam ex parte orientali et abuttat ex parte occidentali super vinetum domini prioris, ut in anno vj^{o} Henrici viij^{vi} patet et reddit per annum iijs viijd. De feodo prioris.

Item Henrico Olyett pro uno tenemento nuper in tenura Willelmi Blande; scituatur in Brodelane, iacet inter tenementum Gilbarti Herrys ex parte australi et tenementum senescalli hospicii ex parte boriali, unum caput abuttat super regiam viam, per copiam ut in anno xij^{o} Henrici viij^{vi} patet et reddit per annum iiijs. De feodo prioris.

From Margaret Pullam <Mr Goodryg> for a close of meadow-land containing 4 acres formerly John Eriswell's as it appears in 14 Edward IV [1474–5], lately Roger Bowtor's as it appears in 18 Henry VII [1502–03], and it lies in an enclosure lately of Thomas Persons, the east head and the west head abut upon the water [running] from St Etheldreda's spring; it abuts on the south side upon the tile kiln close, by copy for a term of years as it appears in 20 Henry VII [1504–05] and renders 4*s* annually. Of the prior's fee.[11]

From the master of the Lady Chapel for a cottage situated in Broad Lane on the west side; \it lies/ next to a tenement of the pittancer of Ely lately in John Davel's tenure on the south side, one head abuts upon the king's highway on the east side and the west head abuts upon the lord prior's vineyard, and renders 10*d* annually. Of the prior's fee.

fo 5v

From Richard Fote for a tenement with an adjoining garden; it lies in Broad Lane on the west side between a tenement of the almoner of Ely on the north side in John Miller's tenure and Richard Dodson's garden on the south side, one head abuts upon the king's highway on the east side and it abuts upon the lord prior's vineyard on the west side, now in Robert Yngram's tenure, annually and renders 14*d* as it appears in 20 Henry VII [1504–05]. Of the prior's fee.

From Richard Wesenam for a tenement next to the aforesaid tenement lately in John Glover's tenure; it lies between Robert Yngram's tenement on the south side and a tenement of the almoner of Ely on the north side, one head abuts upon the king's highway on the east side and it abuts upon the lord prior's vineyard on the west side, and renders 4*s*. Of the prior's fee.

From John Shepherd for a tenement next to the aforesaid tenement lately in John Haltam's tenure; it lies between Richard Wesenam's tenement on the south side and a tenement of the pittancer of Ely on the north side, one head abuts upon the king's highway on the east side and the west head abuts upon the lord prior's vineyard, and renders 5*s* annually. Of the prior's fee.

From Walter Larlyng for \a/ tenement; it lies in Broad Lane, lately in John Mower's tenure between a tenement of the master of the Lady Chapel on the south side and William Salmon's tenement on the north side, one head abuts upon the lord prior's vineyard and it abuts on the north side[12] upon the king's highway, and renders 4*s* annually. Of the prior's fee.

fo 6

From Richard Rechisson for a tenement next to the aforesaid tenement lately in the tenure of John Collys; it lies between a tenement of the almoner of Ely on the south side, and one head abuts upon the king's highway and on the west side it abuts upon the lord prior's vineyard, and renders 4*s* annually at the four terms of the year. Of the prior's fee.

From John Estlyn for a tenement; it lies in Broad Lane, lately in John Tucke's tenure, and it lies between a tenement of the steward of the household on the north side, and abuts upon the king's highway on the east side and one head abuts upon the lord prior's vineyard on the west side, and renders 3*s* 4*d* annually. Of the prior's fee.

From Gilbert Herrys for a tenement lately in Alan Moll's tenure; it lies in Broad Lane between a tenement of the almoner of Ely on the north side in Henry Holiet's tenure, one head abuts upon the king's highway on the east side and it abuts on the west side upon the lord prior's vineyard, as it appears in 6 Henry VIII [1514–15] and renders 3*s* 8*d* annually. Of the prior's fee.

From Henry Olyett for a tenement lately in William Blande's tenure; it lies in Broad Lane, it lies between Gilbert Herrys' tenement on the south side and a tenement of the steward of the household on the north side, one head abuts upon the king's highway, by copy as it appears in 12 Henry VIII [1520–21] and renders 4s annually. Of the prior's fee.

fo 6v
Item Willelmo <Johanne> Replyngall pro quadam parcella tenementi sui nuper Isabelle Rysele quondam Walteri Webber pro quodam camino ibidem ponendo; iacet super corneram vocatam Croylecorner iuxta tenementum elemosinarii eliensis ex parte occidentali, et caput boriale abuttat super regiam viam et caput australe abuttat super vinetum domini prioris, per copiam ad terminum annorum <modo John Krechine> ut in anno *[blank]* et reddit per annum iiijd. De feodo prioris.
Item Thoma Stubbley pro uno tenemento; iacet iuxta tenementum predictum ex parte occidentali et tenementum Johannis Replyngall ex parte orientali; unum caput abuttat super regiam viam ex parte boriali et abuttat super vinetum domini prioris ex parte australi, et reddit per annum vijs. De feodo prioris.
Item Ricardo Baker pro uno tenemento iuxta tenementum predictum nuper in tenura Johannis Trowe; abuttat super regiam viam ex parte boriali et abuttat ex parte australi super vinetum domini prioris, et reddit per annum vijs. De feodo prioris.
Item Willelmo Knyte pro uno tenemento nuper in tenura Roberti Bucke; iacet iuxta tenementum predictum inter tenementum Roberti Blande ex parte occidentali et abuttat super regiam viam ex parte boriali et abuttat super vinetum domini prioris ex parte australi, vijs. De feodo prioris.
Item Willelmo Alowe pro ij^{bus} tenementis iuxta tenementum predictum nuper in tenura Johannis Torner, inter tenementum Willelmi Alowe ex parte occidentali, abuttant super regiam viam ex parte boriali, ut in anno secundo Regis Henrici viij^{vi} et reddunt per annum viijs. De feodo prioris.
Item Johanne Turner pro uno tenemento ibidem, per annum et reddit iiijs. De feodo prioris.
fo 7
Item Gilberto Wettley pro uno tenemento nuper in tenura Willelmi Alowe; iacet iuxta tenementum predictum ex parte orientali et tenementum Willelmi Alowe ex parte occidentali, unum caput abuttat super regiam viam ex parte boriali et abuttat australi super vinetum domini prioris, per copiam ut in anno undecimo Henrici viij patet et reddit per annum ijs viijd. De feodo prioris.
Item Willelmo Alowe pro uno tenemento quondam Bryant iuxta tenementum predictum ex parte orientali et tenementum elemosinarii eliensis ex altera parte; caput australe abuttat super le ortyard et aliud caput super regiam viam, per copiam ut in anno decimo nono Henrici vij^{mi} patet et reddit per annum iijd iiijd. De feodo prioris.
Item Johanne Wythe pro uno tenemento iuxta tenementum predictum nuper in tenura Thome Tomson, ut in anno primo Regis Henrici viij^{vi} patet; et unum caput abuttat super regiam viam ex parte boriali et caput australe abuttat super le orteyard ex parte australi, per copiam ut in anno decimo Regis Henrici viij^{vi} patet et reddit per annum iiijs. De feodo prioris.
Item Johanne Strecfford pro uno tenemento iuxta tenementum predictum ex parte orientali et tenementum elemosinarii eliensis ex parte occidentali; et abuttat super regiam viam ex parte boriali, et abuttat super le orteyard ex parte australi,[13] per copiam ut in anno xxiiij^{mo} Regis Henrici vij^{i} patet et reddit per annum iijs iiijd. De feodo prioris.
fo 7v
Item Margeria Halpeney pro uno tenemento nuper in tenura Margerie Coston; iacet iuxta tenementum predictum ex parte occidentali et tenementum Johannis Bele ex parte orientali, \et/ unum caput abuttat super regiam viam ex parte boriali et abuttat super le orteyard ex parte australi, per annum et reddit iiijs. De feodo prioris.
Item Roberto Belle pro uno tenemento ibidem nuper in tenura Johannis Eriswell; scituatur in vico versus Brodehith inter tenementa elemosinarii eliensis ex utraque parte, abuttat super regiam \viam/ ex parte boriali, per copiam ad terminum xl annorum, hoc anno ij annorum, ut in anno ij^{o} Ricardi iij^{i} patet, iijs iiijd. De feodo prioris.
Item Willelmo Foykes carpentario pro uno tenemento iuxta tenementum predictum nuper in tenura Johannis Barnard coper; iacet inter tenementum Johannis Deye ex parte occidentali et abuttat super regiam viam ex parte boriali et abuttat ex parte australi super le orteyard, et reddit per annum vijs. De feodo prioris.

fo 6v
From William <John> Replyngall for a portion of his tenement lately of Isabel Rysele formerly of Walter Webber to create a right of way there; it lies on a corner called Croyles Corner next to a tenement of the almoner of Ely on the west side, and the north head abuts upon the king's highway and the south head abuts upon the lord prior's vineyard, by copy for a term of years <now John Krechine> as in the *[blank]* year, and renders 4*d* annually. Of the prior's fee.
From Thomas Stubbley for a tenement; it lies next to the aforesaid tenement on the west side and John Replyngall's tenement on the east side; one head abuts upon the king's highway on the north side and it abuts upon the lord prior's vineyard on the south side, and renders 7*s* annually. Of the prior's fee.
From Richard Baker for a tenement next to the aforesaid tenement lately in John Trowe's tenure; it abuts upon the king's highway on the north side and it abuts on the south side upon the lord prior's vineyard, and renders 7*s* annually. Of the prior's fee.
From William Knyte for a tenement lately in Robert Bucke's tenure; it lies next to the aforesaid tenement, between Robert Blande's tenement on the west side and it abuts upon the king's highway on the north side and abuts upon the lord prior's vineyard on the south side, 7*s*. Of the prior's fee.
From William Alowe for two tenements next to the aforesaid tenement lately in John Torner's tenure, between William Alowe's tenement on the west side, they abut upon the king's highway on the north side, as in 2 Henry VIII [1510–11] and render 8*s* annually. Of the prior's fee.
From John Turner for a tenement there, and renders annually 4*s*. Of the prior's fee.

fo 7
From Gilbert Wettley for a tenement lately in William Alowe's tenure; it lies next to the aforesaid tenement on the east side and William Alowe's tenement on the west side, one head abuts upon the king's highway on the north side, and it abuts on the south side upon the lord prior's vineyard, by copy as it appears in 11 Henry VIII [1519–20] and renders 2*s* 8*d* annually. Of the prior's fee.
From William Alowe for a tenement formerly Bryant's next to the aforesaid tenement on the east side and a tenement of the almoner of Ely on the other side; the south head abuts upon the orchard and the other head upon the king's highway, by copy as it appears in 19 Henry VII [1503–04] and renders 3*s* 4*d* annually. Of the prior's fee.
From John Wythe for a tenement next to the aforesaid tenement lately in Thomas Tomson's tenure, as it appears in 1 Henry VIII [1509–10]; and one head abuts upon the king's highway on the north side, and the south head abuts upon the orchard on the south side, by copy as it appears in 10 Henry VIII [1518–19] and renders 4*s* annually. Of the prior's fee.
From John Strecfford for a tenement next to the aforesaid tenement on the east side and a tenement of the almoner of Ely on the west side; and it abuts upon the king's highway on the north side, and it abuts upon the orchard on the south side, by copy as it appears in 24 Henry VII [1508–09] and renders 3*s* 4*d* annually. Of the prior's fee.

fo 7v
From Margery Halpeney for a tenement lately in Margery Coston's tenure; it lies next to the aforesaid tenement on the west side and John Bele's tenement on the east side, \and/ one head abuts upon the king's highway on the north side, and it abuts upon the the orchard on the south side, and renders 4*s* annually. Of the prior's fee.
From Robert Belle for a tenement there lately in John Eriswell's tenure; it lies in the street towards Broad Hithe, between tenements of the almoner of Ely on either side, it abuts upon the king's \highway/ on the north side, by copy for a term of forty years, this year two years remain, as it appears in 2 Richard III [1484–5], 3*s* 4*d*. Of the prior's fee.
From William Foykes carpenter for a tenement next to the aforesaid tenement lately in the tenure of John Barnard *coper*; it lies between John Deye's tenement on the west side, and abuts upon the king's highway on the north side and it abuts upon the orchard on the south side, and renders 7*s* annually. Of the prior's fee.

Item Johanne Day pro uno tenemento iuxta tenementum predictum nuper in tenura Johannis \Day/; et abuttat super gradum lapideum in alta strata versus Brodhyth ex parte boriali et abuttat super le orteyard ex parte australi, per copiam ad terminum annorum ut in anno xj^{mo} Regis Henrici viij^{i} patet, et reddit per annum iiijs. De feodo prioris.
fo 9[14]
Item Willelmo Dopbys pro uno tenemento nuper in tenura Willelmi Nele ut in anno quarto Regis Henrici viij^{vi} patet; scituatur in Brodlane ex parte orientali eiusdem inter tenementum capelle Beate Marie vocatum Storehows ex parte australi et tenementum elemosinarii eliensis in tenura Willelmi Lay ex parte boriali, caput occidentale abuttat super regiam viam, caput orientale super tenementum elemosinarii in tenura Johannis Wattys, ut in anno xiij^{o} Henrici viij^{vi} patet et reddit vjs viijd. De feodo prioris.
Item Thoma Heyward pro uno mesuagio; scituatur in Brodlane nuper in tenura Johannis Clerke ut in anno quarto Henrici vij^{i} patet, iacet inter tenementum Thome Heywad ex parte una et tenementum Edmundi Hennysby ex parte australi, caput occidentale abuttat super regiam viam, ut in anno xij^{mo} Regis Henrici viij^{vi} patet et reddit per annum viijs. De feodo prioris.
Item Edmundo Hennysbey pro uno tenemento nuper in tenura Johannis Watton; iacet in Brodlane iuxta tenementum Thome Heyward ex parte boriali et tenementum Johannis Rose ex parte australi, caput occidentale abuttat super regiam viam, per copiam ut in anno quartodecimo Henrici viij^{vi} patet et reddit per annum iiijs iiijd. De feodo prioris.
Item Willelmo Nelle pro uno vacuo horto nuper Thome Lamberd et Johannis Crose ut in anno primo Ricardi tercii patet; iacet in Brodelane ex opposito tenementi Johannis Rose nuper in tenura Thome Hervy ex parte boriali inter communem venellam ex parte occidentali, uno capite abuttante super magnam ripam versus austrum, per copiam ut in anno *[blank]* et reddit viijd. De feodo prioris.
fo 9v
Item Willelmo Burdon pro uno alneto nuper in tenura rectoris de Norwold et postea Willelmi Corson; iacet inter riveram ex parte occidentali et alnetum Willelmi Sewall ex parte orientali, et commune fossatum ex parte australi, et caput boriale abuttat super riveram predictam, per copiam ut in anno xxiij^{o} Regis Henrici vij^{mi} patet et reddit per annum ixs. De feodo episcopi.
Item Thoma Agas pro uno alneto nuper in tenura Edmundi Winfrey; iacet ultra le ee, inter alnetum Thome Palmer ex parte australi et alnetum Johannis Synkwyn ex parte boriali, per copiam ut in anno septimo Regis Henrici viij^{vi} patet et reddit per annum vjs. De feodo episcopi.
Item Johanne Craye unum mesuagium nuper in tenura Thome Many et Johannis Cobbold ut in anno xxiiij^{o} Henrici vij^{i} patet ad terminum xxx annorum hoc anno xvj annorum, et postea Edward Burd ut in anno quarto Henrici viij^{i} patet, nunc in tenura Johannis Craye ut in anno nono Henrici viij^{vi} patet, et reddit per annum xxs. De feodo prioris.
Item Ricardo Aldered barker pro uno tenemento; scituatur in Ely ad latam ripam inter tenementa elemosinarii eliensis ex utraque parte in tenura Johannis Craye, et abuttat super regiam [viam] ex parte australi, et abuttat boriale super commune fossatum, ut in anno tercio Regis Henrici vij^{mi} patet et reddit per annum xxs. De feodo prioris.
fo 10
Item Johanne Craye pro uno tenemento ibidem nuper in tenura Johannis Cobbold ut in anno xxiij^{mo} Henrici vij patet, et postea Edwardi Burde ut in anno quarto Henrici viij patet; iacet inter tenementa elemosinarii eliensis ex utraque parte, in tenura Angnete Wake ex parte occidentali et tenementum Ricardi Aldered ex parte orientali, abuttat super regiam [viam] ex parte australi, per copiam ut in anno ix^{o} Henrici viij^{vi} patet et reddit per annum xvjs. Feodum prioris.
Item Angneta Wake pro uno tenemento ibidem nuper in tenura Thome Many et Johannis Wrytht ut in anno sexto Regis Henrici vij^{mi} patet; iacet inter tenementa elemosinarii eliensis ex utraque parte, et abuttat super regiam viam ex parte australi et abuttat versus boriam super commune fossatum ibidem, per copiam ut in anno xxiij^{o} Henrici vij^{mi} patet, vjs viijd . De feodo prioris.

From John Day for a tenement next to the aforesaid tenement lately in the tenure of John \Day/; and it abuts upon the stone steps in the highway towards Broad Hithe on the north side, and abuts upon the orchard on the south side, by copy for a term of years, as it appears in 11 Henry VIII [1519–20] and renders 4*s* annually. Of the prior's fee.

fo 9[15]

From William Dopbys for a tenement lately in William Nele's tenure, as it appears in 4 Henry VIII [1512–13]; it lies in Broad Lane on the east side, between a tenement of the Lady Chapel called Storehouse on the south side and a tenement of the almoner of Ely in William Lay's tenure on the north side, the west head abuts upon the king's highway, the east head upon a tenement of the almoner in John Wattys' tenure, as it appears in 13 Henry VIII [1521–2] and renders 6*s* 8*d*. Of the prior's fee.

From Thomas Heyward for a messuage; it lies in Broad Lane lately in John Clerke's tenure as it appears in 4 Henry VII [1488–9], it lies between Thomas Heywad's tenement on one side and Edmund Hennysby's tenement on the south side, the west head abuts upon the king's highway, as it appears in 12 Henry VIII [1520–21] and renders 8*s* annually. Of the prior's fee.

From Edmund Hennysbey for a tenement lately in John Watton's tenure; it lies in Broad Lane next to Thomas Heyward's tenement on the north side and John Rose's tenement on the south side, the west head abuts upon the king's highway, by copy as it appears in 14 Henry VIII [1522–3] and renders 4*s* 4*d* annually. Of the prior's fee.

From William Nelle for a vacant yard lately of Thomas Lamberd and John Crose as it appears in 1 Richard III [1483–4]; it lies in Broad Lane opposite John Rose's tenement lately in Thomas Hervy's tenure on the north side between a common lane on the west side, one head abutting upon the great bank towards the south, by copy as in *[blank]* and renders 8*d*. Of the prior's fee.

fo 9v

From William Burdon for an alder-holt lately in the tenure of the rector of Northwold and afterwards of William Corson; it lies between the river on the west side and William Sewall's alder-holt on the east side, and a common ditch on the south side, and the north side abuts upon the aforesaid river, by copy as it appears in 23 Henry VII [1507–08] and renders 9*s* annually. Of the bishop's fee.

From Thomas Agas for an alder-holt lately in Edmund Winfrey's tenure; it lies beyond the water, between Thomas Palmer's alder-holt on the south side and John Synkwyn's alder-holt on the north side, by copy as it appears in 7 Henry VIII [1515–16] and renders 6*s* annually. Of the bishop's fee.

From John Craye a messuage lately in the tenure of Thomas Many and John Cobbold as it appears in 24 Henry VII [1508–09] for a term of thirty years, this year sixteen years remain, and afterwards of Edward Burd as it appears in 4 Henry VIII [1512–13], now in John Craye's tenure as it appears in 9 Henry VIII [1517–18] and renders 20*s* annually. Of the prior's fee.

From Richard Aldered barker for a tenement; it lies in Ely at the broad bank between tenements of the almoner of Ely on either side in John Craye's tenure, and it abuts upon the king's [highway] on the south side, and the north abuts upon the common ditch,[16] as it appears in 3 Henry VII [1487–8] and renders 20*s* annually. Of the prior's fee.

fo 10

From John Craye for a tenement there lately in John Cobbold's tenure as it appears in 23 Henry VII [1507–08], and afterwards of Edward Burde as it appears in 4 Henry VIII [1512–13]; it lies between tenements of the almoner of Ely on either side, in Agnes Wake's tenure on the west side and Richard Aldered's tenement on the east side, it abuts upon the king's [highway] on the south side, by copy as it appears in 9 Henry VIII [1517–18] and renders 16*s* annually. Prior's fee.

From Agnes Wake for a tenement there lately in the tenure of Thomas Many and John Wrytht, as it appears in 6 Henry VII [1490–91]; it lies between tenements of the almoner of Ely on either side, and abuts upon the king's highway on the south side and abuts towards the north upon the common ditch there, by copy as it appears in 23 Henry VII [1507–08], 6*s* 8*d*. Of the prior's fee.

Item Johanne Wrytht pro uno tenemento nuper in tenura Willelmi Resleys ut in anno *[blank]* Henrici vj^{ti} patet et reddebat per annum vjs, nunc in tenura Johannis Wryth vocato le parler; iacet inter tenementum Angel Wake ex parte orientali et tenementum Johannis Wryth ex parte occidentali, per copiam et reddit per annum iijs iiijd. De feodo prioris.
Item Johanne Wrytht pro quadam parcella gardini supradicti nuper in tenura Thome Martyn quondam in tenura Johannis Burgeys, per copiam et reddit viij d. De feodo prioris.
fo 10 v
Item Thoma Ruscell pro uno gardino nuper in tenura Isabelle Ayleward et Ricardi Heydon ut in anno xviij^{o} Henrici vij^{mi} patet, et continet in longitudine xviij perticas et iij pedes, et in latitudine ij perticas et vij pedes, et caput australe abuttat super communem venellam et aliud caput super commune fossatum, per copiam ad terminum annorum ut in anno undecimo Henrici viij^{vi} patet et reddit per annum ijs. De feodo prioris.
Item Thoma Roscell pro uno tenemento nuper in tenura Willelmi Heydon quondam Ricardi Heydon; scituatur apud Broydhyth, abuttat super regiam viam versus australem et iuxta tenementum vocatum Le Shepe ex parte occidentali, per copiam ad terminum annorum ut in anno xj^{o} Henrici viij^{vi} patet et reddit per annum iiijs. De feodo prioris.
Item Johanne Wayte pro uno tenemento ibidem nuper in tenura Johannis Clerke, et abuttat super regiam viam ex parte australi, abuttat boriali super communem venellam; iacet inter tenementum elemosinarii in tenura Radulfi Heyward ex parte occidentali et tenementum vocatum Le Shype ex parte orientali nuper in tenura Johannis \Crosbys/, ut in anno xx^{mo} Regis Henrici vij^{i} patet per copiam et reddit per annum vjs. De feodo prioris.
Item Radolfo Heywad pro uno tenemento ibidem nuper in tenura Ricardi Wodwroff quondam Crosbys; iacet inter tenementum magistri capelle Beate Marie in tenura Alicie Pomell ex parte occidentali et tenementum elemosinarii eliensis in tenura Johannis Wayte ex parte orientali, abuttat super regiam viam ex parte australi, ut in anno x^{o} Henrici viij^{vi} patet, et reddit vjs. De feodo prioris.
fo 11
Item Roberto Rumney pro uno horto nuper in tenura Radulphi Heywad et Edmundi Nedyng quondam Roberti Barnard ut in anno iij^{o} Henrici vij^{i} patet; scituatur in Leleslane ex parte occidentali, inter vacuam placeam pertinentem domui Sancti Johannis ex parte boriali, et continet in fronte ex parte de Lileslane duas perticas, ut in laudo per copiam ad terminum annorum ut in anno iiij^{to} Regis Henrici viij^{vi} patet et reddit per annum viijd. De feodo prioris.
Item Stephano Wrenche pro uno tenemento nuper Roberti Blomer quondam Johannis Pond ut in anno xiij^{o} Edwardi iiij^{ti} patet; scituatur ex opposito finis borialis de Brodlane inter tenementum Edwardi Burd ex parte orientali et tenementum nuper Townesends ex parte occidentali, et continet in latitudine per regiam viam xj virgas j pedem, et in longitudine xxix virgas et ij pedes, ut in anno xij^{o} Henrici viij^{vi} patet et reddit per annum vjs viijd. De feodo episcopi.
Item Willelmo Sewale pro uno tenemento nuper Thome Emneth; iacet in vico versus \magnam/ ripam inter tenementum elemosinarii eliensis in tenura Johannis Adam ex parte occidentali et tenementum Petri Browne ex parte orientali, caput australe abuttat super vicum predictum, caput boriale super vinetum domini episcopi, per copiam ad terminum lij annorum hoc anno xxviij, ut in anno xiiij Henrici vij^{mi} patet et reddit per annum iijs iiijd. De feodo prioris.
Item Thoma Lokey et Johanne Adam pro uno tenemento quondam in tenura Johanne Millys relicte Roberti Rogers ut in anno iij^{o} Henrici viij patet; scituatur prope le arche inter tenementum Willelmi Sewall ex parte orientali et tenementum Willelmi Palmer ex parte occidentali, ut in anno xij^{mo} Regis Henrici viij^{vi} patet et reddit per annum vs. De feodo prioris.
fo 11v
Item Willelmo Palmer pro uno tenemento iuxta tenementum predictum nuper in tenura Willelmi Hansard; scituatur inter tenementum Johannis Adam ex parte orientali et tenementum Johannis Okyrby ex parte occidentali, abuttat super regiam viam versus Brodhet ex parte australi, ut in anno xj^{mo} Regis [Henrici] viij^{vi} patet per copiam et reddit vs. De feodo prioris.

From John Wrytht for a tenement called the parlour lately in William Resley's tenure, as it appears in *[blank]* Henry VI and rendered 6*s* annually, now in the tenure of John Wryth; it lies between Agnes Wake's tenement on the east side and John Wryth's tenement on the west side, by copy and renders 3*s* 4*d* annually. Of the prior's fee.
From John Wrytht for a piece of the abovesaid garden[17] lately in Thomas Martyn's tenure formerly in John Burgeys' tenure, by copy, and renders 8*d*. Of the prior's fee.
fo 10 v
From Thomas Ruscell for a garden lately in the tenure of Isabel Ayleward and Richard Heydon as it appears in 18 Henry VII [1502–03] and it contains 18 perches and 3 feet in length, and 2 perches and 7 feet in breadth, and the south head abuts upon a common lane and the other head upon the common ditch, by copy for a term of years as it appears in 11 Henry VIII [1519–20] and renders 2*s* annually. Of the prior's fee.
From Thomas Roscell for a tenement lately in the tenure of William Heydon formerly of Richard Heydon; it lies at Broad Hithe, it abuts upon the king's highway towards the south and next to a tenement called The Ship on the west side, by copy for a term of years as it appears in 11 Henry VIII [1519–20] and renders 4*s* annually. Of the prior's fee.
From John Wayte for a tenement there lately in John Clerke's tenure, and it abuts upon the king's highway on the south side, it abuts upon a common lane on the north side; it lies between a tenement of the almoner in Ralph Heyward's tenure on the west side and a tenement called The Ship on the east side lately in the tenure of John Crosby, as it appears in 20 Henry VII [1504–05], by copy and renders 6*s* annually. Of the prior's fee.
From Ralph Heywad for a tenement there lately in Richard Wodwroff's tenure formerly Crosby's; it lies between a tenement of the master of the Lady Chapel in Alice Pomell's tenure on the west side and a tenement of the almoner of Ely in John Wayte's tenure on the east side, it abuts upon the king's highway on the south side, as it appears in 10 Henry VIII [1518–19] and renders 6*s*. Of the prior's fee.
fo 11
From Robert Rumney for a yard lately in the tenure of Ralph Heywad and Edmund Nedyng formerly of Robert Barnard as it appears in 3 Henry VII [1487–8]; it lies in Liles Lane on the west side, between a vacant plot pertaining to the house of St John on the north side, and contains 2 perches in front on Liles Lane, as in the award[18] by copy for a term of years as it appears in 4 Henry VIII [1512–13] and renders 8*d* annually. Of the prior's fee.
From Stephen Wrenche for a tenement lately Robert Blomer's formerly John Pond's as it appears in 13 Edward IV [1473–4]; it lies opposite the north end of Broad Lane between Edward Burd's tenement on the east side and a tenement lately Townesend's on the west side, and it contains 11 yards I foot in breadth along the king's highway, and 29 yards and 2 feet in length, as it appears in 12 Henry VIII [1520–21] and renders 6*s* 8*d* annually. Of the bishop's fee.
From William Sewale for a tenement lately Thomas Emneth's; it lies in the street towards the \great/ bank between a tenement of the almoner of Ely in John Adam's tenure on the west side and Peter Brown's tenement on the east side, the south head abuts upon the aforesaid street, the north head upon the lord bishop's vineyard, by copy for a term of fifty-two years, this year twenty-eight remain, as it appears in 14 Henry VII [1498–9] and renders 3*s* 4*d* annually. Of the prior's fee.
From Thomas Lokey and John Adam for a tenement formerly in the tenure of Joan Millys widow of Robert Rogers as it appears in 3 Henry VIII [1511–12]; it lies near the arch, between William Sewall's tenement on the east side and William Palmer's tenement on the west side, as it appears in 12 Henry VIII [1520–21] and renders 5*s* annually. Of the prior's fee.
fo 11v
From William Palmer for a tenement next to the aforesaid tenement lately in William Hansard's tenure; it lies between John Adam's tenement on the east side and John Okyrby's tenement on the west side, it abuts upon the king's highway towards Broad Hithe on the south side, as it appears in 11 [Henry] VIII [1519–20] by copy and renders 5*s*. Of the prior's fee.

Item Johanne Okyrby pro uno tenemento nuper in tenura Angnete Mony relicte Willelmi Plome; scituatur in vico ducente versus ad latam ripam inter tenementum Ricardi Person pertinens capelle ex parte occidentali et tenementum elemosinarii eliensis nunc in tenura Willelmi Palmer ex parte orientali, abuttat super regiam viam ex parte australi, per copiam ut in anno vj^{o} \Henrici viij^{vi}/ patet et reddit per annum iijs iiijd. De feodo prioris.
Item Willelmo Palmer pro ij^{bus} tenementis nuper in tenura Petri Browne et Andree Polle ut in anno xxj^{mo} Henrici vij patet, et postea Simonis Bloxham, Thome Sigurson; iacent inter tenementum Willelmi Nele ex parte occidentali et tenementum magistri capelle in tenura Johannis Spylman ex parte orientali, abuttant super regiam viam, caput boriale abuttat super vinetum domini episcopi, per copiam ut in anno x^{mo} Regis Henrici viij^{vi} patet et reddunt per annum xs. De feodo prioris.
Item Johanne Baker pro uno tenemento; scituatur in Le Hyerow nuper in tenura Henrici Heth, inter tenementum Willelmi Chapman ex parte occidentali et tenementum Ricardi Blowfyld ex parte orientali, abuttat super regiam viam ex opposito porte elemosinarii eliensis, per copiam ut in anno nono Henrici viij^{vi} patet et reddit per annum xiijs iiijd. De feodo prioris.
fo 12
Item Thoma Buttler pro uno tenemento scituato in Newnham nuper in tenura Roberti Stokyll ut in anno quinto Regis Henrici viij^{vi} patet; iacet inter tenementum Willelmi Sempull ex parte australi et tenementum magistri Sancti Johannis ex parte boriali, abuttat super regiam viam ex parte orientali et abuttat ex parte occidentali super tenementum Willelmi Sempull, per copiam ut in anno Regis Henrici viij^{vi} xj^{o} patet et reddit per annum iijs iiijd. De feodo prioris.
Item Ricardo Galy pro uno tenemento in Newnham quondam in tenura Luce[19] Tayllor; iacet inter tenementum Roberti Writh ex parte boriali et tenementum magistri Sancti Johannis ex parte australi, abuttat super regiam viam ex parte orientali et abuttat ex parte occidentali super tenementum vocatum Lonkgys nunc in manu domini, et reddit vjs viijd. De feodo prioris.
Item Johanne Laye pro ij^{bus} cotagiis sub uno tecto quondam Thome Flexman nuper in tenura Roberti Marchall ut in anno xvj Henrici vij^{mi} patet; scituantur in Neunam inter tenementum capelle Beate Marie in tenura Ricardi Inge ex parte australi et tenementum domini episcopi in tenura Willelmi Percy ex parte boriali, per copiam ut in anno undecimo Regis Henrici viij^{i} patet et reddunt per annum vjs viijd. De feodo prioris.
Item Willelmo Herdyng pro uno tenemento quondam Johannis Howtyng ut in anno xiiij^{o} Edwardi iiij^{ti} patet, postea Ricardi Baker ut in anno xix^{o} Henrici vij patet, nuper in tenura Petri Malet et Clementie Awston ut in anno xj^{mo} Henrici viij^{vi} patet; scituatur in Newnam inter tenementa vocata Redmans ex utraque parte, abuttat [ex parte] australi super regiam viam, abuttat ex parte boriali super le Paradysclose, per copiam ut in anno Henrici viij^{vi} xij patet et reddit per annum iijs iiijd. De feodo prioris.
fo 12v
Item Willelmo Sempull pro una selda nuper in tenura Roberti Crose et Johannis Sempull; iacet in le bocheria[20] inter seldam Ricardi Banke ex una parte et seldam Johannis Alyne ex altera parte, per copiam ad terminum lj annorum ut in anno xv^{mo} Edwardi iiij^{ti} patet et reddit per annum ijs. De feodo episcopi.
Item Willelmo Tylby pro una opella inter domos carnificorum nuper Elene Page ut in anno xxj^{mo} Henrici vij patet; continet in latitudine xij pedes et in longitudine xxx pedes inter opellam elemosinarii ex parte orientali et tenementum Johannis Dey ex parte occidentali, per copiam ut in anno \13/ Henrici viij patet et reddit per annum ijs. De feodo episcopi.
Item Willelmo Tylby pro j opella ibidem nuper in tenura Johannis Crose et Johannis Bryggys ut in anno primo Henrici viij^{vi} patet; iacet inter opellam Willelmi Sempull ex parte orientali et opellam elemosinarii eliensis in tenura Willelmi Tylby ex parte occidentali, abuttat ex parte australi super tenementum Johannis Dey, per copiam ut in anno xiij^{mo} Henrici viij^{vi} patet et reddit per annum ijs. De feodo episcopi.

From John Okyrby for a tenement lately in the tenure of Agnes Mony widow of William Plome; it lies in the street leading towards the broad bank, between a tenement of Richard Person pertaining to the [Lady] Chapel on the west side and a tenement of the almoner of Ely now in William Palmer's tenure on the east side, it abuts upon the king's highway on the south side, by copy as it appears in 6 \Henry VIII/ [1514–15] and renders 3*s* 4*d* annually. Of the prior's fee.

From William Palmer for two tenements lately in the tenure of Peter Brown and Andrew Polle as it appears in 21 Henry VII [1505–06] and afterwards of Simon Bloxham, Thomas Sigurson; they lie between William Nele's tenement on the west side and a tenement of the master of the [Lady] Chapel in John Spylman's tenure on the east side, they abut upon the king's highway, the north head abuts upon the lord bishop's vineyard, by copy as it appears in 10 Henry VIII [1518–19] and they render 10*s* annually. Of the prior's fee.

From John Baker for a tenement; it lies in the High Row lately in Henry Heth's tenure, between William Chapman's tenement on the west side and Richard Blowfyld's tenement on the east side, it abuts upon the king's highway opposite the gate of the almoner of Ely, by copy as it appears in 9 Henry VIII [1517–18] and renders 13*s* 4*d* annually. Of the prior's fee.

fo 12

From Thomas Buttler for a tenement situated in Newnham lately in Robert Stokyll's tenure as it appears in 5 Henry VIII [1513–14]; it lies between William Sempull's tenement on the south side and a tenement of the master of St John on the north side, it abuts upon the king's highway on the east side and abuts on the west side upon William Sempull's tenement, by copy as it appears in 11 Henry VIII [1519–20] and renders 3s 4d annually.Of the prior's fee.

From Richard Galy for a tenement in Newnham formerly in Luke Tayllor's tenure; it lies between Robert Writh's tenement on the north side and a tenement of the master of St John on the south side, it abuts upon the king's highway on the east side and abuts on the west side upon a tenement called Lonkgys' now in the lord's hand, and renders 6*s* 8*d*. Of the prior's fee.

From John Laye for two cottages under one roof formerly Thomas Flexman's lately in Robert Marchall's tenure as it appears in 16 Henry VII [1500–01]; they lie in Newnham between a tenement of the Lady Chapel in Richard Inge's tenure on the south side and a tenement of the lord bishop in William Percy's tenure on the north side, by copy as it appears in 11 Henry VIII [1519–20] and render 6*s* 8*d* annually. Of the prior's fee.

From William Herdyng for a tenement formerly John Howtyng's as it appears in 14 Edward IV [1474–5], afterwards of Richard Baker as it appears in 19 Henry VII [1503–04], lately in the tenure of Peter Malet and Clemence Awston as it appears in 11 Henry VIII [1519–20]; it lies in Newnham between tenements called Redman's on either side, it abuts on the south [side] upon the king's highway, it abuts on the north side upon the Paradise Close, by copy as it appears in 12 Henry VIII [1520–21] and renders 3*s* 4*d* annually. Of the prior's fee.

fo 12v

From William Sempull for a stall lately in the tenure of Robert Crose and John Sempull; it lies in the butchery between Richard Banke's stall on one side and John Alyne's stall on the other side, by copy for a term of fifty-one years, as it appears in 15 Edward IV [1475–6] and renders 2*s* annually. Of the bishop's fee.

From William Tylby for a stall among the butchers' houses, lately Ellen Page's as it appears in 21 Henry VII [1505–06]; it contains 12 feet in breadth and 30 feet in length, between a stall of the almoner on the east side and John Dey's tenement on the west side, by copy as it appears in \13/ Henry VIII [1521–2] and renders 2*s* annually. Of the bishop's fee.

From William Tylby for a stall there lately in the tenure of John Crose and John Bryggys, as it appears in 1 Henry VIII [1509–10]; it lies between William Sempull's stall on the east side and a stall of the almoner of Ely in William Tylby's tenure on the west side, it abuts on the south side upon John Dey's tenement, by copy as it appears in 13 HenryVIII [1521–2] and renders 2*s* annually. Of the bishop's fee.

Item Willelmo Sempull pro una selda ibidem nuper in tenura Johannis Stokyll quondam Roberti Crose; iacet in Le Bocheria, per annum et reddit xijd. De feodo episcopi.
fo 13
Item Johanne Annesley pro uno tenemento cum gardino adiacente in vico vocato Akyrman Strete nuper in tenura Johannis Smytht et Willelmi Asshewoyd ut in anno xx^{mo} Henrici vij^{mi} patet; et iacet inter tenementum Thome Martyn ex parte orientali et tenementum Willelmi Godbed ex parte occidentali, uno capite abuttante super regiam viam ex parte australi, abuttat ex parte boriali super clos de Brays, per copiam ut in anno ix^{o} Henrici viij^{vi} patet et reddit vjs viijd. De feodo prioris.
Item Thoma Wesfeld pro ij^{bus} cotagiis sub uno tecto; iacent super corneram de Cattys Lane quondam in tenura Johannis Waleys ad terminum annorum ut in anno quarto Henrici vij patet; iacent in Cattys Lane, abuttant versus occidentalem super venellam ducentem ad communem pinfald ibidem, versus orientalem super gardinum Johannis Dounham in tenura Willelmi Burdon, per copiam ad terminum annorum hoc anno xxij, et reddunt per annum ut in anno xxiiij^{mo} Regis Henrici octavi patet ijs. De feodo prioris.
Item Johanne Wrythe pro uno tenemento in parochia Beate Marie nuper in tenura Roberti Wryth ad terminum annorum iiij^{xx} ut in anno xvj Edwardi iiij^{ti} patet; et iacet inter tenementum Thome Dowlyng ex parte occidentali et tenementum Willelmi Burdon ex parte orientali, et abuttat super regiam viam ex parte australi, per copiam ad terminum xxxv annorum ut in anno iiij^{to} Henrici viij patet et reddit per annum vijs. De feodo prioris.
Item Thomas Foxke tenet unam vacuam placeam; iacet subtus murum lapideum elemosinarie, et continet in longitudine xxxiij pedes et in latitudine ix pedes, per copiam ad terminum annorum lix, hoc anno xxxj, ut in anno decimo patet Henrici vij^{mi} in libera curia, et reddit per annum iiijd. De feodo prioris.
fo 13v
Item Amabilia Palmer pro uno tenemento scituato in Brode [Lane] ex parte orientali nuper in tenura Thome Palmer ut in anno Regis *[blank]* patet; et iacet inter tenementum senescalli hospicii ex parte australi, abuttat super regiam viam ex parte occidentali, abuttat ex parte orientali super gurgitem in tenura Thome Palmer infra le ee, per copiam ut in anno xj^{mo} Regis Henrici viij^{vi} patet et reddit elemosinario vs. De feodo prioris.
Item pitanciario de Sutton pro uno gardino iacente in Brodelane nuper in tenura Johannis Fordham; iacet inter tenementum pertinens ad officium subprioris eliensis ex parte australi et tenementum pitanciarii de Sutton ex parte boriali, et caput orientale abuttat super regiam viam et caput occidentale super vinetum pitanciarii, et continet in longitudine xxv virgas et in latitudine xvj virgas, ut in anno viij Regis Henrici vj^{ti} patet et reddit xd. De feodo prioris.
[Pro uno gurgite in Lytylportwatur]
Item Johanne Charlys pro una acra pasture infra clausum predicti Johannis Charlys nuper in tenura Johannis Smyth parvi ut in anno xxv^{mo} Regis Henrici vj^{ti} patet; et iacet in parochia Beate Marie iuxta communem venellam ex parte occidentali, uno capite abuttante super clausum sacriste versus austrum et versus boriam super clausuram domini episcopi in tenura Johannis Spyrad, per copiam ut in anno xvij^{mo} Regis Henrici vij patet et reddit per annum xiiijd.
fo 14
Item Henrico Chapman pro uno clauso continente j acram iacente ad finem borialem de Lylesholtys quondam in tenura Alicie[23] Coke ut in anno quarto Henrici vij^{mi} patet; et abuttat versus australem super Bellecrose et versus borialem super Cressewellwey, per copiam ut in anno decimo Regis Henrici viij^{vi} et reddit per annum ijs.
Item Willelmo Sempull pro una acra terre versus Westfene quondam in tenura Gransdens nuper in tenura Roberti Everad; et iacet iuxta tenementum Henrici Stalon nunc in tenura Ricardi Gotobed, per copiam et reddit per annum viijd.

From William Sempull for a stall there lately in John Stokyll's tenure formerly of Robert Crose; it lies in the butchery, and renders 12*d* annually. Of the bishop's fee.

fo 13
From John Annesley for a tenement with an adjoining garden in a street called Acreman Street lately in the tenure of John Smytht and William Asshewoyd as it appears in 20 Henry VII [1504–05]; and it lies between Thomas Martyn's tenement on the east side and William Godbed's tenement on the west side, one head abutting upon the king's highway on the south side, it abuts on the north side upon Brays close, by copy as it appears in 9 Henry VIII [1517–18] and renders 6*s* 8*d*. Of the prior's fee.
From Thomas Wesfeld for two cottages under one roof; they lie on the corner of Cats Lane formerly in John Waleys' tenure for a term of years as it appears in 4 Henry VII [1488–9];[21] they lie in Cats Lane, they abut towards the west upon a lane leading to the common pinfold there, towards the east upon John Dounham's garden in William Burdon's tenure, by copy for a term of years this year twenty-two remain, and render 2*s* annually as it appears in 24 Henry VIII [1532–3].[22] Of the prior's fee.
From John Wryth for a tenement in St Mary's parish lately in Robert Wryth's tenure for a term of eighty years as it appears in 16 Edward IV [1476–7]; and it lies between Thomas Dowlyng's tenement on the west side and William Burdon's tenement on the east side, and it abuts upon the king's highway on the south side, by copy for a term of thirty-five years as it appears in 4 Henry VIII [1512–13] and renders 7*s* annually. Of the prior's fee.
Thomas Foxke holds a vacant plot; it lies below the stone wall of the almonry, and contains 33 feet in length and 9 feet in breadth, by copy for a term of fifty-nine years, thirty-one years remain/ this year, as it appears in 10 Henry VII [1494–5] in the free court and renders 4*d* annually. Of the prior's fee.

fo 13v
From Mabel Palmer for a tenement situated in Broad [Lane] on the east side lately in Thomas Palmer's tenure as it appears in *[blank]*; and it lies between a tenement of the steward of the household on the south side, it abuts upon the king's highway on the west side, it abuts on the east side upon a weir in the river in Thomas Palmer's tenure, by copy as it appears in 11 Henry VIII [1519–20] and renders 5*s* to the almoner. Of the prior's fee.
From the pittancer of Sutton for a garden lying in Broad Lane lately in John Fordham's tenure; it lies between a tenement pertaining to the office of the subprior of Ely on the south side, and a tenement of the pittancer of Sutton on the north side, and the east head abuts upon the king's highway and the west head upon the pittancer's vineyard, and it contains 25 yards in length and 16 yards in breadth, as it appears in 8 Henry VI [1429–30] and renders 10*d*. Of the prior's fee.[24]
[For a weir in Littleport water]
From John Charlys for one acre of pasture within the enclosure of the aforesaid John Charles lately in the tenure of John Smyth junior, as it appears in 25 Henry VI [1446–7]; and it lies in St Mary's parish next to a common lane on the west side, one head abutting upon the sacrist's enclosure towards the south, and towards the north upon the lord bishop's enclosure in John Spyrad's tenure, by copy as it appears in 17 Henry VII [1501–02] and renders 14*d* annually.

fo 14
From Henry Chapman for an enclosure containing one acre lying at the north end of Liles Holt formerly in Alice Coke's tenure at it appears in 4 Henry VII [1488–9]; and it abuts towards the south upon Belle Cross and towards the north upon Cresswell Way, by copy as in 10 Henry VIII [1518–19] and renders 2*s* annually.
From William Sempull for an acre of land towards West Fen formerly in Gransden's tenure lately in Robert Everad's tenure; and it lies next to Henry Stalon's tenement now in Richard Gotobed's tenure, by copy and renders 8*d* annually.

Item senescallo hospicii pro parcella gardini pertinente ad tenementum suum; iacet super corneram de Brodelane vocatam Croyle corner nunc in tenura Willelmi Replyngall, per copiam ut in anno quarto Regis Henrici viij^{vi} patet et reddit per annum ijs. De feodo prioris.
Item eodem senescallo hospicii pro una vacua placea iacente iuxta gardinum pitanciarii de Wysbeche ; scituatur in Brodlane nunc in tenura Willelmi Schelford, per copiam ut in anno tercio Regis Henrici viij^{vi} patet et reddit per annum ijs. De feodo prioris.
fo 14v
Item cellerario eliense pro ij^{bus} acris terre vocatis Brevetorsakyr que iacent in quodam clauso vocato Ketonsclose ex parte occidentali ibidem et reddunt per annum xijd.
Item senescallo hospicii pro ij^{bus} stagnis; iacent in le ortehard iuxta gardinum precentoris eliensis ex parte occidentali et pitanciarii ex altera parte, et reddunt per annum ijs.
[Priore de Speney et custode de Bucton, pro molacione et erogacione]
Item firma de le gaytehows in tempore nundinarum, hoc anno iijs.
Summa xxli ixs vjd
Summa totalis in Ely hoc anno xxijli vs
fo 15
Brame. Item Johanne Downhold pro uno tenemento; scituatur ad rubiam crucem super corneram vocatam Akyrman Strete quondam in tenura Johannis Smyth nunc in tenura Willelmi Hardyng, et reddit per annum ijs. De feodo prioris.
Item Angneta Burdon pro uno gardino iacente in Cattyslane nuper in tenura Johannis Spencer at Stepylgayt ut in anno xvj Regis Edwardi iiij^{ti} patet; scituatur iuxta gardinum Johannis Barburs ex parte occidentali et hortum archidiaconi eliensis ex parte orientali, et reddit per annum iiijd. De feodo prioris.
Item Willelmo Sempull pro una parcella terre iuxta le bernyard elemosinarii eliensis ex parte orientali grangie ibidem; abuttat versus boriam super Sclefordlane et versus austrum super tenementum Ricardi Coke \ut in anno primo Edwardi iiij^{ti} patet/ ante in tenura Roberti Barford per copiam ut in anno sexto Henrici vij^{mi} patet, et reddit per annum vjs viijd. De feodo episcopi.
Item Willelmus Sempull tenet unam vacuam placeam cum grangio superedificato nuper Ricardi Coke ut in anno Edwardi iiij^{ti} primo patet; et continet in latitudine versus austrum per regiam viam iij perticas et iij pedes, et in latitudine versus boriam iij perticas et vij pedes, et in longitudine a regia via versus boriam vj perticas per gardinum Ricardi Coke, per copiam ut in anno vj^{to} Henrici vij patet et reddit ijs. De feodo prioris.
fo 15v
Item Willelmo Sempull pro uno gardino; iacet ex parte occidentali grangii nuper Ricardi Coke, et continet in longitudine iuxta gardinum Johannis Stokyl iiij perticas et ij pedes, per perticam xviij pedes, et versus orientem iiij perticas, et in longitudine versus boriam ij perticas et ij pedes, versus austrum ij perticas per regiam viam ducentem versus rubiam crucem, per copiam ut in anno sexto Henrici vij^{mi} patet et reddit ijd. De feodo prioris.
[Pro uno gurgite in Thetford]
Item Willelmo Sempull pro uno crofto; iacet in Ely iuxta stratam prope rubiam crucem, nuper in tenura Johannis Alen et postea in tenura Ricardi Person per indenturam ad terminum octoginta annorum hoc anno xxvij et reddit per annum ad quatuor terminos xxjs. De feodo prioris.
[Pro firmaria de Brame]
Summa xli vjs ijd
fos 15B–18v
[Well. Pro tenementis in Upwell et Owtwell; pro uno gurgite in Upwell. Firma domorum ibidem: pro terris et tenementis in Upwell, Elme, Marche, Fincham, Wyvelyngton, Bukton, Teryngton. Summa xliiijs vjd obolum]
[Cantebrigia. Pro tenementis et terris; pro tenemento in Hornyngseye. Summa lxxijs xd obolum]

From the steward of the household for a piece of garden pertaining to his tenement; it lies on the corner of Broad Lane called Croyle corner now in William Replyngall's tenure, by copy as it appears in 4 Henry VIII [1512–13] and renders 2*s* annually. Of the prior's fee.
From the same steward of the household for a vacant plot lying next to a garden of the pittancer of Wisbech; it lies in Broad Lane now in William Schelford's tenure, by copy as it appears in 3 Henry VIII [1511–12] and renders 2*s* annually. Of the prior's fee.
fo 14v
From the cellarer of Ely for two acres of land called Brevetors acre that lie in an enclosure called Ketons close, on the west side there, and render 12*d* annually.
From the steward of the household for two ponds; they lie in the orchard next to the garden of the precentor of Ely on the west side and of the pittancer on the other side, and render 2*s* annually.
[From the prior of Spinney and from the keeper of Bucton, for multure and alms]
Rent of the gatehouse at the time of the fair, 3*s* this year.
Total £20 9s 6d
Grand total in Ely this year £22 5s

fo 15
Braham.[25] From John Downhold for a tenement; it lies at the red cross, on the corner called Acreman Street formerly in John Smyth's tenure now in William Hardyng's tenure, and renders 2*s* annually. Of the prior's fee.
From Agnes Burdon for a garden lying in Cats Lane lately in the tenure of John Spencer at Stepylgayt as it appears in 16 Edward IV [1476–7]; it lies next to John Barbur's garden on the west side and a yard of the archdeacon of Ely on the east side, and renders 4*d* annually.Of the prior's fee.[26]
From William Sempull for a piece of land next to the barn yard of the almoner of Ely on the east side of the barn there; it abuts towards the north upon Shendforth Lane, and towards the south upon Richard Coke's tenement \as it appears in 1 Edward IV [1461–2]/ formerly in Robert Barford's tenure, by copy as it appears in 6 Henry VII [1490–91] and renders 6*s* 8*d* annually. Of the bishop's fee.
William Sempull holds a vacant plot with a barn built upon it lately Richard Coke's as it appears in 1 Edward IV [1461–2]; and it contains 3 perches and 3 feet in breadth towards the south along the king's highway, and 3 perches and 7 feet in breadth towards the north, and 7 perches in length from the king's highway towards the north along Richard Coke's garden, by copy as it appears in 6 Henry VII [1490–91] and renders 2*s*. Of the prior's fee.
fo 15v
From William Sempull for a garden; it lies on the west side of a barn lately Richard Coke's, and contains 4 perches and 2 feet in length next to John Stokyll's garden, by the perch of 18 feet,[27] and 4 perches towards the east, and 2 perches and 2 feet in length towards the north, 2 perches towards the south along the king's highway leading towards the red cross, by copy as it appears in 6 Henry VII [1490–91] and renders 2*d*. Of the prior's fee.
[For a weir in Little Thetford]
From William Sempull for a croft; it lies in Ely next to the street near the red cross, lately in John Alen's tenure and afterwards in Richard Person's tenure, by indenture for a term of eighty years this year twenty-seven remain, and it renders 21*s* annually at the four terms. Of the prior's fee.
[For the farm of Braham]
Total: £10 6s 2d

fos 15B–18v
[Welle. For tenements in Upwell and Outwell; for a weir in Upwell. Rent of the houses there: for land and tenements in Upwell, Elm, March, Fincham, Willingham, Buckton, Terrington. Total 44*s* 6½*d*]
[Cambridge. For tenements and lands; for a tenement in Horningsea. Total 72*s* 10½*d*]

fos 19–21v
[Redditus assisi in diversis locis. Summa xjli xvjs iiijd]
fo 22
[Penciones rectorie de Barsham, ecclesiarum de Ympyngton, Sancti Andree in Cantebrigia, Fodeston; anniversarii. Summa lxxvjs viijd]
fos 22v–24
Firma grangii. Item Thoma Makrow pro firma grangii elemosinarii cum omnibus terris et tenementis pratis et pasturis quondam in tenura Thome Galon, ad terminum xxj annorum hoc anno xvj, [ut] per indenturam patet et reddit per annum ad quatuor terminos lxvjs viijd.
[Firma rectorie de Foston; redditus assisi in Sall, Hecham, Telney, Walesoken, Wysbeych, Lincolnia, Cantebrigia] Summa xxxviijs vjd
fos 24v–27
[Anniversarii et erogaciones]
fo 27v
Resolucio redditus ad terminos usuales ut in anno *[blank]* Henrici vj^{ti} patet.
Solutum domino episcopo eliensi ad terminos usuales xvijs iiijd.
Solutum cancellario conventus per annum xjs viijd.
Solutum custodi capelle Beate Marie per annum iijs iiijd.
Solutum sacriste eliensi pro j tenemento quondam Kyllokys vd.
Solutum custodi de Lylesholt in precio j libre piperis per annum xiiijd.
Solutum thesaurario conventus pro j tenemento in Brodlane iiijd.
Solutum custodi de Brays pro iiij acris terre per annum ijs viijd.
[Solutum pro terris apud Brame et in Stretham]
fos 28–29v
[Ad heygabell in Cantebrigia; pro terris]
Summa lxxvjs viijd obolum
[Inventorium factum in decessu fratris Johannis Paate elemosinarii]

fo 30
Rentale de ballivo de Porta renovatum anno regni Regis Henrici viij xiiij^{mo}

[Redditus assisus de manerio de Thetford]
Item Willelmo Hollynshed <Willelmo Styrowde semer> pro uno tenemento; iacet in Brodlane super corneram ex opposito Potters Lane versus Castellheyt quondam in tenura Thome Person nuper in tenura Thome Martyn et reddit per annum ijs. De feodo prioris.
Item Roberto Weterer <Rodulphus Hollande> pro uno tenemento scituato in Walpullane quondam in tenura Johannis Duke; et iacet inter tenementum Thome Dunstabull ex parte occidentali et abuttat ex parte boriali super regiam viam et reddit per annum iiijd. De feodo prioris.
fo 30v
Item Thoma Dunstabull <Raphe Hollande> pro uno tenemento; iacet in Walpull Lane inter tenementum Roberti Weterer ex parte orientali et unum caput abuttat super regiam \viam/ ex parte boriali et reddit per annum xjjd. De feodo prioris.
Item Edmundo Tyler <Willelmo Port> pro tenemento fere ex opposito Catteslane quondam in tenura Andree Somerset et postea Roberti Tyler et Ricardi Hendiman, et reddit per annum iiijd. De feodo prioris.
Item Willelmo Rutter <Robert Martche> pro uno tenemento quondam Johannis Soneman et postea Johannis Custans; iacet versus Westefen inter tenementum Johannis Marche ex parte occidentali et tenementum Ricardi Gotobed ex parte orientali, et abuttat ex parte australi super regiam viam, et reddit per annum xijd. De feodo prioris.

fos 19–21v
[Fixed rents in various places. Total £11 16*s* 4*d*]
fo 22
[Pensions of the rectory of Barsham, of the churches of Impington, of St Andrew in Cambridge, of Foxton; obits. Total 76s 8d]
fos 22v–24
Rent of the barn. From Thomas Makrow for the rent of the almoner's barn with all lands and tenements, meadows and pastures formerly in Thomas Galon's tenure for a term of twenty-one years this year sixteen remain, [as] it appears by indenture and renders 66*s* 8*d* annually at the four terms.
[Rent of the rectory of Foxton; fixed rents in Salle, Heacham, Tilney, Walsoken, Wisbech, Lincoln, Cambridge.] Total 38*s* 6*d*
fos 24v–27
[Obits and alms]
fo 27v
Repayment of rent at the usual terms as it appears in *[blank]* Henry VI.
Paid to the lord bishop of Ely at the usual terms 17*s* 4*d*.
Paid to the chancellor of the convent 11*s* 8*d* annually.
Paid to the keeper of the Lady Chapel 3*s* 4*d* annually.
Paid to the sacrist of Ely for a tenement formerly Kyllokys' 5*d*.
Paid to the keeper of Liles Holt one pound of pepper, worth 14*d* annually.
Paid to the treasurer of the convent for a tenement in Broad Lane 4*d*.
Paid to the keeper of Brays for 4 acres of land, 2*s* 8*d* annually.
[Paid for lands at Braham and in Stretham]
fos 28–29v
[For hagable in Cambridge; for lands]
Total 76s 8½d
[Inventory made on the departure of brother John Paate, almoner][28]

fo 30
The rental of the bailiff of Porta renewed in 14 Henry VIII [1522–3]

[Fixed rent from the manor of Little Thetford]
From William Hollynshed <William Styrowde tailor> for a tenement; it lies in Broad Lane on the corner opposite Potters Lane towards Castle Hithe, formerly in Thomas Person's tenure lately in Thomas Martyn's tenure and renders 2*s* annually. Of the prior's fee.
From Robert Weterer <Ralph Hollande> for a tenement situated in Walpole Lane formerly in John Duke's tenure; and it lies between Thomas Dunstabull's tenement on the west side and it abuts on the north side upon the king's highway, and renders 4*d* annually. Of the prior's fee.
fo 30v
From Thomas Dunstabull <Ralph Hollande> for a tenement; it lies in Walpole Lane between Robert Weterer's tenement on the east side and one head abuts upon the king's \highway/ on the north side and renders 12*d* annually. Of the prior's fee.
From Edmund Tyler <William Port> for a tenement almost opposite Cats Lane formerly in the tenure of Andrew Somerset and afterwards of Robert Tyler and Richard Hendiman, and renders 4*d* annually. Of the prior's fee.
From William Rutter <Robert Martche> for a tenement formerly John Soneman's and afterwards John Custans'; it lies towards West Fen between John Marche's tenement on the west side and Richard Gotobed's tenement on the east side, and it abuts on the south side upon the king's highway, and renders 12*d* annually. Of the prior's fee.

Item custode graciarum de Reddmans pro uno mesuagio; iacet in Newnaham vocato Chesewekes nuper in tenura Ricardi Bakers et reddit per annum xijd. De feodo episcopi.
fo 31
Item sacrista eliensi pro uno tenemento; iacet in vico versus Castell Heyth nuper in tenura Thome Person et reddit per annum iiijd. De feodo prioris.
Item Thoma Palmer pro quadam pecia terre quondam Benedicti Hillok nuper Thome Persons <nunc in tenura Roberti Buck>; et iacet remociori parte tenementi supradicti, in longitudine iuxta tenementum domini prioris usque Potterslane, ut patet in compoto Edwardi iiij[ti] xix[o] et reddit per annum iiijs. De feodo prioris.
Item Roberto Mote pro crofto; iacet in Potterslane nuper in tenura Edmundi Umfrey quondam in tenura Thome Person et reddit per annum unam libram cimini, iiijd. De feodo prioris.
Item Johanne Rose <Edmondi Haynes nunc uxoris> pro tenemento suo quondam Thome Hervys; iacet in Brodlane inter tenementum Amabylie Palmer boriali et tenementum Johannis Ward ex parte australi, et reddit per annum xd. De feodo prioris.
fo 31v
Item infirmario eliensi pro uno tenemento; scituatur in Brod Lane nuper in tenura Johannis Botoll quondam in tenura magistri Thome Getesle et postea Johannis Shepey, et reddit per annum xijd. De feodo prioris.
Item domino Roberto Colvell pro uno tenemento super le Hirowe nuper in tenura Ricardi Blowfeld quondam Johannis Hyver; iacet inter tenementum elemosinarii eliensis ex parte occidentali et tenementum Johannis Synkyn ex parte orientali et reddit xijd. De feodo prioris.
Item custode capelle Beate Marie Virginis pro uno tenemento; iacet in le Brodelane quondam in tenura Johannis Whyte et postea in tenura Willelmi Cooke, et reddit per annum xijd. De feodo prioris.
Item Thoma Dunstabull pro quadam parcella terre capta ad tenementum in Walpull Lane sibi dimissa et heredibus suis per cartam capituli eliensis, et reddit per annum iijd. De feodo prioris.
fo 32
[Pro terris in campis de Ely]
Item pitanciario de Sutton pro j tenemento quondam in tenura Willelmi Dounham; iacet in Brodlane iuxta mesuagium elemosinarii eliensis ex parte australi, et reddit per annum xviijd. De feodo prioris.
Item Margareta Lavynham pro quodam tenemento in Acremanstret quondam Katerine Bramton nunc in tenura Johannis Dunhold et reddit per annum viijd, hoc anno nihil quia iacet ad vastum. De feodo prioris.
fo 32v
[Redditus assisus de manerio de Henny]
Summa xxxs vd
Firma mesuagiorum. Item Johanne Rose <Thomas Blevine> pro uno stagnario in Potterslane nuper in tenura Edmundi Humfrey; et abuttat super Caudewellfene, per copiam ut in anno quinto Regis Henrici viij[vi] patet et reddit viijs. De feodo prioris.
Item Johanne <Willelmo> Lame pro stagnario in Potterslane nuper in tenura Johannis Tooke quondam Welams et postea in tenura Ricardi Overe hoc anno solvebat per annum vjs, nunc per copiam ut in anno nono Henrici octavi patet et reddit per annum iiijs. De feodo prioris.
Item Johanne Rose pro uno tenemento in Potterslane nuper in tenura Johannis Smyth carpentarii et postea Angnete Smyth, per copiam ut in anno secundo Henrici viij[vi] patet et reddit per annum vjs. [De feodo prioris.]
fo 33
Item Thoma Palmer fescher pro uno horto vocato le pondyard cum una domo edificata; scituatur in Potters Lane nuper in tenura Willelmi Palmer Salmon, iacet iuxta tenementum infirmarii eliensis quondam Thome Manys, per copiam ut in anno viij[vo] Henrici viij[vi] patet et reddit viijs. De feodo prioris.

From the keeper of Redman's charity for a messuage; it lies in Newnham called *Chesewekes* lately in Richard Baker's tenure, and renders 12*d* annually. Of the bishop's fee.

fo 31

From the sacrist of Ely for a tenement; it lies in the street towards Castle Hithe lately in Thomas Person's tenure and renders 4*d* annually. Of the prior's fee.

From Thomas Palmer for a piece of land formerly Benedict Hillok's lately Thomas Person's <now in Robert Buck's tenure>; and it lies in the further part of the aforesaid tenement, in length next to the tenement of the lord prior as far as Potters Lane, at it appears in the account in 19 Edward IV [1479–80] and renders 4*s* annually. Of the prior's fee.

From Robert Mote for a croft; it lies in Potters Lane lately in Edmund Umfrey's tenure formerly in Thomas Person's tenure, and renders one pound of cumin annually, 4*d*. Of the prior's fee.

From John Rose <now Edmund Haynes' wife> for his tenement formerly Thomas Hervy's; it lies in Broad Lane between Mabel Palmer's tenement on the north and John Ward's tenement on the south side, and renders 10*d* annually. Of the prior's fee.

fo 31v

From the infirmarer of Ely for a tenement; it lies in Broad Lane lately in John Botoll's tenure formerly in the tenure of master Thomas Getesle and afterwards of John Shepey, and renders 12*d* annually. Of the prior's fee.

From Sir Robert Colvell for a tenement on the High Row lately in the tenure of Richard Blowfeld formerly of John Hyver; it lies between a tenement of the almoner of Ely on the west side and John Synkyn's tenement on the east side and renders 12*d*. Of the prior's fee.

From the keeper of the Lady Chapel for a tenement; it lies in Broad Lane formerly in John Whyte's tenure and afterwards in William Cooke's tenure and renders 12*d* annually. Of the prior's fee.

From Thomas Dunstabull for a piece of land added to a tenement in Walpole Lane bequeathed to him and his heirs by charter of the chapter of Ely priory, and renders 3*d* annually. Of the prior's fee.

fo 32

[For lands in the fields of Ely]

From the pittancer of Sutton for a tenement formerly in William Dounham's tenure; it lies in Broad Lane next to a messuage of the almoner of Ely on the south side and renders 18*d* annually. Of the prior's fee.

From Margaret Lavynham for a tenement in Acreman Street formerly of Katherine Bramton now in John Dunhold's tenure, and renders 8*d* annually, this year nothing because it is waste. Of the prior's fee.

fo 32v

[Fixed rent from the manor of Henny Hill]

Total 30s 5d

Rent of the messuages. From John Rose <Thomas Blevine> for a pond in Potters Lane lately in Edmund Humfrey's tenure; and it abuts upon Caldwell Fen, by copy as it appears in 5 Henry VIII [1513–14] and renders 8*s*. Of the prior's fee.

From John <William> Lame for a pond in Potters Lane lately in John Tooke's tenure formerly Welam's and afterwards in Richard Overe's tenure, this year, it paid 6*s* annually, now by copy as it appears in 9 Henry VIII [1517–18] and renders 4*s* annually. Of the prior's fee.

From John Rose for a tenement in Potters Lane lately in the tenure of John Smyth carpenter and afterwards of Agnes Smyth, by copy as it appears in 2 Henry VIII [1510–11] and renders 6*s* annually. [Of the prior's fee.][29]

fo 33

From Thomas Palmer fisherman for a yard called the pondyard with a house built upon it; it lies in Potters Lane lately in the tenure of William Palmer Salmon, it lies next to a tenement of the infirmarer of Ely formerly Thomas Many's, by copy as it appears in 8 Henry VIII [1516–17] and renders 8*s*. Of the prior's fee.

Item Johanne Rose pro pondyard; iacet in Potters Lane quondam in tenura Henrici Palmer et Johannis Mobbys, et solvebat per annum vjs viijd, nunc per copiam ut in anno *[blank]* Henrici vij patet et reddit per annum iiijs vjd. De feodo prioris.
Item Roberto Motte pro uno stagnario cum ij^bus stagnis in eodem; iacet in Potters Lane nuper in tenura Roberti Orton quondam Thome Canam, per copiam ut in anno xj^mo Henrici viij^vi patet et reddit per annum xijd. De feodo prioris.
Item Thoma Palmer pro uno crofto continente ij acras cum pertinenciis nuper Roberti Rechys, inter terram subprioris ex parte orientali et terram episcopi ex parte occidentali, abuttat super Potterslane ex parte australi et caput boriam super Pynderlane, per copiam ut in anno vicesimo primo Henrici vij^mi patet et reddit per annum vs. De feodo prioris.
fo 33v
Item Thoma Slowe pro uno alneto nuper Willelmi Rede ut \in/ anno xxvj Henrici vj^ti patet; iacet versus altum pontem ex parte boriali et tenementum sacriste ex parte occidentali, et caput australe abuttat super calcetum versus Stuntney, per copiam ut in anno vicesimo nono Regis Henrici vij^mi patet et reddit per annum xviijd. De feodo prioris.
Item Thoma Camam pro uno tenemento nuper Johannis Canam quondam Johannis Bayll, solebat reddere per annum xijs; scituatur in vico ducente versus Castelhithe inter tenementum subprioris ex parte orientali et tenementum magistri capelle ex parte occidentali, abuttat super regiam \viam/ ex parte australi et caput boriale abuttat super vinetum domini prioris, per copiam ut in anno xij^o Henrici vij^mi patet et reddit per annum vjs viijd. De feodo prioris.
Item Ricardo Bryte pro uno tenemento in le Brodlane ex parte occidentali strate ibidem, quondam in tenura Willelmi Shelford quondam Jacobi Schomaker, et solebat reddere per annum vjs viijd, nunc per copiam ut in anno Regis Henrici viij^i tercio patet et reddit per annum vs. De feodo prioris.
Item Willelmo Wryght braser pro uno tenemento quondam in tenura Thome Pope et reddebat per annum iiijs; iacet in Brodelane inter tenementa elemosinarii ex utraque parte per copiam ut in anno iiij^to Henrici viij^vi patet et reddit per annum iijs. De feodo prioris.
fo 34
Item Thoma Manchestre pro uno tenemento in Brodelane ex parte occidentali strate ibidem nuper in tenura Johannis Franches; iacet inter tenementum nuper Margarete Pullam ex parte australi et tenementum Willelmi Yemanson ex parte boriali, per copiam ut in anno xiiij^o Henrici viij^vi patet et reddit per annum xxd. De feodo prioris.
Item Johanne Replyngale pro uno tenemento; scituatur ex parte occidentali de Brodlane super corneram vocatam Croylsecorner quondam in tenura Willelmi Chyppley et Willelmi Brodderer et solebat reddere per annum xxs, nunc per copiam ut in anno quarto Regis Henrici viij^vi patet et reddit per annum vjs. De feodo prioris.
Item Johanne Laci de Lakynheyt pro uno tenemento in Brodelane iuxta tenementum Johannis Replyngayl ex parte boriali et tenementum elemosinarii ex parte australi, abuttat ex parte orientali super Brodlane et ex parte occidentali super le ortard quondam in tenura Willelmi Brodderer et reddit per annum ijs vjd \nuper Browdyer ut in anno xij^o Henrici vij patet/ De feodo prioris.
Item Roberto Symen pro uno tenemento in Brodelane; iacet ex parte orientali strate inter tenementum Johannis Pally ex parte boriali et tenementum Sancti Johannis ex parte australi, quondam solebat reddere per annum vjs viijd; nunc per copiam ut in anno vj^to Regis Henrici viij^vi patet et reddit per annum ijs viijd. De feodo prioris.
fo 34v
Item Roberto Reman de Salterloyd pro uno tenemento; iacet ex parte orientali de Brodlane inter tenementum Amabylie Palmer ex parte australi et tenementum subprioris eliensis ex parte boriali, et reddit per annum vs. De feodo prioris.

From John Rose for a pondyard; it lies in Potters Lane formerly in the tenure of Henry Palmer and John Mobby, and it paid 6*s* 8*d* annually; now by copy as it appears in *[blank]* Henry VII and renders 4*s* 6*d* annually. Of the prior's fee.
From Robert Motte for a pond with two fish tanks in it; it lies in Potters Lane lately in Robert Orton's tenure formerly of Robert Canam, by copy as it appears in 11 Henry VIII [1519–20] and renders 12*d* annually. Of the prior's fee.
From Thomas Palmer for a croft containing two acres with appurtenances lately Robert Rechy's, between land of the subprior on the east side and the bishop's land on the west side, it abuts upon Potters Lane on the south side, and the north head upon Pynder Lane, by copy as it appears in 21 Henry VII [1505–06] and renders 5*s* annually. Of the prior's fee.
fo 33v
From Thomas Slowe for an alder-holt lately William Rede's as it appears \in/ 26 Henry VI [1447–8]; it lies towards the high bridge on the north side and a tenement of the sacrist on the west side, and the south head abuts upon the causeway towards Stuntney, by copy as it appears in 29 Henry VII[30] and renders 18*d* annually. Of the prior's fee.
From Thomas Camam for a tenement lately of John Canam formerly of John Bayll, it paid a rent of 12*s* annually; it lies in the street leading towards Castle Hithe between the subprior's tenement on the east side and a tenement of the master of the [Lady] Chapel on the west side, it abuts upon the king's \highway/ on the south side and the north head abuts upon the lord prior's vineyard, by copy as it appears in 12 Henry VII [1496–7] and renders 6*s* 8*d* annually. Of the prior's fee.
From Richard Bryte for a tenement in the Broad Lane on the west side of the street there, formerly in William Shelford's tenure, formerly of James Schomaker, and it paid a rent of 6*s* 8*d* annually, now by copy as it appears in 3 Henry VIII [1511–12] and renders 5*s* annually. Of the prior's fee.
From William Wryght brewer for a tenement formerly in Thomas Pope's tenure and rendered 4*s* annually; it lies in Broad Lane between tenements of the almoner on either side, by copy as it appears in 4 Henry VIII [1512–13] and renders 3*s* annually. Of the prior's fee.
fo 34
From Thomas Manchestre for a tenement in Broad Lane on the west side of the street there lately in John Franches' tenure; it lies between a tenement lately of Margaret Pullam on the south side and William Yemanson's tenement on the north side, by copy as it appears in 14 Henry VIII [1522–3] and renders 20*d* annually. Of the prior's fee.
From John Replyngale for a tenement; it lies on the west side of Broad Lane on the corner called Croyles corner formerly in the tenure of William Chyppley and William Brodderer, and it paid a rent of 20*s* annually, now by copy as it appears in 4 Henry VIII [1512–13] and renders 6*s* annually. Of the prior's fee.
From John Laci of Lakenheath for a tenement in Broad Lane next to John Replyngayl on the north side and a tenement of the almoner on the south side, it abuts on the east side upon Broad Lane and on the west side upon an orchard formerly in William Brodderer's tenure, and renders 2*s* 6*d* annually \lately Browdyer as it appears in 12 Henry VII [1496–7]/ Of the prior's fee.
From Robert Symen for a tenement in Broad Lane; it lies on the east side of the street between John Pally's tenement on the north side and a tenement of St John's on the south side, it formerly paid a rent of 6*s* 8*d* annually; now by copy as it appears in 6 Henry VIII [1514–15] and renders 2*s* 8*d* annually. Of the prior's fee.
fo 34v
From Robert Reman of *Salterloyd* for a tenement; it lies on the east side of Broad Lane between Mabel Palmer's tenement on the south side and a tenement of the subprior of Ely on the north side, and renders 5*s* annually. Of the prior's fee.

Item Thoma Heyward de Swaffam Markyt pro uno tenemento nuper in tenura Rogeri Pullam quondam in tenura Wonderwodes et reddebat per annum xvijs; iacet in Brodlane iuxta venellam vocatam Segewykelane ex parte boriali et tenementum elemosinarii ex parte australi, per copiam ut in anno xij^{mo} Henrici viij, reddit \viijs viijd/. De feodo episcopi.
Item Johanne Bentley pro quadam vacua placea existente gardino quondam Ade Thorney et solebat reddere xxd per annum; iacet apud latam ripam inter tenementum Johannis Sand ex parte occidentali et continet in longitudine v perticas et in latitudine ij perticas per copiam ut in anno xj^{mo} Henrici viij^{vi} patet et reddit j gallinam, ijd. De feodo prioris.
Item Willelmo Martyn pro uno alneto vocato Oldesegewyk cum fossatis annexatis quondam in tenura Thome Hervy et Johannis Martyn, per copiam ut in anno xiij^{mo} Edwardi iiij^{ti} patet, nunc in tenura Thome Martyn et reddit iijs vjd. \Nunc in tenura Thome Martyn ut in anno xxiiij^{mo} Henrici vij patet/ De feodo episcopi.
fo 35
Item Petro Browne pro uno alneto nuper in tenura Willelmi Alowe quondam Roberti Markanante; iacet ultra reveram iuxta tenementum capelle in tenura Willelmi Hidon et solebat reddere iiijs per annum, nunc per copiam ut in anno xiiij^{mo} Regis Henrici viij^{vi} patet et reddit per annum iijs iiijd. De feodo episcopi.
Item Thoma Gallant pro uno tenemento a retro stallarum carnificum quondam in tenura Andree Bolle et reddebat xiijs iiijd, et postea Willelmi Harman; et iacet inter tenementum hospitalis Sancti Johannis ex parte occidentali, tenementum Johannis Wellys nuper Longys ex parte orientali, per indenturam ad terminum nonaginta novem annorum hoc anno xxij et reddit per annum vjs viijd. De feodo prioris.
Item Katerina Colson pro uno mesuagio cum crofto nuper Roberti Dale; iacet in Newnam inter tenementum domini prioris in tenura Johannis Amany ex parte occidentali et tenementum domini episcopi ex parte orientali, ut in anno xix^{o} Henrici viij patet et reddit vs iiijd. De feodo prioris.
Item Johanne Many pro uno tenemento cum crofto; iacet in Newnam inter tenementum Katerine Colson ex parte orientali, quondam in tenura Johannis Eldersham, per copiam \ut in anno ij^{o} Henrici vij patet/ et reddit per annum iiijs. De feodo prioris.
fo 35v
Item Roberto Urton pro uno tenemento in parochia Beate Marie ; iacet in Cattyslane nuper in tenura Willelmi Chyppley quondam in tenura Ricardi Orcher, per copiam ut in anno xxiij^{mo} Henrici vij^{mi} patet et reddit per annum xijd. De feodo prioris.
Item Johanne Greye pro uno tenemento; iacet in Walpull Lane quondam in tenura Roberti Orton et postea in tenura Ricardi Dente, per copiam ut in anno decimo Regis Henrici viij^{vi} patet et reddit per annum viijs. De feodo prioris.
Item Roberto Orton pro uno horto nuper Willelmi Bawdyn; iacet in Walpull Lane inter tenementum Johannis Greye ex parte occidentali et tenementum Johannis Castell ex parte orientali, et in longitudine a fine boriali usque australem xxxiiij virgas et iij quarteria, et in latitudine in fine boriali xij virgas et dimidiam, per copiam ut in anno quarto Henrici viij^{vi} patet et reddit j caponem, iiijd. De feodo prioris.
Item Roberto Ryrth <William Godbed> pro uno tenemento nuper in tenura Johannis Deumoke postea Thome Carter; iacet in Westefstrete versus Westefen, scituatur ex parte boriali strate ex opposito tenementi Johannis Custans et reddit per annum vs. De feodo prioris.
Summa cxvjs vjd
fos 36–37
[Firma piscariarum. Summa lxxixs xd]
Summa totalis receptarum hoc anno xjli vjs ixd
Nota. Item Johanne Dunhold pro uno tenemento; iacet iuxta corneram de Akermanstrete et reddit per annum vjd, nihil. De feodo prioris.
[Pro uno tenemento in Downham]

From Thomas Heyward of Swaffham Market for a tenement lately in Roger Pullam's tenure formerly in Wonderwode's tenure and it rendered 17*s* annually; it lies in Broad Lane next to a lane called Sedgwick Lane on the north side and a tenement of the almoner on the south side, by copy as in 12 Henry VIII [1520–21] it renders \8*s* 8*d*/. Of the bishop's fee.[31]
From John Bentley for vacant plot being a garden formerly of Adam Thorney and it paid a rent of 20*d* annually; it lies at the broad bank between John Sand's tenement on the west side and contains 5 perches in length and 2 perches in breadth, by copy as it appears in 11 Henry VIII [1519–20] and renders one hen, 2*d*. Of the prior's fee.
From William Martyn for an alder-holt called Old Sedgwick with associated ditches, formerly in the tenure of Thomas Hervy and John Martyn, by copy as it appears in 13 Edward IV [1473–4] now in Thomas Martyn's tenure and renders 3*s* 6*d*. \Now in Thomas Martyn's tenure as it appears in 24 Henry VII [1508–09]/. Of the bishop's fee.
fo 35
From Peter Browne for an alder-holt lately in the tenure of William Alowe formerly of Robert Markanante; it lies beyond the river next to a tenement of the Lady Chapel in William Hidon's tenure and it paid a rent of 4*s* annually, now by copy as it appears in 14 Henry VIII [1522–3] and renders 3*s* 4*d* annually. Of the bishop's fee.
From Thomas Gallant for a tenement behind the butchers' stalls formerly in the tenure of Andrew Bolle and rendered 13*s* 4*d*, and afterwards of William Harman; and it lies between a tenement of St John's hospital on the west side, John Wellys' tenement lately Longys' on the east side, by indenture for a term of ninety-nine years this year twenty-two remain, and renders 6*s* 8*d* annually. Of the prior's fee.
From Katherine Colson for a messuage with a croft lately Robert Dale's; it lies in Newnham between a tenement of the lord prior in John Amany's tenure on the west side and a tenement of the lord bishop on the east side, as it appears in 19 Henry VIII [1527–8][32] and renders 5*s* 4*d*. Of the prior's fee.
From John Many for a tenement with a croft; it lies in Newnham between Katherine Colson's tenement on the east side formerly in John Eldersham's tenure, by copy \as it appears in 2 Henry VII [1486–7]/ and it renders 4*s* annually. Of the prior's fee.
fo 35v
From Robert Urton for a tenement in St Mary's parish; it lies in Cats Lane lately in William Chyppley's tenure formerly in Richard Orcher's tenure, by copy as it appears in 23 Henry VII [1507–08] and renders 12*d* annually. Of the prior's fee.
From John Greye for a tenement ; it lies in Walpole Lane formerly in Robert Orton's tenure and afterwards in Richard Dente's tenure, by copy as it appears in 10 Henry VIII [1518–19] and renders 8*s* annually. Of the prior's fee.
From Robert Orton for a yard lately of William Bawdyn; it lies in Walpole Lane between John Greye's tenement on the west side and John Castell's tenement on the east side, and in length 34¾ yards from the north end to the south, and 12½ yards in breadth at the north end, by copy as it appears in 4 Henry VIII [1512–13] and renders one capon, 4*d*. Of the prior's fee.
From Robert Ryrth <William Godbed> for a tenement lately in the tenure of John Deumoke afterwards of Thomas Carter; it lies in West Fen Street towards West Fen, it lies on the north side of the street opposite John Custans' tenement and renders 5*s* annually. Of the prior's fee.
Total 116s 6d
fos 36–37
[Rent of the fisheries. Total 79s 10d]
Grand total of receipts this year £11 6s 9d
Note. From John Dunhold for a tenement; it lies next to the corner of Acreman Street and renders 6*d* annually, nothing. Of the prior's fee.
[For a tenement in Little Downham]

Nota. Item Johanne Rose pro uno crofto cum ij stagnis; iacet inter terram pertinentem infirmario eliensi nuper in tenura Alani Many quondam Roberti Welyngham et reddit per annum ijs, nihil hoc anno, nihil. De feodo prioris.
Summa iijs
fo 37v
Resolucio cum decasu redditus. Domino episcopo eliensi pro quadam placea apud Segewyke viijd.
Item eidem episcopo pro j alneto vocato Oldesegewyke per annum iiijd.
Item pitanciario de Sutton pro quodam cursu aque de vineto domini iiijd.
Item sacriste eliensi pro quodam alneto iuxta Bryggemede per annum iiijd.
Item elemosinario eliensi pro tenemento quondam Ade Thurmer per annum xviijd.
Item in decasu de manerio de Henny hoc anno et reddebat xijs.
Item feodum ballivo de Porta hoc anno xls.
In stipendia servientium ad Portam hoc anno iiijs.
Summa lixs ijd

fo 38
Rentale de ballivo de Brayes renovatum anno xiiij^{mo} Henrici viij^{vi}

Item Thoma Palmer <modo Roberti Buck> pro uno tenemento; iacet in vico versus Castelheyth inter tenementum sacriste eliensis <modo Laurentii ...> orientali et caput boriale abuttat super regiam viam quondam in tenura Thome Person et Kyllok, et reddit per annum iiijs. De feodo prioris.
Item Thoma Wright pro uno tenemento nuper in tenura Roberti Gabbys quondam in tenura Johannis Duke; et iacet in parochia Beate Marie super corneram vocatam Duke Corner ex opposito tenementi Thome Martyn vocati Lelame, et reddit per annum ad iiij^{or} terminos vjs. De feodo prioris.
Item Curtofero Rechys pro parcella tenementi sui nuper in tenura Ricardi Baker et postea in tenura Thome Prechett; iacet iuxta liberum [tenementum] ex parte australi eiusdem et gardinum Johannis Synkewyn ex parte boriali, per copiam ut in anno decimo nono Regis Henrici vij patet et reddit per annum xvjd. De feodo prioris.
Item Katerina Many pro uno tenemento in Newnam nuper in tenura Ricardi Tymynts inter tenementum pertinens graciis de Redmans ex parte boriali et abuttat ex parte orientali super regiam viam versus Newberns, per annum iiijd. De feodo prioris.
fo 38v
Item Johanne Synkewyn pro uno tenemento nuper in tenura Thome Yon quondam Ricardi Pykenham; iacet in Hyrowe inter Braysgate ex parte orientali et tenementum Roberti Colvell nuper Blowfeld ex parte occidentali et caput australe abuttat super regiam viam, et reddit per annum iijs iiijd. De feodo prioris.
Item magistro domus Sancti Johannis in Ely pro uno tenemento nuper in tenura Johannis Lysters, et reddit per annum ad iiij^{or} terminos vjd. De feodo *[blank]*.
Item Johanne Feltuewell pro una placea cum iij stagnis in Potterslane quondam in tenura Thome Person et reddebat per annum xviijd, nunc in tenura Roberti Moyte, per copiam ut in anno xj^{mo} Regis Henrici viij^{vi} patet et reddit per annum xijd, hoc anno nihil quia ballivus de Porta oneratus eidem. De feodo prioris.
Summa xvs vjd

fo 39
Firma mesuagiorum. Item Thoma Denys pro uno tenemento; scituatur in Newnham super corneram ex opposito super fontem, nuper in tenura Ricardi Baker quondam in tenura Johannis Annesley et postea in tenura Willelmi Baker, per copiam ut in anno tercio Regis Henrici viij patet et reddit per annum vs, ij capones. De feodo episcopi.

Note. From John Rose for a croft with two ponds; it lies between land pertaining to the infirmarer of Ely lately in Alan Many's tenure formerly Robert Welyngham's and renders 2*s* annually, nothing this year, nothing. Of the prior's fee.
Total 3s[33]
fo 37v
Repayment and decay of rent. To the lord bishop of Ely for a plot at Sedgwick 8*d*.
To the same bishop for an alder-holt called Old Sedgwick 4*d* annually.
To the pittancer of Sutton for a watercourse from the lord's vineyard 4d.
To the sacrist of Ely for an alder-holt next to Bridgemead 4*d* annually.
To the almoner of Ely for a tenement formerly Adam Thurmer's 18*d* annually.
In the deficit from the manor of Henny Hill this year, and it should render 12*s*.
The fee for the bailiff of Porta this year 40*s*.
For the wages of the servants at the Porta this year 4*s*.
Total 59s 2d

fo 38
The rental of the bailiff of Brays renewed in 14 Henry VIII [1522–3][34]

From Thomas Palmer <now Robert Buck> for a tenement ; it lies in the street towards Castle Hithe between a tenement of the sacrist of Ely <now Laurence …> on the east, and the north head abuts upon the king's highway, formerly in the tenure of Thomas Person and Kyllok, and renders 4*s* annually. Of the prior's fee.
From Thomas Wright for a tenement lately in Robert Gabby's tenure, formerly in John Duke's tenure; and it lies in St Mary's parish on the corner called Duke's corner, opposite a tenement of Thomas Martyn called The Lamb, and renders 6*s* annually at the four terms. Of the prior's fee.
From Christopher Rechys for part of his tenement lately in Richard Baker's tenure and afterwards in Thomas Pretchett's tenure; it lies next to a free [tenement] on its south side, and John Synkwyn's garden on the north side, by copy as it appears in 19 Henry VII [1503–04] and renders 16*d* annually. Of the prior's fee.
From Katherine Many for a tenement in Newnham lately in Richard Tymynt's tenure, between a tenement pertaining to Redman's charity on the north side and it abuts on the east side upon the king's highway towards New Barns, 4*d* annually. Of the prior's fee.
fo 38v
From John Synkewyn for a tenement lately in the tenure of Thomas Yon, formerly of Richard Pykenham; it lies in High Row between Brays gate on the east side and a tenement of Robert Colvell lately of Blowfeld on the west side and the south head abuts upon the king's highway, and renders 3*s* 4*d* annually. Of the prior's fee.
From the Master of St John's house in Ely for a tenement lately in John Lyster's tenure, and renders 6*d* annually at the four terms. Of the *[blank]* fee.
From John Feltwell for a plot with three ponds in Potters Lane formerly in Thomas Person's tenure, and it rendered 18*d* annually, now in Robert Moyte's tenure by copy as it appears in 11 Henry VIII [1519–20] and renders 12*d* annually, this year nothing because the bailiff of Porta is charged with it. Of the prior's fee.
Total 15s 6d

fo 39
Rent of the messuages. From Thomas Denys for a tenement; it lies in Newnham on the corner opposite the spring, lately in Richard Baker's tenure formerly in John Annesley's tenure and afterwards in William Baker's tenure, by copy as it appears in 3 Henry VIII [1511–12] and renders 5*s*, two capons annually. Of the bishop's fee.

Item Willelmo Ellys pro uno tenemento cum pertinenciis; scituatur in Newnam ex parte boriali strate inter tenementum Thome Agas ex parte orientali nuper in tenura Johannis Crawford et tenementum vocatum Paradis ex parte occidentali et abuttat super regiam viam ex parte australi, per copiam ut in anno Regis Henrici viij^{vi} octavo patet et reddit iijs iiijd. De feodo prioris.
Item Thoma Agas pro uno tenemento cum curtilagio adiacente in Newnham nuper in tenura Henrici Webster; iacet inter tenementum Willelmi Elys ex parte occidentali et tenementum Elene Molte ex parte orientali, abuttat super regiam viam ex parte australi, per copiam ut in anno xij^{mo} Henrici viij^{vi} patet et reddit per annum iijs iiijd. De feodo prioris.
Item Elena Molte pro uno tenemento ibidem in Newnam nuper Roberti Ferthyngton quondam Johannis Heth; iacet inter tenementum Thome Agas ex parte occidentali, per copiam ut in anno xiij^{mo} Henrici viij^{vi} patet et reddit per annum iijs iiijd. De feodo prioris.
fo 39v
Item Willelmo Rechys pro uno tenemento cum curtilagio; iacet in Newnaham ex parte australi strate ibidem ducentis versus Turbesey iuxta tenementum domini prioris ex parte orientali, et caput australe dicti tenementi abuttat super gardinum Johannis Alyn ex parte orientali, et continet in longitudine a gardino Johannis Synkyn ex parte boriali xxxvj virgas, per copiam ut in anno primo Regis Henrici octavi patet et reddit per annum iijs iiijd. De feodo prioris.
Item Ricardo Sanderson pro uno tenemento; scituatur in Newnham nuper in tenura Willelmi Musyke et postea in tenura Thome Maye quondam in tenura *[blank]* per copiam ut in anno xxij^{mo} Regis Henrici vij^{mi} patet et reddit per annum ijs. De feodo prioris.
Item Johanne Maye pro uno crofto; iacet in Newnham, continet dimidiam acram terre inter terras domini episcopi ex utraque parte, uno capite abuttante super viam ducentem versus Lekylporte, per copiam ut in anno terciodecimo Regis Henrici viij^{vi} patet et reddit per annum xijd et j caponem. De feodo prioris.
Item custode graciarum de Redmans pro iij acris prati infra clausuram nuper Ricardi Bakers quondam Thome Person in Newnham vocatam Parradys Close, per annum et reddit ad iiij^{or} terminos vs. De feodo episcopi.
fo 40
Item Thoma Slowe pro uno gardino nuper in tenura Willelmi Rede; iacet iuxta rubiam crucem inter gardinum Johannis Charlys ex parte australi et gardinum Roberti Gapbys ex parte boriali et caput orientale abuttat super regiam viam, per copiam ut in anno xix^{no} Henrici vij patet et reddit per annum xijd. De feodo prioris.
Item Johanne Harison pro uno cotagio cum gardino quondam Johannis Charlys; iacet iuxta rubiam crucem inter gardinum Thome Sloo ex parte boriali et unum toftum nuper Willelmi Bully ex parte australi, per copiam ut in anno secundo Regis Henrici octavi patet et reddit per annum xvjd. De feodo prioris.
Item Thoma Sloo pro uno inclauso cum pertinenciis nuper in tenura Nicholai Tiler quondam in tenura Roberti Gabbys; iacet ad rubiam crucem, vocatur Brayescrofte, per copiam ut in anno vij^{mo} Henrici viij^{vi} patet et reddit per annum vs viijd. De feodo episcopi.
Item Thomas Auston tenet unum croftum vocatum Grauntescrofte nuper in tenura Thome Dowlyng quondam Edmundi Emlyn; iacet in Akyrmanstret versus Downham super corneram ex opposito communis pynfold domini, per copiam ut in anno octavo Regis Henrici viij^{vi} patet et reddit per annum xs. De feodo episcopi.
fo 40v
Item Thoma Dunstabull pro uno clauso nuper in tenura Johannis Castell quondam Denvers, ut in anno xxvj Henrici vj^{ti} patet; iacet in Walpole Lane iuxta manerium de Ketons ex parte occidentali et tenementum liberum eiusdem Thome ex parte orientali, per copiam ut in anno xij^{o} Henrici viij^{vi} patet et reddit per annum ijs.

From William Ellys for a tenement with appurtenances; it lies in Newnham on the north side of the street, between Thomas Agas' tenement on the east side lately in John Crawford's tenure and a tenement called Paradise on the west side and it abuts upon the king's highway on the south side, by copy as it appears in 8 Henry VIII [1516–17] and renders 3*s* 4*d*. Of the prior's fee.
From Thomas Agas for a tenement with an adjoining courtyard in Newnham, lately in Henry Webster's tenure; it lies between William Elys' tenement on the west side and Ellen Molte's tenement on the east side, it abuts upon the king's highway on the south side, by copy as it appears in 12 Henry VIII [1520–21] and renders 3*s* 4*d* annually. Of the prior's fee.
From Ellen Molte for a tenement there in Newnham lately Robert Ferthyngton's formerly John Heth's; it lies between Thomas Agas' tenement on the west side, by copy as it appears in 13 Henry VIII [1521–2] and renders 3*s* 4*d* annually. Of the prior's fee.
fo 39v
From William Rechys for a tenement with a courtyard; it lies in Newnham on the south side of the street there leading towards Turbutsey next to the lord prior's tenement on the east side, and the south head of the said tenement abuts upon John Alyn's garden on the east side, and it contains 36 yards in length from John Synkyn's garden on the north side, by copy as it appears in 1 Henry VIII [1509–10] and renders 3*s* 4*d* annually. Of the prior's fee.
From Richard Sanderson for a tenement; it lies in Newnham, lately in William Musyke's tenure and afterwards in Thomas Maye's tenure formerly in the tenure of *[blank]*, by copy as it appears in 22 Henry VII [1506–07] and renders 2*s* annually. Of the prior's fee.
From John Maye for a croft; it lies in Newnham, it contains ½ acre of land between land of the lord bishop of Ely on either side, one head abutting upon the road leading towards Littleport, by copy as it appears in 13 Henry VIII [1521–2] and renders annually 12*d* and one capon. Of the prior's fee.
From the keeper of Redman's charity for 3 acres of meadow within the enclosure in Newnham called Paradise Close, lately Richard Baker's formerly Thomas Person's, and renders annually 5*s* at the four terms. Of the bishop's fee.

fo 40
From Thomas Slowe for a garden lately in William Rede's tenure; it lies next to the red cross between John Charly's garden on the south side and Robert Gapby's garden on the north side and the east head abuts upon the king's highway, by copy as it appears in 19 Henry VII [1503–04] and renders 12*d* annually. Of the prior's fee.
From John Harison for a cottage with a garden formerly John Charly's; it lies next to the red cross between the garden of Thomas Sloo on the north side and a toft lately William Bully's on the south side, by copy as it appears in 2 Henry VIII [1510–11] and renders 16*d* annually. Of the prior's fee.
From Thomas Sloo for an enclosure with appurtenances lately in Nicholas Tiler's tenure formerly in Robert Gabby's tenure; it lies at the red cross, it is called Brays croft, by copy as it appears in 7 Henry VIII [1515–16] and renders 5*s* 8*d* annually. Of the bishop's fee.
Thomas Auston holds a croft called Grauntes croft lately in Thomas Dowling's tenure formerly Edmund Emlyn's; it lies in Acreman Street towards Little Downham, on the corner opposite the lord's common pinfold, by copy as it appears in 8 Henry VIII [1516–17] and renders 10*s* annually. Of the bishop's fee.

fo 40v
From Thomas Dunstabull for an enclosure lately in John Castell's tenure formerly Denver's, as it appears in 26 Henry VI [1447–8]; it lies in Walpole Lane next to Ketons manor on the west side and a free tenement of the same Thomas on the east side, by copy as it appears in 12 Henry VIII [1520–21] and renders 2*s* annually.

Item Rowland Johnson pro uno mesuagio cum uno gardino in fine boriali nuper in tenura Thome Segurson quondam in tenura Johannis Eswell; iacet inter Braygayte ex parte occidentali et tenementum celerarii eliensis ex parte orientali, per copiam ut in anno nono Regis Henrici viij^{vi} patet et reddit per annum xjs iiijd. De feodo prioris.
Item Willelmo Chapman pro uno grangio cum quadam parcella fundi extra vastum capta; iacet infra manerium de Brays inter gardinum Willelmi Chapman ex parte orientali et abuttat super vinetum domini episcopi ex parte orientali nuper in tenura Johannis Howlet, ut in anno quinto Regis Henrici viij^{vi} patet et reddit per annum iiijs. De feodo episcopi.
Item Johannes Shynkwyn tenet unum parvum gardinum[35] quondam Cutt et postea in tenura Pekenham \ut in anno primo Henrici vj patet, reddit ijs/ nuper in tenura Thome Yon; iacet iuxta tenementum suum ex parte boriali, per copiam ut in anno quinto Regis Henrici viij^{vi} patet et reddit per annum xijd. De feodo episcopi.
fo 41
Item Roberto Colvell pro uno gardino iacente iuxta gardinum Johannis Synkwyn nuper in tenura Thome Yon ex parte australi, per copiam ad terminum lx annorum sine aliqua reparacione unius muri extransverso gardini ibidem nuper in tenura Willelmi Burdon, ut patet in anno nono Regis Henrici viij^{vi} et reddit per annum xijd. De feodo episcopi.
Item Willelmo Chapman pro quadam vacua placea terre iuxta gardinum Roberti Colvell ex parte australi et gardinum Willelmi Chapman ex parte boriali, per annum vjd. De feodo episcopi.
Item Willelmo Chapman pro uno gardino ibidem nuper in tenura Johannis Shynkyn quondam in tenura Thome Yon et reddebat per annum iijs vjd, nunc per copiam Willelmi Chapman ut in anno quarto Regis Henrici octavi patet et reddit per annum ijs. De feodo episcopi.
Item Willelmo Chapman pro uno fundo noviter edificato; iacet infra Brays quondam in tenura Johannis Rasshe et Johannis Bentley, ut in anno xij^{o} Henrici vij patet, inter grangium Thome Ellys modo Willelmi Chapman ex parte australi et unum croftum Willelmi Dey buccher modo in tenura Johannis Adam ex parte boriali, per copiam ut in anno xv^{mo} Henrici vij patet et reddit per annum iijs. De feodo episcopi.
fo 41v
Item Johanne Adam pro uno cotagio cum crofto in Brays Lane nuper in tenura Roberti Tabbot quondam in tenura Willelmi Deye bocher, per copiam ut in anno tercio Henrici viij^{vi} patet et reddit per annum vjs viijd. De feodo episcopi.
Item Johanne Shynkwyn pro licencia cariandi omnia necessaria sua tantum per portas a tenemento quondam in tenura Ricardi Pekynham per copiam ut in anno nono Regis Henrici vj^{ti} patet, et postea in tenura Thome Yon per copiam ut in anno xxxj Regis Henrici vj^{ti} patet, et reddit per annum j caponem ad festum Nativitatis Domini, j caponem. De feodo prioris.
Summa lxxvs xd, iiij capones

fos 41v–43
[Firma terrarum et pratorum in Downham et in campis de Ely]

fos 44–44v
Rentale de Nordeney renovatum in anno regni Regis Henrici octavi xiiij^{mo} pertinens senescallo hospicii

[Redditus assisus. Pro alnetis in Northney et Stunteney; pro firma Norney. Summa vjli vjs iiijd]

From Roland Johnson for a messuage with a garden at the north end lately in Thomas Segurson's tenure formerly in John Eswell's tenure; it lies between Brays gate on the west side and a tenement of the cellarer of Ely on the east side, by copy as it appears in 9 Henry VIII [1517–18] and renders 11*s* 4*d* annually. Of the prior's fee.
From William Chapman for a barn with a piece of land taken from the waste; it lies within Brays manor between William Chapman's garden on the east side, and it abuts upon the lord bishop's vineyard on the east side lately in John Howlet's tenure, as it appears in 5 Henry VIII [1513–14] and renders 4*s* annually. Of the bishop's fee.
John Shynkwyn holds a small garden formerly Cutt's and afterwards in Pekenham's tenure \as it appears in 1 Henry VI [1422–3] it renders 2*s*/ lately in the tenure of Thomas Yon; it lies next to his tenement on the north side, by copy as it appears in 5 Henry VIII [1513–14] and renders 12*d* annually. Of the bishop's fee.
fo 41
From Robert Colvell for a garden lying next to John Synkwyn's garden lately in the tenure of Thomas Yon on the south side, by copy for a term of sixty years without any repair of a wall across the garden there lately in William Burdon's tenure, as it appears in 9 Henry VIII [1517–18] and renders 12*d* annually. Of the bishop's fee.
From William Chapman for a vacant plot of land next to Robert Colvell's garden on the south side and William Chapman's garden on the north side, 6d annually. Of the bishop's fee.
From William Chapman for a garden there lately in John Shynkyn's tenure formerly in the tenure of Thomas Yon and it rendered 3*s* 6*d* annually, now by copy of William Chapman as it appears in 4 Henry VIII [1512–13] and renders 2*s* annually. Of the bishop's fee.
From William Chapman for ground newly built upon; it lies within Brays formerly in the tenure of John Rasshe and John Bentley, as it appears in 12 Henry VII [1496–7] between the barn of Thomas Ellys now William Chapman's on the south side and a croft of William Dey butcher now in John Adam's tenure on the north side, by copy as it appears in 15 Henry VII [1499–1500] and renders 3*s* annually. Of the bishop's fee.
fo 41v
From John Adam for a cottage with a croft in Brays Lane lately in Robert Tabbot's tenure formerly in the tenure of William Deye butcher, by copy as it appears in 3 Henry VIII [1511–12] and renders 6*s* 8*d* annually. Of the bishop's fee.
From John Shynkwyn for permission to carry all his goods only through the gates from a tenement formerly in Richard Pekynham's tenure, by copy as it appears in 9 Henry VI [1430–31], and afterwards in the tenure of Thomas Yon, by copy as it appears in 31 Henry VI [1452–3], and renders one capon annually at Christmas, one capon. Of the prior's fee.
Total 75s 10d, four capons

fos 41v–43
[Rent of lands and meadow in Little Downham and in the fields of Ely]

fos 44–44v
The rental of Nornea renewed in 14 Henry VIII [1522–3] pertaining to the steward of the [prior's] household

[Fixed rent. For alder-holts in Nornea and Stuntney; for the rent of Nornea.[36] Total £6 6*s* 4*d*]

fo 45

Rentale de ballivo de Caxtons in Ely cum Melburn et Cantebrigia renovatum in anno Regis Henrici viij^{vi} xiiij^{mo}

Item Edwardo Burde pro mesuagio suo nuper Eldersham libero in alta strata in Ely versus *[blank]*; quod quidem mesuagium iacet ex opposito le Brodlane inter tenementum elemosinarii eliensis in tenura Stephani Wrenche ex parte occidentali et partem alii mesuagii dicti Edwardi ex parte orientali et reddit per annum xxjd. De feodo prioris.

Item Thoma Wyton pro uno mesuagio suo libero cum gardino adiacente super corneram de Brodlane ex opposito mesuagii Edwardi Burde, ultra redditum assisum pertinentem domino episcopo hoc anno nihil quia nondum levatum, et reddit per annum vjd. De feodo episcopi.

Item Ricardo Ponder pro j mesuagio libero ibidem in alta strata quondam Ricardi Cooke; iacet inter tenementum dicti Thome Wilton ex parte occidentali et iij cotagia pertinentia capelle Beate Marie ex parte orientali, et reddit per annum in precio unius libre piperis, xiiijd. De feodo prioris.

fo 45v

Item elemosinario eliensi pro ij cotagiis sub uno tecto in Brodlane ex parte orientali eiusdem in tenura Willelmi Laye quondam Barkers; iacet inter venellam vocatam Baldokslane ex parte boriali et le storayerd capelle Beate Marie ex parte australi, et reddit in precio j libre piperis, xiiijd. De feodo prioris.

Item Roberto Wylly pro mesuagio suo quondam in tenura Johannis Sendale et postea Rogeri Davy nuper in tenura Willelmi Clerke; iacet apud Castelhith quondam Hartys inter vacuam placeam nuper Willelmi Tylers ex parte orientali et vacuam placeam pertinentem elemosinario ex parte occidentali, et reddit per annum xvjd. De feodo episcopi.

Firma. Item Galfrido Fyscher pro uno tenemento; iacet in Leyleslane iuxta portam de Leylesholt nuper in tenura Thome Benet, et reddebat vs, nunc per copiam ut in anno vj^{to} Henrici viij patet et reddit per annum iiijs. De feodo episcopi.

Item Johanne Okyrby pro uno tenemento ibidem nuper in tenura Willelmi Hansard; iacet inter tenementum Galfridi Fyscher ex parte boriali et tenementum W. Seman quondam Carters ex parte australi, ut in anno ix^{o} Henrici viij patet, reddit iiijs vjd. De feodo episcopi.

Item Willelmo Rudston pro uno alneto; iacet in Medylfen iuxta commune fossatum, et reddit per annum ijd.

fo 46

Item Willelmo Alowe pro uno alneto vocato le asheholt modo gardino Hugonis Spencer nuper Angnete Wayke; iacet iuxta portam de Lylesholt inter tenementum Galfridi Fyscher ex parte australi et continet in circuitu lvj perticas, ut in anno xiiij^{o} Henrici viij^{vi} patet et reddit iijs.

Item Edwardo Burde pro uno clauso continente per estimacionem quinque acras terre sive plus sive minus, quondam Coke nuper in tenura Johannis Ketyll; iacet in Lylesholt inter Belholt et unum alnetum Willelmi Bucke, per copiam ut in anno xij^{o} Henrici viij^{vi} patet et reddit per annum viijs.

Item Willelmo Bucke pro ij acris prati morosi vocati le Haronth in Lylesholt nuper Emmeth ut in anno xxj Edwardi iiij^{ti} patet, inter clausum Edwardi Burde ex parte occidentali[39] et clausum Willelmi Hardyng nuper Bruowd boriali et unum alnetum Thome Agas ex parte australi ut in anno xvij^{mo} Henrici vij^{mi} patet, vjs viijd.

Item Thoma Agas pro iij alnetis quondam in tenura Willelmi Ladd, Ricardi Colson et Halydays in Leylesholt inter alnetum Willelmi Bucke ex parte boriali et alnetum Johannis Adam nuper in tenura Johannis Nedyng \ex/ parte australi, per copiam ut in anno x^{o} Henrici viij patet et reddit per annum xs.

Item Thoma Oxborow pro iiij acris terre ibidem nuper Ricardi Bakers; iacet ex parte orientali de Lylesholt, et reddit per annum xjjs viijd.

fo 45

The rental of the bailiff of Caxtons in Ely with Melbourn and Cambridge renewed in 14 Henry VIII [1522–3][37]

From Edward Burde for his free messuage lately Eldersham's on the highway in Ely towards *[blank]*; this messuage lies opposite Broad Lane between a tenement of the almoner of Ely in Stephen Wrenche's tenure on the west side and part of another messuage of the said Edward on the east side, and renders 21*d* annually. Of the prior's fee.
From Thomas Wyton for his free messuage with an adjoining garden on the corner of Broad Lane opposite Edward Burde's messuage, over and above the fixed rent pertaining to the lord bishop, this year nothing because not yet levied, and renders 6*d* annually. Of the bishop's fee.
From Richard Ponder for a free messuage there on the highway formerly Richard Cooke's; it lies between the said Thomas Wilton's tenement on the west side and three cottages pertaining to the Lady Chapel on the east side, and renders annually the price of one pound of pepper, worth 14*d*. Of the prior's fee.
fo 45v
From the almoner of Ely for two cottages under one roof in Broad Lane on the east side in William Laye's tenure formerly Barker's; it lies between a lane called Baldocks Lane on the north side[38] and the storeyard of the Lady Chapel on the south side, and renders the price of one pound of pepper, 14*d*. Of the prior's fee.
From Robert Wylly for his messuage formerly in John Sendale's tenure and afterwards Roger Davy's lately in William Clerke's tenure; it lies at Castle Hithe formerly Harty's between a vacant plot lately William Tyler's on the east side and a vacant plot pertaining to the almoner on the west side, and renders 16*d* annually. Of the bishop's fee.
Rent. From Geoffrey Fyscher for a tenement; it lies in Liles Lane next to the gate of Liles Holt lately in Thomas Benet's tenure and rendered 5*s*, now by copy as it appears in 6 Henry VIII [1514–15] and renders 4*s* annually. Of the bishop's fee.
From John Okyrby for a tenement there lately in William Hansard's tenure; it lies between Geoffrey Fyscher's tenement on the north side and a tenement of W. Seman formerly Carter's on the south side, as it appears in 9 Henry VIII [1517–18], it renders 4*s* 6*d*. Of the bishop's fee.
From William Rudston for an alder-holt; it lies in Middle Fen next to the common ditch, and renders 2*d* annually.
fo 46
From William Alowe for an alder-holt called the ash-holt now a garden of Hugh Spencer lately of Agnes Wayke; it lies next to the gate of Liles Holt between Geoffrey Fyscher's tenement on the south side, and contains 56 perches in perimeter, as it appears in 14 Henry VIII [1522–3] and renders 3*s*.
From Edward Burde for an enclosure containing by estimation 5 acres of land more or less, formerly Coke's lately in John Ketyll's tenure; it lies in Liles Holt between Bell Holt and an alder-holt of William Bucke, by copy as it appears in 12 Henry VIII [1520–21] and renders 8*s* annually.
From William Bucke for 2 acres of marshy meadow called *le Haronth* in Liles Holt lately Emmeth's as it appears in 21 Edward IV [1481–2] between Edward Burde's enclosure on the west side and William Hardyng's enclosure lately Bruowd's on the north and an alder-holt of Thomas Agas on the south side, as it appears in 17 Henry VII [1501–02], 6*s* 8*d*.
From Thomas Agas for three alder-holts formerly in the tenure of William Ladd, Richard Colson and Halydays, in Liles Holt between William Bucke's alder-holt on the north side and John Adam's alder-holt lately in John Nedyng's tenure \on/ the south side, by copy as it appears in 10 Henry VIII [1518–19] and renders 10*s* annually.
From Thomas Oxborow for four acres of land there lately Richard Baker's; it lies on the east side of Liles Holt, and renders 12*s* 8*d* annually.

fo 46v
Item Johanne Adam pro uno alneto quondam Johannis Nedyng; iacet inter alnetum Johannis Adam quondam in tenura Isabelle Heydon ex parte australi et alnetum Thome Agas quondam Halydas ex parte boriali, et continet in latitudine vij perticas et dimidiam, ut in anno xxiiij Henrici vij^{mi} patet et reddit vjs viijd.
Item Johanne Adam pro alio alneto ibidem nuper in tenura Thome Gallant quondam Isabelle Heydon; iacet inter alnetum dicti Johannis ex parte boriali et alnetum Angnete Wayke et le comyng ex parte australi, ut in anno *[blank]* Henrici viij^{vi} patet et reddit per annum vjs viijd.
Item Angneta Wayke pro uno alneto nuper in tenura Spencer; et iacet in Leylesholt inter alnetum Johannis Adam ex parte boriali et le comyng ex parte australi, et reddit per annum iiijs.
Item Thoma Dowson pro uno tenemento quondam in tenura Johannis Bentley; scituatur in Brodelane super corneram venelle vocate Flexlane, continet per regiam viam novem virgas, per copiam ut in anno viij^{o} Henrici viij^{vi} patet et reddit per annum xxd. De feodo episcopi.
fo 47
Item Johanne Sand pro uno mesuagio cum pertinenciis quondam Biccham nuper Johannis Howlet ut in anno ij Henrici vij patet et reddebat \x/ s; iacet in venella vocata Barkerslane ex parte australi eiusdem, nuper in tenura Johannis Lesuant, per copiam ut in anno secundo Henrici viij patet et reddit vjs viijd. De feodo episcopi.
Summa iiijli vijd
fos 47–48v
[Melburn. Pro tenementis et terris. Summa iijli xixs viijd]
[Cantebrigia. Pro tenementis. Summa xlvijs iiijd]
Summa totalis xli vijs vijd
fo 49
[Resolucio cum pencionibus. Sacriste pro cereo coram feretro Sancte Ethedrede Virginis; stipendia; pro cereo in capella Beate Marie. Summa iiijli xviijd]

fo 49v
Rentale ballivi capelle Beate Marie Virginis in Ely renovatum in anno regni Regis Henrici viij^{vi} xiiij^{mo}

Redditus assisi officiariorum. Item subpriore eliensi pro thesaurario pro uno tenemento quondam Baldok; scituatur super corneram de Brodlane ex parte australi, abuttat super regiam \viam/ versus Castelhyth, et reddit per annum jd. De feodo prioris.
Item sacrista eliensi pro uno tenemento; scituatur apud Castelhyt et reddit per annum ad iiij^{or} terminos usuales viijd. De feodo prioris.
Item elemosinario eliensi pro diversis tenementis; scituantur in Brodlane ex parte occidentali, et reddunt per annum ad iiij^{or} terminos usuales iijs iiijd. De feodo prioris.
Item infirmario eliensi pro uno tenemento in Brodlane; scituatur ex parte orientali ibidem et reddit per annum ad iiij^{or} terminos xijd. De feodo prioris.
Item pitanciario eliensi pro uno tenemento; scituatur in Brodlane ex parte occidentali et reddit per annum ad iiij^{or} terminos usuales ijs. De feodo prioris.
fo 50
Item magistro hospitalis Sancti Johannis Baptiste \in Ely/ pro uno tenemento ibidem; scituatur in parochia Beate Marie, et reddit per annum ad iiij^{or} terminos usuales vijd obolum. De feodo prioris.

fo 46v
From John Adam for an alder-holt formerly John Nedyng's; it lies between John Adam's alder-holt formerly in Isabel Heydon's tenure on the south side and an alder-holt of Thomas Agas formerly Halydas' on the north side, and contains 7½ perches in breadth, as it appears in 24 Henry VII [1508–09] and renders 6*s* 8*d*.
From John Adam for another alder-holt there lately in Thomas Gallant's tenure formerly Isabel Heydon's; it lies between the said John's alder-holt on the north side and Agnes Wayke's alder-holt and the common on the south side, as it appears in *[blank]* Henry VIII and renders 6*s* 8*d* annually.
From Agnes Wayke for an alder-holt lately in Spencer's tenure; and it lies in Liles Holt between John Adam's alder-holt on the north side and the common on the south side, and renders 4*s* annually.
From Thomas Dowson for a tenement formerly in John Bentley's tenure; it lies in Broad Lane on the corner of a lane called Flax Lane, it contains 9 yards along the king's highway, by copy as it appears in 8 Henry VIII [1516–17] and renders 20*d* annually. Of the bishop's fee.
fo 47
From John Sand for a messuage with appurtenances formerly Biccham's lately John Howlet's as it appears in 2 Henry VII [1486–7] and rendered \10/*s*; it lies in a lane called Barkers Lane on the south side, lately in the tenure of John Lesuant, by copy as it appears in 2 Henry VIII [1510–11] and renders 6*s* 8*d*. Of the bishop's fee.
Total £4 7d
fos 47–48v
[Melbourn. For tenements and land. Total £3 19*s* 8*d*]
[Cambridge. For tenements. Total 47*s* 4*d*]
Grand total £10 7s 7d
fo 49
[Money paid out and pensions. To the sacrist for wax at the shrine of St Etheldreda the Virgin; wages; for wax in the Lady Chapel. Total £4 18*d*]

fo 49v
The rental of the bailiff of the Lady Chapel in Ely renewed in 14 Henry VIII [1522–23]

Obedientiaries' fixed rents. From the subprior of Ely, for the treasurer for a tenement formerly Baldok's; it lies on the corner of Broad Lane on the south side, it abuts upon the king's \highway/ towards Castle Hithe, and renders 1*d* annually. Of the prior's fee.
From the sacrist of Ely for a tenement; it lies at Castle Hithe and renders 8*d* annually at the four usual terms. Of the prior's fee.
From the almoner of Ely for various tenements; they lie in Broad Lane on the west side, and render 3*s* 4d annually at the four usual terms. Of the prior's fee.
From the infirmarer of Ely for a tenement in Broad Lane; it lies on the east side there and renders 12*d* annually at the four terms. Of the prior's fee.
From the pittancer of Ely for a tenement; it lies in Broad Lane on the west side and renders 2*s* annually at the four usual terms. Of the prior's fee.
fo 50
From the master of the hospital of St John the Baptist \in Ely/ for a tenement there; it lies in St Mary's parish, and renders 7½*d* annually at the four usual terms. Of the prior's fee.

Redditus assisi in parochia Beate Marie. Item Johanne Sperad pro uno tenemento suo quondam in tenura Johannis Emlyn; iacet inter tenementum capelle Beate Marie in tenura Johannis Podych ex parte orientali et tenementum Willelmi Lane pertinens hospitali Sancti Johannis ex parte occidentali, abuttat super regiam viam, et reddit per annum xiijd. De feodo prioris.
Item Willelmo Sempull pro uno tenemento ibidem; scituatur inter tenementum Johannis Podyh pertinens capelle Beate Marie ex parte occidentali et tenementum magistri Sancti Johannis ex parte orientali, et caput australe abuttat super regiam viam et caput boriale abuttat super clausum Charl' Medylton, et reddit per annum xiijd. De feodo prioris.
Item Roberto Dernell pro uno tenemento quondam in tenura Roberti Tylers nuper Thome Chancelers quondam ij tenementis quondam Alicie Denver \vd/ et Roberti Tilers \vijd/; iacet inter tenementum Johannis Dawkyn ex parte orientali et tenementum Ricardi Boltyn plowwryt ex parte occidentali et abuttat super regiam viam ex parte australi, et reddit xijd. De feodo prioris.
fo 50v
De Johanne Dawkyn pro uno tenemento quondam in tenura Thome Pentur; iacet iuxta tenementum Roberti Darnell ex parte occidentali, tenementum Roberti Roger ex parte orientali, et caput australe abuttat super regiam [viam] et reddit per annum xijd. De feodo prioris.
Item Thoma Fewterer pro uno tenemento suo; scituatur ex opposito Prestyspond inter tenementum Ricardi Colson ex parte orientali et tenementum Anten' Gylder ex parte occidentali, et reddit per annum ad iiij^{or} terminos usuales xijd. De feodo prioris.
Item Willelmo Burdon pro tenemento suo quondam in tenura Johannis Stale; scituatur in parochia Beate Marie inter tenementum Nicholai Tilers ex parte orientali et tenementum elemosinarii eliensis in tenura Johannis Barbur ex parte occidentali, et caput australe abuttat super regiam viam ex opposito le Grene <modo in tenura Thome Rust> et reddit per annum ad iiij^{or} terminos usuales ijd. De feodo prioris.
Item uno tenemento in parva venella quondam Margarete Denver quia dato ad officium custodie capelle predicte et modo dimittitur ad firmam Johanni Colman per copiam ut inferius, et solebat reddere iij grana piperis, nihil. <Modo dimittitur Johanni Adame per copiam pro redditu per annum vijs.> De feodo prioris.
fo 51
Redditus assisi in parochia Sancte Trinitatis. Item Roberto Colvell pro uno tenemento quondam Heywers; scituatur in Heyrow inter tenementum Johannis Synkwyn ex parte orientali et tenementum elemosinarii eliensis ex parte occidentali, abuttat super regiam viam ex parte australi ex opposito portam elemosinarie et reddit iijs. De feodo prioris.
Item Willelmo Neele pro uno tenemento suo; scituatur in vico versus Brodhyth inter tenementum elemosinarii eliensis ex parte orientali et tenementum capelle Beate Marie in tenura Willelmi Hoggeys ex parte occidentali, abuttat super regiam viam ex parte australi, et reddit per annum xijd. De feodo prioris.
Item ij libre cere pro uno tenemento ibidem supra montem quondam in tenura Thome Wheteryche eo quod dato ad officium custodie capelle predicte et modo dimittitur Thome Agas ut inferius, et solebat reddere ij libras cere, nihil. De feodo prioris.
Item Willelmo Wapull pro uno tenemento; scituatur super corneram de Brodlane ex parte boriali inter tenementum Ricardi Ponder ex parte orientali et abuttat ex opposito super tenementum Edwardi Burde ex parte boriali, et reddit ijs. De feodo prioris.
fo 51v
Item Ricardo Ponder pro uno gardino; scituatur apud le comyng ex parte orientali inter alnetum Johannis Adam vocatum Leylesholt ex parte boriali et communem venellam versus dictum comyng ex parte australi, et reddit j rosam. De feodo prioris.

Fixed rent in St Mary's parish. From John Sperad for his tenement formerly in John Emlyn's tenure; it lies between a tenement of the Lady Chapel in John Podych's tenure on the east side and William Lane's tenement pertaining to St John's hospital on the west side, it abuts upon the king's highway and renders 13*d* annually. Of the prior's fee.
From William Sempull for a tenement there; it lies between a tenement of John Podyh pertaining to the Lady Chapel on the west side and a tenement of the master of St John on the east side, and the south head abuts upon the king's highway and the north head abuts upon Charles Medylton's close, and renders 13*d* annually. Of the prior's fee.
From Robert Dernell for a tenement formerly in Robert Tyler's tenure lately Thomas Chanceler's, formerly two tenements formerly of Alice Denver \5*d*/ and of Robert Tiler \7*d*/; it lies between John Dawkyn's tenement on the east side and a tenement of Richard Boltyn ploughwright on the west side and abuts upon the king's highway on the south side, and renders 12*d*. Of the prior's fee.
fo 50v
From John Dawkyn for a tenement formerly in Thomas Pentur's tenure; it lies next to Robert Darnell's tenement on the west side, Robert Roger's tenement on the east side, and the south head abuts upon the king's [highway] and renders 12*d* annually. Of the prior's fee.
From Thomas Fewterer for his tenement; it lies opposite Priests Pond between Richard Colson's tenement on the east side and Anthony Gylder's tenement on the west side, and renders 12*d* annually at the four usual terms. Of the prior's fee.
From William Burdon for his tenement formerly in John Stale's tenure; it lies in St Mary's parish between Nicholas Tiler's tenement on the east side and a tenement of the almoner of Ely in John Barbur's tenure on the west side, and the south head abuts upon the king's highway opposite the Green <now in Thomas Rust's tenure> and renders 2*d* annually at the four usual terms. Of the prior's fee.
From a tenement in a small lane formerly Margaret Denver's, nothing because awarded to the office of keeper of the aforesaid chapel, and it is now demised at farm to John Colman by copy as below, and it used to render three peppercorns. <It is now demised to John Adame by copy for a rent of 7*s* annually.> Of the prior's fee.
fo 51
Fixed rent in Holy Trinity parish. From Robert Colvell for a tenement formerly Heywer's; it lies in High Row between John Synkwyn's tenement on the east side and a tenement of the almoner of Ely on the west side, it abuts upon the king's highway on the south side opposite the almonry gate, and renders 3*s*. Of the prior's fee.
From William Neele for his tenement; it lies in the street towards Broad Hithe between a tenement of the almoner of Ely on the east side and a tenement of the Lady Chapel in William Hoggey's tenure on the west side, it abuts upon the king's highway on the south side, and renders 12*d* annually. Of the prior's fee.
Two pounds of wax for a tenement there on the hill formerly in Thomas Wheteryche's tenure, nothing because awarded to the office of keeper of the aforesaid chapel and it is now demised to Thomas Agas as below, and it rendered two pounds of wax. Of the prior's fee.
From William Wapull for a tenement; it lies on the corner of Broad Lane on the north side between Richard Ponder's tenement on the east side and it abuts upon Edward Burde's tenement opposite on the north side, and renders 2*s*. Of the prior's fee.
fo 51v
From Richard Ponder for a garden; it lies on the common on the east side between an alder-holt of John Adam called Liles Holt on the north side and a common lane towards the said common on the south side, and renders one rose. Of the prior's fee.

Item Ricardo Ellys pro tenemento suo quondam edificato in tenura Thome Person nuper Thome Cutte et postea Thome Palmer; iacet apud Brodeheyth in angulo ex parte \orientali/ tenementi Johannis Adam et Flexlane ex parte boriali, et reddit per annum ad iiij^or^ terminos usuales ijd. De feodo prioris.
Item Ricardo Wesenham pro uno tenemento in Brodlane; iacet ex parte orientali inter tenementum Johannis Rose ex parte boriali et communem venellam versus riveram ex parte australi et unum caput abuttat super regiam viam ex parte occidentali, et reddit per annum ijd. De feodo prioris.
Item Johanne Tucke pro uno tenemento suo; scituatur apud Brodheyth inter Flexlane ex parte boriali et Barkerslane ex parte australi et unum caput abuttat super regiam viam vocatam Monkysheyte, et reddit j rosam. De feodo prioris.
fo 52
Item Thoma Coston pro uno tenemento suo; scituatur in vico versus Brodheyth, iacet inter tenementum capelle Beate Marie in tenura Roberti Bekells ex parte orientali et tenementum capelle predicte ex parte occidentali, et abuttat super gardinum Edwardi Burde ex parte boriali et caput australe abuttat super regiam viam versus Brodhyth, et reddit per annum xijd. De feodo prioris.
Summa xxs iiijd obolum

Firma tenementorum in parochia Beate Marie. Item Johanne Colman pro uno tenemento quondam in tenura Roberti Bardy; scituatur in parochia Beate Marie inter tenementum Thome Tyffe ex parte australi et clausum nuper Johannis Stokyll ex parte boriali unde caput orientale abuttat super clausum predictum et caput occidentale abuttat super clausum nuper Roberti Rogers, per copiam ut in anno v^{o} Henrici viij^{vi} patet et reddit per annum iiijs. De feodo prioris.
Item Thoma Parker pro uno tenemento nuper in tenura Roberti Bardy; iacet ex opposito domus Sancti Johannis cum una acra terre vocata Cattes acra iacente prope Cattyscrose, ut in anno xj^{o} Henrici viij^{vi} patet et reddit per annum vjs viijd. De feodo prioris.
Item Johanne Podych pro uno cotagio nuper in tenura Ricardi Wodborne; scituatur in parochia Beate Marie inter tenementum Willelmi Sempul ex parte orientali et tenementum Johannis Sperad ex parte occidentali et caput australe abuttat super regiam viam, per copiam ut in anno nono Henrici viij patet et reddit per annum xvjd. De feodo prioris.
fo 52v
Item Thoma Auston pro uno tenemento; iacet in parochia Beate Marie inter tenementum Willelmi Cryston ex parte orientali et tenementum nuper Johannis Syer ex parte occidentali uno capite abuttante super regiam viam ex parte boriali, per copiam ut in anno vj^{to} Henrici viij patet et reddit per annum viijs. De feodo prioris.
Item Thoma Wynbuch pro iiij rodis terre in ij peciis iacentibus apud lepynfold in Downham feld, et uno gardino iacente in vico versus Westfen inter tenementum dicti Thome ex parte orientali et clausum nuper in tenura Johannis Townsend ex parte occidentali et caput australe abuttat super regiam viam ex opposito tenementi Johannis Gylberd, per copiam ut in anno xiiij^{mo} Henrici vij patet et reddit per annum xd.
Item Willelmo Burdon pro uno tenemento; iacet super corneram de Cattyslane inter tenementum elemosinarii eliensis in tenura Thome Westfyld ex parte australi et j clausum nuper Johannis Grey ex parte boriali et abuttat super gardinum W. Burdon ex parte orientali et abuttat ex parte occidentali super regiam viam versus Downham, per copiam ut in anno quarto Regis Henrici viij^{vi} patet et reddit per annum xijd. De feodo prioris.
Item Thoma Squery pro uno tenemento; scituatur in Cattyslane nuper in tenura Willelmi Burdon, et reddebat per annum vs ut in anno v^{to} Henrici vij patet, et iacet inter tenementum magistri Sancti Johannis in Ely ex parte occidentali et tenementum nuper Ricardi Watkyns ex parte orientali et abuttat versus boriam super Akyrmanstret et versus austrum super Cattyslane, per copiam ut in anno xiiij^{o} Henrici viij^{vi} patet et reddit per annum iiijs. De feodo episcopi.

From Richard Ellys for his tenement formerly built upon, in Thomas Person's tenure lately Thomas Cutte's and afterwards Thomas Palmer's; it lies at Broad Hithe on the corner on the \east/ side of John Adam's tenement and Flax Lane on the north side, and renders 2*d* annually at the four usual terms. Of the prior's fee.
From Richard Wesenham for a tenement in Broad Lane; it lies on the east side between John Rose's tenement on the north side and a common lane towards the river on the south side and one head abuts upon the king's highway on the west side, and renders 2*d* annually. Of the prior's fee.
From John Tucke for his tenement; it lies at Broad Hithe between Flax Lane on the north side and Barkers Lane on the south side and one head abuts upon the king's highway called Monks' Hithe, and renders one rose. Of the prior's fee.
fo 52
From Thomas Coston for his tenement; it lies in the street towards Broad Hithe, it lies between a tenement of the Lady Chapel in Robert Bekells' tenure on the east side and a tenement of the aforesaid chapel on the west side, and abuts upon Edward Burde's garden on the north side and the south head abuts upon the king's highway towards Broad Hithe, and renders 12*d* annually. Of the prior's fee.
Total: 20s 4½d

Rent of the tenements in St Mary's parish. From John Colman for a tenement formerly in Robert Bardy's tenure; it lies in St Mary's parish between Thomas Tyffe's tenement on the south side and an enclosure lately of John Stokyll on the north side, the east head of which abuts upon the aforesaid enclosure and the west head abuts upon an enclosure lately Robert Rogers', by copy as it appears in 5 Henry VIII [1513–14] and renders 4*s* annually. Of the prior's fee.
From Thomas Parker for a tenement lately in Robert Bardy's tenure; it lies opposite St John's house, with an acre of land called Cats acre lying near Cats cross, as it appears in 11 Henry VIII [1519–20] and renders 6*s* 8*d* annually. Of the prior's fee.
From John Podych for a cottage lately in Richard Wodborne's tenure; it lies in St Mary's parish between William Sempul's tenement on the east side and John Sperad's tenement on the west side and the south head abuts upon the king's highway, by copy as it appears in 9 Henry VIII [1517–18] and renders 16*d* annually. Of the prior's fee.
fo 52v
From Thomas Auston for a tenement; it lies in St Mary's parish between William Cryston's tenement on the east side and a tenement lately John Syer's on the west side, one head abutting upon the king's highway on the north side, by copy as it appears in 6 Henry VIII [1514–15] and renders 8*s* annually. Of the prior's fee.
From Thomas Wynbuch for four roods of land in two pieces lying at the pinfold in Downham Field, and for a garden lying in the street towards West Fen between a tenement of the said Thomas on the east side and an enclosure lately in John Townsend's tenure on the west side and the south head abuts upon the king's highway opposite John Gylberd's tenement, by copy as it appears in 14 Henry VII [1498–9] and renders 10*d* annually.
From William Burdon for a tenement; it lies on the corner of Cats Lane between a tenement of the almoner of Ely in Thomas Westfyld's tenure on the south side and an enclosure lately John Grey's on the north side and it abuts upon W. Burdon's garden on the east side and it abuts on the west side upon the king's highway towards Little Downham, by copy as it appears in 4 Henry VIII [1512–13] and renders 12*d* annually. Of the prior's fee.
From Thomas Squery for a tenement; it lies in Cats Lane lately in William Burdon's tenure, and rendered 5*s* annually as it appears in 5 Henry VII [1489–90], and it lies between a tenement of the master of St John in Ely on the west side and a tenement lately Richard Watkyn's on the east side and abuts towards the north upon Acreman Street and towards the south upon Cats Lane, by copy as it appears in 14 Henry VIII [1522–3] and renders 4*s* annually. Of the bishop's fee.

fo 53
Item Johanne Peye pro uno tenemento; iacet in parochia Beate Marie in Walpull Lane nuper in tenura Willelmi Bawdyn, iacet inter tenementum celerarii eliensis ex parte orientali et tenementum magistri Sancti Johannis in Ely ex parte occidentali, per copiam ut in anno primo Henrici viij patet et reddit per annum iijs iiijd. De feodo prioris.
Item Radulfo Makam pro uno tenemento nuper in tenura Ricardi Fordam; scituatur in parochia Beate Marie inter tenementum Johannis Dane ex parte orientali et tenementum Nicholai Tylers vocatum le Gorge ex parte occidentali, abuttat super regiam viam ex parte australi, per copiam ut in anno xj^{o} Henrici viij patet et reddit per annum ixs ixd. De feodo episcopi.

Firma tenementorum in parochia Sancte Trinitatis. Item Petro Browne pro uno tenemento nuper in tenura Johannis Page; scituatur ex parte boriali de Stepulrowe inter tenementum Willelmi Rudston ex parte orientali et tenementum Johannis Gylbarde ex parte occidentali et caput boriale abuttat super gardinum Lanletredell et caput australe abuttat super regiam viam, ut in anno xj^{o} Henrici viij patet et reddit per annum viijs iiijd. De feodo episcopi.
Item Johanne Deye pro ij seldis in bocheria quondam in tenura Willelmi Adam et nuper Willelmi Deye bocher, per annum et reddit per annum \ijs iiijd/. De feodo episcopi.
fo 53v
Item Johanne Watton pro una opella nuper in tenura Johannis Bregys quondam in tenura Thome Welyn, et reddit per annum ijs iiijd, j libram cere, nunc per copiam ut in anno xiij^{mo} Henrici octavi patet et reddit per annum ijs iiijd. De feodo episcopi.
Item Ricardo Judde pro uno tenemento quondam in tenura Willelmi Adam nuper in tenura Freman; scituatur in Newnam inter tenementum elemosinarii eliensis ex parte boriali et caput orientale abuttat super regiam viam et caput occidentale super gardinum Johannis Wellys, per copiam ut in anno ix^{o} Henrici viij^{vi} patet et reddit per annum vjs viijd. De feodo prioris.
Item Willelmo Gryme pro uno fundo modo domibus superedificato; scituatur in Newnam versus Turbeseye in parva venella versus Cressewell inter communem venellam ex parte occidentali et unum clausum domini episcopi in tenura Johannis Marche, et caput boriale abuttat super regiam viam, ut in anno ix^{o} Henrici vij patet et reddit per annum iiijd. \post Boteler ut in anno xiiij^{o} Henrici vij patet/ <quondam Willelmi Adam [ut] anno Henrici vij ij^{do} patet> De feodo prioris.
Item Ricardo Sanderson pro uno tenemento in Newnam quondam in tenura Johannis Fier nuper Ricardi Seman; iacet inter communem viam versus Cressewell ex parte occidentali et tenementum Thome Agas ex parte orientali et caput boriale abuttat super regiam viam versus Turbeseye, per indenturam ad terminum annorum et reddit per annum iijs iiijd. De feodo episcopi.
fo 54
Item Thoma Martyn pro uno tenemento nuper in tenura Roberti Coye; scituatur in vico versus Brodehith inter tenementum nuper Ricardi Fote ex parte orientali et tenementum modo Thome Martyn ex parte occidentali, abuttat super regiam viam ex parte australi, per copiam ut in anno xviij^{o} Henrici vij^{mi} patet et reddit per annum vs. De feodo domini episcopi.
Item Thoma Hoggys pro uno tenemento ibidem nuper in tenura Ricardi Fote; iacet inter tenementum Thome Martyn ex parte occidentali et tenementum Willelmi Nele ex parte orientali et caput australe abuttat super regiam viam et caput boriale super vinetum domini episcopi, per copiam ut in anno v^{to} Henrici viij^{vi} patet et reddit per annum viijs. De feodo prioris.
Item Thoma Agas pro uno tenemento nuper in tenura Thome Ellys; scituatur in Brodehytward inter tenementum capelle Beate Marie in tenura Ricardi Segerson ex parte orientali et tenementum elemosinarii eliensis ex parte occidentali et caput australe abuttat super regiam viam versus Brodhyth, ut in anno xxiiij^{mo} Henrici vij patet et reddit xs. De feodo prioris.

fo 53
From John Peye for a tenement; it lies in St Mary's parish in Walpole Lane lately in William Bawdyn's tenure, it lies between a tenement of the cellarer of Ely on the east side and a tenement of the master of St John in Ely on the west side, by copy as it appears in 1 Henry VIII [1509–10] and renders 3*s* 4*d* annually. Of the prior's fee.
From Ralph Makam for a tenement lately in Richard Fordam's tenure; it lies in St Mary's parish between John Dane's tenement on the east side and a tenement of Nicholas Tyler called The George on the west side; it abuts upon the king's highway on the south side, by copy as it appears in 11 Henry VIII [1519–20] and renders 9*s* 9*d* annually. Of the bishop's fee.

Rent of the tenements in Holy Trinity parish. From Peter Browne for a tenement lately in John Page's tenure; it lies on the north side of Steeple Row between William Rudston's tenement on the east side and John Gylbarde's tenement on the west side and the north head abuts upon the garden of Lanletredell and the south head abuts upon the king's highway, as it appears in 11 Henry VIII [1519–20] and renders 8*s* 4*d* annually. Of the bishop's fee.
From John Deye for two stalls in the butchery formerly in William Adam's tenure and lately of William Deye butcher, annually and renders annually \2*s* 4*d*/. Of the bishop's fee.
fo 53v
From John Watton for a stall lately in John Bregy's tenure formerly in Thomas Welyn's tenure, and renders 2*s* 4*d*, one pound of wax annually, now by copy as it appears in 13 Henry VIII [1521–2] and renders 2*s* 4*d* annually. Of the bishop's fee.
From Richard Judde for a tenement formerly in William Adam's tenure lately in Freman's tenure; it lies in Newnham between a tenement of the almoner of Ely on the north side and the east head abuts upon the king's highway and the west head upon John Wellys' garden, by copy as it appears in 9 Henry VIII [1517–18] and renders 6*s* 8*d* annually. Of the prior's fee.
From William Gryme for a plot of land on which houses have now been built; it lies in Newnham towards Turbutsey in a small lane towards Cresswell between a common lane on the west side and an enclosure of the lord bishop in John Marche's tenure, and the north head abuts upon the king's highway, as it appears in 9 Henry VII [1493–4] and renders 4*d* annually. \afterwards Boteler as it appears in 14 Henry VII [1498–9]/ <formerly William Adam's [as] it appears in 2 Henry VII [1486–7]> Of the prior's fee.
From Richard Sanderson for a tenement in Newnham formerly in John Fier's tenure lately Richard Seman's; it lies between a common way towards Cresswell on the west side and a tenement of Thomas Agas on the east side and the north head abuts upon the king's highway towards Turbutsey, by indenture for a term of years and renders 3*s* 4*d* annually. Of the bishop's fee.
fo 54
From Thomas Martyn for a tenement lately in Robert Coye's tenure; it lies in the street towards Broad Hithe between a tenement lately Richard Fote's on the east side and a tenement now Thomas Martyn's on the west side, it abuts upon the king's highway on the south side, by copy as it appears in 18 Henry VII [1502–03] and renders 5*s* annually. Of the lord bishop's fee.
From Thomas Hoggys for a tenement there lately in Richard Fote's tenure; it lies between Thomas Martyn's tenement on the west side and William Nele's tenement on the east side and the south head abuts upon the king's highway and the north head upon the lord bishop's vineyard, by copy as it appears in 5 Henry VIII [1513–14] and renders 8s annually. Of the prior's fee.
From Thomas Agas for a tenement lately in the tenure of Thomas Ellys; it lies in Broad Hithe ward between a tenement of the Lady Chapel in Richard Segerson's tenure on the east side and a tenement of the almoner of Ely on the west side and the south head abuts upon the king's highway towards Broad Hithe, as it appears in 24 Henry VII [1508–09] and renders 10*s*. Of the prior's fee.

Item Thoma Segurson pro uno tenemento nuper in tenura Ricardi Person; iacet inter tenementum Thome Agas ex parte occidentali et tenementum elemosinarii eliensis ex parte orientali et caput boriale abuttat super vinetum domini episcopi eliensis et caput australe abuttat super regiam viam ex opposito le asche, ut in anno xij^{mo} Henrici viij patet et reddit vjs. De feodo prioris.
fo 54v
Item Johanne Grene pro uno tenemento; scituatur in vico versus Brodehyth inter tenementum Thome Coston ex parte orientali et tenementum nuper Dokyt in tenura custodis graciarum de Redmans ex parte occidentali et caput australe abuttat super regiam viam, nunc in manu domini, et reddit per annum vjs viijd. De feodo episcopi.
Item Roberto Bekells pro uno tenemento ibidem nuper in tenura Roberti Heyerman; iacet inter tenementum Johannis Grene ex parte occidentali et tenementum Thome Lenakyr ex parte orientali et caput boriale [abuttat] super gardinum Edwardi Burde et caput australe abuttat super regiam viam, per copiam ut in anno xix^{mo} Henrici vij patet et reddit per annum viijs. De feodo episcopi.
Item Thoma Lenakyr pro uno tenemento ibidem inter tenementum Roberti Bekels ex parte occidentali et tenementum magistri capelle Beate Marie in tenura Johannis Spilman ex parte orientali et abuttat ex parte boriali super gardinum E. Burde et caput australe abuttat super regiam viam, per copiam ut in anno x^{o} Henrici viij patet et reddit per annum vs. De feodo episcopi.
Item Johanne Spylman pro uno tenemento ibidem super corneram de Leleslane inter tenementumThome Lenaker ex parte occidentali et Leyslane ex parte orientali et caput boriale abuttat super gardinum Edwardi Burde et abuttat ex parte australi super regiam viam, per copiam ut in anno xiij^{mo} Henrici viij patet, vijs. De feodo episcopi.
fo 55
Item Roberto Rumney pro uno tenemento in Leyleslane nuper in tenura Edmundi Henne inter tenementum Willelmi Seman ex parte boriali, abuttat ex parte occidentali super Leyleslane, per copiam, cum uno gardino nuper in tenura Thome Godlad prope tenementum quondam Johannis Burwell ex opposito Lytell Comon, per copiam ut in anno nono Regis Henrici viij^{vi} patet et reddit per annum vs iiijd. De feodo prioris.
Item Ricardo Ponder pro uno tenemento nuper in tenura Edwardi Heyward; iacet inter tenementum Willelmi Walpol ex parte occidentali et tenementum capelle Beate Marie in tenura uxoris Johannis Pomell ex parte orientali et caput australe abuttat super regiam viam versus Brodheyth, ut in anno xiiij^{mo} Henrici viij^{vi} patet et reddit per annum iiijs. De feodo prioris.
Item uxore Johannis Pomell pro uno tenemento iuxta tenementum Ricardi Ponder ex parte occidentali et tenementum elemosinarii eliensis in tenura Radolfi Heyward ex parte orientali et unum caput abuttat super regiam viam versus Brodheyth, per copiam ut in anno xx^{mo} Regis Henrici vij patet \in libera curia/et reddit per annum xijs,[40] \j libram cere/. De feodo episcopi.
Item Alano Mole pro uno tenemento quondam Ricardi Heydon ut in anno vj^{to} Henrici vij patet et reddebat per annum vjs; et iacet inter tenementum Thome Martyn ex parte occidentali et tenementum Johannis Wryth nuper Wakys ex parte orientali et abuttat super regiam viam versus Brodheyth ex parte australi, ut in anno vij Henrici viij^{vi} patet et reddit per annum iiijs vjd. De feodo domini episcopi.
fo 55v
Item Willelmo Heydon pro uno tenemento; scituatur ultra aquam inter tenementum Thome Swyfte ex parte australi, abuttat super riveram ex parte occidentali, quondam in tenura Willelmi Chapman et reddebat per annum xvjs, nunc in tenura predicti Willelmi per indenturam ad terminum annorum et reddit per annum xiijs iiijd. De feodo episcopi.
Item Johanne Bell pro ij tenementis nuper Willelmi Hall; scituantur inter tenementum Johannis Daye nuper in tenura Edmundi Henne ex parte orientali et tenementum capelle Beate Marie ex parte occidentali et caput australe abuttat super Flexlane et caput boriale abuttat super regiam viam versus Brodheyth ex opposito tenementi Johannis Spylman, ut in anno xiij^{mo} Henrici viij patet et reddit per annum ixs. De feodo prioris.

From Thomas Segurson for a tenement lately in Richard Person's tenure; it lies between a tenement of Thomas Agas on the west side and a tenement of the almoner of Ely on the east side and the north head abuts upon the vineyard of the lord bishop of Ely and the south head abuts upon the king's highway opposite the arch, as it appears in 12 Henry VIII [1520–21] and renders 6*s*. Of the prior's fee.
fo 54v
From John Grene for a tenement; it lies in the street towards Broad Hithe between Thomas Coston's tenement on the east side and a tenement lately Dokyt's in the tenure of the keeper of Redman's charity on the west side and the south head abuts upon the king's highway, now in the lord's hand, and renders 6*s* 8*d* annually. Of the bishop's fee.
From Robert Bekells for a tenement there lately in Robert Heyerman's tenure; it lies between John Grene's tenement on the west side and Thomas Lenakyr's tenement on the east side and the north head [abuts] upon Edward Burde's garden and the south head abuts upon the king's highway, by copy as it appears in 19 Henry VII [1503–04] and renders 8*s* annually. Of the bishop's fee.
From Thomas Lenakyr for a tenement there between Robert Bekels' tenement on the west side and a tenement of the master of the Lady Chapel in John Spilman's tenure on the east side and it abuts on the north side upon E. Burde's garden and the south head abuts upon the king's highway, by copy as it appears in 10 Henry VIII [1518–19] and renders 5*s* annually. Of the bishop's fee.
From John Spylman for a tenement there on the corner of Liles Lane between Thomas Lenaker's tenement on the west side and Liles Lane on the east side and the north head abuts upon Edward Burde's garden and it abuts on the south side upon the king's highway, by copy as it appears in 13 Henry VIII [1521–2], 7*s*. Of the bishop's fee.
fo 55
From Robert Rumney for a tenement in Liles Lane lately in Edmund Henne's tenure between William Seman's tenement on the north side, it abuts on the west side upon Liles Lane, by copy, with a garden lately in Thomas Godlad's tenure near a tenement formerly of John Burwell opposite Little Common, by copy as it appears in 9 Henry VIII [1517–18] and renders 5*s* 4*d* annually. Of the prior's fee.
From Richard Ponder[41] for a tenement lately in Edward Heyward's tenure; it lies between William Walpol's tenement on the west side and a tenement of the Lady Chapel in the tenure of John Pomell's wife on the east side and the south head abuts upon the king's highway towards Broad Hithe, as it appears in 14 Henry VIII [1522–3] and renders 4s annually. Of the prior's fee.
From John Pomell's wife for a tenement next to Richard Ponder's tenement on the west side and a tenement of the almoner of Ely in Ralph Heyward's tenure on the east side and one head abuts upon the king's highway towards Broad Hithe, by copy as it appears in 20 Henry VII [1504–05] \in the free court/ and renders 12*s* annually, \one pound of wax/. Of the bishop's fee.
From Alan Mole for a tenement formerly Richard Heydon's as it appears in 6 Henry VII [1490–91] and rendered 6*s* annually; and it lies between Thomas Martyn's tenement on the west side and John Wryth's tenement lately Wakys' on the east side and abuts upon the king's highway towards Broad Hithe on the south side, as it appears in 7 Henry VIII [1515–16] and renders 4*s* 6*d* annually. Of the lord bishop's fee.
fo 55v
From William Heydon for a tenement ; it lies beyond the water between Thomas Swyfte's tenement on the south side, it abuts upon the river on the west side, formerly in William Chapman's tenure and rendered 16*s* annually, now in the aforesaid William's tenure by indenture for a term of years and renders 13*s* 4*d* annually. Of the bishop's fee.
From John Bell for two tenements lately William Hall's; they lie between John Daye's tenement lately in Edmund Henne's tenure on the east side and a tenement of the Lady Chapel on the west side and the south head abuts upon Flax Lane and the north head abuts upon the king's highway towards Broad Hithe opposite John Spylman's tenement, as it appears in 13 Henry VIII [1521–22] and renders 9*s* annually. Of the prior's fee.

Item Johanne Wythe pro uno tenemento; iacet iuxta tenementum Johannis Bell et tenementum Ricardi Ponder ex parte occidentali et unum caput abuttat super Flexlane et aliud super regiam viam ex parte boriali ex opposito tenementi Thome Lenakyr, per annum et reddit iijs iiijd. De feodo prioris.
Item Thoma Palmer pro uno horto; iacet inter tenementum nuper Mortemers nunc in tenura Johannis Ward ex parte australi et tenementum Johannis Tucke nuper Markant ex parte boriali, per copiam ut in anno xix^o Henrici vij patet et reddit per annum iijs. De feodo prioris.
fo 56
Item Johanne Adams pro uno gardino cum uno pomerio inde edificato; iacet versus Brodhith quondam in tenura Johannis Wyncent, iacet in Flexlane ex parte boriali et tenementum Willelmi Yemanson nuper Sparrowe ex parte australi, uno capite abuttante super communem cursum aque alio capite abuttante super tenementum capelle Beate Marie Virginis, ut in anno xx^mo Henrici vij patet et reddit per annum xvjd. De feodo prioris.
Item Willelmo Yemanson pro uno gardino quondam in tenura Johannis Ketyll nuper vocatum tria gardina; iacet inter gardinum Johannis Bentley ex parte occidentali et caput boriale abuttat super Flexlane nuper in tenura Johannis Replyngall, per copiam ut in anno xiij^mo Henrici viij patet et reddit per annum xviijd. De feodo prioris.
Item Johanne Bentley pro una parcella gardini; iacet in Flexlane nuper in tenura Alicie Mower inter gardinum Willelmi Yemanson ex parte orientali et gardinum Johannis Bentley nuper Bryslond ex parte occidentali et caput boriale abuttat super Flexlane, ut in anno sexto Henrici vij patet et reddit per annum vjd. De feodo prioris.
Item Johanne Bentley pro uno gardino quondam Breysland nuper Roberti Portas; iacet in Flexlane inter gardinum Johannis Bentley ex parte orientali et tenementum capelle Beate Marie ex parte occidentali, per copiam ut in anno iiij^to Henrici viij patet et reddit per annum vjd. De feodo prioris.
fo 56v
Item Willelmo Sande pro uno tenemento scituato in Brodelane; iacet super corneram de Flexlane et tenementum Thome Dawson ex parte boriali et tenementum capelle Beate Marie ex parte australi et caput orientale abuttat super gardinum Johannis Bentley et caput occidentale abuttat super Brodlane, per copiam ut in anno duodecimo Henrici octavi patet et reddit per annum iijs iiijd. De feodo prioris.
Item Johanne Wysbord pro uno tenemento ibidem iijs iiijd; item Matilda Cowper pro uno tenemento iijs iiijd; item Hugone Thurtton pro uno tenemento ibidem iijs iiijd; item Edwardo Foliet pro uno tenemento ibidem iiijs; et predicta tenementa iacent inter tenementum Willelmi Sand ex parte boriali et tenementum Johannis Ward nuper Mortemers ex parte australi, abuttant super gardinum Johannis Bently ex parte orientali et caput occidentale abuttat super Brodlane et reddunt per annum xiiijs. De feodo prioris.
Item Henrico Chapman pro uno tenemento; scituatur ex parte orientali de Brodlane inter tenementum Willelmi Yemanson nuper Sparrows ex parte australi et communem venellam ex parte boriali, uno capite abuttante super gardinum Johannis Adam ex parte orientali et caput occidentale super regiam \viam/, ut in anno iiij^to Henrici viij^vi patet et reddit per annum xs. De feodo prioris.
Item le storeyard capelle nihil quia utensiles capelle conservantur;[42] iacet inter tenementum elemosinarii eliensis in tenura Ricardi Segerson ex parte boriali et caput occidentale abuttat super regiam viam, aliud caput \orientale/ abuttat super gardinum Ricardi Ellys. De feodo prioris.
fo 57
Item Ricardo Ellys pro uno gardino ibidem; scituatur inter le storeyard capelle Beate Marie ex parte occidentali et communem venellam ex parte orientali, per copiam ut in anno primo Henrici viij^vi patet et reddit per annum ijs viijd. De feodo prioris.
Item Johanne Smyth pro uno tenemento quondam Wattons; iacet ex parte occidentali de Brode Lane inter tenementum Thome Lenaker nuper in tenura Thome Cutt ex parte australi et abuttat super regiam viam ex parte orientali et caput occidentale abuttat super le horhard, et reddit per annum ad quatuor terminos usuales iiijs. De feodo prioris.

From John Wythe for a tenement; it lies next to John Bell's tenement and Richard Ponder's tenement on the west side and one head abuts upon Flax Lane and the other upon the king's highway on the north side opposite Thomas Lenakyr's tenement, and renders 3*s* 4*d* annually. Of the prior's fee.
From Thomas Palmer for a yard; it lies between a tenement lately Mortemer's now in John Ward's tenure on the south side and John Tucke's tenement lately Markant's on the north side, by copy as it appears in 19 Henry VII [1503–04] and renders 3*s* annually. Of the prior's fee.
fo 56
From John Adam for a garden with an orchard planted there; it lies towards Broad Hithe formerly in John Wyncent's tenure, it lies in Flax Lane on the north side and William Yemanson's tenement lately Sparrow's on the south side, one head abutting upon the public waterway, the other head abutting upon a tenement of the Lady Chapel, as it appears in 20 Henry VII [1504–05] and renders 16*d* annually. Of the prior's fee.
From William Yemanson for a garden formerly in John Ketyll's tenure lately called three gardens; it lies between John Bentley's garden on the west side and the north head abuts upon Flax Lane lately in John Replyngall's tenure, by copy as it appears in 13 Henry VIII [1521–2] and renders 18*d* annually. Of the prior's fee.
From John Bentley for part of a garden; it lies in Flax Lane lately in Alice Mower's tenure between William Yemanson's garden on the east side and John Bentley's garden lately Bryslond's on the west side and the north head abuts upon Flax Lane, as it appears in 6 Henry VII [1490–91] and renders 6*d* annually. Of the prior's fee.
From John Bentley for a garden formerly Breysland's lately Robert Portas'; it lies in Flax Lane between John Bentley's garden on the east side and a tenement of the Lady Chapel on the west side, by copy as it appears in 4 Henry VIII [1512–13] and renders 6*d* annually. Of the prior's fee.
fo 56v
From William Sande for a tenement lying in Broad Lane; it lies on the corner of Flax Lane and Thomas Dawson's tenement on the north side and a tenement of the Lady Chapel on the south side and the east head abuts upon John Bentley's garden and the west head abuts upon Broad Lane, by copy as it appears in 12 Henry VIII [1520–21] and renders 3*s* 4*d* annually. Of the prior's fee.
From John Wysbord for a tenement there 3*s* 4*d*; from Matilda Cowper for a tenement 3*s* 4*d*; from Hugh Thurtton for a tenement there 3*s* 4*d*; from Edward Foliet for a tenement there 4*s*; and the aforesaid tenements lie between William Sand's tenement on the north side and John Ward's tenement lately Mortemer's on the south side, they abut upon John Bently's garden on the east side and the west head abuts upon Broad Lane and they render 14*s* annually. Of the prior's fee.
From Henry Chapman for a tenement; it lies on the east side of Broad Lane between William Yemanson's tenement lately Sparrow's on the south side and a common lane on the north side, one head abutting upon John Adam's garden on the east side and the west head upon the king's \ highway/, as it appears in 4 Henry VIII [1512–13] and renders 12*s* annually. Of the prior's fee.
The storeyard of the [Lady] Chapel, nothing because the chapel's goods are stored there; it lies between a tenement of the almoner of Ely in Richard Segerson's tenure on the north side and the west head abuts upon the king's highway, the other \east/ head abuts upon a garden of Richard Ellys. Of the prior's fee.
fo 57
From Richard Ellys for a garden there; it lies between the storeyard of the Lady Chapel on the west side and a common lane on the east side, by copy as it appears in 1 Henry VIII [1509–10] and renders 2*s* 8*d* annually. Of the prior's fee.
From John Smyth for a tenement formerly Watton's; it lies on the west side of Broad Lane between Thomas Lenaker's tenement lately in Thomas Cutt's tenure on the south side, and it abuts upon the king's highway on the east side and the west head abuts upon the orchard,[43] and renders 4*s* annually at the four usual terms. Of the prior's fee.

Item Thoma Kyrkysby pro uno tenemento nuper in tenura Johannis Owtyng; iacet in Brode Lane inter tenementum Johannis Slowe ex parte australi et tenementum Thome Lenaker nuper in tenura Thome Cutt ex parte boriali et caput orientale abuttat super regiam viam et caput occidentale super le horthard, et reddit per annum vs. De feodo prioris.
Item Johanne Hall pro uno tenemento ibidem quondam in tenura Willelmi Lysters inter tenementum Johannis Slowe quondam Halpeneys ex parte boriali et tenementum sacriste eliensis ex parte australi et caput orientale abuttat super regiam viam, per copiam ut in anno ix^{o} Henrici viij^{vi} patet et reddit per annum ijs vjd. De feodo prioris.
fo 57v
Item Johanne Haynone pro uno tenemento in Brodlane ex parte occidentali; iacet inter tenementum elemosinarii eliensis ex parte boriali et tenementum Roberti Burne ex parte australi, abuttat super regiam viam et caput occidentale super le venyard, et reddit iijs iiijd. De feodo prioris.
Item Roberto Burne pro uno tenemento ibidem, per copiam ut in anno primo Henrici viij^{vi} patet et reddit per annum ijs iiijd; item Johanne Reynold pro uno tenemento ibidem iijs iiijd; item Ricardo Campyon pro tria tenementa ibidem sub uno tecto tegulato \viijs/; et predicta tenementa iacent inter tenementum Johannis Heynon ex parte boriali et le venardstyle ex parte australi, et abuttant super Brodlane ex parte orientali et abuttant super levenard ex parte occidentali, et reddunt per annum ad iiij^{or} terminos usuales xiijs viijd. De feodo prioris.
Item Ricardo Dodgeson pro uno tenemento cum gardino nuper in tenura Ricardi Holmys; iacet inter tenementum Roberti Ingram nuper Ricardi Fott ex parte boriali et tenementum infirmarii eliensis ex parte australi et caput orientale abuttat super regiam viam et aliud caput super le wenyard, per copiam ut in anno primo Henrici viij^{vi} patet et reddit per annum iiijs. De feodo prioris.
Item Elena Mouse pro uno tenemento in Brode Lane; iacet inter tenementum Johannis Bone ex parte boriali et tenementum nuper Johannis Slowe ex parte australi et abuttat super Brodlane ex parte orientali, per copiam ut in anno xxj^{o} Henrici vij patet et reddit per annum iiijs. De feodo prioris.
fo 58
Item Roberto Mott pro uno tenemento nuper in tenura Edwardi Lane; scituatur in vico versus Castelhith super corneram de Potterslane ex opposito de Brolanesend, per copiam ut in anno Henrici octavi vij patet et reddit per annum vjs viijd. De feodo episcopi.
Item Roberto Wetley pro uno tenemento cum molendino equino ibidem nuper in tenura Alani Knyt; iacet inter tenementumThome Caman ex parte orientali et vacuum fundum pertinentem domo Sancti Johannis ex parte occidentali et abuttat ex parte boriali super vinetum domini prioris et abuttat super regiam viam versus Castelhith ex parte australi, per copiam ut in anno viij^{vo} Henrici viij^{vi} patet et reddit per annum vjs viijd. De feodo prioris.
fos 58–58v
[Firma terrarum in Ely]
Summa totalis xiiijli xjs xjd obolum, j libra cere, ij rose

fo 59
Rentale infirmarii eliensis renovatum anno regni Regis Henrici viij^{vi} xiiij^{o} cum omnibus terris et tenementis in Ely

[Redditus assisi in Bluntesham et Colne, Thetford, Coveney, Hadnam, Tryplowe, Marche]
Item Johanne Rose pro uno gardino cum ij^{bus} stagnis; iacet in Croyslane apud Castelhith nuper in tenura Johannis Buntyng, per copiam ut in anno xij^{mo} Henrici vij patet et reddit per annum iiijs. De feodo prioris.

From Thomas Kyrkysby for a tenement lately in John Owtyng's tenure; it lies in Broad Lane between John Slowe's tenement on the south side and a tenement of Thomas Lenaker lately in Thomas Cutt's tenure on the north side and the east head abuts upon the king's highway and the west head upon the orchard, and renders 5*s* annually. Of the prior's fee.
From John Hall for a tenement there formerly in William Lyster's tenure between a tenement of John Slowe formerly Halpeney's on the north side and a tenement of the sacrist of Ely on the south side and the east head abuts upon the king's highway, by copy as it appears in 9 Henry VIII [1517–18] and renders 2*s* 6*d* annually. Of the prior's fee.
fo 57v
From John Haynone for a tenement in Broad Lane on the west side; it lies between a tenement of the almoner of Ely on the north side and Robert Burne's tenement on the south side, it abuts upon the king's highway and the west head upon the vineyard, and renders 3*s* 4*d*. Of the prior's fee.
From Robert Burne for a tenement there, by copy as it appears in 1 Henry VIII [1509–10] and renders 2*s* 4*d* annually; from John Reynold for a tenement there 3*s* 4*d*; from Richard Campyon for three tenements there under one, tiled, roof \8*s*/; and the aforesaid tenements lie between John Heynon's tenement on the north side and the vineyard stile on the south side, and they abut upon Broad Lane on the east side and they abut upon the vineyard on the west side, and render 13*s* 8*d* annually at the four usual terms. Of the prior's fee.
From Richard Dodgeson for a tenement with a garden lately in Richard Holmys' tenure; it lies between a tenement of Robert Ingram lately Richard Fott's on the north side and a tenement of the infirmarer of Ely on the south side and the east head abuts upon the king's highway and the other head upon the vineyard, by copy as it appears in 1 Henry VIII [1509–10] and renders 4*s* annually. Of the prior's fee.
From Ellen Mouse for a tenement in Broad Lane; it lies between John Bone's tenement on the north side and a tenement lately John Slowe's on the south side and abuts upon Broad Lane on the east side, by copy as it appears in 21 Henry VII [1505–06] and renders 4*s* annually. Of the prior's fee.
fo 58
From Robert Mott for a tenement lately in Edward Lane's tenure; it lies in the street towards Castle Hithe on the corner of Potters Lane opposite Broad Lane's end, by copy as it appears in 7 Henry VIII [1515–16] and renders 6*s* 8*d* annually. Of the bishop's fee.
From Robert Wetley for a tenement with a horsemill there lately in Alan Knyt's tenure; it lies between Thomas Caman's tenement on the east side and a vacant plot pertaining to St John's house on the west side and it abuts on the north side upon the lord prior's vineyard and it abuts upon the king's highway towards Castle Hithe on the south side, by copy as it appears in 8 Henry VIII [1516–17] and renders 6*s* 8*d* annually. Of the prior's fee.
fos 58–58v
[Rent of lands in Ely][44]
Grand total £14 11s 11½d, 1 pound of wax, 2 roses

fo 59
The rental of the infirmarer of Ely renewed in 14 Henry VIII [1522–3] with all lands and tenements in Ely

[Fixed rent in Bluntisham and Colne, Little Thetford, Coveney, Haddenham, Thriplow, March]
From John Rose for a garden with two ponds; it lies in Croyles Lane at Castle Hithe lately in John Buntyng's tenure, by copy as it appears in 12 Henry VII [1496–7] and renders 4*s* annually. Of the prior's fee.

fo 59v
Item Willelmo Cramper pro uno tenemento nuper in tenura Johannis Cheveley; iacet in Potterslane quondam Johannis Writth et reddebat per annum iiijs, iacet inter tenementum Johannis Rose ex parte australi et Croslane ex parte boriali et caput occidentale abuttat super Potterslane, nunc per copiam ut in anno xj° Henrici viij^vi patet et reddit per annum iijs iiijd. De feodo prioris.
Item Johanne Slowe pro uno tenemento in Brodlane ex parte occidentali; iacet inter tenementum elemosinarii eliensis ex parte boriali et tenementum pitanciarii de Sutton ex parte australi et reddit per annum iijs vjd. De feodo prioris.
Item Willelmo Salmon pro uno tenemento in Brodlane ex parte occidentali nuper in tenura Ricardi Sparrow; et iacet inter tenementum domini episcopi nuper in tenura Gregorii Pylche ex una parte et tenementum elemosinarii ex altera parte, caput orientale abuttat super regiam viam et caput occidentale abuttat super vinetum domini prioris, per copiam ut in anno \secundo/ Henrici viij patet et reddit per annum viijs. De feodo prioris.
Item Thoma Browne shegger pro uno tenemento ex parte orientali de Brodlane nuper in tenura Thome Halder et reddit per annum vjs. De feodo prioris.
Item Johanne Yownge pro uno tenemento ibidem super corneram de Berkers Lane nuper in tenura Thome Aldred carpentarii et reddit per annum vjs. De feodo prioris.
Item Thoma Hynchow pro uno tenemento iuxta tenementum predictum in Barkerslane nuper in tenura Thome Aldered carpentarii et reddit per annum vjs. De feodo prioris.
fo 60
Item Thoma Palmer pro uno gardino nuper Mortemers; iacet versus Brodhith inter venellam vocatam Barkerslane ex parte australi et parvam venellam iuxta gardinum Thome Palmer ex parte boriali, caput orientale inde abuttat super tenementum infirmarii eliensis et aliud caput super Barkerslane, per copiam ut in anno xx^mo Henrici vij patet et reddit per annum vd. De feodo prioris.
Item Johanne Benntley pro uno tenemento vocato la Vyne scituato ad latam ripam; iacet inter communes venellas ex utraque parte, nuper in tenura Willelmi Mortimer, et reddebat per annum xxvjs viijd, nunc per copiam ut in anno decimo Henrici viij^vi patet et reddit per annum xvijs. De feodo prioris.
Item Thoma Martyn pro uno alneto; iacet ultra riveram inter alnetum Roberti Talbott ex parte boriali et alnetum Roberti Woddrofe ex parte australi unde caput orientale abuttat super comyngdyke aliud caput super riveram, per copiam ut in anno decimo nono Henrici vij patet et reddit per annum iiijs. De feodo domini episcopi.
Item Edmundo Hennysby pro uno alneto nuper in tenura Roberti Reman; iacet ultra le ee inter tenementum Thome Swyft ex parte boriali et alnetum Thome Writh ex parte australi et caput occidentale abuttat super le ee, per copiam ut in anno xij° Henrici viij patet et reddit per annum vs. De feodo domini episcopi.
fo 60v
Item Johanne Bentley pro uno le storhows iuxta tenementum Johannis Yownge; iacet in Berkers Lane quondam in tenura Johannis Slowe, et reddit per annum ijs. De feodo prioris.
Item Willelmo Rudston pro uno inclauso sive gardino nuper in tenura Thome Heldersam et reddebat per annum iiijs; iacet in Leyslane inter gardinum Edwardi Burde quondam Thome Heldersham ex parte australi et gardinum pertinentem celerario ex parte boriali et abuttat super Leyslane versus orientalem et super vinetum domini episcopi versus occidentalem, per copiam ut in anno xij° Henrici viij patet et reddit per annum ijs. De feodo prioris.
Item Johanne Dey pro uno fundo vacuo quondam edificato; iacet in vico ducente versus altam ripam in longitudine et latitudine inter tenementum Johannis Dey ex parte orientali et tenementum magistri capelle Beate Marie in tenura Johannis Bell ex parte occidentali et abuttat versus boriam super altam viam ex opposito de Leyslane et caput australe abuttat super Flexlane, per copiam ut in anno vij^mo Henrici viij patet et reddit xxd. De feodo prioris.

fo 59v
From William Cramper for a tenement lying in Potters Lane lately in John Cheveley's tenure formerly in John Writth's and rendered 4*s* annually; it lies between John Rose's tenement on the south side and Croyles Lane on the north side and the west head abuts upon Potters Lane, now by copy as it appears in 11 Henry VIII [1519–20] and renders 3*s* 4*d* annually. Of the prior's fee.
From John Slowe for a tenement in Broad Lane on the west side; it lies between a tenement of the almoner of Ely on the north side and a tenement of the pittancer of Sutton on the south side and renders 3*s* 6*d* annually. Of the prior's fee.
From William Salmon for a tenement in Broad Lane on the west side lately in Richard Sparrow's tenure; and it lies between a tenement of the lord bishop lately in Gregory Pylche's tenure on one side and a tenement of the almoner on the other side, the east head abuts upon the king's highway and the west head abuts upon the vineyard of the lord prior, by copy as it appears in \2/ Henry VIII [1510–11] and renders 8*s* annually. Of the prior's fee.
From Thomas Browne *shegger* for a tenement on the east side of Broad Lane lately in Thomas Halder's tenure and renders 6*s* annually. Of the prior's fee.
From John Yownge for a tenement there on the corner of Barkers Lane lately in the tenure of Thomas Aldred carpenter and renders 6*s* annually. Of the prior's fee.
From Thomas Hynchow for a tenement next to the aforesaid tenement in Barkers Lane lately in the tenure of Thomas Aldered carpenter and renders 6s annually. Of the prior's fee.
fo 60
From Thomas Palmer for a garden lately Mortemer's; it lies towards Broad Hithe between a lane called Barkers Lane on the south side and a small lane next to Thomas Palmer's garden on the north side, the east head abuts upon a tenement of the infirmarer of Ely and the other head upon Barkers Lane, by copy as it appears in 20 Henry VII [1504–05] and renders 5*d* annually. Of the prior's fee.
From John Benntley for a tenement called The Vyne lying at the broad bank; it lies between common lanes on either side, lately in William Mortimer's tenure, and rendered 26*s* 8*d* annually, now by copy as it appears in 10 Henry VIII [1518–19] and renders 17*s* annually. Of the prior's fee.
From Thomas Martyn for an alder-holt; it lies beyond the river between Robert Talbott's alder-holt on the north side and Robert Woddrofe's alder-holt on the south side, the east head abuts upon the common dyke the other head upon the river, by copy as it appears in 19 Henry VII [1503–04] and renders 4*s* annually. Of the lord bishop's fee.
From Edmund Hennysby for an alder-holt lately in Robert Reman's tenure; it lies beyond the water between Thomas Swyft's tenement on the north side and Thomas Writh's alder-holt on the south side and the west head abuts upon the water, by copy as it appears in 12 Henry VIII [1520–21] and renders 5*s* annually.Of the lord bishop's fee.
fo 60v
From John Bentley for a storehouse next to John Yownge's tenement; it lies in Barkers Lane formerly in John Slowe's tenure, and renders 2*s* annually. Of the prior's fee.
From William Rudston for a close or garden lately in Thomas Heldersam's tenure and it rendered 4s annually; it lies in Liles Lane between a garden of Edward Burde formerly Thomas Heldersham's on the south side and a garden pertaining to the cellarer on the north side, and abuts upon Liles Lane towards the east and upon the lord bishop's vineyard towards the west, by copy as it appears in 12 Henry VIII [1520–21] and renders 2*s* annually. Of the prior's fee.
From John Dey for a vacant plot formerly built upon; it lies in the street leading towards the public waterway in length and breadth between John Dey's tenement on the east side and a tenement of the master of the Lady Chapel in John Bell's tenure on the west side and it abuts towards the north upon the highway opposite Liles Lane and the south head abuts upon Flax Lane, by copy as it appears in 7 Henry VIII [1515–16] and renders 20*d*. Of the prior's fee.

Item Edmundo Tiler pro una vacua placea quondam edificata, et reddebat per annum vjs; iacet in parochia Beate Marie quondam Hendymans nuper Roberti Tyler, iacet ex opposito occidentalis de Cattyslane in via ducente versus Downham, simul cum una acra terre iuxta le Ronnyngforowhe quondam in tenura Margarete Hacford per annum nuper Roberti Tylers et reddit xxd. \Modo in tenura Edmundi Tyler ut in anno Henrici vij quarto patet, et quondam Roberti Tylers per copiam et reddebat vs ut in anno Henrici vj[ti] xxxij[o] patet in libera curia/ De feodo prioris.
fo 61
Item Henrico Broke pro uno tenemento in parochia Beate Marie scituato in Walpullane quondam Willelmi Tilers et reddebat per annum iiijs vjd; iacet ex parte boriali de Walpullane et abuttat ex opposito tenementi Willelmi Wympull versus occidentalem, per copiam ut in anno quinto Henrici viij[vi] patet et reddit per annum iijs iiijd. De feodo prioris.
Item Henrico Fuller pro uno tenemento iuxta tenementum predictum vocatum le storhows quondam in tenura Johannis Pratt et reddebat per annum iiijs vjd, nunc in tenura Henrici Fuller et reddit per annum iijs vijd. De feodo prioris.
[Pro una piscaria et pro uno botysgang; pro dayria de Quaveney]
fo 61v
[Pro pencionibus ecclesiarum de Melreth et Wycheford; pro firma rectorie de West Wrattyng; redditus assisus pro marisco in Lekylport]
Summa: xxjli xixs iijd

Resolucio redditus. Item sacriste eliensi pro uno tenemento in Walpull Lane quondam Johannis Peyntors et reddit per annum xiiijd.
Item celerario eliensi ac custodi de Ketons pro uno tenemento quondam Hendyman ex opposito finis occidentalis de Catteslane prope viam versus Downham per annum xvjd.
[Pro uno tenemento in Wytgate]
fo 62
[Pro uno crofto in West Wrattyng]
Item pitanciario de Sutton pro parcella gardini capta extra vinetum cum stagno in eadem pro elargacione eiusdem tenementi in tenura Johannis Sompton, pro consensu capituli, nunc in tenura Willelmi Salmon per annum xijd.
[Pro uno alneto in Letelport]
Item elemosinario eliensi pro uno tenemento vocato le Vyne in tenura Johannis Bentley, ijs vjd.
Item ballivo domini prioris pro uno tenemento; iacet in Brodlane super corneram de Barkaslane, per annum xijd.
Summa: xviijs

fo 62v
Rentale precentoris eliensis renovatum anno regni Regis Henrici octavi quintodecimo cum omnibus terris et tenementis ad idem pertinentibus

Item Johanne Gilbard pro parcella tenementi sui quondam Roberti Russell; iacet in parochia Beate Marie versus West Fen iuxta tenementum Willelmi Lege ex parte australi et tenementum dicti Johannis Gilbard ex parte boriali, et reddit per annum vjd. De feodo prioris.
Item Willelmo Legge pro uno tenemento; scituatur in parochia Beate Marie versus Westfen iuxta tenementum Johannis Gilbard ex parte boriali quondam in tenura Thome Hadnam, per copiam ut in anno nono Henrici viij[i] patet et reddit vijs jd. De feodo prioris.
Item Nicholao Tyler pro quadam parcella dicti tenementi Willelmi Legge nuper Roberti Tylers, ad terminum annorum et reddit per annum xijd. De feodo prioris.
Item Agneta Ascham pro uno tenemento; scituatur in Newynham nuper Ricardi Bakers, cum una acra terre in campo versus Wychford et una parcella crofti vocati Chantryrscrofte quondam in tenura

From Edmund Tiler for a vacant plot formerly built upon, and rendered 6s annually; it lies in St Mary's parish formerly Hendyman's lately Robert Tyler's, it lies opposite the west end of Cats Lane in the road leading to Little Downham, together with an acre of land next to the *Ronnyng* furrow formerly in Margaret Hacford's tenure lately Robert Tyler's, and renders 20*d* annually.[45] \now in Edmund Tyler's tenure as it appears in 4 Henry VII [1488–9] and formerly Robert Tyler's by copy and rendered 5*s* as it appears in 32 Henry VI [1453–4] in the free court/ Of the prior's fee.
fo 61
From Henry Broke for a tenement in St Mary's parish lying in Walpole Lane formerly William Tiler's and rendered 4*s* 6*d* annually; it lies on the north side of Walpole Lane and abuts opposite William Wympull's tenement towards the west, by copy as it appears in 5 Henry VIII [1513–14] and renders 3*s* 4*d* annually. Of the prior's fee.
From Henry Fuller for a tenement next to the aforesaid tenement called the storehouse formerly in John Pratt's tenure and rendered 4*s* 6*d* annually, now in Henry Fuller's tenure and renders 3*s* 7*d* annually. Of the prior's fee.
[For a fishery and a *botysgang;*[46] for Quanea dairy]
fo 61v
[For the pensions of the churches of Meldreth and Witchford; for the rent of the rectory of West Wratting; fixed rent for a marsh in Littleport]
Total: £21 19s 3d

Repayment of rent. To the sacrist of Ely for a tenement in Walpole Lane formerly John Peyntor's, and renders 14*d* annually.
To the cellarer of Ely and the keeper of Ketons for a tenement formerly Hendyman's opposite the west end of Cats Lane near the road towards Little Downham, 16*d* annually.
[For a tenement in *Wytgate*]
fo 62
[For a croft in West Wratting]
To the pittancer of Sutton for a piece of garden taken from the vineyard containing a pond, to enlarge the same tenement, in John Sompton's tenure, with the chapter's agreement, now in William Salmon's tenure, 12*d* annually.
[For an alder-holt in Littleport]
To the almoner of Ely for a tenement called The Vyne in John Bentley's tenure, 2*s* 6*d*.
To the lord prior's bailiff for a tenement; it lies in Broad Lane on the corner of Barkers Lane, 12*d* annually.
Total 18s

fo 62v
The rental of the precentor of Ely renewed in 15 Henry VIII [1523–4] with all the lands and tenements pertaining to it

From John Gilbard for part of his tenement formerly Robert Russell's; it lies in St Mary's parish towards West Fen next to William Lege's tenement on the south side and the said John Gilbard's tenement on the north side, and renders 6*d* annually. Of the prior's fee.
From William Legge for a tenement; it lies in St Mary's parish towards West Fen next to John Gilbard's tenement on the north side, formerly in Thomas Hadnam's tenure, by copy as it appears in 9 Henry VIII [1517–18] and renders 7*s* 1*d*. Of the prior's fee.
From Nicholas Tyler for a piece of the said tenement of William Legge lately Robert Tyler's, for a term of years and renders 12*d* annually. Of the prior's fee.
From Agnes Ascham for a tenement; it lies in Newnham lately Richard Baker's, with one acre of land in the field towards Witchford and part of a croft called *Chantryrscrofte* formerly in Nicholas Wase's

Nicholai Wase, et solebat reddere per annum xiijs iiijd, nunc per copiam ut in anno Henrici viij xv^{o} patet et reddit vijs. De feodo prioris.
Item Johanne Synkynge pro uno gardino quondam parcella tenementi predicti nuper in tenura Thome Jon, ad terminum annorum et reddit per annum vjd. De feodo prioris.
fo 63
Item Thoma Cheveley pro uno tenemento cum gardino ad idem pertinente nuper in tenura Johannis Rudston; iacet iuxta tenementum predictum Angnete Ascham ex australi parte sub sigillo capituli, ad terminum annorum cum reparacione eiusdem, et reddit per annum xiijd. De feodo prioris.
Item Amabilia Palmer pro uno tenemento; scituatur in Brodlane ex parte orientali eiusdem et abuttat super gurgitem nuper in tenura Thome Palmer infra le ee versus orientalem et caput occidentale abuttat super regiam viam, per copiam ut in anno xj^{o} Regis Henrici viij^{vi} patet et reddit per annum ijs. De feodo prioris.
[Pro uno alneto in Stuntney; redditus in Huntyngton]
Summa xxiijs ijd
fo 63v–64
[Penciones. Pro firma decimarum in Letilbery et in Pampiswort; pro minucionibus; pro firma rectorie de Impynton]
Summa totalis xxli vijs vjd

Resolucio redditus. Item celerario eliensi pro uno stagno ab eo conducto et reddit per annum xijd.
[Pro uno alneto in Norney]
Summa xvjd

fo 65
Rentale de feretrario eliensi renovatum anno regni Regis Henrici viij^{vi} quintodecimo cum omnibus terris et tenementis ad idem pertinentibus

Item Johanne Gylbard pro uno tenemento; scituatur in parochia Beate Marie versus Westfen nuper Russell quondam Spellers, et reddit per annum iijd. De feodo prioris.
Item celerario eliensi pro uno tenemento; scituatur in parochia Beate Marie, iacet in Walpull Lane quondam in tenura Agnete Ketenis, et reddit per annum xijd. De feodo prioris.
Item custode capelle Beate Marie pro uno tenemento quondam in tenura Johannis Wythe modo Johannis Brouster, et reddit per annum xijd. De feodo prioris.
Item Johanne Wellys capellano pro uno tenemento quondam Johannis Hardyng et postea Johannis Longys; iacet inter tenementum \senescalli hospicii ex parte occidentali/ et tenementum Willelmi Sempull ex parte orientali et abuttat super regiam viam ex parte australi ex opposito le stallys, et reddit per annum iiijd. De feodo prioris.
fo 66
Item Willelmo Yemanson tanner pro uno tenemento quondam Roberti Sparrowe; scituatur in Brode Lane ex parte orientali inter tenementum magistri capelle ex parte boriali et tenementum Willelmi Yemanson ex parte australi quondam in tenura Schepeys et Willelmi Malsters, et reddit per annum vjd. De feodo prioris.
Item subpriore eliensi pro horto columbaris; scituatur versus Castelhith nunc in tenura Thome Palmer, per copiam et reddit per annum vjd. De feodo domini episcopi.
Item Roberto Wylly pro uno tenemento nuper Henrici Wykham; iacet in vico ducente versus Castelhithe super corneram de Potters Lane ex parte orientali ibidem, et reddit per annum vjd. De feodo domini episcopi.
[Pro terris in Schpdam Norff]
Summa totalis iiijs iijd

tenure, and it paid a rent of 13*s* 4*d* annually, now by copy as it appears in 15 Henry VIII [1523–4] and renders 7*s*. Of the prior's fee.
From John Synkynge for a garden formerly part of the aforesaid tenement lately in Thomas Jon's tenure, for a term of years and renders 6*d* annually. Of the prior's fee.
fo 63
From Thomas Cheveley for a tenement with a garden pertaining to it lately in John Rudston's tenure; it lies next to the aforesaid tenement of Agnes Ascham on the south side, under the seal of the chapter for a term of years, with the cost of repairs, and renders 13*d* annually. Of the prior's fee.
From Mabel Palmer for a tenement; it lies in Broad Lane on the east side and abuts upon a weir in the river towards the east, lately in Thomas Palmer's tenure, and the west head abuts upon the king's highway, by copy as it appears in 11 Henry VIII [1519–20] and renders 2*s* annually. Of the prior's fee.
[For an alder-holt in Stuntney; rent in Huntingdon]
Total 23s 2d
fos 63v–64
[Pensions. For the farm of the tithes in Littlebury and Pampisford; for blood-letting; for the rent of Impington rectory]
Grand total £20 7s 6d

Repayment of rent. To the cellarer of Ely for a pond rented from him, and it renders 12*d* annually.
[For an alder-holt in Nornea]
Total 16d

fo 65[47]
The rental of the shrine-keeper of Ely renewed in 15 Henry VIII [1523–4] with all the lands and tenements pertaining to it

From John Gylbard for a tenement; it lies in St Mary's parish towards West Fen lately Russell's formerly Speller's, and renders 3*d* annually. Of the prior's fee.
From the cellarer of Ely for a tenement; it lies in St Mary's parish, it lies in Walpole Lane formerly in Agnes Keten's tenure, and renders 12*d* annually. Of the prior's fee.
From the keeper of the Lady Chapel for a tenement formerly in John Wythe's tenure now John Brouster's, and renders 12*d* annually. Of the prior's fee.
From John Wellys chaplain for a tenement formerly John Hardyng's and afterwards John Longy's; it lies between a tenement \of the steward of the [prior's] household on the west side/[48] and William Sempull's tenement on the east side and abuts upon the king's highway on the south side opposite the stalls, and renders 4*d* annually. Of the prior's fee.
fo 66
From William Yemanson tanner for a tenement formerly Robert Sparrowe's; it lies in Broad Lane on the east side between a tenement of the master of the Lady Chapel on the north side and William Yemanson's tenement on the south side formerly in the tenure of Schepey and William Malster, and renders 6*d* annually. Of the prior's fee.
From the subprior of Ely for the dove yard; it lies towards Castle Hithe now in Thomas Palmer's tenure, by copy and renders 6*d* annually. Of the lord bishop's fee.
From Robert Wylly for a tenement lately Henry Wykham's; it lies in the street leading towards Castle Hithe on the corner of Potters Lane on the east side there, and renders 6*d* annually. Of the lord bishop's fee.
[For lands in Shipdham, Norfolk]
Grand total 4s 3d

fo 66v

Rentale de thesaurario conventus eliensis renovatum anno regni Regis Henrici viij^{vi} quintodecimo cum omnibus tenementis ad idem pertinentibus

Redditus assisi
Item sacrista eliensi pro uno tenemento; scituatur in medio de Brodelane quondam Chestesneys et postea Peyntours, et reddit per annum iiijd. De feodo prioris.
Item elemosinario eliensi pro duobus tenementis, cum vjs pro tenemento Johannis Bakers et vs vjd pro uno tenemento Johannis Lyetotens et ijd pro alio tenemento quondam Rogeri Clerke; scituantur in Brodelane ex parte orientali ibidem et reddunt per annum xjs viijd. De feodo prioris.
Item magistro capelle Beate Marie Virginis in Ely pro iij^{bus} tenementis quondam in tenura Radulphi Coke, Willelmi Lakyngheth et Willelmi Talker; iacent in Brodelane ex parte orientali et reddunt per annum vs. De feodo prioris.
Item elemosinario eliensi pro quadam parcella terre pertinente ad tenementum suum ducentem ad aque ripam nunc in tenura Edmundi Hennesby; iacet in Brodlane ex parte orientali et reddit per annum iiijd. De feodo prioris.
fo 67
Item magistro Walpull pro uno tenemento in Brodelane ex parte occidentali, ex opposito tenementi Willelmi Yemanson tanner quondam Roberti Sparrowe et \Johannis/ Clement, Margarete Topisfeld, et reddit per annum xviijd. De feodo prioris.
Item Willelmo Yemanson barker pro uno tenemento in Brodelane ex parte orientali nuper Roberti Sparrow modo Johannis Wencent barker et Ade Clement; iacet ex opposito tenementi magistri Walpull ex parte occidentali, et reddit per annum xviijd. De feodo prioris.
Item Thoma Chakker pro uno tenemento in Brodelane ex parte occidentali quondam in tenura Johannis Downham modo in tenura Johannis Nelle capellani, et reddit per annum xijd. De feodo prioris.
Summa xxjs iiijd

Firma domorum. Item Elena Clefford pro uno tenemento; iacet in strata versus Castelhith ex parte boriali inter tenementum Thome Canam ex parte occidentali et abuttat super regiam viam ex parte australi ex opposito tenementi quondam Killok in tenura Thome Palmer, per copiam ad terminum annorum et reddit vs. De feodo prioris.
Item Thoma Hardyng pro uno tenemento ibidem iuxta tenementum Elene Clefford ex parte orientali quondam in tenura Nicholai Wryth et reddebat per annum vijs vjd ut in anno xxj^{mo} Henrici vij^{i} patet, nunc in tenura Thome Hardyng per annum et reddit vjs viijd. De feodo prioris.
fo 67v
Item Willelmo Wylkynson pro uno tenemento; scituatur ad finem australem de Brodlane super corneram ad crucem ibidem quondam in tenura Alicie Waklen, per copiam ut in anno Regis Henrici viij^{vi} xiij^{o} patet et reddit per annum iiijs iiijd. De feodo prioris.
Item Thoma Prior pro duobus cotagiis sub uno tecto in Brodelane inter tenementum quondam Cheveleys vocatum le storehows ex parte australi et tenementum Roberti Frewell ex parte boriali, per copiam ut in anno x^{o} Henrici viij patet et reddit per annum iiijs. De feodo prioris.
Item \Ricardo/ Person pro uno tenemento in Brodelane ex parte occidentali inter tenementum quondam in tenura Willelmi Hardyng belman ex parte australi et tenementum vocatum le storhows ex parte boriali, per copiam ut in anno xiiij^{o} Henrici viij^{vi} patet et reddit vijs. De feodo prioris.
Item Johanne Bromell pro uno tenemento in Brodlane ex parte orientali quondam in tenura Johannis Rose vocato le bordidhows; iacet inter tenementum Roberti Reman ex parte australi et tenementum Edmundi Hennysby ex parte boriali, per copiam ut in anno xiiij^{mo} Henrici viij^{vi} patet et reddit per annum xijs. De feodo prioris.

fo 66v

The rental of the treasurer of Ely Priory renewed in 15 Henry VIII [1523–4] with all the tenements pertaining to it

Fixed rents

From the sacrist of Ely for a tenement; it lies in the middle of Broad Lane formerly Chestesney's and afterwards Peyntour's, and renders 4*d* annually. Of the prior's fee.

From the almoner of Ely for two tenements, with 6*s* for John Baker's tenement and 5*s* 6*d* for John Lyetoten's tenement and 2*d* for another tenement formerly Roger Clerke's; they lie in Broad Lane on the east side there and render 11*s* 8*d* annually. Of the prior's fee.

From the master of the Lady Chapel in Ely for three tenements formerly in the tenure of Ralph Coke, William Lakyngheth and William Talker; they lie in Broad Lane on the east side and render 5*s* annually. Of the prior's fee.

From the almoner of Ely for a piece of land pertaining to his tenement extending towards the river bank now in Edmund Hennesby's tenure; it lies in Broad Lane on the east side and renders 4*d* annually. Of the prior's fee.

fo 67

From master Walpull for a tenement in Broad Lane on the west side, opposite a tenement of William Yemanson tanner formerly of Robert Sparrowe and \John/ Clement, Margaret Topisfeld, and renders 18*d* annually. Of the prior's fee.

From William Yemanson barker for a tenement in Broad Lane on the east side lately Robert Sparrow's now of John Wencent barker and Adam Clement; it lies opposite master Walpull's tenement on the west side, and renders 18*d* annually. Of the prior's fee.

From Thomas Chakker for a tenement in Broad Lane on the west side formerly in John Downham's tenure now in the tenure of John Nelle chaplain, and renders 12*d* annually. Of the prior's fee.

Total 21s 4d

Rent of the houses. From Ellen Clefford for a tenement; it lies in the road towards Castle Hithe on the north side between Thomas Canam's tenement on the west side and it abuts upon the king's highway on the south side opposite a tenement formerly Killok's in Thomas Palmer's tenure, by copy for a term of years and renders 5*s*. Of the prior's fee.

From Thomas Hardyng for a tenement there next to Ellen Clefford's tenement on the east side formerly in Nicholas Wryth's tenure and rendered 7*s* 6*d* annually as it appears in 21 Henry VII [1505–06], now in Thomas Hardyng's tenure and renders 6*s* 8*d* annually. Of the prior's fee.

fo 67v

From William Wylkynson for a tenement; it lies at the south end of Broad Lane on the corner at the cross-roads there formerly in Alice Waklen's tenure, by copy as it appears in 13 Henry VIII [1521–2] and renders 4*s* 4*d* annually. Of the prior's fee.

From Thomas Prior for two cottages under one roof in Broad Lane between a tenement formerly Cheveley's called the storehouse on the south side and Robert Frewell's tenement on the north side, by copy as it appears in 10 Henry VIII [1518–19] and renders 4*s* annually. Of the prior's fee.

From \Richard/[49] Person for a tenement in Broad Lane on the west side between a tenement formerly in the tenure of William Hardyng bellman on the south side and a tenement called the storehouse on the north side, by copy as it appears in 14 Henry VIII [1522–3] and renders 7*s*. Of the prior's fee.

From John Bromell for a tenement in Broad Lane on the east side formerly in John Rose's tenure called the boarded house; it lies between Robert Reman's tenement on the south side and Edmund Hennysby's tenement on the north side, by copy as it appears in 14 Henry VIII [1522–3] and renders 12*s* annually. Of the prior's fee.

Item Johanne Wakrell pro uno tenemento vocato le storhows in Brode Lane inter tenementum Thome Prior ex parte boriali et tenementum Ricardi Person ex parte australi, et redditus assisus hoc anno vs. De feodo prioris.
fo 68
Item Thoma Palmer pro uno tenemento cum gardino et stagnis infra Duffushayerd quondam in tenura Johannis Crosse; scituatur in vico versus Castelheyth inter communem venellam vocatam Pinferthyng Lane ex parte occidentali, per copiam ad terminum annorum et reddit per annum xs. De feodo domini episcopi.
[Item infirmario eliensi pro panno lineo, viijd]
Summa liiijs viijd
Summa totalis receptarum lxxvjs

Resolucio redditus. Item magistro capelle Beate Marie Virginis pro uno tenemento quondam Baldok; scituatur super corneram de Brodelane ex parte australi in tenura Willelmi Wilkynson, et reddit per annum jd.
Item domino episcopo eliensi pro uno gardino vocato Dufhoushayerd; scituatur versus Castelhyth in tenura Thome Palmers, et reddit per annum xviijd.
Item magistro feretrario eliensi pro dicto gardino vocato Duffousheyrd versus Castellhyth in tenura Thome Palmer, et reddit per annum vjd.
Summa ijs jd

fo 68v
Rentale de camerario eliensi renovatum anno regni Regis Henrici octavi sextodecimo cum omnibus terris et tenementis

Item Johanne Marche pro uno alneto; scituatur ultra aquam quondam in tenura Thome Hervy nuper Willelmi Marche, per copiam et reddit per annum ad quatuor terminos vs. De feodo episcopi.
Item Roberto Colvell pro uno gardino quondam edificato; scituatur in Schelfordlane inter tenementum Johannis Day pertinens hospitali Sancti Johannis ex parte occidentali et gardina Willelmi Rudston, Willelmi Percy et elemosinarii ex parte orientali et abuttat ex parte australi super tenementa Roberti Colvell et Thome Gallant, abuttat ex parte boriali super Schelfordlane, et reddit xijd. De feodo prioris.
Item Christofero Rechys pro uno tenemento; scituatur in Newnam quondam in tenura Alicie Massengers inter tenementum Johannis March ex parte australi et abuttat super regalem viam, et reddit per annum ijd. De feodo prioris.

fos 69–70
[Pro terris et tenementis in Dounham, Lakynghith, Hawkeston; pro rectoria de Hawkeston cum decima de Newtyn, pro rectoria de Wycham]
[Rydyngsilver percipiendum de hamstallis in Wysebech et Leveryngton; pro terris in Elm]
Summa xxiijli iiijd

Resolucio redditus hoc anno. De domino episcopo eliensi pro uno alneto in Ely ultra aquam nunc in tenura Johannis Marche, iiijd.
[Pro terris in Wycham]
fo 70v
[Pro fraternitate de Schengy; pro procuracione et augmentacione de Wycham et de Hawkeston; pro augmentacione de Newton]
Summa allocacionum viijli vjs xjd

From John Wakrell for a tenement called the storehouse in Broad Lane between Thomas Prior's tenement on the north side and Richard Person's tenement on the south side, and the fixed rent this year is 5*s*. Of the prior's fee.
fo 68
From Thomas Palmer for a tenement with a garden and ponds in dovehouse yard formerly in the tenure of John Crosse; it lies in the street towards Castle Hithe between a common lane called Pinferthyng Lane on the west side, by copy for a term of years and renders 10*s* annually. Of the lord bishop's fee.
[From the infirmarer of Ely for linen cloth, 8*d*]
Total 54s 8d
Grand total of receipts 76s

Repayment of rent. To the master of the Lady Chapel for a tenement formerly Baldok's; it lies on the corner of Broad Lane on the south side in William Wilkynson's tenure, and renders 1*d* annually.
To the lord bishop of Ely for a garden called dovehouse yard; it lies towards Castle Hithe in Thomas Palmer's tenure, and renders 18*d* annually.
To the shrine-keeper of Ely for the said garden called dovehouse yard towards Castle Hithe in Thomas Palmer's tenure, and renders 6*d* annually.
Total 2s 1d

fo 68v
The rental of the chamberlain of Ely renewed in 16 Henry VIII [1524–5] with all the lands and tenements

From John Marche for an alder-holt; it lies beyond the water formerly in Thomas Hervy's tenure lately William Marche's, by copy and renders 5*s* annually at the four terms. Of the bishop's fee.
From Robert Colvell for a garden formerly built upon; it lies in Shendforth Lane between a tenement of John Day pertaining to St John's hospital on the west side and gardens of William Rudston, William Percy and the almoner on the east side and abuts on the south side upon tenements of Robert Colvell and Thomas Gallant, it abuts on the north side upon Shendforth Lane, and renders 12*d*. Of the prior's fee.
From Christopher Rechys for a tenement; it lies in Newnham formerly in Alice Massenger's tenure between John March's tenement on the south side and it abuts upon the king's highway, and renders 2*d* annually. Of the prior's fee.

fos 69–70
[For lands and tenements in Little Downham, Lakenheath, Hauxton; for the rectory of Hauxton with the tithe of Newton, for the rectory of Witcham]
[*Rydyngsilver* to be collected from homesteads in Wisbech and Leverington; for lands in Elm]
Total £23 0s 4d

Repayment of rent this year. The lord bishop of Ely for an alder-holt in Ely beyond the water now in John Marche's tenure, 4d.
[For lands in Witcham]
fo 70v
[For the fraternity of Shingay; for the stewardship and upkeep of Witcham and of Hauxton; for the upkeep of Newton]
Total allowances £8 6s 11d

fo 71
Rentale de pitanciario eliensi renovatum anno regni Regis Henrici octavi sextodecimo cum omnibus terris et tenementis ad idem pertinentibus

Redditus assisi. Item Christofero Rechys pro uno tenemento in Ely nuper in tenura Ricardi Bakers; scituatur in le Heyrow inter tenementum Johannis Marche ex parte occidentali et tenementum Johannis Tomleyn ex parte orientali, et reddit per annum iijs. De feodo prioris.
Item Johanne Tomleyn pro uno tenemento ibidem inter tenementum Christoferi Rechys et tenementum elemosinarii eliensis in tenura Henrici Heth ex parte orientali, abuttat super regiam viam ex parte australi et reddit vs vjd. De feodo episcopi.
Item infirmario eliensi pro uno cursu aque in horto Willelmi Salmon nuper in tenura Ricardi Sparrow, et reddit per annum xijd. De feodo prioris.
Item redditus assisus et firmus pertinens ad gardinum nihil, quia concedimus elemosinario eliensi et successoribus suis pro graciis conventus. De feodo prioris.
fo 71v
Item fratre Thoma Oxborow pro uno stagnario vocato le ponchard quondam vocato le ashholt, per sigillum capituli, vjd.
Item fratre Willelmo Whitfote pro uno gardino; iacet inter gardinum camerarii eliensis ex una parte et le okehard ex altera parte, et reddit per annum ad ij terminos anni vjs viijd.
Item Thoma Galon pro uno gardino; iacet in le orthard \ex/ parte australi tenementi sui, per sigillum conventus, et reddit per annum xijd.
Item magistro capelle Beate Marie Virginis pro uno stagnario et uno tenemento ibidem in Brode Lane quondam Rogeri Mayhewe ubi porte vineti stent, et reddit per annum xijd. De feodo prioris.
[Pro uno tenemento in Wychford]
fo 72
[Pro piscaria in mara de Soham; redditus unius tenementi in Saffham; pro firma terrarum et tenementorum in Kentford; redditus assisi de homagiis de Sutton, Wycham et Wichford; pro terris in Tryplowe]
fo 72v
[Pro bladis decimalibus in Haddam Parva; redditus assisus unius tenementi in Lynn]
Item Willelmo Holished pro capitali mesuagio suo in Brodelane; \iacet/ ex parte orientali nuper in tenura Thome Persons, et reddit per annum xxd.

Firma terrarum et tenementorum in Ely. Item Thoma Gallant pro uno alneto ultra aquam quondam in tenura Thome Yon, ut in anno xiij[mo] Henrici vij patet, et postea in tenura Nicholai Lewen ut in anno secundo Henrici viij patet, et reddit vs.
Item Thoma Bemys pro uno tenemento nuper in tenura Johannis Daniell ut in anno tercio Henrici viij patet; iacet ex parte occidentali de Brodlane ex opposito tenementi Johannis Pally, per copiam ut in anno xj[o] Henrici viij patet et reddit per annum vjs viijd. De feodo prioris.
Item Johanne Rose pro uno tenemento ibidem inter tenementum infirmarii ex parte boriali et tenementum Thome Bemys ex parte australi, per copiam ut in anno xij Henrici viij patet, xiiijd. De feodo prioris.
fo 73
Item Ricardo Dodgeson pro uno le pondyard cum ij stagnis in eodem existentibus; iacet ex parte occidentali de Brodlane subtus le vyneyard, ex opposito mesuagii Thome Hervy modo in tenura Johannis Rose, per copiam ut in anno tercio Henrici viij patet et reddit per annum xvjd.

fo 71

The rental of the pittancer of Ely renewed in 16 Henry VIII [1524–5] with all the lands and tenements pertaining to it

Fixed rents. From Christopher Rechys for a tenement in Ely lately in Richard Baker's tenure; it lies in the High Row between John Marche's tenement on the west side and John Tomleyn's tenement on the east side, and renders 3*s* annually. Of the prior's fee.
From John Tomleyn for a tenement there between Christopher Rechys' tenement and a tenement of the almoner of Ely in Henry Heth's tenure on the east side, it abuts upon the king's highway on the south side and renders 5*s* 6*d*. Of the bishop's fee.
From the infirmarer of Ely for a watercourse in William Salmon's yard lately in Richard Sparrow's tenure and renders 12*d* annually. Of the prior's fee.
Fixed rent pertaining to the garden nothing,[50] because we granted it to the almoner of Ely and his successors for the monks' pocket money.[51] Of the prior's fee.
fo 71v
From brother Thomas Oxborow[52] for a pond called the pondyard formerly called the ash-holt, by seal of the chapter, 6*d*.
From brother William Whitfote[53] for a garden; it lies between the garden of the chamberlain of Ely on one side and the orchard on the other, and renders 6*s* 8*d* annually at the two terms of the year.
From Thomas Galon for a garden; it lies in the orchard \on/ the south side of his tenement, by seal of the convent, and renders 12*d* annually.
From the master of the Lady Chapel for a pond and a tenement there in Broad Lane formerly Roger Mayhewe's where the gates of the vineyard stand, and renders 12*d* annually. Of the prior's fee.
[For a tenement in Witchford]
fo 72
[For a fishery in Soham mere; rent for a tenement in Swaffham; for the rent of lands and tenements in Kentford; fixed rents from the tenantry of Sutton, Witcham and Witchford; for lands in Thriplow]

fo 72v
[For corn-tithes in Hadham Parva; fixed rent for a tenement in Lynn]
From William Holished for his principal messuage in Broad Lane; \it lies/ on the east side lately in Thomas Person's tenure, and renders 20*d* annually.

Rent of land and tenements in Ely. From Thomas Gallant for an alder-holt beyond the water formerly in Thomas Yon's tenure, as it appears in 13 Henry VII [1497–8] and afterwards in Nicholas Lewen's tenure as it appears in 2 Henry VIII [1510–11], and renders 5*s*.
From Thomas Bemys for a tenement lately in John Daniell's tenure as it appears in 3 Henry VIII [1511–12]; it lies on the west side of Broad Lane opposite John Pally's tenement, by copy as it appears in 11 Henry VIII [1519–20] and renders 6*s* 8*d* annually. Of the prior's fee.
From John Rose for a tenement there between a tenement of the infirmarer on the north side and Thomas Bemys' tenement on the south side, by copy as it appears in 12 Henry VIII [1520–21], 14*d*. Of the prior's fee.
fo 73
From Richard Dodgeson for a pondyard containing two ponds; it lies on the west side in Broad Lane below the vineyard, opposite Thomas Hervy's messuage now in John Rose's tenure, by copy as it appears in 3 Henry VIII [1511–12] and renders 16*d* annually.

Item Johanne Ward pro uno tenemento in Brodlane nuper in tenura Thome Whetret nuper edificato; iacet iuxta wyneyerdestyle ex parte boriali et tenementum elemosinarii eliensis ex parte australi, per copiam ut in anno xix[mo] Henrici vij patet et reddit per annum viijd. De feodo prioris.
[Redditus assisus in Ditton; pro firma rectorie de Sutton]
Summa xxijli xvjs viijd
fos 73v–75v
[Redditus assisus in Wysbech. Summa iiijli xijs vjd]
[Firma terrarum et tenementorum in Gyhern; pro caponibus etc. venditis; redditus assisus pro operibus venditis; pro firma rectorie de Wysbych. Summa xvli xvs jd obolum]
[Penciones de rectoriis de Sutborne et de Melton, et de vicaria de Wysbych. Summa xxvjs viijd]
Summa totalis receptarum hoc anno xliiijli xs xjd obolum
fos 76–77
Redditus resolucio. Domino episcopo pro uno alneto vocato Oldesegwyke, iiijd obolum.
[Pro terris in Wysbych; ad lumen in ecclesia de Wysbych]
Item custodi capelle Beate Marie pro uno tenemento in Brodlane, per annum ijs.
Summa iijs quarter
[Decasus redditus terrarum in Wysebech, Leveryngton et alibi. Summa xxjs]
[Frumentum. Redditus pro manerio de Hyhall iuxta Hornyngesey; redditus tenementorum et terrarum in Fen Ditton. Summa j quarter iiij busselli]

fo 77v
Rentale de celerario eliense renovatum anno regni Regis Henrici viij[vi] quintodecimo cum omnibus terris et tenementis ad idem [pertinentibus]

Item precentore eliensi pro uno stagno vocato Cosmers pond; scituatur versus le orthard et reddit per annum xijd.
Item granatore eliensi pro quadam parcella gardini pro grangia granatoris elarganda iuxta le horspond, et reddit per annum ijd.
Summa xiiijd

Rentale de Ketenys renovatum anno regni Regis Henrici octavi sextodecimo cum terris et tenementis ad idem [pertinentibus]

Item senescallo hospicii pro terris et tenementis pertinentibus ad manerium de Brays, et reddit per annum iijs.
Item elemosinario pro iiij[or] acris terre quondam Johannis Walpoll quas idem vendidit dicto elemosinario, et reddunt per annum xviijd.
fo 78
Item infirmario eliensi pro uno tenemento in parochia Beate Marie ex opposito de Cattyslane nunc in tenura Edmundi Tyler, per copiam et reddit xvjd. De feodo prioris.
Item Thoma Wylson pro uno tenemento ibidem iuxta tenementum predictum quondam in tenura Henrici Pope et Thome Tyler, receptum de precio unius libre cimini, hoc anno ijd. De feodo prioris.
Item magistro hospitalis Sancti Johannis in Ely pro uno tenemento quondam Roberti Denwer, et reddit per annum jd obolum. De feodo prioris.
Item Angneta Rumbelow pro uno tenemento libero vacuo in parochia Beate Marie; iacet super corneram de Walpoll Lane versus occidentalem quondam Ricardi Rede, iacens ad finem australem tenementi Ricardi Redde nuper in tenura Ricardi Rumbelow, receptum de precio ij caponum, hoc anno vjd. De feodo prioris.
Item Angneta Wake pro uno tenemento apud Brodhyth quondam Johannis Baxter postea Thome Martyn nuper in tenura Johannis Wryth, receptum de precio unius libre piperis, hoc anno xiiijd.

From John Ward for a tenement in Broad Lane lately in Thomas Whetret's tenure lately built upon; it lies next to the vineyard stile on the north side and a tenement of the almoner of Ely on the south side, by copy as it appears in 19 Henry VII [1503–04] and renders 8*d* annually. Of the prior's fee.
[Fixed rent in Ditton; for the rent of Sutton rectory]
Total £22 16s 8d
fo 73v–75v
[Fixed rents in Wisbech. Total £4 12*s* 6*d*]
[Rent of land and tenements in Guyhirn; for the sale of capons etc.; fixed rent for the sale of labour-services; for the rent of Wisbech rectory. Total £15 15*s* 1½*d*]
[Pensions of the rectories of Sudbourne and Melton, and of Wisbech vicarage. Total 26*s* 8*d*]
Grand total of receipts this year £44 10s 11½d
fos 76–77
Repayment of rent. To the lord bishop for an alder-holt called Old Sedgwick, 4½*d*.
[For land in Wisbech; for a light in Wisbech church]
To the keeper of the Lady Chapel for a tenement in Broad Lane, 2*s* annually.
Total 3s 0¼d
[Decay of rent of lands in Wisbech, Leverington and elsewhere. Total 21*s*]
[Corn. Render for the manor of Eye Hall near Horningsea; rent of tenements and lands in Fen Ditton. Total 1 quarter 4 bushels]

fo 77v
The rental of the cellarer of Ely renewed in 15 Henry VIII [1523–4] with all the lands and tenements [pertaining] to it

From the precentor of Ely for a pond called Cosmers pond; it lies towards the orchard and renders 12*d* annually.
From the granger of Ely for a piece of garden to extend the granger's barn next to the horse-pond, and renders 2*d* annually.
Total 14d

The rental of Ketons renewed in 16 Henry VIII [1524–5] with the lands and tenements [pertaining] to it[54]

From the steward of the [prior's] household for lands and tenements pertaining to the manor of Brays, and renders 3*s* annually.
From the almoner for four acres of land formerly John Walpoll's that he sold to the said almoner, and they render 18*d* annually.
fo 78
From the infirmarer of Ely for a tenement in St Mary's parish opposite Cats Lane now in Edmund Tyler's tenure, by copy and renders 16*d*. Of the prior's fee.
From Thomas Wylson for a tenement there next to the aforesaid tenement formerly in the tenure of Henry Pope and Thomas Tyler, receipt of the price of one pound of cumin, this year 2*d*. Of the prior's fee.
From the master of St John's hospital in Ely for a tenement formerly Robert Denwer's, and renders 1½*d* annually. Of the prior's fee.
From Agnes Rumbelow for a vacant free tenement in St Mary's parish; it lies on the corner of Walpole Lane towards the west formerly Richard Rede's, lying at the south end of Richard Redde's tenement lately in Richard Rumbelow's tenure, receipt of the price of two capons, this year 6*d*. Of the prior's fee.
From Agnes Wake for a tenement at Broad Hithe formerly John Baxter's afterwards Thomas Martyn's lately in John Wryth's tenure, receipt of the price of one pound of pepper, this year 14*d*.

fo 78v
[Pro uno tenemento in Downham]
Item domino episcopo eliensi pro parcella terre de Ketons quolibet anno habenda de manerio de Barton ex antiqua consuetudine ubi pynfald domini episcopi infra Berton modo stat, j carectata feni, hoc anno nihil.
Summa viijs ixd obolum

Firma domorum. Item Roberto Orton pro firma manerii ibidem et xvij acris terre in campis nuper in tenura Thome Tyffe cum uno crofto adiacente ex parte australi de Ketons subtus Berton sic dimissa ad terminum annorum, et reddit per annum xxxjs viijd.
Item Willelmo Wympull seniori pro uno tenemento de novo edificato iacente in Walpollane cum gardino adiacente; scituatur iuxta portam de Ketons ex parte orientali quondam in tenura Johannis Warde, per copiam ut in anno xiiij^{mo} Henrici viij patet et reddit vjs.
fo 79
Item Galfrido Bruet pro uno tenemento in Walpollane ex parte australi nuper in tenura Thome Squery iuxta tenementum nuper Baldwyn ex parte orientali et portam firme de Ketons ex parte occidentali cum libero introitu et exitu ad portam predictam, per copiam ut in anno xij^{mo} Henrici viij patet, iijs.
Item Johanne Makam pro uno tenemento ibidem et reddit per annum iijs iiijd.
Item Thoma Gloser pro uno tenemento ibidem et reddit per annum iijs iiijd.
Item Angneta Atkyn pro uno tenemento ibidem et reddit per annum iijs.
Item Roberto Orton pro uno pomefero nuper in tenura Ricardi Colson prout iacet in longitudine intra murum lapideum manerii de Barton ex parte australi et venellam vocatam Myllane ex parte boriali, per copiam ut in anno nono Henrici viij patet et reddit per annum xijd. De feodo episcopi.
fos 79v–80
[Pro terris pertinentibus ad manerium de Ketons; pro uno alneto et pro terris in Dounham]
Summa cxiiijs
Summa totalis vjli ijs ixd obolum

Resolucio redditus. [Pro uno alneto et pro terris in Dounham]
Item custodi feretrarii Sancte Etheldrede Virginis, per annum xijd.
Item elemosinario eliensi pro Brevytors \acra/; iacet in Ketons crofte ex parte occidentali ibidem et reddit per annum xijs.
[Ad reparacionem calceti de Aldreth]
Summa vjs ijd

fo 80v
Rentale de Othams renovatum anno regni Regis Henrici octavi quintodecimo cum omnibus terris et tenementis ad idem pertinentibus

Item Willelmo Hardyng pro uno tenemento; scituatur in Hyrowe super corneram versus Newnam quondam in tenura Otherpes nuper in tenura Johannis Bruwod <modo in tenura Thome Goderik generosi> et reddit per annum iiijs.
Item Roberto Orton pro uno tenemento in Walpollane super corneram ex parte boriali vocato le Swane quondam in tenura Ricardi Potters, et reddebat per annum xxxs ut in anno tercio Edwardi iiij^{ti} patet, nunc per copiam, xiijs iiijd.
Item Johanne Chorpe pro uno tenemento cum curtilagio adiacente nuper in tenura Roberti Rechys ut in anno xix Henrici vij patet; iacet ex parte boriali de Walpollane inter tenementum Roberti Orton ex parte orientali et [tenementum] celerarii ex parte occidentali, ut in anno xij^{mo} Henrici viij patet per copiam et reddit per annum vs iiijd.

fo 78v
[For a tenement in Little Downham]
From the bishop of Ely for a piece of land of Ketons where the lord bishop's pinfold in Barton now stands, to be held annually of the manor of Barton by ancient custom, one cart-load of hay, this year nothing.
Total 8s 9½d

Rent of the houses. From Robert Orton for the farm of the manor there and 17 acres of land in the fields lately in Thomas Tyffe's tenure with an adjoining croft on the south side of Ketons below Barton demised for a term of years, and renders 31*s* 8*d* annually.
From William Wympull senior for a tenement newly built upon lying in Walpole Lane with an adjoining garden; it lies next to Ketons gate on the east side formerly in John Warde's tenure, by copy as it appears in 14 Henry VIII [1522–3] and renders 6*s*.
fo 79
From Geoffrey Bruet for a tenement in Walpole Lane on the south side lately in Thomas Squery's tenure next to a tenement lately Baldwyn's on the east side and the gate of Ketons farm on the west side with free access through the aforesaid gate, by copy as it appears in 12 Henry VIII [1520–21], 3*s*.
From John Makam for a tenement there and renders 3*s* 4*d* annually.
From Thomas Gloser for a tenement there and renders 3*s* 4*d* annually.
From Agnes Atkyn for a tenement there and renders 3*s* annually.
From Robert Orton for an orchard lately in Richard Colson's tenure as it lies in length within the stone wall of the manor of Barton on the south side and a lane called Mill Lane on the north side, by copy as it appears in 9 Henry VIII [1517–18] and renders 12*d* annually. Of the bishop's fee.
fos 79v–80
[For lands pertaining to Ketons manor; for an alder-holt and lands in Little Downham]
Total 114s
Grand total £6 2s 9½d

Repayment of rent. [For an alder-holt and lands in Little Downham]
To the keeper of the shrine of St Ethedreda the Virgin, 12*d* annually.
To the almoner of Ely for Brevytor's \acre/; it lies in Ketons croft on the west side there and renders 12d annually.
[For the repair of Aldreth causeway]
Total 6s 2d

fo 80v
The rental of Hothams renewed in 15 Henry VIII [1523–4] with all the lands and tenements pertaining to it[55]

From William Hardyng for a tenement; it lies in High Row on the corner towards Newnham formerly in Otherpe's tenure lately in John Bruwod's tenure <now in the tenure of Thomas Goderik gentleman> and renders 4s annually.
From Robert Orton for a tenement called The Swan in Walpole Lane on the corner on the north side formerly in Richard Potter's tenure, and rendered 30*s* annually as it appears in 3 Edward IV [1463–4] now by copy, 13*s* 4*d*.
From John Chorpe for a tenement with an adjoining courtyard lately in Robert Rechy's tenure as it appears in 19 Henry VII [1503–04]; it lies on the north side of Walpole Lane between Robert Orton's tenement on the east side and [a tenement] of the cellarer on the west side, by copy as it appears in 12 Henry VIII [1520–21] and renders 5*s* 4*d* annually.

Item Roberto Markys pro uno tenemento ibidem inter tenementum Johannis Chorpe ex parte orientali et tenementum Johannis Warde ex parte occidentali, et reddit per annum vs.
fo 81
Item Johanne Warde pro uno tenemento ibidem nuper Johannis Warners ut in anno ix^{o} Henrici viij patet; iacet inter tenementum celerarii eliensis ex parte occidentali et tenementum Roberti Markys ex parte orientali et abuttat super regiam viam ex parte australi, per copiam ut in anno xij^{mo} Henrici viij patet et reddit per annum vjs viijd.
Item Johanne Dee pro uno tenemento ibidem quondam in tenura Willelmi Dopson; iacet in Walpollane ex parte boriali nuper in tenura Radulfi Makam, per copiam ut in anno ix^{no} Henrici viij patet et reddit per annum vjs.
Item Johanne Fostard pro tribus cotagiis sub uno tecto nuper in tenura Johannis Warde ut in anno xix^{mo} Henrici vij patet; iacet in Walpollane ex parte boriali inter tenementum Johannis Dee ex parte orientali et tenementum celerarii eliensis ex parte occidentali, per copiam ut in anno xj^{mo} Henrici viij patet et reddit per annum xs.
Item Thoma Gloser pro uno tenemento ibidem nunc in tenura Johannis Ellys; iacet ex parte boriali de Walpollane, et reddit per annum iiijs.

fo 81v
Item Waltero Perse pro uno tenemento nuper in tenura Johannis Pye; iacet in Walpullane inter tenementum Willelmi Baldwyn modo in tenura Johannis Pye ex parte occidentali et tenementum celerarii eliensis ex parte orientali, per copiam ut in anno decimo Henrici viij patet et reddit per annum iijs iiijd.
Item Johanne Adham pro uno tenemento quondam in tenura Johannis Howlet ut in anno \iiij/ Henrici viij patet; scituatur iuxta vinetum domini episcopi ex parte orientali et tenementum de Brays ex parte occidentali et abuttat super regiam viam ex parte australi, per copiam ut in anno xiiij^{mo} Henrici viij patet et reddit xiijs iiijd.
Item Thoma Pepur fuller pro tribus cotagiis; iacent super Ratynrowe iuxta vinetum domini episcopi eliensis prope portas de Brays, continent in longitudine xvj virgas et ij pedes et in latitudine xvij virgas, ut in anno secundo Ricardi tercii patet, modo in tenura Willelmi Bucke et reddunt xs.
Item Willelmo Bucke pro uno [tenemento] ibidem nuper in tenura Margerie Emneth ut in anno xv^{mo} Edwardi quarti patet; dictum tenementum abuttat super le Dudrey versus occidentalem et continet in latitudine quinque virgas et dimidiam, in longitudine a le dudrey usque finem orientalem undecim virgas, per copiam ut in anno secundo Henrici viij patet et reddit per annum iijs viijd.
fo 82
Item Willelmo Bucke pro parcella terre iuxta tenementum predictum nuper Margerie Enneth ut in anno xiiij^{mo} Henrici vij patet; iacet inter tenementum predictum ex parte occidentali et cameram Thome Martyn ex parte orientali et continet in fine occidentali v virgas, in longitudine usque orientalem sex virgas et in fine orientali iiij^{or} virgas et tres quarter, per copiam et reddit per annum iiijd.
[Pro vineto et pro tenementis in London; pro firma manerii de Burdens in Lytylbury]
Summa xxli xiiijs
fo 82v
Redditus resolucio. Domino episcopo eliensi pro uno tenemento iuxta vinetum domini episcopi ex parte boriali eiusdem et reddit per annum xvjd.
Et domino episcopo eliensi pro iiij^{or} cotagiis sub uno tecto; iacent ex parte australi porte vineti domini episcopi eliensis nunc in tenura Willelmi Bucke ut supra, et reddunt per annum xd.
[Pro terris et tenementis in manerio de Burdens in Lytylbury; nigro hostillario ijd]
Summa [blank]

From Robert Markys for a tenement there between John Chorpe's tenement on the east side and John Warde's tenement on the west side, and renders 5*s* annually.
fo 81
From John Warde for a tenement there lately John Warner's as it appears in 9 Henry VIII [1517–18]; it lies between a tenement of the cellarer of Ely on the west side and Robert[56] Markys' tenement on the east side, and abuts upon the king's highway on the south side, by copy as it appears in 12 Henry VIII [1520–21] and renders 6s 8*d* annually.
From John Dee for a tenement there formerly in William Dopson's tenure; it lies in Walpole Lane on the north side lately in Ralph Makam's tenure, by copy as it appears in 9 Henry VIII [1517–18] and renders 6*s* annually.
From John Fostard for three cottages under one roof lately in John Warde's tenure as it appears in 19 Henry VII [1503–04]; it lies in Walpole Lane on the north side between John Dee's tenement on the east side and a tenement of the cellarer of Ely on the west side, by copy as it appears in 11 Henry VIII [1519–20] and renders 10*s* annually.
From Thomas Gloser for a tenement there now in John Ellys' tenure; it lies on the north side of Walpole Lane, and renders 4*s* annually.

fo 81v
From Walter Perse for a tenement lately in John Pye's tenure; it lies in Walpole Lane between William Baldwyn's tenement now in John Pye's tenure on the west side and a tenement of the cellarer of Ely on the east side, by copy as it appears in 10 Henry VIII [1518–19] and renders 3*s* 4*d* annually.
From John Adham for a tenement formerly in John Howlet's tenure as it appears in \4/ Henry VIII [1512–13]; it lies next to the lord bishop's vineyard on the east side and a tenement of Brays on the west side and abuts upon the king's highway on the south side, by copy as it appears in 14 Henry VIII [1522–3] and renders 13*s* 4*d*.
From Thomas Pepur fuller for three cottages; they lie on *Ratynrowe* next to the vineyard of the lord bishop of Ely near the gates of Brays, they contain 16 yards 2 feet in length and 17 yards in breadth, as it appears in 2 Richard III [1484–5], now in William Bucke's tenure and render 10*s*.
From William Bucke for a [tenement] there lately in Margery Emneth's tenure as it appears in 15 Edward IV [1475–6]; the said tenement abuts upon the *dudrey* towards the west and contains 5½ yards in breadth, 11 yards in length from the *dudrey* to the east end, by copy as it appears in 2 Henry VIII [1510–11] and renders 3*s* 8*d* annually.
fo 82
From William Bucke for a piece of land next to the aforesaid tenement lately Margery Enneth's as it appears in 14 Henry VII [1498–9]; it lies between the aforesaid tenement on the west side and Thomas Martyn's chamber on the east side and contains 5 yards at the west head, 6 yards in length to the east and 4¾ yards at the east head, by copy and renders 4*d* annually.
[For a vineyard and tenements in London; for the farm of Burdens manor in Littlebury]
Total £20 14s 0d
fo 82v
Repayment of rent. To the lord bishop of Ely for a tenement next to the lord bishop's vineyard on the north side and renders 16*d* annually.
And to the lord bishop of Ely for four cottages under one roof; they lie on the south side of the gate of the lord bishop of Ely's vineyard, now in William Bucke's tenure as above, and render 10*d* annually.
[For lands and tenements in Burdens manor in Littlebury; 2*d* to the keeper of the Black Hostelry]
Total [blank]

fo 83

Rentale de Stunteneye renovatum anno regni Regis Henrici octavi quintodecimo cum omnibus terris et tenementis ad idem pertinentibus

[Pro uno tenemento et quadam piscaria in Stunteney]
Firma terrarum et tenementorum in Stuntney et Ely ad idem pertinentium
fo 83v–84
[Pro terris et tenementis in Stuntney]
Ely
Item Thoma Bulward pro uno tenemento; scituatur ex parte boriali de Segewyklane et comenn venelle ibidem versus austrum et abuttat super tenementum Thome Wrygth ex parte orientali, per copiam ut in anno xij^mo Henrici viij^vi patet et reddit per annum iijs iiijd. De feodo prioris.
fo 84v
Item Thoma Wryght pro uno tenemento ibidem apud Brodhith in Ely iuxta Segwyke nuper in tenura Willelmi Many cum una wyta ultra aquam ex opposito eiusdem tenementi, per copiam et reddit per annum xs. De feodo prioris.
Item eodem Thoma pro uno alneto ultra ripam nuper in tenura Willelmi Many, per copiam et reddit per annum iiijd. De feodo episcopi.
Item Willelmo Rudston pro uno pomifero cum duobus stagnis, inclauso pertinenti infirmario eliensi ex parte australi et clauso in tenura Lancelet Ridley et cotagium Roberti Rumney ex parte boriali, et abuttat super Leyleslane versus orientalem et abuttat super vinetum domini episcopi versus occidentalem, per copiam ut in anno xij^mo Henrici viij patet et reddit ijs. De feodo prioris.
Item Margareta Wynbush pro uno gardino in parochia Beate Marie; iacet ex parte orientali de Pallyslane, continet unam acram et dimidiam terre quondam Baldewyns, per copiam et reddit per annum ijs viijd. De feodo episcopi.
fo 85
[Pro piscaria de Neykereswer et pro uno botysgang; pro firma maneriorum de Stuntney et de Thorney]
Summa totalis xxvjli obolum
fo 85v
[Pro piscariis: nihil]

Resolucio redditus
[Pro Nykerswere]
Solutum domino episcopo eliensi pro una vacua placea in Lyleslane ex parte occidentali strate nunc in tenura Willelmi Ruston et reddit per annum viijd.
Solutum eidem domino episcopo pro uno gardino; iacet iuxta le Paleslane in parochia Beate Marie Virginis modo in tenura Margarete Wynbush nuper Baldewyn, et reddit per annum xijd. De feodo episcopi.
fo 86
Solutum domino episcopo eliensi pro uno alneto ultra ripam nuper in tenura Willelmi Many modo in tenura Thome Wrytht et reddit per annum iiijd.
Solutum ad calcetum de Alderhyth pro les tylkylnes et reddit per annum iiijd.
Summa xijs iiijd

fos 86v–88

Rentale de Wynteworth renovatur anno regni Regis Henrici octavi quintodecimo terrarum et tenementorum ad idem pertinentibus

fo 83

The rental of Stuntney renewed in 15 Henry VIII [1523–4] with all the lands and tenements pertaining to it

[For a tenement and a fishery in Stuntney]
Rent of lands and tenements in Stuntney and Ely pertaining to it
fo 83v–84
[For lands and tenements in Stuntney]
Ely
From Thomas Bulward for a tenement; it lies on the north side of Sedgwick Lane and the common lane there [is] towards the south, and it abuts upon Thomas Wrygth's tenement on the east side, by copy as it appears in 12 Henry VIII [1520–21] and renders 3*s* 4*d* annually. Of the prior's fee.

fo 84v
From Thomas Wryght for a tenement there at Broad Hithe in Ely next to Sedgwick lately in William Many's tenure with a wite beyond the water opposite the same tenement, by copy and renders 10*s* annually. Of the prior's fee.
From the same Thomas for an alder-holt beyond the water lately in William Many's tenure, by copy and renders 4*d* annually. Of the bishop's fee.
From William Rudston for an orchard with two ponds, an enclosure pertaining to the infirmarer on the south side and an enclosure in Lancelot Ridley's tenure and Robert Rumney's cottage on the north side, and it abuts upon Liles Lane on the east and upon the lord bishop's vineyard on the west, by copy as it appears in 12 Henry VIII [1520–21] and renders 2*s*. Of the prior's fee.
From Margaret Wynbush for a garden in St Mary's parish; it lies on the east side of Palace Lane, it contains 1½ acres of land formerly Baldewyn's, by copy and renders 2*s* 8*d* annually. Of the bishop's fee.
fo 85
[For the fishery of *Neykereswer* and for a *botysgang*; for the rent of the manors of Stuntney and Thorney]
Grand total £26 0s 0½ d
fo 85v
[For fisheries: nothing]

Repayment of rent
[For *Nykerswere*]
Paid to the lord bishop of Ely for a vacant plot in Liles Lane on the west side of the street now in William Ruston's tenure and renders 8*d* annually.
Paid to the same bishop of Ely for a garden; it lies next to Palace Lane in the parish of St Mary the Virgin now in Margaret Wynbush's tenure lately Baldewyn's, and renders 12*d* annually. Of the bishop's fee.
fo 86
Paid to the lord bishop of Ely for an alder-holt beyond the bank lately in William Many's tenure now in Thomas Wrytht's tenure and renders 4*d* annually.
Paid[57] for Aldreth causeway for the tile-kilns and renders 4d annually.
Total 12s 4d

fos 86v–88[58]

The rental of Wentworth renewed in 15 Henry VIII of the lands and tenements pertaining to it

fo 88v

Rentale de ballivo sacriste eliensis pro terris et tenementis in Ely renovatum anno regni Regis Henrici 8^{vi} decimo quinto

De curia tenta die mercurii proxime ante festum dominice in Ramis Palmarum anno regni Regis Henrici vj^{ti} decimo sexto patet Johannes Duke et Mary uxor eius ceperunt de ballivo prioris unum clausum; iacet ex parte australi campanile ecclesie eliensis prout includitur cum muris lapideis circumquaque, et reddit ballivo per annum ad officium sacriste ijs.

fos 93–95

Rentale de Cotnam, anno Henrici $viij^{vi}$ xxix^{no}

fos 96–119

Rentale de Sutton renovatum anno regni Regis Henrici $viij^{vi}$ xix^{no}

fos 120–122

Rentale de Mepall renovatum anno regni Regis Henrici viij xx^{mo}

fos 123v–126v

Anno xxiij. Rentale de Wycfford

fos 127v–128v

Rentale de Sottherton

fos 129–132v

Rentale de Blunsham et Eryt, anno $xxiij^{cio}$

fos 133–137v

Meldret Rentall renewd anno Henrici viiij xxix^{no}

fos 138–143v

Rentale de Melburn, anno Regis xxix^{no}

fos 144v–147v

[Summary on facing page]

fo 88v

The rental of the bailiff of the sacrist of Ely for lands and tenements in Ely renewed in 15 Henry VIII [1523–4][59]

According to the court held on the Wednesday preceding Palm Sunday in 16 Henry VI [2 April 1438] it appears that John Duke and Mary his wife received a close from the prior's bailiff; it lies on the south side of the tower of the cathedral, as it is surrounded with stone walls, and renders to the bailiff 2s annually for the sacrist.

fos 93–95

The rental of Cottenham, 29 Henry VIII [1537–8]

fos 96–119[60]

The rental of Sutton renewed 19 Henry VIII [1527–8]

fos 120–122

The rental of Mepal renewed 20 Henry VIII [1528–9]

fos 123v–126v[61]

Year 23. The rental of Witchford [1531–2]

fos 127v–128v

The rental of *Sottherton*

fos 129–132v

The rental of Bluntisham and Earith, year 23 [1531–2]

fos 133–137v

Meldreth rental renewed 29 Henry VIII [1537–8]

fos 138–143v

The rental of Melbourn, year 29 [1537–8]

fo 144v

Receipts dated 32 Henry VIII [1540–41] and 18 Henry VIII [1526–7]

fo 145

List of bishops of Ely, from John Hotham to Nicholas West

fo 145v

Aid to accounting: calculation of annual payment on the basis of daily payment

fo 146

Receipts

fos 146v–147v

Table giving sums of money from 1*d* to £1000 in French, with the equivalent in Roman numerals superscript. Examples of addition

Receipts

NOTES

[1] 'Aicie'

[2] 'clus'

[3] Richard Redman was bishop of Ely 1501–05; he left 100 marks to be distributed among the poor: J. Bentham, *The History and Antiquities of the Conventual and Cathedral Church of Ely* (Cambridge, 1771), p. 185.

[4] 'bishop's' *[deleted]*

[5] This is the first of many references to enclosures, a process begun on a small scale in the fifteenth century; an inquiry of 1548 provides evidence for the situation at Ely: W.M. Palmer, *Enclosures at Ely, Downham and Littleport AD 1548* (Transactions of the Cambridgeshire and Huntingdonshire Archaeological Society, 5, 1936), 369–84.

[6] 'b' in the left margin, alongside this entry.

[7] 'a' in the left margin alongside this entry.

[8] Smale's corner in 1417: H, fo 21v.

[9] 'claso'

[10] 'cluac'

[11] In the margin, to the right of this entry 'Mr John Goderik bought it from Master Sperard, now in Cranford's tenure, now in decay' *[Latin]*; the site of the tile kiln close occurs in the 1417 survey, at the south end of Potters Lane.

[12] The manuscript has 'north', this should be 'east'.

[13] 'super australem le orteyard'

[14] Folio 8 has been excised, the stub is just visible along the gutter; this suggests that several entries are lost.

[15] See note 14.

[16] The ditch north of Broad Hithe, the 'ancient lode' in 1417: H fo 15.

[17] The previous entries do not mention a garden; this may refer to the next entry.

[18] This presumably refers to the holding listed in the 1417 survey (H, fo 15v) where the holding comprises two cottages with a street frontage of 2 perches less ½ yard.

[19] 'Luci'

[20] 'lebcher'

[21] 'VIII' corrected to 'VII' (*vijj* corrected to *vij*).

[22] The year postdates the date of this rental; in view of the correction made to the regnal date in the first part of this entry, 24 Henry VII [1508–9] is more likely.

[23] 'Aic'

[24] The holdings of the pittancer of Sutton can be traced back to the thirteenth century, and the title 'pittancer of Sutton' to the fourteenth (see Introduction); the monks' vineyard was managed by the pittancer: CUL EDC 1/F/8.

[25] In 1362, Alan of Walsingham, then prior, awarded the income from the Braham estate to the almoner: BL Egerton 3047, fo 244.

[26] 'bishop's' *[deleted]*

[27] The perch of 18 feet was used for measuring fen ground: CUL EDC 8A/1/15.

[28] John Paate relinquished the office of almoner in 1511–12 and died in 1526: J. Greatrex, *Biographical Register of the English Cathedral Priories of the Province of Canterbury, c.1066 to 1540* (Oxford, 1997), pp. 429–30; the inventory lists the contents of the chamber, chapel, hall, kitchen, cellar and storehouse in the almoner's department.

[29] The foot of the page has been trimmed, the top of the words remain, suggesting 'prior's fee'.

[30] The date is incorrect, Henry VII reigned for twenty-four years.

[31] 'prior's' *[deleted]*

[32] The date is later than that given at the head of this rental.

[33] This is the expected income; the rental records that these holdings yielded nothing.

[34] Brays estate was acquired by the priory in the early fourteenth century (see Introduction); the main house stood north of the market place: F.R. Chapman, ed., *Sacrist Rolls of Ely* (2 vols, Cambridge, 1907), i, p. 155.
[35] 'garn' expanded to 'gardinum'; the word occurs in full in the second entry on this folio, and in the second entry on fo 41.
[36] See map 1.
[37] Caxtons manor in Melbourn had been acquired by the prior and convent in 1392: Evans, *Medieval Estate*, p. 17.
[38] 'south' *[deleted]*
[39] 'od'
[40] 'x', followed by 'ij' *[inserted]*
[41] 'Edward H' *[deleted]*
[42] 'conservand'
[43] The monastic orchard.
[44] In the fields of Ely and Little Downham.
[45] '8d' (*viijd*) *[deleted]*
[46] 'Botysgang' occurs in the marginalia of the 1250 survey as 'bootgonges' where these refer to a fishery that involves the use of boats: R fo 2.
[47] fo 65 is on the verso of fo 64.
[48] 'of the Master of St John on the south side' (*Magistri Sancti Johannis ex parte australi*) *[deleted]*.
[49] 'John' *[deleted]*
[50] The monastic garden, presumably.
[51] In the visitation injunctions of 1307, *gracie* are defined as money given out to the monks for their essential needs (*illa pecunia que vocatur gracie solita distribui inter fratres pro suis necessitatibus*): S.J.A. Evans, ed., *Ely Chapter Ordinances and Visitation Records: 1241–1515* (The Camden Miscellany, Third Series, 17, 1940), p. 34.
[52] A monk at Ely who held the offices of granger, pittancer, sacrist and cellarer between 1509–10 and his death in 1528–9: Greatrex, *Biographical Register*, p. 429.
[53] A monk at Ely who had been granger in 1500: Greatrex, *Biographical Register*, p. 460.
[54] The manor of Ketons stood on the south side of Silver Street; the cellarer had bought it in the later fourteenth century (see Introduction).
[55] John Hotham, bishop of Ely 1316–37, had granted to the monastery lands and tenements in Ely, later called 'le Cellarers Rents' (see Introduction).
[56] 'John' *[deleted]*
[57] 'to the lord bishop of Ely' *[deleted]*
[58] Six folios have been excised between fos 87 and 94 and the stubs are visible in the gutter; fos 88–93v have been inserted in their place; they are in a more cursive hand, on uniformly shorter pages; fos 88 and 93 are blank.
[59] This entry for the sacrist's rental is on an inserted page; the table of contents at the beginning of the volume (see Introduction) has 'Sacrist in Ely' on fo 89, followed by 'Cottenham' on fo 93, suggesting that four of the six lost folios contained the rental of sacrist's holdings in Ely.
[60] There are ten fos 119, numbered 119, 119(2)–(10), on standard size pages and apparently in the same hand as the main part of the manuscript.
[61] fos 122v–123 are blank, as are fos 127 and 144.

BIBLIOGRAPHY

MANUSCRIPTS

British Library

Cotton Claudius C XI, fos 25–312: survey of the manors of the bishop of Ely 1250; fos 321–32v: arbitration and town survey 1417
Cotton Tiberius B II, fos 86–233v: survey of the manors of the bishop of Ely 1222
Cotton Vespasian A XIX, fos 61–98v: arbitration and town survey 1417
Egerton 3047: First part of a fifteenth-century priory cartulary (the second part is now MS Ashmole 801)
Harleian 329, fos 1–32: arbitration and two versions of the town survey 1417

Cambridgeshire Record Office

T/E/AT 1: List of tolls to be paid at the Stone Bridge and Soham turnpike gates, 1764–5

Cambridge University Library

Add. MSS 2948, fos 9–22v: transcript of BL Cotton Vespasian A XIX by James Bentham
EDC 1/A/2: Almoner's cartulary
EDC 1/B1/: Miscellaneous medieval deeds and charters
EDC 1/C/7: Sixteenth-century priory rentals
EDC 1/C/8: Arbitration forming the first part of the 1417 survey
EDC 1/F/1 to 14: Obedientiary account rolls
EDC 1/F/1/: Almoner's account rolls
EDC 1/F/2/: Cellarer's account rolls
EDC 1/F/8/: Pittancer's account rolls
EDC 1/F/10/: Sacrist's account rolls
EDC 1/F/14/: Infirmarer's account roll
EDC 2/2A/1: Order Book 1550–1643
EDC 4/6/2: John Bacon, Manuscript record of cathedral restorations 1818–71
EDC 4/6/3: John Bacon, Manuscript record of college restorations 1818–71
EDC 8A/1/13: Survey book of the college and town of Ely 1649
EDC 8A/1/15: Part of a verdict of the jury at the court of survey, Ely Porta and Brays 1649
EDR D 10/1/1 and 2: Ely Barton account rolls
EDR G2/1: Bishop Wren's transcripts
EDR G3/27, fos 1–206: survey of the manors of the bishop of Ely 1250
EDR G3/28: 'Liber M', priory cartulary compiled in the fourteenth century

Gonville and Caius College, Cambridge

MS 489/485, fos 19–366: survey of the manors of the bishop of Ely 1250

Public Record Office

C66/401, membranes 5–1: arbitration and town survey 1417
E 143/9/2, membrane 36: inventory of the bishop's manors 1356–8, Ely

PRINTED PRIMARY SOURCES

Blake, E. O., ed., *Liber Eliensis* (Camden Society, Third Series, 92, 1962)
Bradshaw, H. and Wordsworth, C., eds, *Statutes of Lincoln Cathedral* (2 vols, Cambridge, 1892–7)
Calendar of Inquisitions Miscellaneous 3 (HMSO, 1937)
Calendar of Liberate Rolls 1245–1251 (HMSO, 1937)
Calendar of Patent Rolls 1292–1436 (37 vols, HMSO, 1891–1914)
Chapman, F. R., ed., *Sacrist Rolls of Ely* (2 vols, Cambridge, 1907)
Evans, S. J. A., ed., *Ely chapter ordinances and visitation records: 1241–1515* (The Camden Miscellany, Third Series, 17, 1940)
Fairweather, J.,trans., *Liber Eliensis: a history of the Isle of Ely from the seventh century to the twelfth* (Woodbridge, 2005)
Giles, J. A., trans., *Matthew Paris's English History* (3 vols, 1852–4)
Karn, N., ed., *Ely 1109–1197* (English Episcopal Acta, 31, 2005)
Letters and Papers Foreign and Domestic 1533–4 (2 vols, HMSO, 1882–3)
Love, R. C., ed. and trans., *Goscelin of Saint-Bertin: the hagiography of the female saints of Ely* (Oxford Medieval Texts, Oxford, 2004)
Rumble, A., ed., *Domesday Book: Cambridgeshire* (History from the Sources. Domesday Book, 18, 1981)

SECONDARY WORKS

Alexander, M., 'A medieval and post-medieval street frontage: investigations at Forehill, Ely', *Proc. Cambridge Antiq. Soc.*, 92 (2003), 135–82
Aston, M., *Thomas Arundel: a study of church life in the reign of Richard II* (Oxford, 1967)
Atherton, I., ' The Dean and Chapter, Reformation to Restoration: 1541–1660' in Meadows and Ramsay, *Ely Cathedral*, pp. 169–92
Atkinson, T.D., *An architectural history of the Benedictine monastery of St Etheldreda at Ely* (2 vols, Cambridge, 1933)
Ayers, B. S., 'The cathedral site before 1096' in I. Atherton, E. Fernie, C. Harper-Bill and H. Smith, eds, *Norwich Cathedral: church, city and diocese, 1096–1996* (1996), pp. 59–72
Baker, A. R. H., 'Evidence in the "Nonarum Inquisitiones" of contracting arable lands in England during the early fourteenth century', *Economic History Review*, Second Series, 19, no. 3 (1966), 518–32
Bendall, S., *The earliest known map of Ely: John Speed's survey map of 1607* (Ely, 2009)
Bentham, J., *The history and antiquities of the conventual and cathedral church of Ely* (Cambridge, 1771)
Bishop, T. A. M., ' Monastic demesnes and the Statute of Mortmain', *English Historical Review*, 49 (1934), 303–6
Cessford, C., Alexander, M. and Dickens, A., *Between Broad Street and the Great Ouse: waterfront archaeology in Ely* (E. Anglian Archaeol., 114, 2006)
Chatwin, C. P., *British regional geology. East Anglia and adjoining areas* (HMSO, 1961)
Clarke, H. and Carter, A., *Excavations in King's Lynn 1963–1970* (1977)
Connor, R. D., *The weights and measures of England* (HMSO, 1987)
Cook, M., *Medieval bridges* (Princes Risborough, 1998)
Crosby, E. U., *Bishop and Chapter in twelfth-century England: a study of the* Mensa Episcopalis (Cambridge, 1994)
Crosby, J. H., 'Ely episcopal manor', *Fenland Notes and Queries*, 3 (1897), 190–96, 275–9
Darby, H. C., *The medieval fenland* (Newton Abbot, 2nd edition 1974)

Dixon, P., 'The monastic buildings at Ely' in Meadows and Ramsay, *Ely Cathedral*, pp. 143–55
Douglas, D. C., *The social structure of medieval East Anglia* (Oxford, 1927)
Draper, P., 'Bishop Northwold and the cult of St Etheldreda' in *Medieval art and architecture at Ely Cathedral* (British Archaeol. Assn Trans, 2, 1979), pp. 8–27
Dyer, A., *Decline and growth in English towns, 1400–1640* (1991)
Dyer, C., 'Peasants and Farmers: rural settlements and landscapes in an age of transition' in D. Gaimster and P. Stamper, eds, *The age of transition: the archaeology of English culture 1400–1600* (Oxford, 1997), pp. 61–76
Evans, S., *The medieval estate of the cathedral priory of Ely: a preliminary survey* (Ely, 1973)
Fowler, G., 'Fenland waterways, past and present. South Level District. Part I', *PCAS*, 33 (1933), 108–28
Gallois, R. W., *Geology of the country around Ely* (British Geological Survey, Memoir for 1:50000 geological sheet 173, 1988)
Geological maps of England and Wales (solid and drift) 1:50000 (1980, 1981), sheets 173 and 188
Graham, R., 'The administration of the diocese of Ely during the vacancies of the see, 1298–9 and 1302–3', *Trans Royal Historical Soc.*, 4th series, 12 (1929), 49–74
Greatrex, J., *Biographical register of the English cathedral priories of the Province of Canterbury, c. 1066–1540* (Oxford, 1997)
Greatrex, J., 'Benedictine observance at Ely: the intellectual, liturgical and spiritual evidence considered' in Meadows and Ramsay, *Ely Cathedral*, pp. 77–93
Hall, D., *The Fenland Project, Number 6: The South-Western Cambridgeshire Fenlands* (E. Anglian Archaeol., 56, 1992)
Hall, D., *The Fenland Project, Number 10: Cambridgeshire Survey, Isle of Ely and Wisbech* (E. Anglian Archaeol., 79, 1996)
Harvey, P. D. A., *Manorial records* (1999)
Holton-Krayenbuhl, A. P. B., ed., *The Three Blackbirds: a medieval house in Ely Cambridgeshire* (Ely, 1984; revised edition, Ely, 2009)
Holton-Krayenbuhl, A., 'Excavations on the Paddock, Ely, Cambs.', *PCAS*, 77 (1988), 119–123
Holton-Krayenbuhl, A., Cocke, T. and Malim, T., 'Ely Cathedral precincts: the north range', *PCAS*, 78 (1989), 47–69
Holton-Krayenbuhl, A., 'The infirmary complex at Ely', *Archaeol. Journ.*, 154 (1997), 118–72
Holton-Krayenbuhl, A., 'The Prior's Lodgings at Ely', *Archaeol. Journ.*, 156 (1999), 294–341
Kershaw, I., 'The Great Famine and Agrarian Crisis in England 1315–1322' in R.H. Hilton, ed., *Peasants, knights and heretics* (Cambridge, 1976), pp. 85–132
Keynes, S., 'Ely Abbey 672–1109' in Meadows and Ramsay, *Ely Cathedral*, pp. 3–58
Kirby, T., 'Railways' in T. Kirby and S. Oosthuizen, eds, *An atlas of Cambridgeshire and Huntingdonshire history* (Cambridge, 2000), no. 68
Knowles, D., *The monastic order in England* (Cambridge, 2nd edition, 1963)
Mackreth, D., *Peterborough history and guide* (Stroud, 1994)
Meadows, P., 'The Priors of Ely' in Meadows and Ramsay, *Ely Cathedral*, pp. 392–400
Meadows, P., 'Dean and Chapter restored 1660–1836' in Meadows and Ramsay, *Ely Cathedral*, pp. 193–212
Meadows, P. and Ramsay, N., eds, *A history of Ely Cathedral* (Woodbridge, 2003)
Miller, E., *The abbey and bishopric of Ely* (Cambridge, 1951)
Miller, E., and Hatcher, J., *Medieval England: rural society and economic change 1086–1348* (1978)
Mortimer, R., Regan, R. and Lucy, S., *The Saxon and Medieval settlement at West Fen Road, Ely: the Ashwell Site* (E. Anglian Archaeol., 110, 2005)
Neilson, N., *Customary rents* (Oxford, 1910)

Owen, D. M., *Ely records: a handlist of the records of the Bishop and Archdeacon of Ely* (Cambridge and Chichester, 1971)
Owen, D., 'The Muniments of Ely Cathedral Priory' in C.N.L. Brooke et al., eds, *Church and government in the middle ages* (Cambridge, 1976), pp. 157–76
Owen, D., 'Ely 1109–1539: priory, community and town' in Meadows and Ramsay, *Ely Cathedral*, pp. 59–75
Palmer, W. M., 'The village gilds of Cambridgeshire', *Trans Cambs. and Hunts. Archaeol. Soc.*, 1 (1904), 330–402
Palmer, W. M., 'The hospitals of St John the Baptist and St Mary Magdalene at Ely, part II', *PCAS*, 36 (1936), 76–108
Palmer, W. M., 'Enclosures at Ely, Downham and Littleport. AD 1548', *Trans Cambs. and Hunts. Archaeol. Soc.*, 5 (1936), 369–84
Parker, V., *The making of King's Lynn* (London and Chichester, 1971)
Raban, S., *Mortmain legislation and the English church 1279–1500* (Cambridge, 1982)
Ramsay, N., 'The library and archives 1109–1541' in Meadows and Ramsay, *Ely Cathedral*, pp. 157–68
Ramsay, N., 'The library and archives 1541–1836' in Meadows and Ramsay, *Ely Cathedral*, pp. 259–79
Snape, R. H., *English monastic finances in the later middle ages* (Cambridge, 1926)
Spoerry, P., *Ely wares* (E. Anglian Archaeol., 122, 2008)
Stewart, D. J., *On the architectural history of Ely Cathedral* (1868)
Stewart, D. J., 'Distribution of the buildings of the dissolved monastery at Ely', *Archaeol. Journ.*, 54 (1897), 174–85
Stone, D., *Decision-making in medieval agriculture* (Oxford, 2005)
Sykes, N., 'The dynamics of status symbols: wildfowl exploitation in England AD 410–1550', *Archaeol. Journ.*, 161 (2004), 82–105
Victoria History of the Counties of England, The: Cambridgeshire and the Isle of Ely (10 vols, 1938–2002)
Wells, S., *The history of the drainage of the Great Level of the fen called Bedford Level* (2 vols, 1828–30)
Wharton, H., *Anglia sacra* (2 vols, 1691)

UNPUBLISHED REPORTS

Fearn, K., Archaeological evaluation of the Old Gaol, Lynn Road, Ely (Historic Buildings Survey Group, 1994)
Fearn, K. et al., The south-west transept of Ely Cathedral: archaeological interpretation (unpublished archive report, 1995): CUL EDC 4/10B/3
Lindley, P.G., The monastic cathedral at Ely *c.* 1320–*c.* 1350: art and patronage in medieval East Anglia (Unpublished Ph.D. thesis, 2 vols, Cambridge, 1985)
McConnell, D. et al., 25 Broad Street, Ely, Cambridgeshire (Archaeological Solutions Ltd Report 1991, 2005)
Regan, R.M. and Alexander, M., Archaeological Investigations: the Old Bishop's Palace, Ely (CAU Report 141, 1995)
Reynolds, T., A medieval waterfront at The Maltings, Ely (AFU Report 096, 1994)
Whittaker, P. Archaeological excavation at King's School, Ely, Cambridgeshire (CAU Report 343, 1999)

Index